Paradoxes of Peace

Social History, Popular Culture, and Politics in Germany
Geoff Eley, Series Editor

Paradoxes of Peace

German Peace Movements since 1945

Alice Holmes Cooper

Ann Arbor

THE UNIVERSITY OF MICHIGAN PRESS

Copyright © by the University of Michigan 1996
All rights reserved
Published in the United States of America by
The University of Michigan Press
Manufactured in the United States of America
⊝ Printed on acid-free paper

1999   1998   1997   1996   4   3   2   1

A CIP catalog record for this book is available from the British Library.

Library of Congress Cataloging-in-Publication Data

Cooper, Alice Holmes, 1955–
    Paradoxes of peace : German peace movements since 1945 / Alice
Holmes Cooper.
        p.   cm. — (Social history, popular culture, and politics in
    Germany)
    Includes bibliographical references and index.
    ISBN 0-472-10624-4 (alk. paper)
    1. Peace movements—Germany—History—20th century.   2. Germany—
Politics and government—1945–1990.   I. Title. II. Series.
JX1961.G3C66   1995
327.1′72′0943—dc20   94-48681
                                                                             CIP

To My Family, Old and New

Acknowledgments

This book would not have been possible without the help of many people and institutions. I was most fortunate to spend a year as a Research Associate at Georgetown University's Center for German and European Studies. I wish to thank Samuel Barnes and Gregory Flynn for making that year possible and for the intellectual stimulation I enjoyed at the Center. Many thanks also go to the American Institute for Contemporary German Studies, where I spent a semester as a Visiting Fellow. I wish to thank Gerald Livingston and Lily Gardner Feldman, along with the Institute's staff, for what was again a very stimulating experience. I would also like to thank the University of Virginia for its financial support, in particular the Summer Grant Committee and the Sesquicentennial Program.

For the use of the cover photo I would like to thank the German Information Center, New York. For their help in shepherding my book from manuscript to published volume I thank Geoff Eley, Ellen Bauerle, and others at the University of Michigan Press.

I owe a great debt to friends and colleagues for their friendship, moral support, and comments on the manuscript. I would like to express my gratitude to my former colleagues at the University of Virginia and my new colleagues at the University of Mississippi. Heartfelt appreciation also goes to Mabel Berezin, Clay Clemens, Lynn Duggan, Richard Eichenberg, Robert Fishman, Art Gunlicks, Paulette Kurzer, David Meyer, Allan Mitchell, Joyce Mushaben, Barbara Pfetsch, Michaela Richter, Thomas Rochon, and Christian Tuschhoff. I would also like to specially thank Peter Hall, Stanley Hoffmann, and Andrei Markovits for their continued support of this long project. Thanks too are due to Susan Kastenmayer Hennigan for her able research assistance.

Finally, I would like to thank my parents and my brother and sister and their families for their lifelong support of my endeavors. Most of all, I would like to thank my husband, whose affection for me and belief in this book never wavered.

Contents

Acronyms

AGDF	Aktionsgemeinschaft Dienst für den Frieden
APO	Ausserparlamentarische Opposition
AS/F	Aktion Sühnezeichen/Friedensdienste
BBU	Bundesverband Bürgerinitiativen Unweltschutz
BDKJ	Bund der Deutschen Katholischen Jugend
BMZ	Bundesministerium für wirtschaftliche Zusammenarbeit
BUF	Bundeskonferenz Unabhängiger Friedensgruppen
CDU/CSU	Christlich-Demokratische Union/Christlich-Soziale Union
CSCE	Conference on Security and Cooperation in Europe
DDR	Deutsche Demokratische Republik
DFG	Deutsche Friedensgesellschaft
DFG-VK	Deutsche Friedensgesellschaft-Vereinigte Kriegsdienstgegner
DFU	Deutsche Friedensunion
DGB	Deutscher Gewerkschaftsbund
DKP	Deutsche Kommunistische Partei
EDC	European Defense Community
EEC	European Economic Community
EKD	Evangelische Kirche in Deutschland
ERW	Enhanced Radiation Weapon
ESG	Evangelische Studentengemeinde
EU	European Union
FDP	Freie Demokratische Partei
FöGA	Föderation gewaltfreier Aktionsgruppen
GHI	Gustav Heinemann Initiative
GVP	Gesamtdeutsche Volkspartei
IdK	Internationale der Kriegsdienstverweigerer
IFIAS	Initiative für Frieden, Internationalen Ausgleich und Sicherheit

IFSH	Institut für Friedensforschung und Sicherheitspolitik
IKvU	Initiative Kirche von Unten
INF	Intermediate Range Nuclear Force
JUDOS	Jungdemokraten
JUSOS	Jungsozialisten
KdA	Kampf dem Atomtod
KPD	Kommunistische Partei Deutschlands
KfA	Kampagne für Abrüstung
KfDA	Kampagne für Demokratie und Abrüstung
KGD	Komitee für Grundrechte und Demokratie
KOFAZ	Komitee für Frieden, Abrüstung und Zusammenarbeit
MBFR	Multilateral and Balanced Force Reductions
MLF	Multilateral Nuclear Force
NAACP	National Association for the Advancement of Colored People
NATO	North Atlantic Treaty Organization
ORL	Ohne Rüstung Leben
SALT	Strategic Arms Limitations Talks
SDAJ	Sozialistische Deutsche Arbeiterjugend
SDI	Strategic Defense Initiative
SDS	Sozialistischer Deutscher Studentenbund
SED	Sozialistische Einheitspartei Deutschlands
SPD	Sozialdemokratische Partei Deutschlands
SRP	Sozialistische Reichspartei
UN	United Nations
VK	Verband der Kriegsdienstverweigerer
VVN	Vereinigung der Verfolgten des Naziregimes-Bund der Antifaschisten
WEU	West European Union
ZU	Koordinationsstelle ziviler Ungehorsam

CHAPTER 1

Introduction

Through their challenge to parties and other orthodox political institutions, social movements have periodically transformed the political landscape in Western democracies. Stemming most recently from the turmoil of the 1960s, protest movements attacked both politics and policy. Demanding democratic participation and self-determination in political, social, and economic spheres, they challenged traditional channels of representation and participation like parties. They also emphasized whole new policy fields, such as ecology, women's rights, and nontraditional defense approaches—again upsetting the more traditional focus on economic growth and high-tech military might. Like many of their forerunners, the new movements questioned the very legitimacy and effectiveness of the political and economic system.

In many European countries, the peace movements of the 1980s typified these broader processes. Their immediate focus was relatively narrow: opposition to the missile deployments proposed by the 1979 double-track decision of the North Atlantic Treaty Organization (NATO).[1] As the movements unfolded, however, they challenged central assumptions of Western defense policy, as well as the highly elitist nature of defense policy making. Debate surrounding a policy decision quickly widened into discussion of the fundamentals of national security and democracy itself. Nowhere was this debate more virulent than in West Germany.

The 1980s movement, however, was by no means the first incidence of peace protest in Germany. Peace movements recurringly played an integral role in West German politics for the entire postwar period, from the end of World War II in 1945 to the end of West Germany in 1990. From the anti-rearmament and antinuclear movements of the 1950s to the Easter March movement *(Ostermarschbewegung)* of the 1960s and, in particular, the massive antinuclear mobilization of the 1980s, peace movements

---

1. See chapter 4 for further discussion of the NATO decision.

accompanied all phases of West German foreign policy. In the meantime, East German peace movements contributed to the demise of the communist regime.[2]

Since unification in 1990, the peace movement's impact on public opinion, party platforms, and defense policy has compounded Germany's difficulties in defining its new international role in the post–cold war world. No longer directly threatened by nuclear weapons or hampered by territorial division and an exposed geostrategic position between East and West, united Germany has the economic potential to become a major power in international affairs despite problems stemming from unification. Yet Germany so far hesitates to engage in military activity beyond the defense of NATO territory. Although it may well eventually do so, the difficulties in building a new consensus around military missions beyond the NATO area reflect the peace movement's legacy.

For roughly forty years, German security choices were dominated by the East-West conflict and the possibility of nuclear confrontation on German soil. From 1945 to 1990, West Germany lived on the front line of the cold war. It was the "checkpoint Charlie" of the West politically, militarily, economically, and ideologically. NATO's nuclear and conventional strategies were designed to defend Western Europe and prevent war. Had war, however—especially nuclear war—ever broken out in the European theater, it would have distinguished only haphazardly among its German victims. In what would have been the most "total" of all wars, all West Germans would have been equally threatened, with no distinctions by class, gender, age, or political partisanship.

Yet only certain people at certain times mobilized against this potential threat. What explains the ebb and flow of peace protest in the postwar period, the alternation between periods of mass mobilization and quiescence? What explains the composition of movement activism—the involvement of certain groups but not others? What explains differences in organizational structure and strategy over time? How have peace movements contributed to united Germany's difficulties in defining its new international role?

After considering alternative theories of social movements, this book

---

2. For reasons of space and scope, this book does not address East Germany's peace movement or other opposition groups. See, among the many works on the East German transformation, Andrei Markovits and Philip Gorski, *The German Left: Red, Green, and Beyond* (New York: Oxford University Press, 1993), chap. 8; Angela Schou, *Die Friedensbewegung in der DDR* (Aalborg: Aalborg Universitetsforlag, 1986); Dirk Philipsen, *We Were the People: Voices from East Germany's Revolutionary Autumn of 1989* (Durham, N.C.: Duke University Press, 1993); Robert Goeckel, *The Lutheran Church and the East German State: Political Conflict and Change under Ulbricht and Honecker* (Ithaca: Cornell University Press, 1990).

adopts a "political process" framework. My argument is three-pronged. First, the timing, duration, and size of peace mobilization cycles reflect the mix of opportunities and constraints provided by the public policy process and other aspects of domestic and international politics. Second, framing of defense issues by institutions and extraparliamentary groups strongly influences the composition of movement activism. Finally, adequate organizational capacities depend on the availability of autonomous extra-parliamentary networks.

Peace movements are "public good" movements in that they are concerned with the provision of a good—"peace"—equally shared by all sectors of society. (This does not mean, of course, that all citizens agree on how to achieve peace, or on the salience of peace in comparison with other values.) On the whole, the political process framework has been used primarily to analyze citizenship movements pursuing greater rights for disadvantaged minorities. I, however, explore the framework's applicability to a different type of movement—one concerned with providing a broadly-shared public good rather than rights for a specific group.

Social Movement Literature

"The analysis of collective action is a risky adventure," admits Charles Tilly. "For one thing, there are too many experts around."[3] Lacunae in our knowledge have not remained because of a lack of scholarly attention. Indeed, the field of social movement literature is vast and varied. In the course of its development, social movement literature has tried to subsume under one heading such diverse subjects as religious sects, racial and class movements, the 1968 student protest movements, and the "new" social movements of the 1970s and 1980s. For our purposes, we will look at three types of recent social movement literature. First, many scholars look for structural causes of social movements, investigating broad social changes at the macrolevel that stimulate protest. Second, the resource mobilization school has a more microlevel focus, looking at both individual and organizational actors in the process of mobilization. Third, the political process framework takes a mesolevel tack, explaining social movements as a function of their specific domestic political contexts.

Modernization and Social Movements

In their search for the structural causes of social movements, several important groups of scholars have linked such movements to broad

---

3. Charles Tilly, *From Mobilization to Revolution* (Reading, Mass.: Addison-Wesley Publishing Company, 1978), 5.

processes of modernization. Although the various groups differ very significantly from one another, their work shares an underlying logic. For each, modernization brings about broad social change, which in turn stimulates a psychological reaction among the populace. Social movements erupt when this psychological effect reaches a sufficient aggregate level. We will look at three variants on this theme: early theories of anomie, Inglehart's theory of value change, and European theories of a crisis of modernization.

Theories in the 1950s and early 1960s stressed the "mass" and "deviant" aspects of protest movements and attributed them to anomie, alienation, and dislocation caused by modernization. Claus Offe notes that for such theorists as Kornhauser and Smelser,[4] "social 'uprootedness' of the alienated and the marginal was the key explanatory idea."[5] Further variants emphasize other links between social change and protest.[6] Crane Brinton, for example, explains revolutions as the result of perceived discrepancies between class accomplishments in one area (such as economic advance) and stagnation in class position in another area (such as political influence).[7] The concept of *relative deprivation* attributes protest to dissatisfaction caused by perceived gaps between expectations and the possibility of fulfilling them.[8]

Subsequent research, however, has largely refuted these early theories. Numerous studies have shown that social movement participants are by no means the isolated, anomic individuals posited by the classical model. On the contrary, participants are generally highly integrated into groups of all sorts and often into society itself. Resource mobilization theory (discussed later in this chapter) demonstrates that movements require at least a minimum level of organization. Marsh and Kaase, moreover, find that unconventional political protesters are highly involved in conventional politics as well.[9] Furthermore, social movement participants

---

4. W. Kornhauser, *The Politics of Mass Society* (New York: Free Press, 1976); Neil Smelser, *Theory of Collective Behavior* (New York: The Free Press, 1963).

5. Claus Offe, "New Social Movements: Challenging the Boundaries of Institutional Politics," *Social Research* 52, no. 4 (1985): 839.

6. For a review of this literature see Infratest, *Politischer Protest in der sozialwissenschaftlichen Literatur* (Stuttgart: Kohlhammer, 1978).

7. Crane Brinton, *The Anatomy of Revolution* (New York: Knopf, 1965).

8. Ted Gurr, *Why Men Rebel* (Princeton: Princeton University Press, 1969).

9. Alan Marsh and Max Kaase, "Measuring Political Action," and Max Kaase and Alan Marsh, "Political Action Repertory: Changes Over Time and a New Typology," both in *Political Action: Mass Participation in Five Western Democracies,* ed. Samuel Barnes, Max Kaase, et al. (Beverly Hills, Calif.: Sage Publications, 1979), 57–96 and 137–66, respectively.

often do not come from the most economically deprived sectors of society but instead are "middle-class radicals."[10]

Though very different, the theory of value change and that of crisis of modernization also link social movements to modernization, with its attendant social, economic, and political change. Devised in the 1970s and after, these theories attempt to explain the "new" social movements that began with the student movements of the late 1960s and include the ecology, feminist, and peace movements present today. While disagreement persists over just how new these movements are and of what their newness consists, a few common characteristics can be noted. First, whatever their forerunners, they all began during or after the student unrest of 1968. Second, the new movements' main actors generally come from the same socioeconomic groups—namely, the young, the highly educated, and the middle class. Third, the movements' themes (e.g., ecology, feminism, and civil rights) are new in that they depart from the traditional conflicts surrounding class, regional, ethnic, or religious cleavages. Finally, the new social movements employ "unconventional" tactics. Though they have not eschewed such conventional behavior as voting or parliamentary lobbying, they tend to rely much more on extraparliamentary action, ranging from demonstrations to blockades and occupations.

The theories of value change and crisis of modernization overlap in the logic of their arguments, but with important differences. Both relate broad social, economic, and political changes to shifts in values, which in turn increase propensity for protest among those groups whose values have most departed from traditional frameworks. The two schools differ, however, in their accounts of how this value change took place. For theorists of value change, changing conditions of socialization produce value change in new generations. Postwar peace and prosperity stimulated "postmaterialist" values among the younger generations, creating new political demands around which social movements form. Although these new values are related to prior objective changes, value change occurs through socialization, without conscious reflection by those involved. To the extent that social movements result from conscious appreciation of objectively existing problems, this appreciation is filtered through a prior change in values.

In contrast, for theorists of a crisis of modernization, the new movements constitute a defense of human needs against the onslaughts of economic and social modernization. The environment changes, while people retain their original needs. Social movements arise when individuals consciously experience the effects of change. Their reactions to change result

---

10. Frank Parkin, *Middle Class Radicalism* (Cambridge: Cambridge University Press, 1968).

from perceptions that anyone could have, given the requisite cognitive abilities, although education and employment in the tertiary sector increase such sensibilities. Change impinges on basic human needs (for integral social structures; for freedom from threats to survival, such as ecological disaster and nuclear war; etc.)—needs that are intrinsic to human nature rather than products of recent value change. Changes in values occur only *after* people recognize contradictions or problems and then reject the "system" that "caused" the problems.

Ronald Inglehart is the best-known proponent of the value change school, which holds that value shifts take place across generations independently of their conscious experience.[11] His basic formulation posits two categories of values: "materialist" values based on material and physical security, and "postmaterialist" values based on social, aesthetic, and intellectual gratification. Young people socialized in times of scarcity acquire materialist values, while those socialized during peace and prosperity acquire postmaterialist ones. Inglehart then explains the rise of new social movements on the basis of value change. Postwar generations have postmaterialist values, and protest forms around new political demands reflecting these new values.

Others have expanded on Inglehart's idea with respect to political themes and forms of political action. Baker, Dalton, and Hildebrandt link values to the salience of specific political issues in West German politics during the 1970s.[12] They demonstrate that Inglehart's postmaterialists are most concerned with "new politics issues" like liberal treatment of foreign workers in Germany or worker participation in industry, while his materialists focus primarily on economic and security issues, traditional religious concerns, and German reunification.

In similar fashion, Barnes and Kaase et al. have investigated the forms of political action preferred by the people most likely to participate in the new social movements.[13] Much of the young, educated, and postmaterialist middle class, as well as a smaller portion of the rest of the populace, has changed its style of political participation. In addition to con-

---

11. Ronald Inglehart, "The Silent Revolution in Europe: Intergenerational Change in Post-Industrial Societies," *American Political Science Review* 65 (1971): 991–1017; *The Silent Revolution: Changing Values and Political Styles Among Western Publics* (Princeton: Princeton University Press, 1977); and *Culture Shifts* (Princeton: Princeton University Press, 1990).

12. Kendall Baker, Russell Dalton, and Kai Hildebrandt, *Germany Transformed: Political Culture and the New Politics* (Cambridge, Mass.: Harvard University Press, 1981). For more recent data and more comparative analysis, see Russell Dalton, *Citizen Politics in Western Democracies: Public Opinion and Political Parties in the United States, Great Britain, West Germany, and France* (Chatham, N.J.: Chatham House Publishers, 1988).

13. Samuel Barnes, Max Kaase, et al., *Political Action: Mass Participation in Five Western Democracies* (Beverly Hills, Calif.: Sage Publications, 1979).

ventional political activity, it is willing to employ "unconventional" methods of political action.

As for the German peace movement of the 1980s, polling data indeed links support for the movement with postmaterialist values. The Eurobarometer 17 poll of 1982[14] reveals that 28.7 percent of the peace movement's active supporters held postmaterialist values, whereas only 5 percent of its opponents did so. While only 23 percent of the peace movement's supporters held materialist values, 34 percent of its opponents did. Finally, 41 percent of the peace movement's supporters fell into the category of mixed values, with 54 percent of its opponents also falling into this category. On the basis of this survey, Mueller-Rommel and Watts conclude that a relatively strong bivariate relationship exists between active support of new social movements and postmaterialist values.[15] In further supporting evidence, Inglehart finds that postmaterialists in Germany approve strongly of the peace movement three times as frequently as materialists and say they are a member twenty times as often.[16]

The value change theory helps explain why the young are more highly represented in the 1980s peace movement than any other generation. However, a further look at the Eurobarometer survey reveals that age is not as closely related to attitudes toward the deployment of new missiles as Inglehart's theory might suggest. Inglehart would predict that older generations have stronger security needs than younger ones and that they would thus be more likely to support strengthened defense systems. But a breakdown of the population by age cohort shows that at least 42 percent of *every* age category approved strongly or somewhat of the peace movement, while no more than 35 percent of any age category disapproved. To be sure, 61 to 70 percent of the younger generations (15–34 years old in 1982) approved of the peace movement. Of the generations that experienced World War II during their formative years, however, 50 to 60 percent also approved strongly or somewhat, whereas only 20 to 33 percent disapproved to any degree. Thus over half of the people that should have had the strongest security needs approved of a movement that, according to its critics,

---

14. Jacques-Rene Rabier, Helene Riffault, and Ronald Inglehart, *Euro-barometer 17: Energy and the Future, April 1982*, 1st ICPSR ed. (Ann Arbor, Mich.: Inter-University Consortium for Political and Social Research, 1983), machine-readable data file; cited in Ferdinand Müller-Rommel and Nicholas Watts, "Zur elektoralen Verankerung der Anhaenger neuer sozialer Bewegungen: Eine vorlaeufige Forschungsnotiz," in *Politische Willensbildung und Interessenvermittlung: Verhandlungen der Fachtagung der DVPW vom 11.–13. Oktober 1983 in Mannheim*, ed. Juergen Falter, Christian Fenner, and Michael Greven (Opladen: Westdeutscher Verlag, 1984), 602–9, here 604.

15. Müller-Rommel and Watts, "Zur elektoralen Verankerung," 604.

16. Ronald Inglehart, "Generational Change and the Future of the Atlantic Alliance," *PS* 17 (summer 1984): 525–35, here 531.

threatened German security. Moreover, the percentage of this war-traumatized generation that voiced approval of the peace movement was slightly higher than the percentage of the generation that immediately followed it. The generation socialized during the late 1940s and 1950s approved of the peace movement by only 48 percent.[17]

Inglehart's theory poses other, very intriguing questions as well. Noting that West German social movements since 1968 have been primarily populated by relatively young, well-educated activists employed in the service sector or other niches outside the market economy, most scholars accept the link between social movement participation and prosperity in some form. The nature of that link, however, is subject to debate. Insofar as prosperity has engendered social movement participation, is it affluence in an activist's formative years—or in his or her current economic situation—that plays the decisive role?[18] If socialization is the key to postmaterialist political activism, what exactly is the socializing agent—the general environment of peace and prosperity that shapes people's subconscious value hierarchy, or more specific experiences or events that shape impressionable minds? What shaped the minds of young activists in the 1960s and 1970s—"peace" or the more specific experiences of détente and the Vietnam War?

While Inglehart's theory implies that social movements arise as a natural consequence of postwar economic change, others view social movements as symptomatic of a crisis of modernity. German theorists have contributed heavily to this school, with Habermas providing the philosophical foundation.[19] In Habermas's view, new social movements reflect legitimation crises in advanced capitalism and represent a reaction against a "colonization of the life-world," or the expanded intervention of the state and economy into new reaches of life. Modernization implies increasing differentiation between the political and economic system, on the one hand, and the sociocultural "life-world," on the other. As Alan Scott notes, new movements defensively "resist the extension of technical rationality into all spheres of social life (inner colonization)." In addition to this defensive impulse, new social movements also have a progressive function, for "at the same time they continue to demand higher levels of rational

---

17. Rabier, Riffault, and Inglehart, *Euro-barometer 17*, contains cross-tabulations of age classes and approval/disapproval variables. The ranges in the percentages given in the preceding text result from combining two age cohorts in the case of the younger generations (15–24 and 25–34 year olds) and two age cohorts in the case of the generation that experienced World War II (45–54 and 55–64 year olds).

18. Claus Offe, "New Social Movements," 850–51.

19. Jürgen Habermas, *Legitimation Crisis* (London: Heinemann, 1976); and *The Theory of Communicative Action*, vol. 2 (Boston: Beacon Press, 1987).

justification in the moral and cultural spheres" (a "communicative morality" stimulated by rationalization of economic and social life). Breaking with traditional deference toward state action, they "demand that politics be rationally presented and justified."[20]

In more concrete terms, new social movements result from an objective crisis of the modernization process, as modernization brings about increasing technological risks to society. Increased risks have reduced popular support for technological and economic progress, in the eyes of Habermas's followers. In their view, new social and political conflicts have arisen as the costs of modernization become more apparent. They think that by the 1970s the negative by-products of industrialization had produced a critical level of threat to society. Pollution and nuclear weapons threatened the physical foundations of life, while destruction of traditional social settings undermined sources of meaning. Given the political system's inability to adequately resolve these problems, many people perceive a crisis and have joined the new social movements in response, especially those directly affected by the adverse consequences of modernization and those who have developed a special sensitivity to these problems as a result of a general shift in values—social workers, teachers, ministers, doctors, and social scientists.[21]

Both Inglehart and Habermas set out to explain the new social movements from the late 1960s on and to do so in terms of very broad macrolevel political, social, and economic change. They serve us well by alerting us to the broad frameworks of postwar politics, within which social movements have arisen and must operate. Valuable as these contributions are, several problems remain. Neither school can adequately explain protest in the 1950s—in particular the significant peace protest of that decade, which occurred before either generational value change or a crisis of modernization had set in. Neither school can account for the institutional anchoring of the peace movement—why it is so much more firmly ensconced in the Protestant than in the Catholic church or why it finds so much more support on the left than on the right among all generations. Whatever their ultimate validity, neither theory tells us enough about how social movements evolve in the context of their own polity, who actually joins them within the confines of broad demographic variables, or the timing of their ebb and flow.

---

20. Alan Scott, *Ideology and the New Social Movements* (London: Unwin Hyman, 1990), 72.

21. Karl-Werner Brand, Detlef Büsser, and Dieter Rucht, *Aufbruch in eine andere Gesellschaft: Neue Soziale Bewegungen in der Bundesrepublik* (Frankfurt: Campus Verlag, 1983).

Resource Mobilization and Social Movements

Resource mobilization theory takes an actor-centered approach, studying the contributions of individuals and organizations to the rise and fall of social movements. It takes issue with the theories discussed in the preceding section of this chapter, because it accords grievances only secondary importance. It presumes that grievances always exist, whereas movements emerge only when they have mobilized enough resources. In its classic formulation by McCarthy and Zald, "there is always enough discontent in any society to supply the grass-roots support for a movement if the movement is effectively organized and has at its disposal the power and resources of some established elite group. . . . the amount of activity directed toward goal accomplishment is crudely a function of the resources controlled by an organization."[22] For McCarthy and Zald, essential movement resources include legitimacy, money, facilities, labor, and support from external allies.[23] Freeman adds publicity, expertise, access to networks and decision makers, and inclusion in the polity.[24]

Resource mobilization theory thus studies the processes by which organizations acquire and deploy resources, based on several key assumptions. First, organizations are the key players in social movements and must mobilize followers or members. Oberschall, for example, notes that movements develop organizational bases by drawing on preexisting organizational structures: either traditional (e.g., tribal) forms of community or networks of secondary groups based on special interests.[25] Mobilization can ensue quite rapidly when bloc recruitment is possible, as entire groups are drawn into a larger movement organization.[26] Preexisting social networks also provide fertile grounds for individual recruitment. McAdam describes the role of "micromobilization contexts" in stimulating individual participation in movements. Small groups provide a setting for attach-

---

22. John McCarthy and Mayer Zald, "Resource Mobilization and Social Movements: A Partial Theory," in *Social Movements in an Organizational Society*, ed. Mayer Zald and John McCarthy (New Brunswick, N.J.: Transaction Books, 1987), 15–49, here 18, 19, and 22.

23. McCarthy and Zald, "Resource Mobilization," 22.

24. Jo Freeman, "Resource Mobilization and Strategy: A Model for Analyzing Social Movement Organization Actions," in *The Dynamics of Social Movements,* ed. Mayer Zald and John McCarthy (Cambridge: Winthrop Publishers, 1979), 167–90, here 174.

25. Anthony Oberschall, *Social Conflict and Social Movements* (Englewood Cliffs, N.J.: Prentice-Hall, 1973), 119.

26. Ibid., 125.

ing meaning to events and supply rudimentary organization and leadership.[27]

Second, social movement participation entails, at a minimum, opportunity costs of time and money, and it often involves the risk of arrest or physical harm. Scholars addressing this problem have developed a "rational choice" perspective, which assumes, according to Oberschall, that "a rational challenger will participate or continue participating in a challenge if his net benefit is greater than zero, but that he will abandon the challenge if his net benefit is zero or negative."[28] Moreover, organizations must somehow overcome the "free-rider" temptation to let others do the work while still enjoying the fruits of successful collective action.[29] Scholars have good news, however, on this front. Fireman and Gamson, for example, find that Olson's utilitarian logic does not apply as readily to social movements as it does to organizations pursuing "selfish" interests.[30] Instead, social movement mobilization can draw on solidarity and consciousness of common interests. Finkel, Muller, and Opp find that belief in the moral duty to participate, belief in the essential contribution of individual participation to group success, and belief in the possibility of group success also motivate individuals to overcome the free-rider temptation.[31]

Third, movements need communication networks both among groups within the movement and between the movement and the broader public. The media often serve as a movement's best communication device, helping it communicate with its followers, reach out to potential recruits, and neutralize potential opponents. Getting useful media coverage, however, may be problematic for a movement. Molotch ascribes to the media a bias against social movements, partly because the media's owners or managers are close to ruling elites, and partly because social movements fall outside the procedures of routine news collection.[32]

Fourth, movements must develop successful tactics, but they face

27. Doug McAdam, "Micromobilization Contexts and Recruitment to Activism," in *From Structure to Action: Comparing Social Movement Research across Cultures,* ed. Bert Klandermans, Hanspeter Kriesi, and Sidney Tarrow (Greenwich, Conn.: JAI Press, 1988), 125–55, here 135.

28. Anthony Oberschall, "Protracted Conflict," in *The Dynamics of Social Movements,* ed. Zald and McCarthy, 45–71, here 52.

29. Mancur Olson, *The Logic of Collective Action: Public Goods and the Theory of Groups,* Cambridge: Harvard University Press, 1965).

30. Bruce Fireman and William Gamson, "Utilitarian Logic in the Resource Mobilization Perspective," in *The Dynamics of Social Movements,* ed. Zald and McCarthy, 8–45.

31. Steven Finkel, Edward Muller, and Karl-Dieter Opp, "Personal Influence, Collective Rationality, and Mass Political Action," *American Political Science Review* 83, no. 3 (Sept. 1989): 885–903.

32. Harvey Molotch, "Media and Movements," in *The Dynamics of Social Movements,* ed. Zald and McCarthy, 71–94.

numerous constraints in doing so. Movements need forms of action that reinforce the commitment of their activists, attract media attention, mobilize potential followers, and influence government policy. These are often conflicting requirements, however, so movements develop a palette of action forms.[33] Movement strategists face other constraints as well. Governments or countermovements may try to hinder or repress the movement.[34] Values, past experiences, reference groups, and the movement's structure itself may constrain available choices of strategy.[35] The range of action forms actually available to a movement, moreover, is constrained by the repertoire of action prevailing in a country at any given time, defined by patterns of repression, prevailing standards of right and justice, and so on.[36]

Fifth, movements must define their relationships to other actors in the polity. Whether the support of external elites harms a movement or is instead a precondition for its emergence has been debated in resource mobilization literature. Oberschall, for example, assumes that deprived groups are too weak to launch successful challenges on their own and thus require the help of external allies like churches, foundations, or the government.[37] McAdam, on the other hand, demonstrates that external elite support was absent until the American civil rights movement had already mounted a successful challenge, which rested instead on the strength of indigenous organization.[38]

Resource mobilization theory has contributed a great deal to our general understanding of the problems movements face and of some of the crucial elements of their rise and success. Unquestionably, a movement without sufficient resources would never get off the ground or achieve any kind of impact. Several problems arise, however, when resource mobilization serves as the sole explanation of social movements.

First, in some cases, the timing of a social movement's emergence shows no relationship to any specific rise in the resources the theory considers important, a rise that catalyzes a movement that was otherwise ready to happen. The timing of German peace movements in both the

---

33. Thomas Rochon, *Mobilizing for Peace: The Antinuclear Movements in Western Europe* (Princeton: Princeton University Press, 1988), chap. 5.

34. Gary Marx, "External Efforts to Damage or Facilitate Social Movements: Some Patterns, Explanations, Outcomes, and Complications," in *The Dynamics of Social Movements,* ed. Zald and McCarthy, 94–125.

35. Freeman, "Resource Mobilization and Strategy," 177.

36. Charles Tilly, "Repertoires of Contention in America and Britain, 1750–1830," in *The Dynamics of Social Movements,* ed. Zald and McCarthy, 126–55.

37. Oberschall, *Social Conflict and Social Movements,* 214.

38. Doug McAdam, *Political Process and the Development of Black Insurgency 1930–1970* (Chicago: University of Chicago Press, Chicago, 1982), chap. 6.

1950s and the 1980s, for example, must be explained by factors other than a rise in resources "essential" to the movement. More generally, while the theory rightly points to the importance of resources, it does not account for their genesis, for why they increase or decrease in availability. According to McAdam, the theory's closest answer is that the availability of resources varies according to "shifting patterns of elite largess."[39]

Second, resource mobilization theory assumes that grievances are constant factors of political life, at least among disadvantaged populations or groups with neglected causes. But grievances do not always exist as constant factors. Minorities may consistently suffer objective disadvantages, but they may not perceive their situation as unjust. Similarly, in the case of peace movements, nuclear weapons always pose a danger to the human race in principle, but most of the time, the populace of their host countries lives reasonably comfortably with them. Only occasionally do nuclear weapons become such a salient issue that they constitute a grievance strong enough to mobilize ordinary people or even political activists.

Finally, resource mobilization theory's stress on organization is vindicated by the experiences of many movements. For movements of disadvantaged minorities, mobilization can begin with preexisting indigenous organizations of the minority in question. In the case of movements pursuing a more broadly shared "public" good (e.g., peace or ecology), however, there is no "indigenous" group. In such cases, resource mobilization theory can not explain which groups provide the most fertile field for mobilization.

Toward an Alternate Explanation: A "Political Process" Approach for a Public-Goods Movement

Modernization theories of macrolevel social and economic change provide clues about the broad framework in which social movements arise. Resource mobilization theory instructs us about their organizational and infrastructure requirements. Central questions, however, still remain concerning our movements of interest: German peace movements since 1945.[40]

Whereas many protest movements pursue expanded rights for disadvantaged social groups, peace movements belong to a different category—those movements concerned with the provision of goods shared equally by

---

39. Ibid., 21.

40. Given the lack of organizational continuity between the several sustained episodes of peace protest since 1945, perhaps it would be a mistake to speak of *the* peace movement for this period. There are, however, considerable thematic and personnel continuities connecting the various episodes, as well as a number of discontinuities.

all sectors of society. In this sense, peace movements are *public-goods movements,* despite political conflict over how to achieve peace, or the salience of peace in comparison with other values, such as a democratic political order or human rights. Nevertheless, peace is a public good in that it is enjoyed by all or none. Indeed, peace was perhaps the purest public good in what used to be the two Germanies—small, densely populated countries on the front line of two confrontational military alliances equipped with nuclear weapons. Neither nuclear nor conventional war in Europe would have made distinctions between Germans on the basis of class, gender, age, or region. Thus apart from the hazards of chance, peace was a good that everyone shared equally or no one enjoyed at all.

Nonetheless, peace movements enjoyed only periodic success at large-scale mobilization and were populated (especially at their activist cores) by only certain groups. We return, therefore, to our initial questions. First, given the constant potential threat of nuclear destruction, what explains the timing of peace protest's ebb and flow, its varying levels of mobilization and quiescence? Second, since there is no "natural" constituency, no "indigenous" social group for a peace movement, what explains the composition of its activist core—the involvement of some groups and not others? Third, what explains variations in the movement's organizational structure and strategy, and what did each contribute to the movement?

To explore these questions, we turn to a body of theory that focuses on three core elements in analyzing social movements. Some scholars specifically call the combination of these three a political process approach.[41] Even if the term *political process* is not explicitly used, moreover, the core elements (alone or in combination) also constitute key analytic categories in a considerable body of recent work on European social movements.[42] This approach views social movements as arising above all from the dynamics of their own polity, or, in McAdam's terms, as the process by which otherwise excluded groups periodically attain political leverage by overcoming the environmental constraints that normally

---

41. McAdam, *Political Process*; Christian Joppke, *Mobilizing against Nuclear Energy: A Comparison of West Germany and the United States* (Berkeley: University of California Press, 1993); Anne Costain, *Inviting Women's Rebellion: A Political Process Interpretation of the Women's Movement* (Baltimore: Johns Hopkins University Press, 1992).

42. Bert Klandermans, Hanspeter Kriesi, and Sidney Tarrow, eds., *From Structure to Action: Comparing Social Movement Research across Cultures* (Greenwich, Conn.: JAI Press, 1988); Russell Dalton and Manfred Kuechler, eds., *Challenging the Political Order: New Social and Political Movements in Western Democracies* (Oxford: Polity Press, 1990); and Sidney Tarrow, *Democracy and Disorder: Protest and Politics in Italy 1965–75* (Oxford: Clarendon Press, 1989).

inhibit them from insurgency.[43] A political process approach contains three elements: the political environment that constrains or permits insurgency (the political opportunity structure), the transformation of consciousness required to launch and sustain a social movement, and the organizational networks necessary for protest.

Political Opportunity Structure

A movement's political opportunity structure is made up of the factors in its broader environment that facilitate or hinder its emergence and success. Improvements in political opportunities should help a movement emerge or succeed, whereas a movement should suffer when its opportunities deteriorate. A political opportunity structure is, scholars agree, a set of factors conditioning a movement's chances. Thus far, however, students of social movements have proven unable to specify a finite set of factors that would constitute the opportunity structure for each and every movement. Instead, its content varies from movement to movement, due to the sheer heterogeneity of movements, polities, and historical circumstances.

Political opportunity structures vary in both structural and conjunctural terms.[44] Structural features of a political system are by definition relatively constant, and they change only incrementally if at all. Structural features become especially important when comparing movements occurring in different countries or other geographical units. Kitschelt's classic study of antinuclear power movements in four countries demonstrates the importance of structural factors for the strategies and impact of antinuclear movements.[45] In "open" and/or "weak" systems, movements adopt assimilative strategies and attempt to work through established institutions, because the latter offer multiple points of access during the formulation and implementation stages of policy making, respectively. In contrast,

---

43. McAdam, *Political Process,* chap. 3.

44. This distinction is well developed by William Gamson and David Meyer, "The Framing of Political Opportunity" (paper presented at the annual meeting of the American Sociological Association, Pittsburgh, Pa., Aug. 1992).

45. Herbert Kitschelt, "Political Opportunity Structures and Political Protest: Anti-Nuclear Movements in Four Democracies," *British Journal of Political Science* 16 (1986): 57–85. Kitschelt distinguishes between "open" and "closed" political systems on the "input" side of policy making and between "strong" and "weak" states in terms of policy "output," or implementation. Openness of the political system depends on the number of political parties or factions articulating demands in electoral politics, the capacity of the legislature to develop policies independently of the executive, the extent of pluralism in interest intermediation, and the capacity for building effective policy coalitions. State "strength" in policy implementation depends on the degree of state centralization, government control over market participants, and the independence of the judiciary and its authority to resolve political conflicts.

"closed" and/or "strong" systems encourage confrontational strategies conducted outside established channels, because of their very limited points of access for outside actors during either stage of policy making.

Comparing movements across time within a given country and analyzing a specific movement's trajectory, in contrast, require examination of conjunctural aspects of political opportunity, dynamic features of politics that vary widely from one period to the next. For most movements, these dynamic elements of political opportunity consist of political, social, and economic processes that shape the power resources of movement actors over time. Tarrow's complex study of Italian protest in the 1960s and 1970s relates the rise of protest to improved political opportunities, which removed previous structural obstacles to insurgency. For example, as Italy moved to "mature capitalism," the labor market tightened and gave workers new leverage. At the same time, the end of conservative political hegemony and the socialists' entry into government opened space for new political demands by revealing divisions within governing elites while also reducing the new coalition's willingness to repress protest.[46] Similarly, in his comparison of peasant mobilization in Central American countries, Brockett discusses a number of conjunctural elements of political opportunity, including changes in support by external (often church-based) allies, the regime's capacity to repress insurgency, and elite fragmentation and conflict.[47]

Compared with peace movements in other countries, German peace movements confirm Kitschelt's thesis that a closed political system will lead to extraparliamentary movements with confrontational strategies.[48] Despite certain limits on the national government's power (e.g., federalism and coalition government),[49] Germany's policy-making structures constitute a relatively closed system. They offer little access to policy making to interests not already represented by the parliamentary parties or by the peak associations involved in Germany's moderately corporatist system.[50]

---

46. Tarrow, *Democracy and Disorder*, chap. 2.

47. Charles Brockett, "The Structure of Political Opportunities and Peasant Mobilization in Central America," *Comparative Politics* 23, no. 3 (1991): 253–74.

48. L. Marvin Overby, "West European Peace Movements: An Application of Kitschelt's Political Opportunity Structures Thesis," *West European Politics* 13, no. 1 (Jan. 1990): 1–11.

49. Peter Katzenstein, *Policy and Politics in West Germany* (Philadelphia, Pa.: Temple University Press, 1987).

50. As Overby notes, the "class structure of its parties, the weakness of its legislature and the insulation of its executive branch are all indicative of a fairly inaccessible input struc-

The relatively closed German political system has been a constant structural feature of West German peace movements across the decades and explains their largely extraparliamentary and confrontational character.

Understanding the historical ebb and flow of German peace protest over time, however, requires considering political opportunities of a more variable, conjunctural sort. For German peace movements, then, the question becomes: Are there factors that explain varying levels of peace mobilization across more than four decades—that is, the relatively stunted peace movements of the 1950s and 1960s, the virtual absence of peace protest during the 1970s, the explosive peace mobilization of the early 1980s, and its waning thereafter? For most social movements, the most important political opportunities are those that affect the power resources of otherwise disadvantaged groups in their attempts to attain expanded rights or improve their economic status. For peace movements, however, the issue is *not* improved legal or economic status for the citizens involved, since they generally belong to the middle class and already enjoy incorporation into conventional politics. Instead, peace movements (like ecology movements) pursue issues that lack adequate representation through established institutions and channels. Thus peace movements stand out because they need favorable political opportunities for their issue, since most people accommodate themselves to nuclear weapons most of the time.

Comparisons of peace movement mobilization across time reveal five key factors of political opportunity. The first three concern the issue itself—the salience of the issue, the credibility of the movement's positions in comparison to those of the government, and the extent to which the movement serves as the chief mouthpiece for opposition to government policy. First, mobilization for peace protest requires a salient defense issue because the general public pays little attention to security matters except when significant weapons decisions or unfolding military conflicts are on the active political agenda. Peace movements thus depend heavily on the policy process of their own governments or, in the West, of NATO to present them with significant nuclear weapons procurement plans, which temporarily turn nuclear weapons into salient political issues. Peace move-

---

ture" ("West European Peace Movements," 3). On the "output," or implementation, side of policy making, Germany does offer some access to outside interests or opinions, particularly through the court system, which has led to some assimilative strategies by opposition groups during this part of the process. Since defense decisions are implemented supranationally at the NATO level, however, this avenue of influence is closed to peace movements once decisions have been reached.

ments can not ordinarily launch an "issue-attention cycle"[51] concerning defense issues on their own, without the help of government proposals to acquire new weapons systems or make some other major change in security policy.

Second, once the movement has a salient issue to work with, its arguments must also seem credible to the public if it is to mobilize on a broad scale. The movement's credibility depends on congruence between its prescriptions for security, on the one hand, and popular perceptions of the international environment, on the other. This congruence in turn depends on such things as the public's perception of friend and foe, whether popular fear of war outweighs perceptions of enemy threat, and the presence or absence of accepted nonmilitary alternatives to security.

Third, the movement's monopoly on opposition to government policy facilitates mobilization, whereas institutionalization of the peace movement's positions tends to reduce mobilization. On the one hand, parties and other institutional allies contribute organizational resources to movements. This cooperation can be quite useful when protest is not yet embedded in the broader political culture, and it does not necessarily reduce mobilization in the short run when defense issues are salient. On the other hand, in the longer run, institutionalization of a social movement's positions in conventional politics often demobilizes the movement's participants, and alliances with parties and other institutions may render the movement dependent on their continued willingness to represent it. Movements fare best when they can both mobilize independently of parties and serve as the chief mouthpieces for opposition to government policy.

The fourth key factor of political opportunity is that peace movements benefit from a high propensity toward extraparliamentary activity (a high protest potential) in the populace at large and from a political culture generally supportive of protest as a means of articulating interests or opinions. However, for peace movements to benefit from high levels of popular mobilization, their issue must take priority over other potentially competing concerns. Finally, the fifth key factor of political opportunity is that peace mobilization is facilitated when the government's policy "package" (its most prominent and most interrelated economic, social, and foreign policies, etc.) is already under stress across the board. Disappointment with a broad range of government policies enlarges the currently available protest potential and makes breaking with defense policy less politically or psychologically dissonant. In contrast, the broad public is unlikely to protest against defense policy when it supports government policy as a whole in rising numbers.

---

51. Anthony Downs, "Up and Down with Ecology—the 'Issue-Attention Cycle,' " *Public Interest* 28 (summer 1972): 38–50.

While the above elements of political opportunity would plausibly govern the chances of peace movements in most countries, the West German case had a particular twist all its own. Since 1945, both government defense policy and peace movements in (West) Germany have been closely bound up with the "German question," which had at least three aspects: first, how could Germany overcome its postwar division, and what territorial borders should it have; second, how should Germany's previous military aggressiveness be contained in the postwar order; and third, what sort of domestic political arrangements were necessary to ensure, this time, the success of democracy? In every era, these questions became intertwined with issues of security and peace, giving West German peace movements a flavor unique in Europe.

As we will see, the overall configuration of these factors goes a long way to explain variations in mobilization over the decades. In the 1950s and 1960s, their configuration as a whole was somewhat, but only weakly, favorable, and the movements of these decades remained relatively stunted. In the 1970s, the weakness of these factors went hand in hand with the virtual absence of peace protest. In the early 1980s, however, the overall configuration of these factors was quite favorable and contributed to the biggest peace movement in German history.

Ideological Resources and the Creation of Peace Constituencies

Resource mobilization theory originally assumed that dissatisfaction was a relatively constant feature of political life, and it correspondingly accorded grievances only secondary importance in the emergence of social movements.[52] More recent work, however, has reevaluated the contribution of subjective assessments to mobilization. As McAdam notes, an improved political opportunity structure provides a structural potential for social movements but is not in itself sufficient to launch one: "Mediating between opportunity and action are people and the subjective meanings they attach to their situations."[53] People must make the conscious decision to participate in social movements. For any given individual, many "extraneous" influences, such as curiosity, rebellion against parental views, or the actions of peers, may play a role. Viewed as a whole, however, movements come to share a collective consciousness, despite factionalism, diverging individual agendas, and sheer ideological diversity. Without this shared consciousness, people will not act together, and movements will not emerge.

52. McCarthy and Zald, "Resource Mobilization," 15–49.
53. McAdam, *Political Process,* 48.

How does this shared consciousness form? Scholars studying citizenship movements often stress the growth of consciousness among the disadvantaged group in question, which frequently focuses on the injustice the group suffers in terms of norms of equality or autonomy prevailing in the larger society. In order to launch insurgency, McAdam maintains, disadvantaged groups must first undergo "cognitive liberation," by realizing that their situation is unjust and that remedy is possible.[54] Similarly, Klein argues that the emergence of the American women's movement presupposed a change in consciousness on the part of women—in particular, development of a group identity and rejection of traditional, biologically defined roles.[55]

Peace movements also depend on a cognitive process, but on one very different from those that occur among disadvantaged groups. People do not join peace movements because they share a common disadvantaged status or belong to an oppressed minority. Instead, a peace movement's constituencies are ideologically determined, on the basis of common convictions. At the level of sympathizers and occasional participants, ideological mobilization occurs as people come to perceive an urgent nuclear threat to their own personal survival. To establish this urgency, the peace movement must establish the plausibility of its strategic-military analysis vis-à-vis the government's and must capture the moral high ground on defense issues. The peace movement must thus engage in what Bert Klandermans calls "consensus mobilization," spreading its point of view through petitions, information stands, discussion forums, and the like.[56]

For the movement's activist core, the process of ideological self-definition is more complex, and it sheds light on how the movement constitutes itself. The core of the movement grows as, in Klandermans's terms, "consensus formation" takes place—an "unplanned convergence of meaning" that occurs as defense issues are discussed within and among subcultural networks.[57] For core activist groups, the question becomes: Are there factors that explain why some groups become involved while others do not? As we will see in subsequent chapters, groups become involved in peace protest when they have access to "interpretive frames" that invite such participation.

---

54. Ibid.
55. Ethel Klein, "The Diffusion of Consciousness in the United States and Western Europe," in *The Women's Movements in the United States and Western Europe,* ed. Mary Katzenstein and Carol Mueller (Philadelphia, Pa.: Temple University Press, 1987), 23–43.
56. Bert Klandermans, "The Formation and Mobilization of Consensus," in *From Structure to Action: Comparing Social Movement Research across Cultures,* ed. Bert Klandermans, Hanspeter Kriesi, and Sidney Tarrow (Greenwich, Conn.: JAI Press, 1988), 173–96.
57. Ibid., 175.

At their core, German peace movements have always consisted of a coalition of preexisting politically active groups. Very few of these groups, however, were founded explicitly as "peace" groups. The vast majority were religious groups, party or union subgroups, or groups that came from the extraparliamentary left, such as feminists or ecologists. Although these groups shared a general opposition to the status quo, their writings reveal quite group-specific reasons for their opposition to government defense policy. On a more or less individual basis, these groups joined the peace movement as they realized that peace was central to their prior concerns. Groups coming from mainstream institutions like parties, churches, or unions based their peace activism on interpretive frames drawn from their own institutions. Social Democratic peace activists in the 1980s, for example, based their opposition to new missiles on their party's official policy of détente, arguing that peace in Europe rested on East-West dialogue and that new missiles would endanger this process. Groups coming from the extraparliamentary left joined the peace movement when they discovered an issue overlap between the missile question and their own central concerns. Ecology groups, for example, became active when they determined that nuclear weapons threatened the environment just as much as the nuclear power plants whose construction they had so ardently fought.

Thus movements actively produce meaning as their coalition of activists grows. As groups discover links between peace and their own concerns, they join the movement and at the same time expand its ideological underpinnings. In other words, as groups join, the movement develops a "cognitive identity," based on a shared body of beliefs about politics, as well as more specific complaints about defense issues.[58] As a broad panoply of groups makes peace its common cause, the movement as a whole develops a multifaceted, richly textured rationale for opposing government policy, here termed the movement's *ideological resources*. In the process, a narrowly defined defense issue—whether to acquire certain nuclear weapons systems—becomes much broader as it becomes linked with all manner of additional concerns. At the same time, peace becomes all the more worth fighting for when it becomes linked to political morality, feminism, ecology, and the like.[59]

---

58. The term *cognitive identity* comes from Ron Eyerman and Andrew Jamison, *Social Movements: A Cognitive Approach* (University Park, Pa.: Pennsylvania State University Press, 1991), chap. 3.

59. Snow and Benford use the term *framing* to describe this process of structuring meaning, or attaching meanings to events and conditions. See David Snow and Robert Benford, "Ideology, Frame Resonance, and Participant Mobilization," in *From Structure to Action*, ed. Klandermans, Kriesi, and Tarrow, 197–217.

Organization

The political process approach emphasizes the importance of organization for a movement's success and argues (in agreement with resource mobilization theory) that social movements can not exist without a certain level of organization. The nature of a movement's organization, moreover, constrains the type of tactics it can effectively employ.[60] Are there factors that determined the organizational structure and strategy of German peace movements in any given episode of sustained mass mobilization, and did variations in organizational structure contribute to movement effectiveness? Launching the American civil rights movement required the growth of an indigenous black organizational network, composed of Southern black churches, colleges, and chapters of the National Association for the Advancement of Colored People (NAACP).[61] Because they were public-goods movements, however, the capacity of peace movements to organize did not depend on the development of indigenous organization within a deprived group, since there is no "indigenous" population for a peace movement. Instead, German peace movements experienced two different sources of organizational potential over time.

In the 1950s, there were relatively few autonomous groups in the extraparliamentary arena, and the peace movement of that decade had little choice but to rely on parties and unions for its main organizational resources. Starting in the 1960s, however, the peace movement itself built a stronger extraparliamentary organization, and over time, it was increasingly able to draw on protest networks autonomous from any established political or social institution. The two types of organization had very different consequences for the respective movements' effectiveness. The peace movement of the 1950s had difficulty mobilizing until parties and unions saw fit to join its efforts, and it disintegrated when these institutions severed their links. An autonomous organizational infrastructure characterized subsequent movements. This infrastructure allowed the movements to mobilize even when virtually no established political institutions sup-

---

60. Freeman notes that many movements run into trouble when they attempt to pursue strategies incompatible with their structures. Decentralized movements, for example, are restricted to activities that small groups can perform without extensive divisions of labor, like educational or service projects at the local level. Nationwide organizations, however, sometimes have trouble decentralizing their strategy. The National Organization of Women, for example, had trouble pursuing the Equal Rights Amendment on the state level with the requisite speed, because it lacked state-level chapters. Despite its national and local chapters already in existence, creating state chapters proved time-consuming. See Freeman, "Resource Mobilization and Strategy," 184.

61. McAdam, *Political Process,* chap. 5.

ported them,[62] and it permitted organizational maintenance for as long as the groups involved saw fit. As we shall see in chapters 3 and 4, the evolution of the German polity in the 1960s and 1970s made possible the organizational infrastructure of protest on which these later peace movements drew.

The factors influencing peace movements discussed in this chapter provide a foundation for analysis of peace movements in West Germany (from 1945 to 1989) and their role in the new unified Germany. As we will see in subsequent chapters, peace movements most successfully mobilize the populace and influence politics when three main factors converge: when the larger political environment favors mobilization, when the movement develops an ideology capable of transforming popular consciousness and attracting a broad coalition of activists, and when the movement enjoys organizational autonomy from parties and other social institutions.

---

62. They drew on subgroups within these institutions but were not dependent on the institutions themselves.

CHAPTER 2

The 1950s: Burning Issues
but Stunted Protest

According to several social movement theories discussed in chapter 1, the 1950s peace movement should never have happened. Few Germans had escaped the war unscathed, and no postwar generation had yet experienced peace or prosperity long enough to develop postmaterialist values or a "new politics" orientation. The majority of the populace did indeed crave security, as the theory of value change would predict. Nevertheless, substantial numbers participated in the peace movement despite its rejection of rearmament and nuclear weapons. Likewise, in Habermas's terms, processes of modernization, rationalization, bureaucratization, and "colonization of the life-world" had by no means reached their height yet, and they are generally not advanced as explanations for peace movements in the 1950s.

Understanding the peace movement of the 1950s requires looking at its political opportunity structure, its ideological resources, and its organizational structure. The movement arose despite an uneven political opportunity structure, but it remained stunted compared to later movements. (At its high point, around 325,000 people participated in its demonstrations,[1] whereas the 1980s movement attracted 2–4 million in a single week in 1983.)[2] The 1950s movement developed considerable ideological resources, but their credibility suffered in the political environment of the time. It mobilized a diverse set of oppositional groups, but problems in its organization and strategy left the movement vulnerable to collapse. In this chapter, we will seek to explain why the peace movement was launched in

---

1. Hans Karl Rupp, *Außerparlamentarische Opposition in der Ära Adenauer* (Cologne: Pahl-Rugenstein, 1980), 191.

2. Joyce Mushaben, "Grassroots and *Gewaltfreie Aktion:* A Study of Mass Mobilization Strategies in the West German Peace Movement," *Journal of Peace Research* 23, no. 2, (1986): 141–55, here 143.

the 1950s, who peopled its activist core, and how it fared—what constraints on mobilization it faced, why its impact on politics and policy remained limited, and why it ultimately disintegrated.

Launching the 1950s Peace Movement

Two policy decisions directly catalyzed peace protest in the 1950s—rearmament and nuclear weapons on German soil. Because their high salience catalyzed the peace movement's emergence and enhanced its capacity to mobilize, these policy decisions represented the few favorable elements of political opportunity in the 1950s, a time otherwise bleak for protest movements of any sort. The 1950s were a defining decade for West German politics, a time in which political, economic, and social institutions assumed their basic (though not immutable) contours.

As chancellor from 1949 to 1963, Konrad Adenauer left an indelible mark on the young republic. The Adenauer era consolidated West German democracy, based on a new parliamentary political order, a revived capitalist economy complemented by an increasingly generous welfare state, and a foreign policy of military, political, and economic integration into larger Western structures. These three pillars of the new democracy became so integrally related that they constituted a political and policy package in the minds of Adenauer himself, his supporters, and his opponents alike. Thus opposition to one pillar of the package (Western military integration—or, specifically, rearmament and nuclear weapons) was part of, and a vehicle for, opposition to the Adenauer era more broadly. As a consequence, a brief sketch of the Adenauer era will facilitate examination of peace protest in the 1950s—its political opportunities, the issues it addressed, its organizational and strategic dilemmas, and its ultimately limited impact.

The 1950s saw the consolidation of a new parliamentary order. Despite Germany's prior experience with authoritarian regimes and the failure of the Weimar Republic's experiment with democracy, West Germany's parliamentary system quickly proved itself a paragon of democratic stability. This stability was partly achieved through the design of political institutions. To avoid the abuses of power and the governmental instability that had scuttled the Weimar Republic, the Basic Law[3] both constrained the power of national governments (e.g., through a Constitutional Court exercising judicial review and through a federal system with important rights reserved for the states) and promoted their stability and effectiveness (e.g., by preventing the chancellor's easy removal at the whim

---

3. The Basic Law was for all intents and purposes West Germany's constitution. Its name implied its provisional nature until reunification might come to pass.

of the cabinet).[4] Electoral law also contributed to stability. In a system of overall proportional representation,[5] each party must receive 5 percent of the total vote to get any seats at all. For much of the time, this requirement restricted the number of parties represented in the Bundestag (parliament) to a "manageable" three or four, thereby facilitating coalition formation and durability.

The transformation of the party system also contributed to political stability and moderation. In the course of the 1950s, the party spectrum narrowed and concentrated itself around right and left poles as two major "catch-all" parties developed. Since they eschewed the democratic order, the Constitutional Court banned the neo-Nazi Sozialistische Reichspartei (SRP) and the Communist Party (Kommunistische Partei Deutschlands, or KPD), narrowing the party spectrum on both ends. In addition, the conservative Christlich-Demokratische Union/Christlich-Soziale Union (CDU/CSU) attracted a wide variety of industrial, middle-class, working-class, religious, and agrarian interests, absorbing in the process a variety of small parties on the right.[6] The CDU/CSU reaped the rewards of Adenauer's policy successes and electoral strategy by continually increasing its share of the vote in federal elections.[7]

The CDU/CSU's success on the right mirrored the Social Democrats' electoral stagnation on the left. Over the course of the 1950s, the Sozialdemokratische Partei Deutschlands (SPD) drew the necessary conclusions and underwent its own evolution toward a catch-all party. With no communist competitor on its left, the SPD felt freer to move toward the center of the political spectrum, moderating its image and its program. In 1959 the SPD presented its historic Godesberg Program, in which it cast

---

4. Governments remain in office until replaced through electoral defeat or through a "constructive vote of no confidence" in the Bundestag, which must elect a new chancellor before withdrawing its confidence from the old one.

5. Despite its complicated two-vote procedures, Germany effectively enjoys a system of proportional representation, modified by the "5 percent hurdle."

6. During the Empire and Weimar Republic, numerous parties had devoted themselves to narrow class, regional, or religious interests. After the war, in contrast, the CDU/CSU directed its appeal to both Protestants and Catholics, overcoming the confessional divide that had earlier splintered the nonsocialist vote. The CDU/CSU also bridged class barriers, attracting most of the rural and urban middle classes and even many workers. Finally, the CDU/CSU pitched its appeal to regional interests, particularly to a Bavarian regional party and to the expellees from former German lands in the East. Thus CDU/CSU was able to absorb small right-wing parties, which succumbed to the 5 percent electoral hurdle, Adenauer's successful policies, and his explicitly catch-all strategy. See R. E. M. Irving, *The Christian Democratic Parties of Western Europe* (London: Allen and Unwin, 1979), chap. 4.

7. William Chandler, "Party System Transformations in the Federal Republic of Germany," in *Parties and Party Systems in Liberal Democracies,* ed. Steven Wolinetz (New York: Routledge, 1988), 59–83.

off its Marxist "ballast" and declared its support for West Germany's capitalist economy and national defense. Thus by 1961 only three parties still enjoyed parliamentary representation: the conservative CDU/CSU, the liberal Freie Demokratische Partei (FDP), and the social democratic SPD.

In the economic sphere, two major developments stand out: the emergence of the "social-market economy" and the "economic miracle." Adenauer and his economics minister, Ludwig Erhard, initiated a market economy moderated by a (initially limited) welfare state. Government intervention was admittedly substantial when it came to subsidies and tax advantages for agriculture and industry, monetary policy, and public sector employment. German industry and banking, moreover, remained highly concentrated despite Allied efforts at decartelization. Nonetheless, the economy remained fundamentally capitalist in terms of property relations. Both the currency reform of 1948 and the "equalization of burdens" law of 1952, moreover, tended to reestablish earlier patterns of wealth and asset distribution and to protect ownership of property that had survived the war.[8]

Despite the extreme hardship of the early postwar years, the 1950s gradually witnessed Germany's "economic miracle," with average growth rates of 7–8 percent. Many factors contributed to the enormous economic dynamism of the period. The worldwide economic boom of the 1950s paved the way for the rapid growth of Germany's export sector, while reconstruction of housing, transportation, and consumer items provided high domestic demand. Government tax policy favored capital formation, while the undervalued currency underwrote the export boom. Immigration of highly skilled labor from East Germany prevented labor shortages, and a very low strike rate enhanced overall productivity. Wages grew rapidly, despite the high unemployment of the first five to ten postwar years, but not faster than productivity gains.[9]

Complementing the establishment of a parliamentary order and social-market economy, foreign policy constituted the final leg of Adenauer's political and policy trio. Here, too, the 1950s defined basic structures and policies for the next several decades. West Germany joined NATO in 1955 and created a new army, the Bundeswehr. Three years later, the Parliament voted to station American tactical nuclear weapons on German soil. These acts officially incorporated West Germany into West-

---

8. Christoph Klessmann, *Die doppelte Staatsgründung* (Göttingen: Vandenhoeck and Ruprecht, 1982), 188–91, 240–43.

9. Michael Kreile, "West Germany: The Dynamics of Expansion," in *Between Power and Plenty: Foreign Economic Policy of Advanced Industrial States,* ed. Peter Katzenstein (Madison: University of Wisconsin Press, 1986), 191–224.

ern defense structures, part of Adenauer's broader strategy to integrate the country politically, militarily, and economically into the West. Departing from the frequently aggressive nationalism of Germany's past, Adenauer's policy of Western integration reflected a supranationalist foreign-policy vision.[10] The road to these decisions was long and hotly debated, both domestically and in international politics.[11] These foreign policy issues provided the catalysts for peace protest in the 1950s.

Few observers in 1945 would have predicted German rearmament so soon after World War II. Initial Allied plans emphasized the demilitarization and denazification of Germany and, at their most extreme, the dismantling of its industry. Nonetheless, by 1949 the West had agreed to the Federal Republic's creation, and in 1955 it accepted West German rearmament and NATO membership. Germany's very existence and inclusion in NATO came about through the convergence of international developments and Adenauer's strategies. By the late 1940s, the West was embroiled in the cold war with the Soviet Union and its allies, which was heightened in the early 1950s by the Korean War. German rearmament suddenly appeared essential to America's containment policy in Europe.

West German rearmament served Adenauer's political agenda just as effectively as it fit into the West's military strategy. Rearmament and NATO membership served as vehicles for regaining almost full sovereignty from foreign occupation,[12] which made West Germany almost equal to the other West European countries in international affairs. In effect, Adenauer traded occupation status for the interdependence of military integration into the Western Alliance. Rearmament and NATO membership were integral to Adenauer's plan for German integration into the West in all senses—military, political, economic, and cultural.[13] Close ties to the other Western democracies, Adenauer felt, would provide the foundation for a liberal-democratic social order in West Germany and would help the

---

10. Dirk Verheyen, *The German Question: A Cultural, Historical, and Geopolitical Exploration* (Boulder, Colo.: Westview Press, 1991), 110.

11. Catherine Kelleher, *Germany and the Politics of Nuclear Weapons* (New York: Columbia University Press, 1975).

12. Arnulf Baring, *Aussenpolitik in Adenauers Kanzlerdemokratie: Bonns Beitrag zur Europäischen Verteidigungsgemeinschaft* (Munich: Oldenbourg Verlag, 1969), 124. Marc Cioc confirms this point in his *Pax Atomica: The Nuclear Defense Debate in West Germany during the Adenauer Era* (New York: Columbia University Press, 1988), 14.

13. Arnulf Baring attributes Adenauer's commitment to Germany's integration with the West to his roots in the Rhineland and his antipathy to Prussia for related historical reasons. His commitment thus seems to have stemmed as much from his personal predilections as from pragmatic or realpolitik considerations of Germany's situation. See Baring, *Aussenpolitik in Adenauers Kanzlerdemokratie,* 48–58.

country resist the dangers emanating from the Soviet Union.[14] Moreover, rearmament played a role in Adenauer's domestic agenda as well, since military and economic integration with the West privileged the restoration of capitalism in West Germany and helped contain pressures for economic and social reform in any socialist direction.[15] Finally, German rearmament had its uses against potential internal communist subversion.[16]

West Germany's acquisition of nuclear weapons shared broad similarities with the country's rearmament—both represented a convergence of American/NATO military strategies and Adenauer's political aims. The alliance initially relied heavily on "massive retaliation," using American nuclear power to deter Soviet conventional aggression. The Soviets' emerging nuclear arsenal, however, increasingly called this strategy into question. Since NATO considered significant increases in conventional troop levels politically infeasible, it decided in 1954 to equip its troops with tactical nuclear weapons. According to Hanrieder and Auton, these weapons "were expected to make up for America's gradual loss of its nuclear monopoly by providing an additional 'firebreak' between conventional provocation and all-out nuclear war."[17]

In addition to these military considerations, Adenauer had political reasons for wanting tactical nuclear weapons on German soil once they had been incorporated into NATO strategy. In particular, he wanted to keep Germany on an equal footing with the rest of the European NATO countries and to prevent any inferiority of status that would make Germany more vulnerable to Soviet expansionist pressure. Finally, Adenauer wanted to use German acceptance of nuclear weapons to counterbalance the Anglo-American "special relationship" and French efforts at continental dominance.[18]

In short, the Adenauer era saw the consolidation of parliamentary democracy and the social-market economy, complemented by his policy of *Westbindung,* the integration of West Germany militarily, politically, and economically (through the European Economic Community [EEC]) into Western Europe. On the plus side, Adenauer provided a plausible solution to two components of the German question. First, he oversaw the intro-

---

14. Helga Haftendorn, *Sicherheit und Entspannung: Zur Außenpolitik der Bundesrepublik Deutschland 1955–1982* (Baden-Baden: Nomos Verlagsgesellschaft, 1986), 70.

15. William Graf, *The German Left since 1945: Socialism and Social Democracy in the German Federal Republic* (New York: Oleander Press, 1976), 100.

16. Joachim Hütter, *SPD und nationale Sicherheit: Internationale und innenpolitische Determinanten des Wandels der sozialdemokratischen Sicherheitspolitik 1959–1961* (Meisenheim am Glan: Verlag Anton Hain, 1975), 58.

17. Wolfram Hanrieder and Graeme Auton, *The Foreign Policies of West Germany, France, and Britain* (Englewood Cliffs, N.J.: Prentice Hall, 1980), 6; Cioc, *Pax Atomica,* 3–7.

18. Haftendorn, *Sicherheit und Entspannung,* 163–65.

duction of a restructured democratic order, one more likely to endure than the Weimar Republic and more likely to permanently overcome the uncertainties of the authoritarian legacy. Second, Western integration had resulted in at least partial national sovereignty after the experience of occupation. Furthermore, West German membership in NATO guaranteed the containment of Germany's military potential and thus addressed another ghost of Germany's past.

Laudable as these accomplishments were, however, they did not come without costs. West Germany's integration into the West left two important aspects of the German question glaringly unresolved. First, West Germany's national sovereignty remained incomplete, especially in the area of national security. West Germany remained profoundly dependent on the United States for its security and lacked national control over its armed forces. Second and even more important was the unresolved problem of German division. West Germany achieved its integration into Western Europe at the widely perceived cost of making German reunification more difficult or even impossible.

According to Wolfram Hanrieder, there was a fundamental contradiction between West German foreign policy goals in the East and its goals in the West. Western integration brought security, partial sovereignty, prosperity, and a stable democratic order; but at the same time, it sealed German division. To be sure, conservatives denied that Western integration and reunification were incompatible. They assumed that the West supported reunification and that the balance of power would shift to the West, permitting reunification on Western terms. In the short term, however, the Soviet bloc refused to dissolve with the requisite dispatch. Despite a series of four-power conferences (the United States, Britain, France, and the Soviet Union) and the "Stalin note" of 1952, which offered the tantalizing prospect of reunification and "guarantees" of democracy in exchange for a neutralized Germany, West German membership in NATO ultimately reduced whatever willingness the Soviets might have had to relinquish "their" Germany. At the same time, both Adenauer and the Western powers rejected German neutralization as the price for reunification. Under these circumstances, German unification perforce remained a merely rhetorical goal.[19]

In the 1950s, rearmament, NATO membership, and nuclear weapons proved highly salient issues for a variety of reasons, providing the peace movement with its most positive element of political opportunity. The importance of these issues in defining the fundamental orientation of West German foreign policy, along with the parade of corresponding proposals

19. Wolfram Hanrieder, *Germany, America, Europe* (New Haven: Yale University Press, 1990), part 2.

and treaties, kept them in nearly continuous public view for most of the decade.[20] Successive four-power failures to resolve German division kept the German question formally open, while West Germany's integration into NATO and other Western structures increasingly precluded reunification in the near future. Because of their impact on chances for reunification, rearmament and nuclear weapons enjoyed heightened salience in the public view, allowing the peace movement to link them to the unresolved German question. In the meantime, the Berlin crises, and other cold war developments reflected superpower tensions and brought home the possibility of another European war.

Discussion of rearmament in the early 1950s invoked fresh and vivid memories of the last war. Later, scientists explosively brought the issue of nuclear weapons home to the public. In 1957, eighteen of West Germany's most famous nuclear scientists (the "Göttingen 18") warned publicly against the destructive powers of tactical nuclear weapons. Their vivid depictions of nuclear explosions over Germany recalled Hiroshima's fate and made clear the possibility of Germany's sharing it. Their warning had all the more impact because the political culture of the times was not accustomed to scientists' taking positions critical of government policy.[21] The media devoted ample space to the issue throughout the decade. Finally, rearmament in both East and West Germany raised the prospect of a German "civil war" in the context of a broader East-West struggle.

Framing the Issues: The Composition of the 1950s Peace Movement

Rearmament, NATO membership, and nuclear weapons provided a series of grievances that catalyzed the 1950s peace movement. The movement brought together the "losers" of the 1950s, whose hopes for far-reaching reform were being dashed by Adenauer's conservative policies. In the process, the peace movement became part of the larger struggle to resist the consolidation of the postwar era. These "losers" consisted primarily of traditional pacifist groups, neutralist intellectuals, Protestant groups, and

---

20. For example, the Pleven Plan and the proposed European Defense Community stirred debate before NATO membership was finally arrived at, while the Radford Plan and the Carte Blanche exercises stirred additional debate along the way.

21. Signers included Nobel prize winners Max Born, Otto Hahn, Werner Heisenberg, and Max von Laue. See Rupp, *Außerparlamentarische Opposition,* 73–78; Hans-Josef Legrand, "Friedensbewegungen in der Geschichte der Bundesrepublik Deutschland: Ein Überblick zur Entwicklung bis Ende der siebziger Jahre," in *Friedensbewegungen: Entwicklung und Folgen in der Bundesrepublik Deutschland, Europa, und den USA,* ed. Josef Janning, Hans-Josef Legrand, and Helmut Zander (Cologne: Verlag Wissenschaft und Politik, 1987), 19–35.

the labor movement.[22] The struggle against rearmament, NATO membership, and nuclear weapons was part of a larger struggle for political and economic reform, both for its own sake and to prevent a revival of fascism by breaking with the previous political, economic, and military relationships considered responsible. In practice, this meant resisting Adenauer's policies, which these groups felt revived dangerous structures responsible for past evils, or which failed to address Germany's needs in the new, bipolar world order.[23]

Pacifist and neutralist involvement was straightforward and predictable, but the bulk of the 1950s peace movement came from the Protestant Church and the labor movement. Given the strength of popular opposition to rearmament and especially to nuclear weapons, why was movement activism particularly concentrated there? After all, 71 percent of CDU members expressed opposition to nuclear weapons,[24] and a significant portion of those members must have been Catholic given the disproportionate Catholic vote for the CDU/CSU. Yet neither CDU/CSU voters (of whatever denomination) nor Catholics (of whatever party affiliation) were more than marginally represented in the peace movement of the 1950s, at least as identifiable groups.

Much of the populace professed itself against Adenauer's security measures in polls, presumably due to horrifying memories of the last war and fear of another. In addition to such sentiments, however, Protestants, the labor movement, neutralists, and pacifists had ideological resources that further motivated them to protest: traditions, ideological leanings, or concerns perceived as overlapping with security issues, based on interpretive frameworks derived from their own institutions. Thus the terms in which the peace movement's constituent groups discussed security issues

---

22. These groups retained remnants of the antimilitarism and anticapitalism that predominated in the public mood right after the war. Containing social democrats, communists, and bourgeois party representatives, grassroots groups called *antifas* (antifascist committees) emerged in the general upheaval surrounding the end of the war and the collapse of the Nazi regime in 1945. By the summer of 1945, however, they had been banned by the occupiers or integrated into party and union formations. Their ideas, however, lived on in their new contexts, mixing with older traditions. In this context, see Lothar Rolke, *Protestbewegungen in der Bundesrepublik* (Opladen: Westdeutscher Verlag, 1987), 117–33.

23. For accounts of the anti-rearmament movement, see Fritz Krause, *Antimilitaristische Opposition in der BRD 1949–1955* (Frankfurt: Verlag Marxistische Blätter, 1971), which, despite Marxist polemics, does not differ from other treatments of the period in its rendition of facts; and Eckart Dietzfelbinger, *Die westdeutsche Friedensbewegung 1948–1955: Die Protestaktionen gegen die Remilitarisierung der Bundesrepublik Deutschland* (Cologne: Pahl-Rugenstein, 1984). On the antinuclear movement, see Rupp, *Außerparlamentarische Opposition*, and Cioc, *Pax Atomica*.

24. Rupp, *Außerparlamentarische Opposition*, 285.

give insight into their motivations for participating, as groups if not as individuals, and thereby into the movement's composition.

The peace movement had three primary diagnostic frames in terms of which they opposed rearmament and nuclear weapons. First, Protestants launched the frame of redemption, arguing that the moral consequences of German guilt for World War II ruled out rearmament and nuclear weapons. Second, the labor movement discussed security issues using the frame of democratization of both society and the economy, arguing that Adenauer's security policies would endanger domestic democracy by reviving the armed forces' traditional antidemocratic militarism and would reinforce capitalism. For them, the fight against remilitarization was part of the struggle against the social-market economy. Third, Protestants and Social Democrats addressed foreign policy in terms of the German question, maintaining that Western military integration would seal German division. They and a number of small independent neutralist groups proposed German neutrality as a means for overcoming national division and bringing peace to Europe. In contrast, neither the Catholic Church nor the CDU provided interpretive frames on which their members could have drawn to motivate protest. Catholics and conservatives would have had to leave their own camps, crossing considerable political and ideological distances, if they had wanted to participate in peace protest.

The Protestant Church and the Peace Movement

Why have Protestants repeatedly been at the forefront of West German peace protest since 1945? Why have explicitly Protestant groups and countless local groups for which an individual Protestant church provided the physical or spiritual center played significant roles in the movement's various leadership structures? In addition to the military requirements of defense, West German debates over security policy have always focused on much broader issues, including the place of morality in politics and defense, the proper role of West Germany in the world, and the relationship of political to military factors in Germany's security policy. To this complex of issues, West Germany's Protestant Church, the Evangelische Kirche in Deutschland (EKD), contributed the notion that German historical guilt resulting from World War II had important implications for postwar foreign policy. Protestant peace groups have explicitly justified their peace protest in terms of this notion of redemption.

Protestants' role in postwar peace movements reflects the Protestant Church's redefinition of its relationship to politics and the state. The Protestant Church inherited the Lutheran tradition of obedience to the state, and yet it became a bastion of peace protest. Fascism and World War II provided the shocks that turned German Protestantism around. After the war, the church reevaluated its relationship to the state and society. Its repentance for its role in the Third Reich laid the foundation for a new Protestant approach to political morality and to defense issues.

For centuries the Protestant Church constituted one of the mainstays of the Prussian, and subsequently German, monarchical order. In the 1800s, German nationalism and unification swept the church along in the general tide of enthusiasm.[25] The church's traditional doctrine of obedience to the state reflected its social and administrative ties to the state. After World War I, the fall of the old imperial order weakened the church's position within the state, which led the clergy to reject the Weimar Republic and ally itself with the conservative forces that undermined it.[26] Much of the Protestant clergy supported Hitler's rise to power,[27] and many joined the Deutsche Christen (German Christians), an organization of Protestant clergy directly subordinated to the state.[28] Protestant clergy extended the same support to the German war effort, at least as revealed in public statements and sermons.[29]

By the early 1950s, however, many Protestants were active in the anti-rearmament movement and participated heavily in all subsequent peace movements. Their activism reflected the Protestant Church's fundamental redefinition of its relationship to politics and the state. The foundations for Protestant political activism were set in the first few years immediately following the war. They consisted of a doctrinal rethinking, namely, the innovative admission that the church had a political, as well as spiritual, responsibility. The church drew two conclusions from the disaster of the

---

25. Karl Kupisch, *Zwischen Idealismus und Massendemokratie: Eine Geschichte der evangelischen Kirche in Deutschland von 1815–1945* (Berlin: Lettner Verlag, 1955), 85.

26. Ibid., 145–47.

27. As many as 80 percent of the Protestant clergy were opposed to the Weimar Republic. See Robert P. Ericksen, "The Barmen Synod and Its Declaration: A Historical Synopsis," in *The Church Confronts the Nazis: Barmen Then and Now,* ed. Hubert Locke (New York: Edwin Mellen Press, 1984), 27–93, here 34.

28. The Deutsche Christen won one-third of the seats to the leadership of the *Altpreußische Union,* the Prussian Church (Kupisch, *Zwischen Idealismus und Massendemokratie,* 189). Just after Hitler's rise to power, the Deutsche Christen received 60–80 percent of the vote (Ericksen, "The Barmen Synod and Its Declaration," 49).

29. This statement comes from an essay on the Protestant Church's reaction to the Third Reich, but it may also refer to Catholics (Ericksen, "The Barmen Synod and Its Declaration," 83). The next essay in the same volume states that the vast majority of German clergy of both churches welcomed Hitler (John Conway, "The German Church Struggle: Its Making and Meaning," in *The Church Confronts the Nazis,* ed. Hubert Locke, 93–145, here 95).

Third Reich: the church could no longer leave the state to its own devices under the premise of full state sovereignty in the political realm; and the church's duty was to keep politics within the bounds of morality and Christian principles. The church's assumption of political responsibility meant a break with two Lutheran traditions. The EKD partially abandoned the *Zwei-Reiche-Lehre* (two-realm doctrine) of leaving politics to the state and significantly weakened its traditionally uncritical relationship to the state. These changes took shape in a series of meetings and statements in the late 1940s.[30]

The mark of the Bekennende Kirche (Confessing Church) on Protestant "new thinking" was evident from the beginning. The Bekennende Kirche had its roots in Protestant attempts to ward off Nazi penetration of the church. Despite their affection for the nationalist and authoritarian tendencies of National Socialism, many clergy resented the Nazis' blatant interference in church affairs. By January 1934, some 7,000 (one-third to one-half) of Germany's Protestant pastors had joined the Pfarrernotbund (Pastors' Emergency League) founded by Martin Niemöller in 1933.[31] Later in 1934, the Bekennende Kirche was founded in the town of Barmen. Its *Barmer Erklärung* (Barmen Declaration) affirmed the church's right to control its own affairs,[32] implicitly challenging the Nazis' claim to absolute power by denying that the state had doctrinal jurisdiction over the church, or that the church could become an organ of the state. The Bekennende Kirche's resistance to the Nazis, however, did not necessarily extend to the war or to other policies unrelated to church affairs.[33] Although individual members of the Bekennende Kirche attacked the Nazis, it never became a center of resistance to the Third Reich, and only a few Protestant churchmen joined the broader German Resistance.[34]

Soon after the end of the war, however, Protestants began to realize what the Third Reich had meant for Germany. Bishop T. Wurm called an assembly at the town of Treysa to reconstitute and reorganize the Protes-

---

30. Although the EKD committed itself to a new political responsibility, the EKD leadership was often split on the concrete implications of this new responsibility.

31. Ericksen, "The Barmen Synod and Its Declaration," 51.

32. Conway, "The German Church Struggle," 105. For an English version of the Erklärung, see Locke, *The Church Confronts the Nazis*, 19–25.

33. According to Robert Ericksen, the Barmen Declaration did not oppose National Socialism or Hitler ("The Barmen Synod and Its Declaration," 77).

34. Conway, "The German Church Struggle," 106, 111. Johanna Vogel calls the Protestant Church at best a "resistance movement against its will." See Vogel, *Kirche und Wiederbewaffnung: Die Haltung der Evangelischen Kirche in Deutschland in den Auseinandersetzungen um die Wiederbewaffnung der Bundesrepublik 1949–1956* (Göttingen: Vandenhoeck and Ruprecht, 1978): 34, 35.

tant Church's structure and liturgy.[35] Calls for purges and broad spiritual reconstruction accompanied this more concrete task. By August of 1945 the Reichsbruderrat, an organ of the Confessing Church, had issued one of the first calls to this larger mission. It declared that the Protestant Church had to reestablish itself according to the *Bekenntnisse* (creed) found in the Barmen Declaration. The tone and content of its "Wort an die Pfarrer" (Message to pastors) revealed the anguish of the authors and their willingness to draw appropriate consequences. As it noted, the unmeasurable abyss of guilt incurred through the Third Reich threatened the very body and soul of the German people. Luckily, the Barmen Declaration provided standards for action, forbidding in particular a return to the blurred boundaries between church and state of the past.[36]

Such churchly deliberations had their greatest public impact in the famous *Stuttgarter Schuldbekenntnis* (Stuttgart Declaration of Guilt). Issued by the EKD church council, it provided a new basis for the Protestant Church's role in society and for its political and spiritual authority. It declared that the church shared the guilt of the German people, and it stressed the suffering that the Germans had brought on other peoples. The Protestant Church accused itself of not having witnessed its creed more courageously, vowing to begin anew and undergo thorough cleansing.[37]

According to Frederic Spotts, the statement had a profound impact on Germany. Proclaimed to the public in countless speeches and writings by prominent leaders of the Protestant Church,[38] it challenged the broad public to face the guilt question. Spotts feels that the EKD thereby became the

> only group to associate itself with the German people in a sense of collective responsibility for the Third Reich and its acts. . . . [Moreover,] the church was able to begin to put into practice what had been set in train at Barmen—a radical new concept of the church's role in society. The core of this idea was that the church's moral responsibility to the nation entailed a political responsibility and—implicit but most important of all—that this political responsibility lies not in passive

---

35. *Kirchliches Jahrbuch für die Evangelische Kirche in Deutschland,* ed. Joachim Beckmann (Gütersloh: C. Bertelsmann Verlag, 1950), 72–75:1, 2.

36. "Beschluss des Reichbruderrates in Frankfurt a.M. zur Kirchenleitung" and "Wort an die Pfarrer," *Kirchliches Jahrbuch* 72–75:2–4 and 4–7.

37. "Erklärung des Rates der Evangelischen Kirche in Deutschland gegenüber den Vertretern des ökumenischen Rates der Kirchen," *Kirchliches Jahrbuch* 72–75:26–27.

38. Martin Niemöller in particular "took the EKD's message to the German people in these stormy months," according to Joachim Beckmann, editor of the EKD's official chronicle, the *Kirchliche Jahrbücher.* See Niemöller's speech "Zur gegenwärtigen Aufgabe der evangelischen Christenheit, Predigt über 1. Joh. 4, 9–14," *Kirchliches Jahrbuch* 72–75:29–42.

obedience, but in independent judgement of the acts of the state. Though imperfectly realized, this ideal transformed German Protestantism into a generally progressive institution of postwar German public life and one through which, despite internal restorative tendencies, political dissent could be expressed.[39]

Just as the Confessing Church had represented only part of the Protestant clergy during the Third Reich, however, only part of the Protestant leadership after the war desired the change in direction outlined by the Stuttgart Declaration. Two factions vied for leadership within the church. The two fronts consisted, roughly speaking, of relatively traditional Lutherans, on the one hand, and the successors of the Bekennende Kirche, on the other. In addition to their roots in recent history, the two fronts reflected theological differences as well, generally described as Lutheran and Barthian. Karl Barth's followers envisaged a complete religious penetration of the public/political realm and its subjection to the requirement of obedience to Christ. Barthians drew justifications for militant political involvement from this doctrine. Lutherans continued their traditional interpretation of the two-realm doctrine, with its differentiation between the spiritual and worldly regiments of Christ. The mundane political realm enjoys a certain autonomy in this view, which precludes directly derived Christian opinion on political questions.[40]

Only the Barthian successors of the Confessing Church wanted a radical renewal of the Protestant Church on the basis of the Barmen Declaration. This radical front was represented by such groups as the Reichsbruderrat, which later became the Bruderrat der EKD, and the Kirchlich-Theologische Arbeitsgemeinschaft für Deutschland. Whereas the Bekennende Kirche had included some moderate and even conservative Lutherans during the war, its successor organizations after the war gradually shed those not agreeing with the (by then) central figures, Karl

---

39. Frederic Spotts, *The Churches and Politics in West Germany* (Middletown, Conn.: Wesleyan University Press, 1973), 11, 12. Joachim Beckmann, the EKD's official chronicler, notes the "great resonance" that greeted the statement's release, as well as the controversy over the "guilt question" that it inspired. He quotes statements by five regional church synods that support the Stuttgart statement, having selected them because they were "particularly impressive and characteristic" (*Kirchliches Jahrbuch* 72–75:29, 42–59). Some later Protestants, however, criticized the EKD for not having changed its direction even more radically, in particular on social and economic questions. Werner Jochmann, for example, accuses the EKD of failure to take its Stuttgart statement sufficiently to heart. See Werner Jochmann, "Zur politischen Orientierung der deutschen Protestanten nach 1945," in *Christen in der Demokratie,* ed. Heinrich Albertz and Joachim Thomsen (Wuppertal: Peter Hammer Verlag, 1978), 175–95, here 175–78.

40. Martin Honecker, "Kontroversen um den Frieden in der evangelischen Kirche und Theologie," *Politische Studien* 33, no. 261 (Jan./Feb. 1982), 17–25.

Barth and Martin Niemöller. Although weaker in numbers, this more radical front dominated the leadership in the earliest postwar years, in part because of the recognition they enjoyed abroad as leaders of the Protestant "resistance" to the Third Reich.[41] Werner Jochmann suggests that only the successors to the Confessing Church took the Stuttgart call to repentance seriously, while many accepted it only with reservations, and the majority of ordinary believers rejected it.[42] This fundamental division within the postwar Protestant Church surfaced repeatedly, particularly in defense policy debates virulent enough to endanger the EKD's very unity.

Whatever its immediate reception, however, the Stuttgart Declaration unquestionably had a long-term impact. Many Protestants subsequently referred to it and echoed its themes. The statement gave radical critics within the EKD a standard against which conservative tendencies could be criticized. The church's new attitude toward politics pushed it to confront controversial political issues as an institution. This led to severe conflict within the EKD because of the wide spectrum of opinion present in the Protestant clergy and laity. The Stuttgart Declaration did not spell out any specific program, so debate over the nature of church responsibility (i.e., whether a truly Christian position on concrete political issues could be found) became embedded in the larger debates that split the German public and the EKD in the 1950s and after. The EKD's internal debate over the foreign policy controversies of the 1950s and afterward had a specifically Protestant flavor. In defense debates, the EKD as an official institution was never fully in the camp of either side. Significant EKD minorities, however, actively participated in all postwar peace movements, and some prominent church leaders belonged to the core leadership. The Stuttgart statement prepared the doctrinal path for such participation.

Protestants Debate Rearmament and Nuclear Weapons

The Stuttgart Declaration established guilt from the fascist past as a standard for political morality, which found its first application to a defense issue in the rearmament debate. The notions of guilt and redemption provided a specifically Protestant motivation for participation in the anti-rearmament movement. Protestant arguments against rearmament revolved around the physical and moral damage inflicted by previous German armies and the moral imperative to stake out a new course. The primary theme was the foreign-policy consequences of repentance for the Third Reich.

Gustav Heinemann provided a dramatic illustration of this Protestant

---

41. Vogel, *Kirche und Wiederbewaffnung,* 37–41.
42. Jochmann, "Zur politischen Orientierung der deutschen Protestanten nach 1945," 175–78.

argument when he resigned his post in Adenauer's cabinet and his membership in the CDU over the rearmament issue. In his statement "Deutsche Sicherheit" (German security), Heinemann argued that disarmament represented God's punishment for recent German crimes. Although Germany could not remain disarmed forever, it was God's will that it was presently without weapons.[43] Similarly,the Kirchliche Bruderschaft, a committee within the Confessing Church, issued a statement in which it maintained that repentance essentially forbad a German army. God had not humiliated Germany only to let her yearn for riches and power again, without looking for a new way to recover humanity, love, and morality. The Bruderschaft did not want Germans to consider using force to restore what the war had taken away—East German political freedom and former German territories in the East. War would only bring destruction and represent denial of repentance and faith.[44] A later statement again advocated renouncing rearmament as a sign of repentance for the role of German armies in the past. Many Christians, it noted, wanted to appoint the German people the protector of Western culture, even though it had recently betrayed the West through support for fascism. This consciousness of guilt had not yet become common property to all Christians. Christians had to confess to this repentance, even if it seemed inopportune to the powers that be.[45]

Protestant statements against rearmament contained a mix of religiously derived opposition and political arguments common to the anti-rearmament movement as a whole. While the government spoke of Soviet expansionary tendencies, Protestant rearmament opponents denied that the Soviets were a greater danger than war itself. A high church official, Präses Wilm, noted that Hitler too had claimed that every war was defensive. The Germans faced Russian hostility because Germany had attacked Russia, not because of a power vacuum.[46] Rearmament opponents feared German entanglement in the East-West conflict and believed that the superpowers' arms buildup would inevitably lead to war.[47] Since arms acquisitions contain an inherent dynamism pushing for their use, arming would bring the very war it was German duty to prevent. Protestant re-

---

43. *Deutsche Sicherheit,* pamphlet by Gustav Heinemann, *Kirchliches Jahrbuch* 77:179–86.

44. "Handreichung an die Gemeinden zur Wiederaufrüstung," *Kirchliches Jahrbuch* 77:171.

45. "Was haben wir Christen in Westdeutschland heute für die Erhaltung des Friedens zu tun?" *Kirchliches Jahrbuch* 80:34–38.

46. Präses der Evangelischen Kirche von Westfalen, speech at the Männertag in Dortmund, 23. Sept. 1951, *Kirchliches Jahrbuch* 78:159–70.

47. "Erklärung der 'Kirchlich-Theologischen Arbeitsgemeinschaft,'" *Kirchliches Jahrbuch* 77:161–62.

armament opponents also worried that remilitarization would amount to a radical division of Germany and could result in civil war.[48] Some joined in the anti-rearmament movement's broader call for neutralism.

Debate over nuclear weapons for the Bundeswehr continued political discussion within the EKD. Initial Protestant arguments against nuclear weapons were directed against nuclear weapons per se. As the Kampf dem Atomtod (Fight Atomic Death) campaign picked up steam across West Germany, the campaign's political questions began to permeate the intra-EKD discussion as well. The question of Christian morality vis-à-vis nuclear weapons was a constant theme throughout the period.

One of the more emphatic statements came from the Konvent der Kirchlichen Bruderschaft im Rheinland, which maintained that God gave humankind the freedom and duty to preserve and protect earthly life. Humankind was not allowed to threaten the lives of millions, not even for the sake of freedom or social justice, for life belongs to God. It was illusory to expect nuclear weapons to preserve life, peace, and freedom, as they are destructive in principle. Therefore no purpose justified their use or production.[49] The leadership of the Rhineland Protestant Church "radically condemned" weapons of mass destruction,[50] as did the Synode der Evangelischen Kirche der Union.[51] Another classic statement came from the Kirchliche Bruderschaft in the Rhineland and Westphalia. Nuclear weapons, it maintained, made "defensive" war an illusion, because nuclear strategy meant accepting the destruction of one's own people, not to mention the enemy's whole populace. Nuclear weapons were inappropriate to political struggles, and a Christian could only reject them unconditionally. Even preparing for nuclear war was a sin against God and man, and Christians should refuse to do so.[52]

Not all Protestants agreed with such positions on either rearmament or nuclear weapons. Many of their arguments reflected a more traditional Lutheran perspective, as well as more conservative political leanings. Protestant delegates to the CDU's party convention of 1950 stressed that

---

48. "Handreichung an die Gemeinden zur Wiederaufrüstung," *Kirchliches Jahrbuch* 77:169–74.

49. "Erklärung des Konvents der Kirchlichen Bruderschaft im Rheinland zur atomaren Bewaffnung," *Kirchliches Jahrbuch* 84:86–87.

50. "Erklärung der Kirchenleitung der Evangelischen Kirche im Rheinland," *Kirchliches Jahrbuch* 84:89.

51. "Beschluss der Synode der Evangelischen Kirche der Union," *Kirchliches Jahrbuch* 84:95. See also "Anfrage an die Synode der Evangelischen Kirche in Deutschland," *Kirchliches Jahrbuch* 85:30–33; and the speech by synod member Vogel during synodal debate on nuclear weapons, *Kirchliches Jahrbuch* 85:51–55.

52. "Anfrage an die Synode der Evangelischen Kirche in Deutschland," *Kirchliches Jahrbuch* 85:30–33.

the CDU was working for German reconstruction on a Christian basis, and they blamed German division on the power hunger of bolshevism.[53] In a separate statement, clergy and laymen denied that the Christian duty of brotherly love required renouncing violence at any price. Saying that the Germans were not permitted to protect themselves against the Soviet threat would be a self-imposed act of contrition, rather than one required by God.[54] The traditional Lutheran provincial churches *(Landeskirchen)* also charged that the EKD was overstepping its bounds and becoming "too politicized."[55] The Lutherans wanted to revive the two-realms doctrine that decisions on political matters fell to those with an official mandate.[56] Controversy revolved around whether the Protestant Church's assumption of political responsibility could lead to explicit positions on concrete questions and whether such positions could be binding for all Christians. The Theologischer Konvent der Bekenntnisgemeinschaft von Hannover, for example, charged Niemöller (a rearmament opponent) with not respecting the border between theological and political judgement, thereby giving subjective political judgement the quality of an absolutely binding judgement of faith.[57] With regard to nuclear weapons too, Adenauer's supporters argued that his defense policies were compatible with Christian principles. Probst Hans Asmussen argued that church leaders were usurping political leaders' tasks when they took such strong stands on political questions. He argued that a threat came from Soviet intentions toward German property, freedom, and so on,[58] and he implied that nuclear weapons might be necessary to meet this threat. Likewise, the Evangelische Oberkirchenrat in Stuttgart maintained that rejecting deterrence could bring the war everyone wanted to avoid.[59]

Rearmament opponents, in contrast, pushed the Protestant Church to take an unambiguous position against rearmament and denied that they were improperly mixing politics and religion. They accused Adenauer's

---

53. "Entschliessung der evangelischen Delegierten," *Kirchliches Jahrbuch* 77:190–91.

54. "Wehrbeitrag und christliches Gewissen," *Kirchliches Jahrbuch* 79:14–17.

55. Wolf Werner Rausch and Christian Walther, eds., *Evangelische Kirche in Deutschland und die Wiederaufrüstungsdiskussion in der Bundesrepublik 1950–1955* (Gütersloh: Gütersloher Verlagshaus Gerd Mohn, 1978), 67.

56. Ibid., 99.

57. "Stellungnahme des Theologischen Konvents der Bekenntnisgemeinschaft der Evangelisch-lutherischen Landeskirche Hannovers zu der Flugschrift 'An die Gewehre? Nein,' " *Kirchliches Jahrbuch* 77:196–210.

58. Probst Hans Asmussen, open letter dated 14 Mar. 1958, *Kirchliches Jahrbuch* 85:34–36.

59. "Rundschreiben des Evangelischen Oberkirchenrat in Stuttgart," *Kirchliches Jahrbuch* 86:94.

Protestant supporters of claiming binding insight on the nature of political "realities," from which they deduced positions "compatible" with Christian faith.[60]

The Protestant Church's Official Stances

From the 1950s on, the EKD participated actively in postwar security debates, which divided the church as deeply as they did the society at large. At every stage, a significant and vocal minority of Protestants participated in peace protest. Official church pronouncements generally represented a compromise, after very heated debate, between the proponents and opponents of the government's policy. The EKD's statements represented the church as an institution but were never binding on all members. The compromises embedded in church pronouncements generally acknowledged both sides' positions as legitimately derived from Christian faith. Thus although official EKD pronouncements never granted *exclusive* validity to peace movement values and positions, they confirmed them by recognizing them as legitimately Christian. The EKD thereby gave organizational expression to peace movement views and contributed to a melding of religious belief and political positions.

The EKD as a whole developed positions on war in general, but it did not always do so for specific defense issues, because divisions were so deep that they threatened the very unity of the church. The cold war and the gradual evolution of two German states, moreover, questioned the EKD's organizational unity across the East-West divide. Germany's traditional confessional balance made German division all the more difficult for the church. Nearly half of all German Protestants lived on the eastern side of the Iron Curtain, where many of the traditionally most important regional churches were located. It was no coincidence that many of the most passionate proponents of reunification and accommodation toward Eastern Europe came from the Protestant camp.[61]

The initial years of the cold war (1947–50) became a prelude to the rearmament debate proper. Given Germany's political impotence during the occupation, the EKD reviewed its relationship to war and peace in general. Its general renunciation of war as an instrument of political conflict suffered little contradiction.[62] The EKD as an institution first decried the horrors of war in a statement issued at its founding conference in 1948 in

---

60. "Fragen an die Entschliessung 'Wehrbeitrag und christliches Gewissen,' " *Kirchliches Jahrbuch* 79:18–21.

61. Vogel, *Kirche und Wiederbewaffnung,* 70.

62. Ibid., 64.

Eisenach, a city that later became part of East Germany.[63] Its conciliatory message was echoed by the statement of the synod at its meeting in Berlin-Weißensee in April 1950. Both called on Christians to view other nations as brothers and sisters rather than enemies. Above all, Germans should not fall prey to delusions that another war could solve their problems. The church's mission was to proclaim God's peace through Christ and to search for peace with all who seek it. In the Berlin-Weißensee statement, the church also called for a just peace treaty to bring an official end to World War II and to allow German unity in freedom.

The outbreak of the Korean War unleashed a second phase of the rearmament debate that continued from 1950 to 1954 and in which the concrete question of a West German army became salient.[64] At the EKD's lay assembly (Kirchentag) in August 1950, the EKD Council issued a statement on rearmament whose key formulation was frequently quoted by rearmament opponents. It stated simply that it could not support remilitarization of either West or East Germany ("Einer Remilitarisierung Deutschlands können wir das Wort nicht reden, weder was den Westen noch was den Osten anlangt"). The church's duty instead was to call for an end to the arms race and a search for peaceful solutions to political problems. The council's statement also showed the legacy of the Third Reich when it called for resistance to propaganda, hate, and "angst-psychosis." No government, it maintained, would be tempted to break the peace if it met decided domestic opposition. The Korean War showed that national division threatened peace. Thus it had to remain unthinkable that Germans would shoot at Germans.[65] The EKD Synod confirmed this line once again at its Elbingerode meeting in 1952, stressing peace and spiritual reorientation.[66]

By 1955, however, the EKD as an institution had decided against tak-

---

63. The Eisenach statement was influenced by the *Darmstädter Wort* of 1947 by the Bruderrat of the EKD, which considered itself the postwar continuation of the Bekennende Kirche (Vogel, *Kirche und Wiederbewaffnung*, 74). For the text of the Eisenach "Wort der Evangelischen Kirche in Deutschland zum Frieden," see *Kirchliches Jahrbuch* 72–75:185–86. For the synodal statement, see "Das Wort zum Frieden," *Kirchliches Jahrbuch* 77:7–10.

64. Vogel, *Kirche und Wiederbewaffnung*, 64.

65. "Der Rat der EKD zur Frage der Wiederaufrüstung," *Kirchliches Jahrbuch* 77:165–66.

66. In language typical for the EKD of the period, the synod maintained that "God . . . still asks us about our reorientation and change of mind. . . . His word has warned us against belief in the stronger batallions. . . . Today we call . . . again to deeds of peace. We are not in the position to prescribe decisions to politicians . . . but we ask all concerned . . . to create no further faits accompli that would lead to hardening the division of our people and the terrible consequences thereof for the whole world" ("Kundgebung der Synode der EKD," *Kirchliches Jahrbuch* 79:83–85.)

ing an official stance on the rearmament issue itself. The EKD's Council maintained that no binding directive on the issue could be derived from the Scriptures and that therefore the rearmament decision had to be left to the political realm.[67] With these statements, the EKD implicitly confirmed the traditional, Lutheran, two-realms doctrine of the church's limited political involvement and in effect supported Adenauer's rearmament policy by not opposing it.

Thus even the EKD's early official statements on peace were never as radical as those of the most ardent opponents of rearmament. They took, however, a middle position that left the latter sufficient psychological and doctrinal space within the church to carry on unhampered. The statements' conscious application of the lessons of the fascist past to problems of peace reflected the general thrust of Protestant peace activists. Although the church later refused to take an official position on the concrete issue of rearmament, Protestant peace activists often used the church's emphasis on peace and its early opposition to rearmament to support their positions.

Again reflecting the divisions within its ranks, the Protestant Church officially took a middle position on nuclear weapons in its "Heidelberg Theses" of 1959, which were subsequently considered among the most important contributions to nuclear ethics by the EKD. The church acknowledged both absolute rejection of nuclear weapons and support for deterrence doctrine as compatible with Christian principles. The "Heidelberg Theses" began by arguing that peace was the prerequisite of life itself in the technical age. In the past, the doctrine of just war had deemed war permissible when waged to ward off greater evil. This doctrine was invalidated for nuclear war, however, which destroys what it means to protect. Nuclear weapons had made war morally intolerable despite dangers to law and freedom.

In theses 6–8, the most quoted and influential theses, the church expressed its "middle position." In line with the first five theses, it recognized renunciation of nuclear weapons as a Christian action; Christians had to consider seriously whether their renunciation, regardless of consequences, was not a command of God. However, the church also recognized deterrence as an attempt to secure peace in freedom. The "Heidelberg Theses" described this position as "still possible for a Christian," but only under the condition that the sole goal was to preserve peace and avoid

---

67. "Wort des Rates der EKiD und der Kirchenkonferenz 'Um die Wiedervereinigung des deutschen Volkes,' 2.2.1955," *Kirchliches Jahrbuch* 82:15; "Wort der Synode der EKiD an die Gemeinden in Ost und West, Espelkamp, 11.3.1955," *Kirchliches Jahrbuch* 82:47–49.

using nuclear weapons. They further emphasized the temporary nature of its acceptability as a Christian position.[68]

Once again, official church positions represented a compromise between radical and conservative Protestant positions. As before, they lent partial support to peace activists and left them room within the church. Indeed, the "Heidelberg Theses" leaned toward the antinuclear position. They fully supported rejection of nuclear weapons as Christian, whereas they called deterrence only "temporarily" Christian.

The EKD's final contribution to defense debates in the 1950s concerned its relationship to the new West German army, the Bundeswehr, after its creation. Two problems manifested themselves for the EKD: whether to supply the Bundeswehr with military chaplains, and whether to support conscientious objection as a principle and push for its realization as an individual right.

The question of providing Protestant military chaplains arose in 1957, when the EKD and the government negotiated a treaty regulating such chaplains. The EKD Synod agreed in principle that the church had to provide religious services to soldiers, as it did to all Protestants, regardless of occupation or status. The previous attachment of the Prussian Protestant Church to the Prussian army, however, made providing military chaplains to the Bundeswehr a sensitive issue.[69] Because the treaty specified that military chaplains would be civil servants and would be administered by the ministry of defense, fears arose that a "military church" *(Militärkirche)* under the direction of the state would arise, with an organizational life independent of the EKD. Some also asked what the church's message could possibly be to soldiers in an army equipped with nuclear weapons— what should a chaplain advise in questions of modern war?[70] Despite these reservations, however, the treaty was accepted by a large majority of the synod.[71]

Although the EKD agreed to provide religious support to soldiers through an institutional link to the Bundeswehr, it also firmly supported conscientious objection as a principle and as an individual right. Parts of the EKD went further. Calls for conscientious objection as a Christian moral duty came from peace groups within the church, especially in the context of debate over nuclear weapons. In 1955 the Bremen regional lay

68. See the report of the academic commission formed by Prelate Kunst of the Evangelische Studiengemeinschaft, *Kirchliches Jahrbuch* 86:100–106.

69. Karl Kupisch, *Kirchengeschichte,* vol. 5, *Das Zeitalter der Revolutionen und Weltkriege* (Stuttgart: Verlag W. Kohlhammer, 1975), 132.

70. See the editor's commentary on a synodal debate on the issue, *Kirchliches Jahrbuch* 84:23.

71. See the editor's commentary on the treaty's passage, *Kirchliches Jahrbuch* 84:40.

assembly (Bremer Kirchentag) issued a statement calling for conscientious objection to all military service on the basis of Christian conscience. Referring to the synod's declaration at the 1950 Berlin-Weißensee meeting, the Kirchentag declared that nuclear weapons had turned war in the contemporary period into mass murder and thus that anyone using military instruments was on a path to murder.[72]

Although the EKD as a whole did not go so far as to *require* conscientious objection, it did stand up for the right to it, thereby overcoming German Protestantism's traditional notion that conscientious objection was impossible for a Christian.[73] In 1955 the EKD Council unanimously passed a statement asking the state to protect conscientious objectors out of respect for human dignity and as a sign of the state's self-limitation. The statement revealed the extent to which the EKD's thinking had changed under the weight of the fascist experience and developments in weapons technology. The church, it noted, saw war no longer merely as an "evil" (as in the nineteenth century) but rather as a sin against God's will, and it thus doubted whether a "just war" was possible at all. While conscientious objection was not required of all Christians, the statement recognized it as a valid Christian position. It also recognized the state's duty to protect citizens, but it denied that this included a *universal* military draft. In light of the recent experience of totalitarianism and total war, universal conscription might go beyond the legitimate authority of the democratic state if it forced people to fight against their conscience.[74]

More than ten years later, the 1967 Kirchentag reinforced the view that both military service and conscientious objection were justifiable Christian positions. The Kirchentag's formula "in service of peace with and without weapons" [Friedensdienst mit und ohne Waffen] meant equal recognition of conscientious objectors and those performing military service, according to a later, more or less official interpretation.[75] Both the "Heidelberg Theses" of 1959 and the 1967 Kirchentag recognized conscientious objection and military service as equally valid Christian positions, thus condoning but not requiring religious pacifism. In the 1960s the church emphasized that the alternative service required of conscientious objectors could be more than a mere "substitute service" *(Ersatzdienst)* and could actively contribute a "service to peace" *(Friedensdienst),*

---

72. *Kirchliches Jahrbuch* 82:4, 5.

73. "Ratschlag zur gesetzlichen Regelung des Schutzes der Kriegsdienstverweigerer," *Kirchliches Jahrbuch* 82:72–77.

74. Ibid.

75. Kirchenkanzlei der EKD, *Frieden wahren, fördern und erneuern: Eine Denkschrift der Evangelischen Kirche in Deutschland,* (Gütersloh: Gütersloher Verlagshaus Gerd Mohn, 1981), 34.

thereby giving it equal moral weight with military service. Conscientious objection within the EKD acquired an additional thrust when the student movement of 1968 politicized it in society at large.[76]

The Labor Movement and Peace Protest

Much of the labor movement vehemently opposed Adenauer's defense policies—an opposition reflecting both the movement's negative experiences with the German military prior to 1945 and its hopes for political and economic reform thereafter. In the Wilhelminian era the Social Democrats and unions did not oppose national defense in principle. They did, however, sharply condemn militarism as a pillar of the authoritarian state and antidemocratic attitudes, and their stance was reinforced by Engel's call for elimination of standing armies as instruments of repression by the ruling class. The kaiser and military officers, for their part, saw the SPD and unions as "vaterlandslose Gesellen" (loosely translated, unpatriotic vagabonds) and hoped that military service would serve as the "school of the nation" by indoctrinating the working class with "appropriate" social values. Thus although the labor movement was refused fundamental political rights (witnessed most blatantly by the antisocialist laws of the 1880s), workers performed military service in defense of the "fatherland."

Not surprisingly, many workers came to view the army as part of the state's repression of labor interests. The military's role in the Weimar Republic reinforced this view, particularly when the Kapp Putsch revealed that the army protected the republic much less valiantly against threats from the right than it had from earlier revolts on the left. Weimar's Social Democratic governments, however, declined for various reasons to undertake a thorough reform of the army. The final source of labor's antimilitarism was the officer corps' support for the Third Reich, which suppressed labor unions and parties alike, and whose military campaigns brought suffering to workers as both soldiers and civilians.[77]

Lessons drawn from past experience significantly influenced labor's thinking on security policy during the 1950s. Labor's attitude toward the military reflected its larger hopes for a fundamental transformation of society, which meant overcoming the trio of evils—capitalism, national-

---

76. Bernd Kubbig, *Kirche und Kriegsdienstverweigerung in der BRD* (Stuttgart: Verlag W. Kohlhammer, 1974).

77. Ernst-Dieter Köpper, *Gewerkschaften und Aussenpolitik* (Frankfurt: Campus Verlag, 1982), chap. 4; Christoph Butterwegge and Heinz-Gerd Hofschen, *Sozialdemokratie, Krieg und Frieden: Die Stellung der SPD zur Friedensfrage von den Anfängen bis zur Gegenwart* (Heilbronn: Distel Verlag, 1984), chaps. 1–4; Gordon Craig, *The Germans* (New York: Oxford University Press, 1978), chap. 11.

ism, and militarism—that, in labor's eyes, had contributed to the Third Reich. At its most ambitious, labor envisioned transforming capitalism through socialization of key industries and other measures, overcoming nationalism through European unity (with supranational labor codetermination), and resisting militarism through pacifism.[78] Thus during the 1950s, it was particularly Social Democrats, communists, and unions who combined the struggle against rearmament, NATO membership, and nuclear weapons with their broader struggle to mold the new republic in their image. In the process, they provided the peace movements of the 1950s and afterward with ideological resources, by embedding specific defense issues in the broader frame of democratization of politics, society, and the economy. Although the three wings of the labor movement overlapped to some extent in their foreign policy outlook and personnel, each had its own internal dynamics.

The Communist Party

The Communist Party, the KPD, was the only branch of the labor movement that unambiguously opposed rearmament and that tried to build a united labor front against it. Although they had lost much of their membership and especially much of their leadership to the Third Reich, the Communist resistance to fascism created sympathy and influence for the party in the immediate postwar years, particularly among workers. After 1948, however, the party found itself driven out of local and regional governments and out of unions and other bodies representing workers in factories. The KPD therefore campaigned more aggressively for its notion of democracy and refused to support the Basic Law.

The KPD also unequivocally opposed rearmament in the most militant tones throughout the 1950s. While still in parliament, the KPD introduced numerous measures opposing everything from Western military integration to production of military materials, until its failure to overcome the newly introduced "five percent hurdle" in the 1953 elections cost the party its parliamentary representation. Outside of parliament, the KPD supported all phases of the peace movement with whatever means possible,[79] spearheading in particular the unofficial popular referenda on rearmament and anti-rearmament activity among workers in factories.[80]

The KPD had several reasons for taking part in the peace movement. Ideologically, it maintained that rearmament would reinforce the power of capital against labor, enable West German "imperialists" to annex the

---

78. Köpper, *Gewerkschaften und Aussenpolitik*, chaps. 1–4.
79. Dietzfelbinger, *Die westdeutsche Friedensbewegung 1948–1955*, 218–24.
80. Lorenz Knorr, *Geschichte der Friedensbewegung in der Bundesrepublik* (Cologne: Pahl-Rugenstein, 1983).

German Democratic Republic and reconquer lost German territories, and intensify the cold war against Eastern Europe and the Soviet Union. Thus peace movement work was part of the party's striving for reunification in accordance with the East German communist regime's preferences, which West German rearmament would endanger. On the domestic front, the KPD tried to organize the anti-rearmament movement as an expression of the larger class struggle, based on its cadre organization, factory groups, and union functionaries. To this end, the party tried (with limited success) to form alliances with other anti-rearmament forces.[81]

The Unions
The West German unions reconstituted themselves after the war as sixteen industrial unions, united by an overarching federated structure, the Deutscher Gewerkschaftsbund (DGB). In the early postwar years, the unions' vision of a democratic Germany emphasized socialization of key economic sectors and parity labor participation in decision making at every level of the economy, from the shop floor and company boardrooms to national economic planning agencies. Actual developments, however, fell far short of union hopes. The social-market economy ended labor's hopes for broad reform of economic and social relations.[82] Codetermination and the Works Constitution Law provided for labor's incorporation into relatively cooperative industrial relations. Although the unions got their much-wanted voice in management, the terms of the actual legislation represented decisive union defeats. To be sure, the Codetermination Law of 1951 represented a partial victory for the unions, as it granted labor half of all seats on firms' supervisory boards in the coal, iron, and steel industries. After 1951, however, the political tide turned against the unions. In particular, the Works Constitution Law of 1952 inflicted a major defeat on the unions, for it gave labor only one-third, rather than one-half, of the seats on corporate boards in the industries involved.[83]

After these setbacks and the SPD's poor electoral showing in the 1949 and 1953 federal elections, the unions abandoned goals involving large-scale transformation of capitalism and pursued more immediate material issues, concentrating increasingly on a "growth pact" with employers in the interests of improving standards of living and working

---

81. Rolke, *Protestbewegungen in der Bundesrepublik,* 164.
82. Andrei Markovits, *The Politics of the West German Trade Unions* (Cambridge: Cambridge University Press, 1986), chap. 3.
83. Katzenstein, *Policy and Politics in West Germany,* 132.

conditions.[84] Union programs often still contained critiques of capitalism and the old goals of socialization and planning, but in practice, unions assisted labor's increasing integration into the existing economic order. This process culminated temporarily in the unions' Düsseldorf Program *(Grundsatzprogramm)* of 1963.[85] The unions' centralized organization, moreover, left little room for rank-and-file militancy.

In the 1950s, the DGB's leadership pursued a policy of constructive cooperation with the government, hoping that Adenauer would support the unions' proposals for economic democracy in exchange for their support of his foreign policy. This policy of constructive cooperation also explains the DGB leadership's willingness to support in principle a West German defense contribution in the context of a West European army. Hans Böckler, the DGB's first leader, considered rearmament inevitable,[86] and subsequent leaders expressed support at various times.

The executive committee *(Vorstand)* leaned toward cautious support for a West German defense contribution for several reasons. First, the DGB's leadership felt that protecting democracy in Germany required facing the international realities of the cold war. It adopted twin goals of securing democracy at home while protecting it militarily from external threats. Second, the DGB's leadership (particularly Ludwig Rosenberg) calculated that by supporting rearmament, the unions could help ensure the postwar military's democratic character through their close contacts to the Dienststelle Blank (which was in charge of establishing the new armed forces). The union leadership considered parliamentary control of the armed forces and their integration into a larger European alliance sufficient to contain the military's threat to democracy. Such a role would also further Rosenberg's vision of the unions' becoming a supporting pillar of the new state and extending economic codetermination into the political realm. In this endeavor, the unions could not afford to be accused of aiding communism by opposing rearmament, given Adenauer's penchant for painting his opponents as objective protagonists of Soviet policy. Third, the DGB's leadership hoped to exchange their support of rearmament for Adenauer's help in securing full labor parity in codetermination and on the shop floor through a union-friendly Works Constitution Law,

---

84. Charles Maier, "The Politics of Productivity: Foundations of American International Economic Policy after World War II," in *Between Power and Plenty: Foreign Economic Policy of Advanced Industrial States,* ed. Peter Katzenstein (Madison: University of Wisconsin Press, 1986), 23–50.

85. Christoph Klessmann, *Zwei Staaten, Eine Nation: Deutsche Geschichte 1955–1970* (Göttingen: Vandenhoeck and Ruprecht, 1988), 126–30.

86. Baring, *Aussenpolitik in Adenauer's Kanzlerdemokratie,* 197.

a not entirely successful calculation. Finally, Allied willingness to take responsibility for West German security and contact with the American unions encouraged DGB support for rearmament.[87]

Although the union rank and file was used to internal discipline, in the case of rearmament a substantial portion revolted against the leadership. This split on rearmament corresponded to a larger historical split, reaching back into the nineteenth century, between the labor movement leadership's pragmatic pursuit of reforms within the existing system and the orientation of the rank and file toward fundamental system transformation, with the unions as a "countervailing force" *(Gegenmacht)* to the status quo. The rank and file stood, furthermore, under the influence of the SPD and, to some extent, the Communists, both of which opposed rearmament. Both the leadership and the union members agreed that West Germany had to secure itself against all internal or external threats and that the Soviet Union was an imperialist and militarist power. Important union opponents of rearmament like Theo Pirker and Erwin Essl, however, denied that a Stalinist seizure of power was possible in West Germany or Western Europe and maintained that American strength made Soviet military invasion unlikely.

Rearmament was thus unnecessary on that score and contained many dangers. In particular, the rank and file feared that a new army would bring a revival of militarism, which would unavoidably threaten domestic democracy and pose a security threat for the whole world. Already disappointed that capitalism had been reestablished after the war, the union opposition viewed rearmament as a second instance of restoring the past and thus saw in opposition to rearmament a last chance to deflect a second rise of fascism. On the economic front, union opposition feared that Adenauer would use the new army against the unions to defeat their struggle for a new order and that economic planning for rearmament would subordinate the economy to the needs of arms production. The costs of rearmament, moreover, would be born by workers and would depress their standard of living. In foreign policy, rearmament would reduce West Germany's autonomy by tying the country to American policy without giving Germany equal influence in the alliance, and it was thus not in the national interest. West German rearmament would also harden East-West bloc formation and increase international tensions (without noticeably improving Western defense) and would hinder reunification.[88]

Taking any strong stand would have threatened the DGB's unity, and its nonsectarian and nonpartisan status as the labor movement's umbrella

---

87. Köpper, *Gewerkschaften und Aussenpolitik,* chap. 3.

88. Ibid.; Gerard Braunthal, "West German Unions and Disarmament," *Political Science Quarterly* 73, no. 1 (1958): 82–99.

organization dictated against strong positions anyway. The DGB's leadership found itself subject to contradictory demands from all sides, however, as the CDU and the Christian unionists pressed it to support Adenauer, while the SPD, the Communists, and much of the DGB's membership pressed it to oppose him. Although there were some early rumblings against remilitarization from the DGB leadership, the Korean War, its desire for Adenauer's help in passing codetermination laws, and its traditional orientation to the state soon moved the leadership to support a West German defense contribution against potential Soviet aggression. Opposition to rearmament within the unions eventually forced the leadership to reject rearmament temporarily until all possibilities for negotiating German reunification had been exhausted.

The DGB membership had thus gotten its leadership to modify its position, but it waited in vain for any concrete measures against rearmament. Although several union leaders participated in the Paulskirche rally in 1955 against rearmament, they did so as individuals rather than as DGB representatives.[89] Even when popular mobilization reached its height, the DGB leadership refrained from calling for a political general strike, as it did not want to violate the antiplebiscitary elements of the Basic Law. In the eyes of many activists, the DGB leadership's support for the Paulskirche movement *(Paulskirchebewegung)* was merely tactical to avoid alienating its membership and to channel unrest, and it did nothing to secure the movement's success.[90]

The Social Democratic Party

The SPD spent the 1950s searching for a viable security policy, caught between electoral pressures for a security policy that reflected international realities, on the one hand, and concerns for reunification, domestic democracy, and rank-and-file pacifism, on the other. Like the unions, the SPD associated rearmament and nuclear weapons with the frame of democratization, but it stressed even more the key issues of the German question—national sovereignty and, above all, reunification. The party considered rearmament incompatible with both reunification and democracy, and it promoted policies that it hoped would assure West German security without endangering either. In retrospect the newly created Bundeswehr proved no threat to the young democracy, but at the time, the SPD feared that any new army might once again harbor antidemocratic tendencies.

---

89. Köpper, *Gewerkschaften und Aussenpolitik,* chap. 4.
90. Theo Pirker, *Die Blinde Macht: Die Gewerkschaftsbewegung in der Bundesrepublik* (Berlin: Olle and Wolter, 1979).

As the 1950s wore on, the incompatibility between German reunification and West German integration into Western military structures became increasingly apparent. The SPD resisted integration precisely because it hardened German division. The SPD's alternative security concepts made provisions for German reunification. Since they were based on German neutralization, however, they failed, in the eyes of many, to provide adequate security against the Soviet threat. Although the 1950s saw intermittent reductions of superpower tensions, the hardening military blocs did not permit an equal emphasis on reunification and security.[91]

The SPD's increasingly devastating electoral defeats, moreover, increased pressure on the party to revamp its security policy, which was held partially responsible for the dismal showing. But the party's rank and file vehemently opposed rearmament and nuclear weapons and exerted considerable pressure on the leadership to oppose them throughout the decade. All these counterpressures affected Social Democratic security policy in the 1950s and account for the SPD's erratic participation in that decade's peace protest.

Kurt Schumacher dominated the postwar SPD until his death in 1952. The pathos of his suffering during the Third Reich inspired tremendous respect; he personified the best of Social Democratic resistance to the Nazis. His intense personality and organizational skills enabled him to weed out his rivals within the party and create a loyal following.[92] In the immediate postwar period, he envisioned a democratic and socialist Europe, to which a free and unified Germany would belong as an equal partner.[93] Though he distrusted the Western occupation powers, Schumacher distrusted the Soviet Union even more, especially after East German communists forced a merger with local Social Democrats to form the Socialist Unity Party (SED).[94] Schumacher opposed an isolated or nationalistic Germany and pictured a social-democratic federation of European states that would serve as a "third force" between the superpowers.[95] A "policy of strength" based on the economic and social attractiveness of Germany's western zones, he hoped, would bring about German

---

91. Haftendorn, *Sicherheit und Entspannung,* 87.

92. Lewis Edinger, *Kurt Schumacher: A Study in Personality and Political Behavior* (Stanford: Stanford University Press, 1965).

93. Haftendorn, *Sicherheit und Entspannung,* 87; Hütter, *SPD und nationale Sicherheit,* 59.

94. Gordon Drummond, *The German Social Democrats in Opposition, 1949–1960: The Case Against Rearmament* (Norman, Okla.: University of Oklahoma Press, 1982), 22.

95. Ibid., 23, 24.

reunification on the basis of democratic socialism, obviating the choice between reunification with communism and division with democracy.[96]

By the late 1940s, such dreams faded as European division hardened and the superpowers began building rival military blocs. The Soviets' first nuclear explosion and the outbreak of the Korean War stimulated Schumacher to revise his position. Whereas he had previously rejected any German rearmament because it could make the occupation powers less willing to negotiate German reunification, he was now open to rearmament for precisely the opposite reason—that rearmament provided a possible lever for committing the Allies to reunification.[97] In addition, Schumacher demanded a strategy of forward defense, because only carrying the battle forward into Eastern Europe would spare Germany the fate of itself becoming a battlefield. Such a strategy, Schumacher felt, would give West Germany equal protection within an alliance, since it would suffer no more destruction than other members.[98]

Schumacher agreed with Adenauer on the existence of a Soviet threat, the need for strong defenses, and aversion to German neutrality.[99] He opposed, however, Adenauer's willingness to join a Western defense structure without, as he thought, adequate Allied commitments to German reunification. Indeed, Hütter considers 1952–55 a time of "priority of reunification over alliances."[100] Although by late 1950 Schumacher was ready to support the creation of a German army under certain conditions, the conditions were not met before his death. When it became clear that the Western Allies were not pushing strongly for reunification, Schumacher stiffened his opposition to rearmament and berated Adenauer for accepting Western military integration before German reunification had been guaranteed. He launched the SPD's standard argument that rearmament would threaten chances for German reunification.[101]

The SPD's reaction to the proposed European Defense Community (EDC) in 1952 rested on these arguments. Fritz Erler, a budding SPD defense specialist, worried about Germany's second-class status in the EDC, because it alone had to assign all its military forces to the European

---

96. Hütter, *SPD und nationale Sicherheit,* 59; Wolfram Wette, "Sozialdemokratische Sicherheitspolitik in historischer Perspektive," in *Jungsozialisten und Jungdemokraten zur Friedens- und Sicherheitspolitik,* ed. Reiner Steinweg (Frankfurt: Suhrkamp Verlag, 1977), 22–42, here 35.

97. Haftendorn, *Sicherheit und Entspannung,* 88.

98. Ibid., 88–89; Udo Löwke, *Für den Fall, daß . . .: Die Haltung der SPD zur Wehrfrage 1949–1953* (Hannover: Verlag für Literatur und Zeitgeschehen, 1969), 61, 67.

99. See Löwke, *Für den Fall, daß . . .,* 14–30, on Schumacher's anticommunism, which only hardened as superpower relations worsened.

100. Hütter, *SPD und nationale Sicherheit,* 52.

101. Drummond, *The German Social Democrats in Opposition,* 65.

army.[102] Most emphatically, however, the SPD argued that the primary goal of German foreign policy had to be German reunification. Since the EDC did nothing to advance this goal, the SPD opposed it. As time went on, the Social Democrats raised this conditional opposition to an absolute truth. Trying to avoid both "an unconditional no to any military contribution, which would make us a satellite of Soviet policy, and an unconditional yes to the treaties, which would make us a satellite of American policy,"[103] the SPD hoped that four-power negotiations might lead to a settlement that allowed both German security and reunification.

Erich Ollenhauer chaired the SPD after Schumacher's death. He shared, and thereby reinforced, the antimilitary sentiments of the rank and file. He also continued Schumacher's policy of opposition, since conditions for support had not been met by any of the defense schemes under consideration.[104] In the Bundestag debates over NATO membership in 1954, Ollenhauer castigated reliance on military factors as the basis of Western unity and argued that comprehensive social security would strengthen the free world more than German rearmament. Furthermore, signs of détente and Soviet talk of four-power negotiations meant that West Germany should not assume any new military obligations that would preclude progress on reunification. After all, as Erler maintained in the same debate, the Soviets would agree to German reunification only if Germany would not join a military alliance directed against them.[105]

If the SPD leadership was intransigent in its opposition to the EDC and NATO, the party membership was even more so. Early on, Schumacher met strong anti-rearmament sentiment within the SPD's executive committee *(Vorstand)*,[106] reinforced by surveys consistently showing large majorities against rearmament, as well as electoral gains at the expense of the CDU in three state-level *(Landtag)* elections in 1950, where the SPD based its campaign largely on the rearmament issue.[107] By the mid-1950s, to be sure, a group of "reformers" was forming around Brandt, Wehner, and Erler, who wanted the SPD to formulate a security policy that provided for military defense. The party rank and file, however, was having none of it and applied pressure on the leadership tantamount to a veto over policy change. The party took Schumacher and later Ollenhauer at their word that the SPD would accept rearmament only if certain condi-

---

102. Ibid., 84–87; Löwke, *Für den Fall, daß . . .*, 96, 99.

103. Cited in Drummond, *The German Social Democrats in Opposition*, 90.

104. Drummond, *The German Social Democrats in Opposition*, 59; Löwke, *Für den Fall, daß . . .*, 11–14.

105. Drummond, *The German Social Democrats in Opposition*, 130–31.

106. Hartmut Soell, *Fritz Erler: Eine politische Biographie*, vol. 1 (Berlin: Verlag J. H. W. Dietz, 1976), 571 n. 154.

107. Drummond, *The German Social Democrats in Opposition*, 56.

tions were met, and it focused on the reasons for opposition rather than the necessity, in principle, of military defense.[108] In addition to concerns about reunification, the SPD viewed foreign policy as a major determinant of postwar domestic social structure, as did the CDU, since military and economic integration with the West would strongly facilitate the emerging capitalist order and hinder the construction of a socialist order.[109] In addition, the party maintained pacifist traditions left over from the prewar period.

All these sentiments came to the fore at party conventions and in the SPD's theoretical journal, the *Neue Gesellschaft*. At the 1954 party congress in Berlin, Ollenhauer argued that a new army posed a potential threat to democracy and that Adenauer's support of America helped restore capitalist privileges. The SPD rejected the European Defense Community, not because it opposed defending democracy or West Germany in principle, but because of reunification's central importance. Ollenhauer expressed confidence that the Berlin four-powers conference had not sealed the division of Germany despite its lack of results, and he maintained that German policy must promote negotiations and international détente. Most significantly, he confirmed that Germany belonged to the West but had to find the best German contribution to Western strength in the face of superpower rivalry and German division. German interests lay in not hardening the fronts, which would be the result of joining military alliances.[110]

For most delegates who contributed to the convention's foreign policy discussion, Ollenhauer's speech represented a comfortable minimum of militancy on the rearmament question. Of the thirty-four delegates who spoke, twenty-four were against rearmament and received the most applause (as recorded in the congress protocols).[111] The problems rearmament posed for reunification were by far the most-cited reason for opposing it. Heinz Kühn, for example, argued that joining military alliances would strengthen the bloc system and make reunification less likely. The SPD should therefore support an alliance only when a party congress had determined that negotiations had no hope.[112] Fritz Baade found that Ger-

---

108. Ibid., 47–48; Löwke, *Für den Fall, daß . . .*, 105, 116.

109. Drummond, *The German Social Democrats in Opposition*, 6.

110. Vorstand der SPD, *Protokoll der Verhandlungen des Parteitages der Sozialdemokratischen Partei Deutschlands vom 20. bis 24. Juli, 1954 in Berlin* (N.p., 1954), 53–70.

111. For the text of the delegates' statements on rearmament at the 1954 Berlin convention, see Vorstand der SPD, *Protokoll der Verhandlungen* 1954:71–143.

112. Johann von Rantzau too argued against tying West Germany rigidly into an alliance against the East, which would eliminate Soviet incentives for negotiations on

man divisions could do little to hold off a Soviet attack. The only effective defense was therefore prevention of war itself. Germany could best contribute to security by being part of a general disarmament movement; this was the only true realpolitik. Others, like Willi Dohr, felt that rearmament was senseless in the atomic age and that the money could be better spent on social problems. Olaf Radke and others pointed to the dangers an army could pose to democracy, either directly, as an institution, if militarism revived, or because the government could assume sweeping powers in military emergencies. Thus the rank and file's opposition to rearmament typified the large majority of the party and the leadership.[113]

Despite all opposition, West Germany joined NATO, and rearmament duly took place. But even then the SPD rank and file pressed the leadership to act against the government's defense policy. Over one-fourth of the resolutions submitted by local party organizations to the Munich convention of 1956 concerned rearmament; one-third still pressed for total opposition and urged use of any means necessary to block its implementation.[114] A further complication resulted from SPD cooperation with the CDU in parliamentary committees to determine the shape and organizational details of the Bundeswehr, although most of the SPD still opposed a new army. Particularly influential was Fritz Erler, one of the SPD's few military experts and chairman of the party's "working group" on security questions. His group worked on parliamentary control of the armed forces, rules for allowing the army to intervene in domestic politics, protection of soldiers' civil rights, and screening of army officers. Because of

---

reunification. It would also stimulate a Soviet military buildup that would lead to a dangerous situation on the Elbe river. Although Germany belonged to the West economically and culturally and should have had military ties too, it did not belong one-sidedly to a Western pact. See Johann Albrecht von Rantzau, "Zweiseitige Pakte und deutsche Mittellage," *Neue Gesellschaft* 2, no. 1 (Jan./Feb. 1955): 10–15.

113. Several articles in the 1955 issues of *Neue Gesellschaft* also discussed the problem of ensuring democratic structures and the influence of any new army, citing the potential dangers a German army could pose to the new democracy. See Julius Deutsch, "Alte Reichswehr oder Neues Volksheer?" and Georg Wünsch, "Deutschland und Europa," *Neue Gesellschaft* 2, no. 3 (May/June 1955), 48–50, 51–54. See also Hans Joachim Langenbach, "Sozialdemokratie und Wehrpolitik," *Neue Gesellschaft* 2, no. 1 (Jan./Feb. 1955): 38–43; and Werner Picht, "Staatsbürger in Uniform?" and Willi Henkel, "Ein Leitbild und seine Möglichkeiten," *Neue Gesellschaft* 2, no. 2 (Mar./Apr. 1955), 53–61, 61–62.

114. Vorstand der SPD, *Protokoll der Verhandlungen des Parteitages der Sozialdemokratischen Partei Deutschlands* (N.p., 1956).

the SPD's representation in Bundestag security policy committees, it was able to introduce a number of amendments to the government's *Soldatengesetz* (law concerning soldiers). Nevertheless, conflict over whether to vote for this legislation proved sharply divisive to the SPD's Bundestag *Fraktion* (parliamentary caucus), as well as to the larger party.[115]

As with West Germany as a whole, within the SPD the rearmament question led into the nuclear weapons issue without noticeable pause. In each case, the bulk of the party vehemently opposed Adenauer's policy, and the leadership's position in turn was not far removed from that of the rank and file. While the late 1950s saw the rise of "reformers" within the leadership, who wanted to make SPD defense policies more acceptable to the electorate by adapting them to West German realities, even they cloaked their substantive policy departures solidly within the rank and file's rhetorical framework.

The SPD had been a major force behind the broader anti-rearmament movement, at least in its final phase as the Paulskirche movement. Local party organizations were heavily involved in movement activities, and Ollenhauer himself helped plan the mass rally at the Frankfurt Paulskirche and was one of the featured speakers. Likewise, as nuclear weapons became controversial, the popular movement Kampf dem Atomtod (KdA) sprang up in opposition. The Social Democrats threw themselves energetically into the fray, and their sheer numbers were instrumental in launching the movement. In January 1958, the SPD leaders called on party members to take up the KdA campaign as their central political cause, and top SPD leaders—Ollenhauer, Carlo Schmid, and Walter Menzel—helped organize the KdA's top committee and central activities.[116] The KdA far surpassed the SPD's earlier attempts to use extra-parliamentary means against the government. In comparison with the Paulskirche anti-rearmament movement, the party mobilized more manpower and resources, and the KdA campaign evoked a greater sense of involvement among the rank and file than any previous issue.[117]

At the 1958 convention, party leaders and convention delegates were in broad agreement on their rejection of nuclear weapons for the West German army. The convention's resolution asked the party to fight its implementation with "all constitutional means" inside and outside Parlia-

---

115. Drummond, *The German Social Democrats in Opposition,* 159–63.
116. Rupp, *Außerparlamentarische Opposition,* 130 and passim.
117. Drummond, *The German Social Democrats in Opposition,* 227.

ment.[118] Ollenhauer expressed the whole party's sentiments. Nuclear weapons rendered war as an instrument of policy meaningless and, given German division, were irresponsible. The right course for West Germany was reunification through détente and a security system that would take Europe out of the current military pacts.[119] Delegates came out time after time against nuclear weapons and for continuing the antinuclear campaign, citing all the familiar reasons: the dangers of nuclear weapons and the futility of nuclear defense for Germany, the priority of social spending over defense acquisitions, and, above all, the danger of reinforcing the military pact structures and thereby German division.[120]

Nineteen fifty-eight marked the high point of the SPD's support for peace protest. As is discussed in chapter 3, a scant year later the historic Godesberg Program proclaimed the party's support for national defense. In 1960, Herbert Wehner's speech to the Bundestag made clear that this commitment included support for NATO membership and nuclear weapons, and thus for Adenauer's policy of Western military integration.

Neutralist Security Proposals in the 1950s

Given their concerns for reunification and the desire to escape superpower confrontation, most parts of the 1950s peace movement supported neutralization, or a bloc-free status, in exchange for German unification. The Social Democrats worked out the most detailed proposals in this respect. Nonpartisan neutralist groups also offered suggestions, while Protestant peace activists supported the concept in general terms.

The SPD's antialliance and antinuclear commitment found its complement in the concept of a collective (European) security system.[121] The

---

118. "Für eine Welt der Freiheit und des Friedens," convention resolution found in Vorstand der SPD, *Protokoll der Verhandlungen des Parteitags der Sozialdemokratischen Partei Deutschlands vom 18. bis 23. Mai in Stuttgart* (Hannover-Bonn: Neuer Vorwärtsverlag, 1958), 481–82. This formulation received some criticism because it implied that the SPD leadership would not call for more radical means, such as a general strike. See Drummond, *The German Social Democrats in Opposition,* 234.

119. Erich Ollenhauer, "Frieden und Freiheit durch sozialistischer Politik," in Vorstand der SPD, *Protokoll der Verhandlungen* 1958:36–51.

120. Vorstand der SPD, *Protokoll der Verhandlungen* 1958:52–175. See also Ihno Krumpelt, "Braucht Westdeutschland taktische A-Waffen?" *Neue Gesellschaft* 5, no. 1 (1958): 42–47; Erich Ollenhauer, "Stuttgart—Parteitag der Klärung," *Neue Gesellschaft* 5, no. 3 (1958): 167–71; Fritz Erler, "Möglichkeiten einer Politik der Disengagement," *Neue Gesellschaft* 5, no. 6 (1958): 435–41.

121. The idea had its roots in proposals for a European security system in the 1920s and 1940s (Haftendorn, *Sicherheit und Entspannung,* 91). It did not attain full development until the mid- to late 1950s, although as Löwke notes, the idea first appeared in the 1952 party con-

SPD hoped such a system could both reunite Germany and protect it against Soviet domination. Disarmament and détente could reduce the acute danger facing Europe and could also improve the superpowers' relationship. Because of the Berlin crisis of 1958, the SPD considered détente a precondition for regulating political and military questions. Indeed, Hütter calls the SPD's policy from 1955–60 the period of "reunification through détente."[122] A collective security system would have transformed the bloc system, which could conceivably have made German reunification possible.[123]

The *Deutschlandplan* (plan for Germany) of 1959 marked the idea's final expression as official SPD policy.[124] It enjoyed, however, only a brief half-year of glory before being quietly shelved on the adoption of the Godesberg Program and the SPD's change of course toward NATO. The *Deutschlandplan* argued that since the German question and European security were related, they both had to be attacked at their common root. The *Deutschlandplan* proposed to do just this and drew explicitly on similar proposals by George Kennan and the Polish foreign minister Rapacki. The SPD's plan called for a four-power commission to work out a European security system and peace treaty for all of Germany. It further proposed a "détente zone" of both Germanies, Poland, Czechoslovakia, and Hungary, in which arms limitations would be imposed and from which foreign troops would be withdrawn. These countries would not have their own nuclear weapons, and those belonging to foreign troops would also be withdrawn. A collective security agreement, sponsored by the superpowers, would guarantee the security of the countries in the détente zone and would remove those countries from NATO and the Warsaw Pact. The *Deutschlandplan*'s final section dealt with German reunification. Given the proposed security arrangements, it assumed, neither superpower would

---

vention's *Aktionsprogramm* and was increasingly fleshed out between 1953 and 1955 (*Für den Fall, daß . . .,* 125). In 1958 the idea received copious mention at the Stuttgart party convention.

122. Hütter, *SPD und nationale Sicherheit,* 57.

123. All specialists on SPD security policy of this period include discussions of the collective security system idea. See Hütter, *SPD und nationale Sicherheit,* 65–75; Haftendorn, *Sicherheit und Entspannung,* 92–95; Drummond, *The German Social Democrats in Opposition,* 188–203; and Soell, *Fritz Erler,* 340, 376. See also Lothar Wilker, *Die Sicherheitspolitik der SPD 1956–1966: Zwischen Wiedervereinigungs- und Bündnisorientierung* (Bonn: Verlag Neue Gesellschaft, 1977), 26–39.

124. Vorstand der SPD, ed., *Deutschlandplan der SPD—Kommentare, Argumente, Begründungen* (booklet, Bonn: N.p., Apr. 1959), 5–11.

mind ceding "its" Germany. The *Deutschlandplan* thus was a last attempt to restore unity through military détente and arms control, by including all of Germany in a collective security system. The Godesberg Program sealed the demise of the *Deutschlandplan* by recognizing the principle of *West* German security.

The idea of German military neutrality attracted support far beyond the Social Democrats. This support for neutrality was organized in ad hoc groups that made up for their small size and number by their sheer diversity and the high profile of some of their leaders. Drawn primarily from secular middle-class circles, neutralist groups encompassed widely diverse views of politics and neutrality itself. Perhaps the most prominent among them was the nonpartisan Nauheimer Kreis (Nauheim Circle), founded by a Würzburg University history professor, Ulrich Noack, and composed of politicians, academics, and other intellectuals.

Noack felt that avoiding war in Central Europe and overcoming Germany's division required a political solution that would create stable conditions in Europe. Since absorbing all of Germany into either superpower's bloc would destroy the unstable equilibrium between the two, Noack advocated that Germany be made neutral and demilitarized, foreign troops be withdrawn, and an internationally guaranteed buffer between the superpowers be established, comprising, at a minimum, Finland, Switzerland, Germany, and Austria. Noack carried his campaign for German neutralization to audiences ranging from the American military government to the Vatican, the Soviets, and the German Democratic Republic, but he met with poor reception. The East Germans criticized him for underestimating the West's aggressive intentions against the Soviet Union, while the CDU/CSU accused him of working with the "East" and banned him from the party in 1951.[125]

Another major, but very different, neutralist group was Wolf Schenke's Dritte Front. Kurt Tauber identifies Schenke as a "former chief editor of the Hitler Youth organ *Wille und Macht* and the Far East correspondent of the *Völkische Beobachter*."[126] Schenke sought a "third way" between the superpowers in terms of culture, social order, and military alignments. In his view, both American materialism and bolshevism were equally foreign to traditional German and European culture, which melded Greek, Roman, Christian, and Teutonic roots. Neutrality not only would secure peace but also would break Germany's postwar "spiritual bondage." Schenke hoped to synthesize personal freedom and social jus-

---

125. Rainer Dohse, *Der Dritte Weg: Neutralitätsbestrebungen in Westdeutschland zwischen 1945 und 1955* (Hamburg: Holsten Verlag, 1974), chap. 3.

126. Kurt Tauber, *Beyond Eagle and Swastika: German Nationalism since 1945* (Middletown, Conn.: Wesleyan University Press, 1967), 171.

tice and to arrive at a just social order that would enable Germany to resist communism and maintain its national unity and political freedom. Moreover, only neutral status would create the foreign policy framework for a domestic order independent of both East and West. The Dritte Front's program thus originated in nationalist rather than pacifist attitudes. Correspondingly, the Dritte Front was the only major neutralist group to support armed rather than unarmed neutrality. Other right-wing support for neutralism came from small neofascist parties like the Nationale Partei Deutschlands and the Sozialistische Reichspartei.[127]

Finally, democratic pacifists from religious circles, such as Martin Niemöller, Gustav Heinemann, and Helene Wessel, supported neutralization of Germany from a moral and political perspective. Martin Niemöller, for example, maintained that Germans belonged to neither East nor West. In his view, the issue was not choosing between the two camps but rather deciding whether Germany would become a battlefield or bridge between them. God was primarily concerned with people; neither Western culture and freedoms nor Eastern social justice were worth more.[128]

The Dogs That Did Not Bark in the Night: Catholics and Peace Protest

The absence of Catholic participation in the 1950s peace movement reinforces the importance of group-specific interpretive frames for involvement in peace protest. In the 1950s, Catholics were conspicuous by their absence from the peace movement, particularly as recognizable groups, but also as prominent individuals. This did not stem from lack of Catholic opposition to Adenauer's defense policies in principle. On the contrary, in the early 1950s, there was observable discomfort with rearmament in Catholic lay associations. Polls revealed, moreover, that in 1958, 71 percent of conservative (CDU/CSU) voters opposed nuclear missile launching sites on German territory,[129] and a considerable number of those voters must have been Catholic, given the disproportionate Catholic vote for Adenauer's party (not to mention likely opposition among Social Democratic Catholics).

As described earlier in this chapter, Protestants based their opposition to rearmament and nuclear weapons on the interpretive frames of guilt and redemption, drawn from the EKD's discussion of fascism and war. Catholics, in contrast, lacked interpretive frames from their own

---

127. Ibid., 173–75.
128. *Kirchliches Jahrbuch* 77:162–65. See also *Kirchliches Jahrbuch* 77:169–71.
129. Rupp, *Außerparlamentarische Opposition*, 285.

church that could have provided a bridge to peace protest, due to the two churches' differences in doctrine and organizational structure. Catholic doctrine developed differently from Protestant doctrine in the postwar period. These differences were especially apparent in Catholic treatment of German guilt and its foreign policy consequences, the Catholic Church's relationship to the Adenauer government and the CDU, its relative indifference to German reunification, and its relationship to conscientious objection. The Catholic Church's hierarchical structure and control of its lay associations, moreover, left much less room for opposition groups to form and act within the church.

Impediments to Catholic Participation in the Peace Movement

In the 1950s, active Catholic opposition to rearmament and nuclear weapons hardly existed. Catholics laid less emphasis on German historical guilt and its foreign policy implications than did Protestants, and they did not associate the guilt question with defense issues. Catholic disinterest in the matter was somewhat surprising given the initial support for Hitler by the vast majority of the clergy. After World War I, the German Catholic Church did not support the Weimar Republic but instead remained conservative, monarchist, and antiliberal. The Third Reich appealed to Catholics in the beginning, for it seemed to realize their vision of an integrated, predemocratic, preliberal, and paternalistic society. Catholic and Third Reich negotiation of the Concordat—which seemed to secure Catholic civil rights violated by previous regimes—and the Center Party's unanimous vote for the Enabling Act of 1933 contributed to National Socialist consolidation of power. Neither event strengthened Catholic will to resist the Nazis' program; indeed, both seemed to signify the new regime's acceptability and the hope for a modus vivendi.[130]

Soon thereafter, however, Hitler moved to consolidate his power over the church, imprisoning some priests and disbanding lay organizations. Catholic leaders resisted Nazi organizational control of the church, however, and organizational integrity spared them the humiliation of absorption into the "German Christians" like their Protestant counterparts.[131] Several bishops also shielded numerous intended victims from Nazi extermination. This resistance, nonetheless, had its limits. At the national level, the Catholic hierarchy remained loyal to the regime. While a minority of clergy wanted a more vigorous campaign against the Nazis, the bishops limited themselves to a legalistic interpretation of the Concordat. While

---

130. Spotts, *The Churches and Politics in Germany,* 27, 28.
131. Ibid., 28–29.

Catholics defended Catholic interests, they supported the Third Reich in foreign and economic policy, persecution of minorities, and repudiation of democracy.[132]

Thus although German Protestantism was more thoroughly compromised by the fascist experience, the Catholic Church's behavior during the Third Reich shared important similarities. Nothing on the Catholic side after the war, however, corresponded to the Protestant Church's Stuttgart Declaration of Guilt. According to some observers, the German Catholic Church in fact evaded its share of responsibility for National Socialism. Spotts maintains that the church showed "not a trace of regret," emphasizing instead its resistance; the bishops apparently felt no debt of repentance.[133] The Third Reich thus had little evident impact in the Catholic Church, in comparison to the radical change in outlook it effected on the Protestant Church (EKD). Others have pointed to a few bishops' statements that Catholics bore some guilt from the Nazi period, but generally the church considered itself freed from twelve years of resistance and struggle.[134] In any event, these few statements had less effect on Catholic thinking than corresponding statements by Protestant leaders. Catholic treatment of the guilt question removed from the Catholic agenda one theme that led many Protestants to oppose rearmament and nuclear weapons.

Another inhibition came from Catholicism's close link to Adenauer's party. Whereas the Protestant Church committed itself to a more critical relationship to the state after the war, the Catholic Church entered a close relationship with the West German state without precedent in German history, illustrated both by the tight links between the Catholic hierarchy and the Adenauer government and by the highly disproportional Catholic vote for the CDU/CSU.[135] This close relationship during the 1950s and early 1960s fully integrated (West) German Catholics into the (West) German state and democracy for the first time ever, while Catholic voting behavior played a stabilizing role in the early West German party system and

---

132. Conway, "The German Church Struggle," 111–31.

133. Spotts, *The Churches and Politics in Germany*, 30.

134. Anselm Doering-Manteuffel, *Katholizismus und Wiederbewaffnung: Die Haltung der deutschen Katholiken gegenüber der Wehrfrage 1948–1955* (Mainz: Matthias-Grünewald-Verlag, 1981), 42. Doering-Manteuffel's book is by far the most detailed treatment of Catholics and rearmament.

135. For a discussion of the ideological basis of postwar political Catholicism, see Gerhard Kraiker, *Politischer Katholizismus in der BRD: Eine ideologiekritische Analyse* (Stuttgart: Verlag W. Kohlhammer, 1972).

state.[136] Such a relationship no doubt inhibited Catholic opposition to Adenauer's policies, including his defense policy.

In contrast to the Protestants, the Catholics exhibited a lack of passionate concern for reunification, which removed a further motivation that Catholics might otherwise have had for opposition to Adenauer's defense policies. Catholics did not express particular concern about conflicts between Western military integration and German reunification, nor did they press for a change in Germany's policies toward Eastern Europe. This relative indifference stemmed from the traditional Rhineland and south German demographic concentration and regional orientation of German Catholics and from the corresponding lack of Catholics in East Germany and the lost territories. West European integration likewise appealed more strongly to Catholics than to Protestants in the 1950s because of the traditional Catholic attachment to the "Christian West."[137]

A final factor in Catholic support for Adenauer's defense policies lay in papal positions of the 1950s, when lay obedience to church authorities was still uncontested. Pope Pius XII maintained the doctrine of just war and the duty of states to defend themselves. Although he condemned *offensive* war, in 1948 the pope enunciated the right of Christian states to defend essential goods.[138] This created a Catholic front line against the Soviet Union, reinforced during the cold war by the ideological opposition of Christianity and "atheistic bolshevism," Eastern European treatment of Catholics, and papal prohibition of Catholic membership in communist parties.[139] When it came to rearmament, the policy preferences of the German Catholic hierarchy and papal pronouncements on war converged neatly. Papal statements, moreover, set strict parameters to the German

---

136. Karl Forster, "Der deutsche Katholizismus in der Bundesrepublik Deutschland," in *Der soziale und politische Katholizismus: Entwicklungslinien in Deutschland 1803–1963,* ed. Anton Rauscher (Munich: Gunter Olzog Verlag, 1981), 209–64, here 222–32.

137. Doering-Manteuffel, *Katholizismus und Wiederbewaffnung,* 98–108. Heinz Hürten concurs on the importance of Catholic emphasis on supranational, European, and Western ties to brothers in faith in other countries as a major ideological basis for Catholic support of rearmament. See his essay "Zur Haltung des deutschen Katholizismus gegenüber der Sicherheits- und Bündnispolitik der Bundesrepublik Deutschland 1948–1960," in *Katholizismus im politischen System der Bundesrepublik 1949–1963,* ed. Albrecht Langner (Paderborn: Ferdinand Schöningh, 1978), 83–102. Hürten makes the interesting additional point that Catholics felt close to France after World War II, which made them receptive to the idea of European integration. Protestants became closer to England through the ecumenical movement, which did not have the same effect.

138. See the papal Christmas message of 1948 in *Herder Korrespondenz* 3, no. 4 (Jan. 1949): 162–66.

139. Doering-Manteuffel, *Katholizismus und Wiederbewaffnung,* 1–32. See "Können Christen mit Kommunisten zusammenarbeiten," *Herder Korrespondenz* 3, no. 6 (Mar. 1949): 279–81, for the prohibition of Catholics' working with communists in any way.

Catholic Church's discussion of rearmament, in particular making out-right pacifism nearly impossible. It is difficult to imagine Catholics in this period arguing, as did pacifist circles of the Protestant Church, that God demanded abstinence from all military activity as a sign of repentance for the past.

Catholics and the Rearmament Debate

These factors combined to inhibit organized Catholic participation in the peace movements of the 1950s, which is all the more striking since many Catholics initially shared the antimilitarism rampant in German society after the war. Before the outbreak of the Korean War, leading Catholic lay journals opposed the various rearmament proposals floated by Adenauer. As late as February 1950, a widely read lay journal revealed that 91 percent of its readers were against military service of any kind.[140] This sentiment, however, reversed itself under the influence of the impediments mentioned in the preceding section of this chapter and the church hierarchy's pressure on lay organizations. In fact, German Catholicism supported rearmament earlier and more decidedly than other groups in German society. A pivotal event was a sermon by Cardinal Frings, the president of the German bish-ops' conference. Frings reminded people of the pope's 1948 message, emphasizing that peace depended on maintaining the order dictated by God and that states had the duty to defend this order. Other bishops and the major organs of the Catholic press soon began to support Frings' posi-tion on rearmament, bringing the episcopate formally into the discussion of defense issues as a church. Pressure grew for conformity within Catholi-cism, and independent voices rapidly lost influence. Catholic support for Adenauer's defense policies thus accorded with binding moral-theological doctrine and also stemmed from other conservative economic and social policies that Catholics favored vis-à-vis Social Democratic alternatives.[141]

Catholic opponents of rearmament existed but did not form a recog-nizable wing within the church that could have opposed the hierarchy's pressure for unity or forced a recognition of pluralism as occurred in the EKD. A few lone individuals like Reinhold Schneider, who felt that the Christian's only weapon was nonviolence, opposed rearmament for reli-gious reasons. Other Catholic pacifists, like Klara Fassbinder, maintained the traditions of the Catholic peace movement left over from the Weimar Republic. Publicists in such journals as the *Frankfurter Hefte* (in particu-lar Walter Dirks and Eugen Kogon) expressed political opposition to rear-mament, using arguments common to the anti-rearmament movement as

---

140. *Mann in der Zeit* 3, no. 2 (Feb. 1950); cited in Doering-Manteuffel, *Katholizismus und Wiederbewaffnung,* 80.

141. Doering-Manteuffel, *Katholizismus und Wiederbewaffnung,* 59–179.

a whole but devoid of any specifically Catholic character.[142] Anti-rearmament sentiments within such lay organizations as the Federation of German Catholic Youth (BDKJ) were also politically rather than religiously motivated, which reduced their effectiveness given the binding nature of church doctrine. The BDKJ leadership, furthermore, quickly squelched this opposition, forbidding members of the organization to contradict church doctrine.

Thus rearmament opponents did not enjoy any broad effect within German Catholicism. At no time did nonconformists form a coherent organization that could have challenged the church's demand for unity. In contrast, the Protestant Church freely condoned a number of political positions in an attempt to maintain its organizational unity. Catholic opponents were only a small part of the domestic opposition to rearmament and could not change the broad Catholic support for rearmament policy. Their opposition was further limited because it was primarily politically rather than religiously motivated and thus could not challenge Catholic doctrine on the subject.[143]

Catholics and the Nuclear Weapons Debate
The tight bond between the West German Catholic Church and the Adenauer government continued to hold during the controversy over nuclear weapons in the late 1950s. While there was some discussion within the church, it did not approach the intensity or divisiveness of Protestant debate.[144] Opposition groups like those in the EKD simply did not exist in the Catholic Church, and opposition to nuclear weapons remained a negligible quantity.[145] The Catholic hierarchy and the vast majority of theologians unconditionally supported Western integration and containment of communism. The doctrine of just war retained its validity for the German Catholic hierarchy, for whom it could apparently encompass nuclear as well as conventional weapons.[146]

The German hierarchy's position reflected the church's continued

---

142. See, for example, Eugen Kogon, "Das Gespenst der deutschen Remilitarisierung," in *Frankfurter Hefte* 5, no. 1 (Jan. 1950): 2–3. See also Martin Stankowski, *Linkskatholizismus nach 1945: Die Presse oppositioneller Katholiken in der Auseinandersetzung für eine demokratische und sozialistische Gesellschaft* (Cologne: Pahl-Rugenstein Verlag, 1974), 118–20.

143. Doering-Manteuffel, *Katholizismus und Wiederbewaffnung,* 165–85.

144. Reinhold Lehmann, "Abrüstung, die tödliche Verschwendung," in *Kirche in der Gesellschaft: der katholische Beitrag 1978/79,* ed. Jürgen Wichmann (Munich: Günter Olzog Verlag, 1978), 19–33, here 21.

145. Kubbig, *Kirche und Kriegsdienstverweigerung,* 93–96.

146. Honecker, "Kontroversen um den Frieden," 17–25.

close relationship to the Adenauer government,[147] and its support for Adenauer's policies hindered Catholic opposition to nuclear weapons. As Walter Dirks, a lonely Catholic dissident, noted, this relationship prevented Catholics from speaking openly against Adenauer either within church synods or in Bonn's political circles, despite the presence of Catholics in the SPD, laity who disapproved of nuclear weapons, and prominent Catholic dissidents like himself. The church treated nonconformists like traitors rather than like Christian brothers, and its emphasis on Catholic unity again inhibited organized opposition among German Catholics.[148]

Some prominent Catholic theologians, moreover, interpreted papal statements as permitting possession and even use of nuclear weapons under some conditions.[149] In 1958 seven moral theologians published "Ein katholisches Wort zur atomaren Rüstung," which was widely distributed among the population and reprinted in a widely read Catholic journal.[150] The statement amounted to a moral and theological justification of Adenauer's policy and carried considerable authority since its authors belonged to the doctrinal body (Lehramt) of the church.[151]

Catholic opponents to nuclear weapons thus failed to become an effective force within the church and did little to dent Catholic political unity behind Adenauer's policies.[152] Those Catholics arguing on political grounds (such as military considerations or German reunification) were not identifiably "Catholic" in their opposition.[153] Dissident theologians, to be sure, denied that nuclear weapons could be permissible instruments of defense under just war doctrine, because in the use of nuclear weapons, civilian death seemed inherent rather than a relatively restricted by-product.[154] Such theologians, however, used abstract and philosophical/theological terms, without the poignancy of Protestant opponents, who linked politics and religion much more directly and emphatically. Thus although

147. Hürten, "Zur Haltung des deutschen Katholizismus," 98.

148. Walter Dirks, "Die Gefahr der Gleichschaltung," *Frankfurter Hefte* 13, no. 6 (June 1959): 379–91.

149. The most prominent example of this interpretation is Gustav Gundlach, "Die Lehre Pius XII vom modernen Krieg," *Stimmen der Zeit,* Apr. 1959; reprinted in *Kann der atomarer Verteidgungskrieg ein gerechter Krieg sein?,* ed. Karl Forster (Munich: Karl Zink Verlag, 1960), 105–34.

150. *Herder Korrespondenz* 12, no. 9 (June 1958): 395–97.

151. Walter Dirks, "Die Gefahr der Gleichschaltung."

152. Karl Forster, "Der deutsche Katholizismus," 234–37.

153. Eugen Kogon, "Zehn politische Argumente gegen die atomare Bewaffnung der Bundeswehr," *Frankfurter Hefte* 13, no. 6 (June 1958): 377–79. Kogon and Walter Dirks had a whole series of such articles in this journal during the nuclear weapons controversy.

154. Karl Peters, "Probleme der Atomrüstung," in *Atomare Kampfmittel und christliche Ethik: Diskussionsbeiträge deutscher Katholiken* (Munich: Kösel Verlag, 1960), 40–59. See also Clemens Münster, "Verantwortlich für Kernwaffen," 59–76 in the same book.

Catholic opponents to nuclear weapons did exist, they did not combine political and religious arguments in a singularly Catholic manner that might have spurred other Catholics to opposition on the basis of their religious identity.[155]

How the Movement Fared: Mobilization Constraints and Organizational Difficulties

The 1950s peace movement failed in a number of senses. First and most immediately, it failed to prevent the policies it opposed, from rearmament and NATO membership to nuclear weapons. Second, although the movement temporarily democratized the political agenda on security issues by forcing plentiful debate, its positions did not become institutionalized in mainstream politics. Instead, German rearmament, NATO membership, and nuclear weapons became moot points, with the Social Democrats conspicuously shedding opposition to them and the neutralist Gesamtdeutsche Volkspartei (GVP) failing to overcome electoral marginality. Finally, the 1950s movement failed the test of organizational survival. Once the SPD and DGB pulled out, the movement's main organizational apparatus dissolved. When opposition to nuclear weapons resumed in the 1960s, it was carried by new organizations.

The peace movement's failures stemmed from limited political opportunity and from problems with organization and strategy. The salience of defense issues and the receding likelihood of reunification, in addition to public opinion surveys that revealed considerable popular opposition to rearmament and nuclear weapons, opened political opportunities for peace protest. But those opportunities remained limited because of numerous factors that hampered the peace movement's efforts to translate this potential mobilization into actual mobilization. In addition, internal organizational and strategic contradictions plagued the movement's efforts.

Limited Political Opportunity Constrains Mobilization

Although inseparable from other elements of postwar German politics, Adenauer's decisions to rearm, join NATO, and station nuclear weapons had the most direct impact on the rise of the 1950s peace movement. These decisions created urgent grievances across most of the 1950s, which both catalyzed the movement's emergence and provided it with its most important resource for popular mobilization. Opinion surveys,

---

155. For an exception to this general rule, see Clemens Münster, "Atomare Verteidigung und Christliche Verantwortung," in *Kann der atomare Verteidigungskrieg ein gerechter Krieg sein?* ed. Karl Forster (Munich: Karl Zink Verlag, 1960), 73–105.

moreover, revealed a potentially mobilizable reservoir of public support. In the end, however, limited political opportunities constrained the movement's growth.

Despite perceptions of a Soviet threat, the populace remained highly ambivalent toward a new West German army, NATO membership, and nuclear weapons, and it thus represented a large reservoir of potential mobilization. This potential revealed itself in numerous opinion surveys and in the diffuse sentiment of *ohne mich,* or "count me out," observable in all strata of the population in the early 1950s.[156] During the rearmament debate, over half of the populace believed that the Soviet Union would be responsible for any new world war, and approximately two-thirds perceived a Soviet threat. Far fewer, however, supported rearmament or NATO membership, although support grew as the 1950s progressed.

In 1950–51 only 36 percent felt that the Atlantic Alliance would secure peace, and just over 25 percent felt that the Alliance would in fact increase the danger of war. Only 38 percent of the men were willing to become soldiers in the event of an attack "from the East," and only 36 percent of the women were willing to see their relatives become soldiers. Only 45 percent of the populace supported defending West Germany against an Eastern attack, whereas 26 percent thought it was better to let the country be "overrun," and 29 percent were undecided. By 1954 outright opposition to German troops in a West European army had fallen to 36 percent, down from 50 percent in 1951, but firm support for German troops in a West European army amounted to only 33 percent, with the rest in "it depends" or "don't know" categories. By 1955 support for NATO membership had risen to 45 percent of the populace, but 35 percent still preferred neutralization.[157]

The HICOG surveys (commissioned by the American Office of the High Commissioner in Germany) showed similar ranges and fluctuations of opinion. Between 1950 and 1955, support for a German military contribution to a Western alliance ranged (nonlinear) from 45 to 60 percent of the populace, with opposition between 25 and 45 percent. By the account of the HICOG surveys, support for neutrality ranged from 20 percent to almost 50 percent, though with a generally downward tendency.[158] Likewise, virtually all qualitative studies of the anti-rearmament movement

---

156. Karl Otto, "Der Widerstand gegen die Wiederbewaffnung der Bundesrepublik," in *Unsere Bundeswehr? Zum 25jährigen Bestehen einer umstrittenen Institution,* ed. Reiner Steinweg (Frankfurt: Suhrkamp Verlag, 1981), 52–105, here 70.

157. Elizabeth Noelle and Erich Neumann, *Jahrbuch der öffentlichen Meinung 1947–1955* (Allensbach am Bodensee: Verlag für Demoskopie, 1956), 347–73.

158. Anna Merritt and Richard Merritt, eds., *Public Opinion in Semisovereign Germany: The HICOG Surveys, 1949–1955* (Urbana: University of Illinois Press, 1980), 19–31 and passim.

comment on the antimilitarism rampant among the populace. Deutsch and Edinger observed a decided lack of enthusiasm for rearmament, noting at best a "reluctant acceptance."[159]

Later in the 1950s, public opinion opposed nuclear weapons in Germany even more strongly than it had remilitarization and thus provided even more fertile soil for opposition movements. From 1955 to 1957, according to Werner Feld, only about one-fourth of respondents supported "continuing the current western defense concept based on the Alliance of Western Europe and the US." Around 30 percent preferred "a general defense concept which included the US and the Soviet Union," while around 20 percent favored neutrality.[160] By 1957, 64 to 72 percent of respondents to various surveys opposed nuclear weapons for the German army, while support had fallen to around 15 percent.[161] In 1958, opposition to missile launching sites on German territory was even higher. SPD supporters were nearly unanimous in their disapproval (90 percent), and opposition was also surprisingly high among CDU supporters (71 percent).[162]

Popular opposition to Adenauer's policies represented a sizable mobilization potential, and various Soviet hints (serious or not) that it might let Germany reunify in exchange for neutral military status provided further temptations. Actual mobilization, however, remained extremely limited. In the early 1950s, Baring maintains, no "broad stream" of articulated opinion emerged to challenge the Adenauer government; and Cioc observes that "no event illustrated public passivity better than the much publicized 'Paulskirche movement.' "[163] Demonstrations reached a participant level of 325,000 during the campaign against nuclear weapons in 1958, but this show of opposition was still small compared to the several million participants later mobilized in the early 1980s.[164]

Despite the high salience of defense issues, several factors inhibited the peace movement's ability to convert mobilization potential into actual participation in movement activities. The international situation limited public acceptance of important parts of the peace movement's message,

159. Karl Deutsch and Lewis Edinger, *Germany Rejoins the Powers* (Stanford: Stanford University Press, 1959), 29.

160. Werner Feld, "Aufrüstung und europäisch-amerikanische Spannungen—bricht die Allianz zusammen?" *Journal für Sozialforschung* 3 (1984): 293–312, here 298.

161. Rupp, *Außerparlamentarische Opposition,* 89; Noelle and Neumann, *Jahrbuch der öffentlichen Meinung 1947–1955,* 471.

162. Rupp, *Außerparlamentarische Opposition,* 285.

163. Baring, *Aussenpolitik in Adenauers Kanzlerdemokratie,* 220; Cioc, *Pax Atomica,* 38.

164. Rupp, *Außerparlamentarische Opposition,* 191; Mushaben, "Grassroots and Gewaltfreie Aktionen," 141–53.

because the cold war strongly affected popular attitudes toward the Soviet Union and the United States. Traditional anticommunism, reinforced by Soviet behavior after World War II, restricted support for the movement's alternative defense proposals—neutralization and a demilitarized Central European zone. Despite its unease with remilitarization and nuclear weapons, only about one-third of the general populace consistently expressed support for neutralization as an alternative (see the polling figures outlined earlier in this section). Given the continuance of the cold war, the continual influx of refugees from East Germany, and the suppression of the East German and Hungarian revolts against their respective communist regimes (in 1953 and 1956, respectively), the movement's "diagnostic" frames (i.e., reasons why Adenauer's policies were "bad" for Germany) resonated much more strongly with the public than its "prescriptive" frames (neutralization and demilitarization).[165] In particular, perception of the Soviet threat and the high level of East-West tensions created needs for military security that only NATO membership could provide, despite discomfort with the rearmament and nuclear weapons intended to ensure that security.

At the same time, West German attitudes toward America were becoming increasingly positive. Although American bombing raids and occupation policies initially created distrust and resentment, these sentiments soon gave way to an idealized image of the United States as a strong, benevolent friend. Three experiences contributed to the idealization of America in the 1950s: its gift of democracy to West Germany after the war, support for German economic recovery through the Marshall Plan and other measures, and its military assistance to West Germany during the Berlin crises of 1948 and 1958–61.[166] Indeed, surveys recorded that 80 percent of West Germans wanted close relations with the United States, whereas only 20 percent supported close relations with the Soviet Union.[167] These America-friendly attitudes discouraged participation in peace protest against NATO membership and American nuclear weapons stationed in West Germany, while the absence of anti-Americanism removed one incentive for protest that was to appear in later decades.

Anticommunism directed toward the domestic left complemented mistrust of the Soviets. Adenauer skillfully exploited the presence of communists in the peace movement. He labeled the movement a front organi-

---

165. On diagnostic and prescriptive frames, see Snow and Benford, "Ideology, Frame Resonance, and Participant Mobilization," 197–218.

166. Harald Müller and Thomas Risse-Kappen, "Origins of Estrangement: The Peace Movement and the Changed Image of America in West Germany," *International Security* 12, no. 1 (summer 1987): 52–88, here 74.

167. Noelle and Neumann, *Jahrbuch der öffentlichen Meinung 1947–1955,* 331–32.

zation for the Soviet Union and East Germany, calling it "Moscow's fifth column," "useful idiots," and so on.[168] Given the anticommunism of the 1950s, it is safe to assume that such depictions deterred participation by tentative supporters.

Subcultural divisions within society served as another limiting factor. Protestants and the labor movement were the most visible elements of the peace movement, and the latter provided its numerical bulk. Active movement participation would have required that the middle class mingle with the working class and that Catholics make common cause with Protestants. Historical precedent did not generally support such cooperation, which would have meant crossing subcultural or religious lines.[169] Since, moreover, the middle class and Catholics overwhelmingly voted for the governing parties, movement participation would have meant traversing considerable political distances in order to cooperate with opposition parties on this one issue. The political culture of the 1950s made such action unlikely. Almond and Verba found a moderately high political distance between supporters of the two major parties, expressed in a relatively low percentage of "open partisans" (people emotionally involved in elections but not so intensely partisan as to avoid relations with the opposing parties' supporters) and relatively high levels of "intense" partisanship (emotional involvement in elections and sharp division from supporters of other parties).[170]

Additional elements of West German political culture in the 1950s reduced the overall protest potential, including the potential for peace movements. In general, protest was not yet part of German political culture. Histories of the period report virtually no extraparliamentary protest of any size, whereas histories of later periods feature such protest prominently. The political system provided few avenues for citizen influence outside of voting or conventional party activity, while the populace mistrusted political activity outside established institutions and exhibited relatively low levels of "citizen" (as opposed to "subject") orientations.[171] Moreover, the multifaceted conservativism of the 1950s worked against popular participation in opposition movements of any kind. To be sure,

---

168. Rolke, *Protestbewegungen in der Bundesrepublik,* 180–81.

169. According to Helga Grebing, the various bourgeois and working-class subcultures had partially reconstituted themselves after World War II, although they no longer enjoyed their former strength and had been regionally intersected by the demographic upheavals of postwar migration from East Germany and the former eastern territories ("Die Parteien," in *Die Bundesrepublik Deutschland: Geschichte in drei Bänden,* vol. 1, *Politik,* ed. Wolfgang Benz (Frankfurt: Fischer Taschenbuch Verlag, 1983), 126–91.)

170. Gabriel Almond and Sidney Verba, *The Civic Culture: Political Attitudes and Democracy in Five Nations* (Boston: Little, Brown and Company, 1965), 114–15.

171. Ibid., chap. 7.

the collapse of the Nazi regime and the mass migrations after the war partially disturbed traditional religious and regional identities. However, despite the apparent possibilities for a new society, the human toll of the Third Reich, the war, and the immediate postwar years served to depoliticize society, as people turned to reconstructing family and professional life. These upheavals also encouraged restabilization of inherited values and political behavior. Popular literature and music of the time mirrored this desire for a return to normalcy, for peace and quiet, and for a *heile Welt*, a world of safety and succor. Return to normalcy often meant a resurgence of traditional conservatism and a return to private life after the mass mobilization of the Third Reich.[172]

Finally, the overall popularity of Adenauer's government limited the peace movement's capacity for mobilization. The peace movement could capitalize on popular unease with rearmament and nuclear weapons but could not plausibly match Adenauer's accomplishments in the political and economic realms. Adenauer presented his policies as an integral whole, maintaining that democratic stability and economic recovery also required tight military integration with the West. By obvious implication, refusing the latter would also mean surrendering the former. Adenauer claimed, and generally received, full credit for West Germany's spectacular economic recovery and unexpected prosperity.[173] The CDU's 1957 election campaign slogan "No Experiments" (and the absolute majority it attained) corresponded to the high value the populace placed on military security, political rehabilitation, and prosperity, despite its unease with the instruments of security (rearmament, etc.). Economic prosperity and anti-communism gradually eclipsed discussion of alternatives in politics, the economy, and defense. As Joppke notes, "In the political culture of postwar Germany, whose autocratic and dictatorial past had discredited any unambiguous identification with national traditions, economic growth provided an ersatz consensus."[174] Thus demonstrations against Adenauer's foreign policy would have conflicted with the populace's increasing electoral support for his political and economic accomplishments, despite unease with rearmament. The peace movement could offer no alternative integral policy package whose appeal could match Adenauer's.

---

172. Christoph Klessmann, *Zwei Staaten, Eine Nation,* chap. 1.

173. Sixty to 75 percent of survey respondents expressed satisfaction with him or his government between 1950 and 1955 (Merritt and Merritt, *Public Opinion in Semisovereign Germany,* 14), and the CDU/CSU's electoral share increased from 30 percent to 50 percent of the vote between 1949 and 1957 (Chandler, "Party System Transformations in the Federal Republic of Germany," 64.)

174. Joppke, *Mobilizing against Nuclear Energy,* 92.

Organizational Contradictions

In addition to the peace movement's limited political opportunities, organizational difficulties restricted its effectiveness as well. The movement
needed an organizational structure that could stabilize and unify the diffuse protest groups opposing government policy. Such an organizational
structure failed to materialize for several reasons. First, because of the
weakness of autonomous extraparliamentary groups and the lack of networks among them, the 1950s peace movement had to rely heavily on
established political institutions, primarily the SPD and the union federation (DGB). Given the SPD and DGB leaderships' ambivalence toward
official participation, however, this dependence hampered the formation
of a nationally organized movement and reduced mobilization until those
organizations were fully involved, and it resulted in the movement's disintegration when those organizations later withdrew their support. Second,
difficulties in cooperation between the various wings limited the movement's cohesion, due in particular to the desire of the noncommunists in
the movement to maintain distance from communists.

The peace movement of the 1950s initiated an organizational pattern
typical of postwar West German peace protest. Like many other social
movements, it did not create a single, large, bureaucratic organization that
members joined as individuals. Instead, interested groups formed ad hoc
coalitions, which devised strategies and coordinated action to combat government policies. These ad hoc coalitions served as the leadership for
peace movements and were backed up by the organizational strength of
the constituent groups. Because of the SPD and DGB leaderships' reluctance to commit themselves to the peace movement, and the noncommunists' unwillingness to cooperate with communists, however, the anti-rearmament movement lacked a nationwide coalition of all important actors
during its early and middle phases (from 1951 to 1954).

The various wings of the movement conducted their own, separate,
protest actions.[175] The SPD concentrated on the parliamentary arena,
using Bundestag debates to considerable rhetorical advantage. Its other
tactics brought less success. It called in vain for new elections, arguing
that, because rearmament was not on the political agenda in 1949, the 1949
elections had not given the Adenauer government a mandate for such a
serious commitment. In addition, the SPD launched a *Feststellungsklage*
(suit requesting declaratory judgement), asking the Constitutional Court
to rule on whether German membership in the European Defense Community (EDC) violated the Basic Law, in which case ratifying the EDC

---

175. Dietzfelbinger, *Die westdeutsche Friedensbewegung 1948–1955.*

would have required a two-thirds majority, and the SPD would have been able to block it. (In the end, after a counter case by the government, the Constitutional Court did not rule on the question.)[176] Communists conducted their own conferences and two unofficial referenda. These referenda were technically illegal, having been banned by the government on the grounds that the Basic Law did not provide for them, and their communist sponsorship undermined the democratic order. (The first, in 1951–52, was a smashing propaganda success, as 94 percent of those polled were against rearmament. The second, in 1955, was much less favorable to the movement, as only 50–60 percent sided with the peace movement.)[177] Finally, middle-class neutralists struggled to hold their own conferences, organized a nationwide youth march, and briefly formed an anti-rearmament party, the Gesamtdeutsche Volkspartei, which disappeared after receiving 1.2 percent of the vote in the 1953 elections.[178]

Although the Social Democratic and union leaderships conditionally opposed rearmament, they remained reluctant to engage in extraparliamentary action until quite late. Reinforced by his intense commitment to parliamentary democracy, Schumacher's view of democracy left little room for "radical" or "grassroots" politics. "For him," according to Markovits and Gorski, "plebiscitary or movement politics were strongly reminiscent of Nazism and therefore illegitimate as a political strategy."[179] Finally, however, pressure from the rank and file forced the hand of the SPD and DGB's leaderships, who feared that they would otherwise be unable to channel this pressure into "responsible" forms of protest. Only in 1955 did the SPD and DGB officially take part in the anti-rearmament movement, finally joining forces with the middle-class and church-based wings of the movement (though still intentionally excluding communists from joint action). As a result, the Paulskirche movement, with its thousands of rallies and demonstrations, overwhelmingly surpassed all previous protest actions organized by various subsections of the movement.[180] Crowned by the rally in the Frankfurt Paulskirche (St. Paul's Church), it used pamphlets, placards, torch parades, and rallies to inform the West German public about the political effects of the NATO membership and the need for pan-German negotiations and to collect signatures for the

---

176. Dennis Bark and David Gress, *A History of West Germany*, vol. 1 (Oxford: Blackwell, 1989), 316–17.

177. Dietzfelbinger, *Die westdeutsche Friedensbewegung 1948–1955*, 105, 194.

178. Gerhard Ritter and Merith Niehuss, *Wahlen in der Bundesrepublik Deutschland* (Munich: Verlag C. H. Beck, 1987), 74.

179. Markovits and Gorski, *The German Left*, 39.

180. Dietzfelbinger, *Die westdeutsche Friedensbewegung 1948–1955*, 194.

Deutsches Manifesto petition.[181] Soon, however, the Bundestag voted to join NATO, and the issue was moot.

In the later 1950s, the Kampf dem Atomtod protest against nuclear weapons acquired more centralized and more durable organization, partly because the activists involved had learned that coherent action depended on SPD and union involvement. In this effort, spearheaded by the Social Democrats, representatives of the various participating constituencies formed a national committee, complemented by similar regional and local committees.[182] Whereas in the early 1950s the SPD's leadership avoided overt cooperation with the peace movement, in the later 1950s it chose the opposite strategy. Putting itself in the forefront of the antinuclear organizational efforts, the SPD's leadership instigated the formation of the Central Committee and used its dominance to keep tight control over the movement. To this purpose, socialist and union leaders secured key positions within regional and city committees.[183] Numerous appeals and resolutions provided an opportunity to garner public expressions of elite support, while a series of rallies mobilized mass participation. During the spring of 1958, demonstrations took place in over half of all larger cities (with populations over 200,000), in which at least 325,000 people took part.[184] Unofficial strikes broke out, although the DGB union leadership held back from the notion of a general strike and thwarted even a five-minute symbolic strike.[185]

Although the movement did eventually manage to mobilize nationwide protest, internal organizational and strategic contradictions reduced the movement's immediate punch and doomed its long-term survival. The 1950s movement faced two fundamental organizational dilemmas. The first dilemma arose because, as noted earlier in this chapter, the movement drew heavily on the SPD and DGB for mass mobilization, organizational structure, leadership, and political visibility. The movement had little choice, since the few existing autonomous groups proved unable to match the SPD and DGB's capacities in these regards. Thus in the strongest phases of the 1950s peace protest, mobilization occurred from above, guided by the SPD and DGB leaderships.

However, the SPD and DGB leaderships found themselves caught between the rank and file's very strong desire for involvement in the peace movement, on the one hand, and, on the other, pressures to desist from such involvement—stemming from fear of electoral stagnation in the SPD

---

181. Ibid., 182.
182. Rupp, *Außerparlamentarische Opposition,* chaps. 4, 5.
183. Cioc, *Pax Atomica,* 118.
184. Rupp, *Außerparlamentarische Opposition,* 191.
185. Ibid., chap. 5.

and threats to organizational unity in the DGB. As a result, neither the SPD's nor the DGB's leadership was fully committed to the movement during the 1950s. This ambivalence resulted in mobilization that depended on strategic calculations of these organizations rather than on its own internal dynamic, which was disadvantageous for several reasons. For one thing, until 1955 the SPD and DGB leaderships' distance from the rest of the movement robbed the movement of unified organization. In addition, both organizations tried to restrain the movement's more radical impulses, restricting its range of protest forms (already tame by later standards).

Concerned to protect their public images of moderation, legality, and commitment to the democratic order, the SPD and DGB tried to channel movement energies into parliamentary forms of action as long as possible, while suppressing the plebiscitary tactics (like unofficial referenda) and confrontational strategies (like political strikes) supported by other parts of the movement. In 1952, for example, the SPD distanced itself officially from extraparliamentary means and even supported Adenauer's ban on unofficial referenda, on the grounds that they were unconstitutional and the whole idea was communist-led.[186] Ironically, later in the 1950s the SPD and DGB leadership tried to steer the antinuclear campaign toward a referendum, which the Constitutional Court subsequently banned. This irony developed as the labor movement leadership came to view even illegal referenda as more containable than the political strikes demanded by large parts of the rank and file, despite high public support for them.[187] Finally, in 1959–60 the SPD abandoned opposition to Western military integration and nuclear weapons altogether. Having failed to develop adequate organizational structures independent of the SPD or DGB, the movement disintegrated when those organizations withdrew their support.

A second strand of incoherence for the movement was the limited ability of its main wings to cooperate with one another on joint activities. The movement's various wings often conducted separate rather than joint actions, and they devoted considerable energy to maintaining "appropriate" distance from one another.[188] Given Adenauer's strategy of associating the movement with the "red menace" and given active repressive measures to disrupt peace movement activities on the grounds that they represented communist "machinations," this separatism reflected the quite understandable reluctance of mainstream forces to associate themselves with the Communist Party and affiliated groups. In particular, both the SPD and the DGB were reluctant to cooperate with the Communist Party

---

186. Fritz Krause, *Antimilitaristische Opposition in der BRD 1949–1955* (Frankfurt: Verlag Marxistische Blätter, 1971), 45.

187. Graf, *The German Left since 1945*, chap. 6.

188. Rolke, *Protestbewegungen in der Bundesrepublik*, part 3, chap. 1.

(KPD) and its affiliated organizations. This reluctance made organizational cohesion and coalition building within the movement more difficult. Although it benefited substantially from the Communists' organizational capacities, the rest of the movement generally refused to form an explicitly united front with the KPD or its affiliated groups. For example, the SPD leadership opposed local "unity committees" containing communists, local social democrats, and nonpartisans.[189] The SPD leadership even limited its contact to the "bourgeois" wing of the anti-rearmament movement until its later phases, avoiding cooperation with the Protestant-based Notgemeinschaft für den Frieden Europas, and forbidding dual memberships between it and the party, apparently out of fear that competing parties might arise out of such groups.[190] In fact, the Gesamtdeutsche Volkspartei did emerge from the Notgemeinschaft, although it failed to overcome electoral marginality.

Middle-class neutralist groups maintained similar distance from communists and thus contributed to the peace movement's overall lack of unity. These groups were also divided among themselves. Numerous neutralist organizations existed, ranging from right-wing parties (the Nationale Partei Deutschlands and the Sozialistische Reichspartei), to democratic pacifists from religious circles (e.g., Martin Niemöller, Helene Wessel, and Gustav Heinemann), and to the far-left and apparently communist-guided Sozialdemokratische Aktion and Neutrales Deutschland.[191] Uniting such diverse groups into a single organization with a common program proved impossible despite several attempts. The Deutscher Kongress of 1951–52, attended by some thirty-five neutralist organizations, was unable to overcome the divisions between pacifist supporters of *unarmed* neutrality on the left and right-leaning supporters of *armed* neutrality concerned primarily with national sovereignty and independence. The search for a common position was further complicated by some groups' insistence on distancing the congress's positions from all Soviet policies.[192] In the context of the cold war, however, neutralism supporters of whatever stripe suffered from the similarity between their positions and Soviet proposals, dooming them to political marginality.

The final phase of the 1950s peace movement, the Kampf dem Atomtod against nuclear weapons, ebbed away quite soon after its high point in the summer of 1958. The main cause of its rapid demise was the withdrawal of the Social Democrats' support. After its parliamentary defeat on

---

189. Dietzfelbinger, *Die westdeutsche Friedensbewegung 1948–1955,* 100.
190. Peter Molt, "Die neutralistische Opposition" (Ph.D. diss., University of Heidelberg, 1956), 73; cited in Rupp, *Außerparlamentarische Opposition,* 61.
191. Tauber, *Beyond Eagle and Swastika,* 173–75.
192. Dohse, *Der Dritte Weg,* chap. 7.

the nuclear weapons issue, the Constitutional Court's banning of the unofficial referendum, and its disappointing showing in the July 1958 Nordrhein-Westfalen *Landtag* elections, the SPD leadership saw itself confronted with several interrelated choices. Most narrowly, it could continue active opposition to nuclear weapons despite their impending arrival, or it could pursue enlargement of its electoral share by dropping this "pointless" opposition. More broadly, it could remain a class-based "worker" party or gradually make the switch to a "catch-all" party. In the late 1950s the SPD showed unmistakable signs of pursuing the catch-all party strategy, a process that culminated formally in the Godesberg Program (see chapter 3). As a result, the SPD's commitment to extraparliamentary activity diminished dramatically. A second blow to the movement was the government's anticommunist offensive, both through direct measures and through the founding of the Anti-Antinuclear Weapons Committee and the Committee to Save Freedom. The Kampf dem Atomtod remained formally in existence for some time, as did several other antinuclear groups, but to very little effect.[193]

The peace movement of the 1950s was catalyzed by a series of fundamental decisions to rearm West Germany and tie it to the West, in the context of the other fundamental outlines of the West German system—parliamentary democracy and a social-market economy. The movement united the various political forces against these developments, drawing particularly on interpretive frames of redemption, democratization, and the German question. Although it performed respectably, it remained hampered by limited protest potential in society at large, an incompatibility between its message and the times, and insoluble organizational dilemmas. However, although it forwent success, the movement did not remain without effect on subsequent West German politics. It launched peace protest as a recurrent theme in extraparliamentary protest, in part by tying it to the durable (but flexible) interpretive frames on which it drew, and by creating a core of activists dedicated to antimilitarist and antinuclear issues. It also taught them the necessity of autonomous extraparliamentary organizational structures, lessons that did not go unheeded in the decades to come.

---

193. Rolke, *Protestbewegungen in der Bundesrepublik,* 190–92.

CHAPTER 3

The 1960s: Peace Protest in Competition with Other Issues

In terms of the social movement theories discussed in the first chapter, peace protest in the 1960s was far more possible than in the 1950s. By the 1960s, the first real postwar generation had grown to early adulthood, and postmaterialist values had begun to emerge. West Germany was undergoing rapid structural change, moreover, as economic modernization enlarged the tertiary sector and society became increasingly secular. The combination of socialization during rising prosperity, societal secularization, and mass entry into tertiary-sector employment contributed to value change that distinguished the postwar generation's most educated segments most decidedly from older generations.

This new postwar cohort significantly enlarged West Germany's protest potential and changed its structure, adding a large educated, left-leaning, middle-class element to the traditional labor movement component. In addition, the new generation began to perceive a crisis of modernization as it read the Frankfurt School's critiques of industrial society, a process that became much more pronounced in the 1970s. Finally, resources for protest of all kinds increased as the media gave more space to dissidence, and extraparliamentary groups built organizational structures and experimented with protest forms outside of conventional political institutions.

These developments decisively shaped protest in the 1960s, giving it a new quality. Their impact can most readily be seen when they, along with other factors, are filtered through the political process approach. Our troika of political opportunity structure, ideological resources, and organizational infrastructure will once again illuminate developments, as we look at what launched protest and when, the composition of the movement, and its impact and ultimate decline.

In the 1960s conditions for peace protest were quite different than they had been a decade earlier, and they set different, though equally serious, limits to peace protest. Compared to the 325,000 people mobilized against nuclear weapons in 1958, the Easter Marches of the 1960s, which topped at 150,000 participants, look small indeed.[1] The political opportunity structure improved significantly for protest in general, ideological resources gained in richness and credibility, and capacity for organizational autonomy grew markedly. However, the movement lacked a galvanizing peace issue comparable to the introduction of nuclear weapons in the 1950s and had to share some of its demands for a new foreign policy with the SPD and others. In the end, peace became submerged in other issues and in a much broader wave of protest, and the peace movement met its demise when the broader extraparliamentary opposition disintegrated.

Launching Peace and Other Protest in the 1960s

Wedged, in retrospect, between the Adenauer era of the 1950s and the Social Democratic era of the 1970s, the politics of the 1960s combined new developments with apparent stagnation. Adenauer himself retired as chancellor, and both domestic and international politics underwent considerable transformation. Thus the Adenauer era began to unravel, transforming the political landscape and raising new issues concerning domestic political arrangements, economic policy, and foreign policy. These issues became intermingled with the overriding theme of the period: the nature and direction of West German democracy, including both its domestic and foreign policy components. These new issues and the changes that put them on the agenda created new opportunities for protest in general, although they limited opportunities for peace protest in particular. Understanding political opportunities for peace protest in the 1960s thus requires a look at both domestic politics and foreign policy.

Domestic Politics in the 1960s

Changes in the political arena raised questions about whether West German democracy was drifting toward renewed authoritarianism, one of the defining protest issues of the 1960s. The 1950s were characterized by Adenauer's uninterrupted tenure as chancellor; "minimal winning" governing coalitions (usually containing the liberal Free Democrats [FDP]), with the SPD as the major opposition party; and the coalescence of the party system around two poles representing distinct alternatives. During

---

1. Karl Otto, *Vom Ostermarsch zur APO: Geschichte der ausserparlamentarischen Opposition in der Bundesrepublik 1960–1970* (Frankfurt: Campus Verlag, 1982), 147.

the 1960s the formal structures of the parliamentary system did not change, but the actual functioning of parliament, its governing coalitions, and the party system did. The Bundestag ceased debating the fundamentals of foreign policy and appeared to be losing its capacity to check the executive branch. In the meantime, the SPD's function as an opposition party declined as it shifted its policy positions and electoral strategy toward the political center. These two trends reached their peak in the Grand Coalition, in which the CDU and SPD governed jointly from 1966 to 1969.

Adenauer's resignation as chancellor in 1963 and the breakup of the conservative-liberal coalition in 1966 were intertwined processes, and both contributed to the formation of the Grand Coalition. Adenauer resigned under pressure from his own party. His fall from grace had many reasons, including the CDU's substantial electoral losses in the 1961 parliamentary election and anger over his manipulation of the party during the election of the federal president in 1959. In addition, the Berlin Wall brought the failure of his reunification policy into full view, and the FDP made his resignation a condition for reentering the conservative-liberal coalition after the 1961 elections.

Ludwig Erhard succeeded Adenauer and continued the coalition with the FDP. As economics minister and architect of the "economic miracle" in the 1950s, Erhard ironically found himself chancellor during the Federal Republic's first real, and sudden, recession. Conflict over how to counteract the unusually large deficit led to the breakup of the conservative-liberal coalition, when the FDP allowed budget negotiations to fail. In October 1966, the FDP resigned from the government and went into opposition, bringing on Erhard's fall as well.[2]

The FDP's resignation from the government provided the immediate catalyst for the Grand Coalition, but its formation would not have been possible without the substantial transformation of the SPD in the late 1950s and early 1960s, including its new, young, and charismatic candidate Willy Brandt (mayor of Berlin, whose popularity rose with his forceful reaction to the Wall). Officially launched by the landmark Godesberg Program of 1959, the SPD began a process of party modernization. In an effort to break out of its electoral stagnation in the "30 percent ghetto," the SPD modified its domestic and foreign policy positions in a move toward the political center. Most scholars agree that the SPD's Godesberg Program represented a major turning point in the party's history. It jettisoned two key SPD positions that many considered responsible for the

---

2. Klessmann, *Zwei Staaten, Eine Nation,* chap. 3.

party's poor postwar electoral performance: nationalization of key industries (and the Marxist rhetoric accompanying this demand)[3] and opposition to NATO.

The Godesberg Program also reflected the ascendance of the "reformer wing" within the party, including Willy Brandt, Fritz Erler, Herbert Wehner, and Helmut Schmidt, who gradually penetrated the party's executive committee *(Vorstand)*. Too young to play significant roles before the Third Reich, after 1960 they took over the party's leadership from the older guard of Ollenhauer's generation. In addition to their more moderate views on economic policy, they became key policy innovators and party spokespersons on defense questions, gradually edging party resolutions more toward their views on defense in the late 1950s. The party's left, with its strong pacifist component, correspondingly slipped from its earlier dominant position.[4]

The Godesberg Program marked the SPD's acceptance of *Landesverteidigung*, or *West German* national defense and its armed forces, but did not yet make any positive commitment to NATO. Six months later, however, the SPD leadership explicitly confirmed the party's support for NATO as the context of "national defense" efforts. In June 1960, Herbert Wehner announced the SPD's support of NATO and willingness to work with the governing CDU on a "common foreign policy."[5] His speech before the Bundestag is properly called historic, for it represented the real break from the 1950s. Reiterating the SPD's new position at the Hannover party convention later that year, Wehner noted that approaching nuclear parity had fundamentally changed superpower relations, and thereby had foreclosed certain alternatives for the German question, along with the European regional order that could conceivably have come into being during the 1950s. Thus West German participation in NATO remained a given until a better alternative arrived, and it would enjoy the SPD's backing.[6] The new "reformist" leadership (Brandt, Schmidt, and Erler) echoed

---

3. See, for example, David Childs, *From Schumacher to Brandt: The Story of German Socialism 1945–1965* (Oxford: Pergamon Press, 1966), chap. 6; and Harold Kent Schellenger, *The SPD in the Bonn Republic: A Socialist Party Modernizes* (The Hague: Martius Nijhoff, 1968), chap. 2.

4. On the rise of the "experts" see, for example, Wilker, *Die Sicherheitspolitik der SPD 1956–1966,* 16–25.

5. See excerpts of Wehner's speech in Butterwegge and Hofschen, *Sozialdemokratie, Krieg und Frieden,* 322–23.

6. Vorstand der SPD, *Protokoll der Verhandlungen und Anträge vom Parteitag der Sozialdemokratischen Partei Deutschlands in Hannover, 21. bis 25. November 1960* (Bonn: Neuer Vorwärts-Verlag, 1960), 104–15, 117–27.

Wehner's commitment to NATO's defense strategy, including its reliance on nuclear deterrence.[7]

The SPD's new political centrism made it possible for the CDU to consider the party a viable coalition partner. Indeed, although normally each other's chief competitors, both parties had compelling reasons to form the coalition. For the SPD, the Grand Coalition rewarded its strategy of modernization and gave the party a chance to prove itself in government for the first time in the postwar period. For the CDU, the Grand Coalition represented its only chance to stay in government. The size of the Grand Coalition, moreover, gave the government the image of national consensus and the two-thirds majority necessary to amend the constitution, helpful in endeavors like the controversial Emergency Laws.

The Grand Coalition prompted many people to wonder whether West German democracy was starting down the slippery slope to renewed authoritarianism. The Grand Coalition's formation seemed to violate important democratic principles. It lacked a specific electoral mandate, and it de facto eliminated effective parliamentary opposition, since the FDP was too small to block constitutional changes or launch parliamentary investigations. It also raised issues of intraparty democracy. Not only did significant portions of both the CDU and the SPD oppose the Grand Coalition, but many SPD members were indignant over the undemocratic way the decision had been reached, as it had been blessed by the party's leadership *(Fraktion, Parteirat,* and *Vorstand)* without rank-and-file input until after the fact.

Controversies concerning the Grand Coalition's impact on democracy did not stop with its formation but instead were continually raised by its policies, of which the Emergency Laws were the most notable example. The government regarded the emergency legislation as an overdue assumption of West German sovereignty (from the Allied occupation) over emergency powers in crisis situations. As we will see later in this chapter, the extraparliamentary opposition saw the emergency legislation as a relapse into an authoritarian past and as an acute danger to democracy. Indeed, although the SPD supported emergency legislation in principle, opposition from unions, its own left wing, and other sources led the party to press successfully for "democratic" modifications concerning distinctions between external and domestic emergencies, limitations on government powers to restrict fundamental rights, restrictions on using the army during domestic emergencies, and guarantees of the right to strike.[8]

Developments in the economic realm were as dramatic as those in

---

7. For Schmidt's speech, see ibid., 141. For Erler and Brandt's speeches, see ibid., 547–57.

8. Klessmann, *Zwei Staaten, Eine Nation,* 247.

politics. Following the rapid growth of the "miracle" 1950s, the economy began to reveal structural weaknesses, and it slid into the first postwar recession in 1966. Although mild by historical comparison, the recession had significant psychological and political consequences. Psychologically, it shook the public's confidence in the hitherto seemingly invincible growth. Politically, it contributed to the Grand Coalition's formation and to passage of legislation that significantly expanded the government's capacity for economic intervention. Some of these policy measures reinforced the left's suspicions of increasing authoritarianism in politics and the economy.

In particular, the Stability and Growth Law gave the government new powers to intervene in the economy and changed the priorities of economic policy. With "global steering" as its new watchword, the government officially committed itself to medium-range planning and to steering the business cycle through demand management and deficit spending if necessary. A second crucial component of this new economic policy was "Concerted Action," a quasi-institutionalized forum of business, labor, government, the Bundesbank, and independent experts. Intended as a mechanism for exchange of information concerning the "macro" state of the economy, concerted action was also expected to set guidelines for wage increases by persuading unions to moderate their demands and thereby help keep down inflation.[9] The extraparliamentary and labor left, however, considered Concerted Action and the *formierte Gesellschaft* (formed society) to be government attempts to steer social actors—harking back to Nazi "coordination" policies—and thus to be veiled authoritarianism.[10]

Foreign Policy in the 1960s

The Grand Coalition and its new economic policy spelled the end of the Adenauer era in domestic politics and the economy. In foreign relations too, the 1960s looked significantly different from the 1950s. First, budding superpower détente, nuclear parity, and East-West arms control initiatives began to reduce tensions in Europe, at least compared to the 1950s. As a result, the German question changed under the impact of the Berlin crises and Allied responses and in the light of the superpowers' growing interest in maintaining the European status quo. These changes rendered West Germany's policy toward Eastern Europe and East Germany increasingly implausible, but Adenauer and Erhard resisted revising it to meet the

---

9. Markovits, *The Politics of the West German Trade Unions*, 27.

10. Tilman Fichter and Siegward Lönnendonker, *Kleine Geschichte des SDS* (Berlin: Rotbuch Verlag, 1977), 83. See also Klaus Hinrich Hennings, "West Germany," in *The European Economy*, ed. Andreas Boltho (New York: Oxford University Press, 1982).

changing times. A new *Ostpolitik* (policy toward Eastern Europe) became one of West Germany's burning foreign policy issues of the decade, although the Grand Coalition made some progress on this front. Second, the Nuclear Non-Proliferation Treaty and the possibility of West German participation in the proposed Multilateral Nuclear Force (MLF) raised the perennial question of German control over nuclear weapons. Finally, the Vietnam War and the Second Vatican Council undermined America's image among parts of the populace, leading to questions about the basic nature of the NATO alliance.

During the 1960s, changes in the international system rendered Adenauer's dual policies of Western integration and reunification increasingly inconsistent. In the 1950s, West Germany's integration into Western structures enjoyed a surface compatibility with its approach to reunification, since the Western allies supported the latter rhetorically if not in deed. In the 1960s, however, West German reunification policy became glaringly implausible, since international developments radically undermined its key premises. The West, and particularly the United States, clearly no longer supported the assumption of an "open status quo," since it took various steps that recognized and solidified European and German division. American "roll-back" policy had already failed to dislodge communist regimes from Eastern Europe, for the United States had not come to East Germany or Hungary's aid during their respective 1953 and 1956 revolts (or to Czechoslovakia's in 1968). To make matters worse, President Kennedy reacted to the construction of the Berlin Wall in 1961 by defending Western rights in *West* Berlin, leaving the Soviets to their own devices in East Berlin and East Germany. Moreover, the extended phase of superpower détente that followed the Cuban missile crisis of 1962 and the Test-Ban Treaty of 1963 reinforced superpower respect for the status quo, since both sides realized that superpower confrontation carried the risk of mutual destruction.

These developments inflicted on Adenauer's policies a slow death through incremental undermining. By the 1960s, America's preference for European stability meant that it shared with the Soviet Union and even East Germany a common interest in continued German division, which undermined the (at least nominal) American commitment to reunification in the 1950s. The construction of the Berlin Wall and the Allied response to it meant the failure of Adenauer's long-term reunification policy. This failure had ramifications for other German positions. Adenauer had made East-West détente and arms control conditional on progress on the German question. The NATO countries' increasing willingness to accept the status quo, however, forced his successors to give up this linkage or risk isolation within the Alliance. Germany was forced to accept détente and

arms control, such as they were in the 1960s, although they helped legitimize the status quo in Europe without resolving the problem of German
division.[11]

These problems made a new Ostpolitik one of the burning issues of
West German foreign policy in the 1960s. Indeed, by 1963, when Erhard
became chancellor, stagnation in West Germany's Eastern policies had
caused widespread dissatisfaction. Foreign Minister Gerhard Schröder
initiated an "opening to the East" and started German trade missions with
most Eastern European countries except East Germany. Nonetheless,
Bonn still refused to accept the Oder-Neisse line (the East German-Polish
border) and maintained the Hallstein Doctrine (which denied East Germany legal recognition and endeavored to isolate it diplomatically). Constrained by legalistic traditions and conservative elements of the CDU, the
Erhard government could not countenance anything that implied recognition of East Germany.[12]

Reflecting the increasing frustration with the stagnation of the CDU's
policy toward the East, the Protestant Church and the SPD issued stirring
calls for a new Ostpolitik in the early and mid-1960s, which were echoed
by the left-liberal media. As an institution, the Protestant Church's pioneering contribution to the emerging Ostpolitik debate consisted of its
"Vertriebenendenkschrift" of 1965, which attracted more attention and
roused more passions than any previous EKD statement.[13] More than
250,000 copies were printed, and the essay was discussed in the press and
in public discussions. This "Essay on the Refugees from the East" (about
Germans driven out of Eastern Europe after World War II) called for a
new foreign policy. It argued that accepting the reality of German division
and postwar territorial borders for the foreseeable future would speed reconciliation with Eastern Europe and in turn contribute to international
stability and to a future "peace order" *(Friedensordnung)*. Discussion of
German policy toward Eastern Europe revolved around the same underlying themes that had dominated previous debates—in particular, German
guilt from World War II and acceptance of its political and moral consequences. In the context of Ostpolitik, accepting the consequences of the
Third Reich meant reconciliation and détente rather than confrontation,
and peaceful (even antimilitaristic) approaches to Eastern Europe rather
than revanchism.

The essay acknowledged that the territorial losses and forced popula-

---

11. Haftendorn, *Sicherheit und Entspannung*; and Hanrieder, *Germany, America, Europe,* chap. 6.

12. Hanrieder, *Germany, America, Europe,* 182.

13. The *Denkschrift* bore the official title of *Die Lage der Vertriebenen und das Verhält-nis des deutschen Volkes zu seinen östlichen Nachbarn.* See *Kirchliches Jahrbuch* 92:48–61.

tion transfers suffered by Germany after World War II had violated international law, but it pitted political arguments against the legal issues to which conservatives both inside and outside the government held so tightly. The Poles, it noted, had suffered grave injustice during the Nazi regime, so Germans had a special duty to respect the Polish right to existence *(Lebensrecht)*. It was impossible to reclaim lost territories twenty years after the fact, as Poland had incorporated them into its economic system. One could not satisfy the German "right to homeland" by expelling Poles now. Thus just resting on legal positions was fruitless, while blindly pursuing German interests and rights threatened peace. One had to look for a political settlement, which would make possible a peaceful future. A new, international peace order required truth and justice, mutual consideration of interests, and the will to reconciliation. Willingness to accept the consequences of guilt and to compensate for injustice had to be embedded in German policy toward its eastern neighbors.

One classic Social Democratic appeal for a new Ostpolitik was Egon Bahr's address to the Protestant Academy in Tutzing in 1963.[14] His catchphrase "change through rapprochement" *(Wandel durch Annäherung)* described the SPD's new approach to reunification, namely, making the German-German border more permeable by improving relations with the East German government. For Bahr, the presuppositions for reunification lay in a good relationship with the Soviet Union. Overcoming the status quo paradoxically required good East-West relations, which for the time being meant accepting the status quo. West Germany had to give up its previous all-or-nothing policy and depend on a process of small steps and many stages to bring about reunification. East Germany could not be removed from the Soviet sphere of influence, which meant dealing with the despised SED regime. Trade, moreover, could help improve East German living standards.

Starting in 1966, the Grand Coalition fared somewhat better in its Eastern policy. Willy Brandt became foreign minister, and the SPD had long pressed for a more open and innovative policy toward East Germany. Chancellor Kiesinger's recognition that East-West détente and arms control measures were the best path to reunification (rather than conditional on it) represented a major policy departure. Reunification became the eventual, rather than immediate, goal of Ostpolitik, with emphasis on improving living conditions for the East German populace in the meantime. The Grand Coalition relaxed (without abolishing) the Hallstein Doctrine to permit full diplomatic relations with the Eastern European states, declared the Munich Agreement of 1938 (in which Czechoslovakia ceded

---

14. "Wandel durch Annäherung: Rede zur Deutschlandpolitik in Tutzing am 15. Juli 1963," in Butterwegge and Hofschen, *Sozialdemokratie, Krieg und Frieden,* 325–27.

territory to Germany) to be no longer valid, and even implied that Bonn would accept the Oder-Neisse line as the Polish border with a future united Germany. These new approaches lay partial groundwork for the treaties of the 1970s, although during the 1960s they remained somewhat hesitant steps.[15] Griffith pronounces the Grand Coalition's Ostpolitik "not very successful," largely because Brandt pushed for more concessions to Eastern Europe than the CDU was willing to grant. As Griffith notes, "the result was that the Grand Coalition postponed the crucial issues, in particular recognition of the status quo, in favor of concentrating on improving the atmosphere and progress on peripheral problems."[16]

If the West Germans faced challenges to their reunification policy from changes in superpower relations, they had an equally portentous task of adaptation in the realm of strategic doctrine and defense. With the new "flexible response" doctrine, the Kennedy administration hoped to reverse the tendency toward reliance on strategic and tactical nuclear weapons. In order to avoid a choice between two equally unpalatable options (doing nothing or else making a nuclear strike and facing a possible Soviet counterstrike), Kennedy wanted the West prepared for a more flexible and "graduated" scale of responses, in order to be able to give, according to Hanrieder and Auton, "a credible retaliatory response to every possible level of provocation."[17] From the German perspective, this doctrine countenanced the possibility of a limited conventional war in Europe, which for Germany essentially meant total war. The envisaged conventional buildup, moreover, meant increased defense spending and might still not ensure adequate defense, while at the same time it made the threat of a nuclear strike less plausible.[18] Although the West Germans eventually went along with the changes, disagreements over them provided fertile ground for transatlantic tensions.

Another contentious issue was sharing nuclear control, or at least nuclear planning, within NATO. Proposals for a Multilateral Nuclear Force (MLF) were the outcome of this debate but were in the end scuttled by the United States. As noted by Hanrieder, the MLF "envisaged the creation under a multilateral NATO authority of a seaborne nuclear force."[19]

---

15. Hanrieder, *Germany, America, Europe*, 171–94; William Griffith, *The Ostpolitik of the Federal Republic of Germany* (Cambridge: MIT Press, 1978), chap. 4.

16. Griffith, *The Ostpolitik of the Federal Republic of Germany*, 137.

17. Hanrieder and Auton, *The Foreign Policies of West Germany, France, and Britain*, 11.

18. See Hanrieder, *Germany, America, Europe*, chap. 2, on how flexible response expressed the divergence between U.S. and German security interests.

19. Hanrieder, *Germany, America, Europe*, 45. The MLF concept tried to satisfy many

The German interest in the MLF stemmed from the symbolic reaffirmations that joint ownership of nuclear forces implied. The MLF would have reconfirmed the German position in the NATO alliance despite the shift from the cold war tensions of the 1950s to the more peaceful coexistence of the 1960s. The CDU also wanted bargaining leverage on reunification issues vis-à-vis the Soviets, and they were hoping to trade renunciation of nuclear ambitions for Soviet cooperation on reunification.[20] German interest in nuclear sharing raised suspicions at home and abroad about German intentions, reinforced by Germany's initial reluctance to sign the Nuclear Non-Proliferation Treaty. In particular, the Erhard government hoped to use opposition to the treaty as further leverage with the Soviets on the reunification issue. Later, the Grand Coalition expressed concerns that signing the treaty would hinder German participation in joint nuclear planning.[21]

As with Ostpolitik, the SPD pioneered the promotion of arms control in German politics as well, displaying much more enthusiasm than the CDU. Genuine as the SPD's new commitment to NATO was, the party leadership nonetheless immediately placed it in the context of détente and arms control. After 1959, arms control assumed its own security value in SPD thinking, shedding its association with disengagement and reunification.[22] Indeed, the SPD gave up directly linking security with reunification. Protecting peace and freedom took priority over reunification after 1959, and the SPD shifted its focus to war prevention through arms stabilization within the bipolar international constellation.[23] In effect, the SPD made a direct transition from its opposition role of the 1950s to the position later embodied in NATO's Harmel Report of 1967, namely, that security policy consisted equally of military defense (through

---

competing demands. According to Hanrieder, the MLF did little to reassure Europeans of American willingness to defend them, since the United States would have retained a veto over use and since both European and American experts questioned the military adequacy of surface deployment at sea. The French, for their part, worried that the United States would gain more influence in NATO through British participation in the MLF, and they preferred a French-dominated European defense arrangement that would tie Germany to France rather than to the United States. The United States hoped that the MLF would stem the tide of nuclear proliferation, without having to relinquish its own monopoly on control of the "buttons." (Hanrieder, *Germany, America, Europe*, chap. 1; see also Cioc, *Pax Atomica*, 148.)

20. Hanrieder, *Germany, America, Europe*, 47.

21. Hanrieder and Auton, *The Foreign Policies of West Germany, France, and Britain*, 16.

22. Wilker, *Die Sicherheitspolitik der SPD 1956–1966*, 57–60.

23. Hütter, *SPD und nationale Sicherheit*, 78, 79.

NATO) and détente. As defense expert Fritz Erler argued at the 1960 party convention, the relatively secure situation since 1945 had been based on balanced deterrence between the superpowers, but this balance was not stable in the long run. Arms control would help reduce tensions and would improve the climate for further disarmament. National defense and arms control belonged together, and Germany would contribute to both.[24]

By professing allegiance to NATO, the SPD leadership had abandoned the direct linkage of security and reunification that had typified their proposals for Central European military disengagement in the 1950s. At the same time, party leaders began to argue that détente and arms control would reduce political tensions, which could pave the way for movement on the German question.[25] Brandt in particular suggested that reunification could eventually be embedded in a broader détente process. For example, Brandt entitled his speech at the 1962 party convention "Dynamic Policy as [a] Common German Task." The German question, he noted, no longer occupied center stage in world politics, and the West would not take risks for German reunification. The only way to effect movement on the German question was to make the superpowers see that German division stood in the way of peace. Reduction of East-West tensions had become the most important precondition for realizing German self-determination, which provided a further incentive to support all efforts toward arms control and détente.[26]

The third change in West Germany's foreign policy environment during the 1960s was shifts in popular images of the two superpowers. Although these shifts became much more pronounced in the 1970s, they already started to break down the popular consensus on foreign policy that Adenauer had enjoyed in the 1950s (except, of course, in the peace movement). On the one hand, the Soviet doctrinal shift from world revolution to peaceful coexistence toned down the East-West ideological confrontation, cracking, if not shattering, the anticommunism fundamental to West German popular attitudes in the 1950s.[27] On the other hand, the American civil rights movement, the Vietnam War, and the Second Vatican Council challenged popular images of the United States and led to questions concerning NATO's very nature and purpose.

The civil rights movement raised questions about American domestic

---

24. Vorstand der SPD, *Protokoll der Verhandlungen* 1960:117–24.

25. Haftendorn, *Sicherheit und Entspannung,* 193–95; Wilker, *Die Sicherheitspolitik der SPD 1956–1966,* 199–205.

26. Vorstand der SPD, *Protokoll der Verhandlungen und Anträge vom Parteitag der Sozialdemokratischen Partei Deutschlands in Köln vom 26. bis 30. Mai 1962* (Bonn: Neuer Vorwärts-Verlag, 1962), 80, 81.

27. Haftendorn, *Sicherheit und Entspannung.*

politics in what had been considered the paragon of democracy. Criticism of America's conduct in the Vietnam War heated up as President Johnson escalated both the number of American troops fighting in Vietnam and the bombing of North Vietnam. Much of European youth endorsed the formula "Vietnam is the Spain of our generation," while others went further in condemning any society that made such barbarism possible, be it European or American. Although it quickly retreated from this position, even the normally anticommunist *Bild Zeitung* once criticized the war in terms that reflected the opinions of an increasingly large spectrum of the West German populace: "We should tell Washington quite clearly that the Germans don't want to go to Vietnam. . . . As everywhere in the world, in Vietnam also the right to self-determination applies, even if free elections there should not turn out favorable to the Americans. . . . We cannot trample underfoot in other parts of the world the right that we demand for the Germans in the East and must therefore stand aside from this 'dirty war.' "[28] Allensbach pollsters found American prestige stained among large sectors of the German population. In November 1968, a full 36 percent of respondents said that their esteem for the United States had decreased during the last year or so, of which 22 percent cited Vietnam as the principal reason.[29] Finally, developments in the Catholic Church damaged America's image, due to its position as the world's major capitalist power of the times. Statements from Popes John XXIII and Paul VI, together with Vatican II, placed more emphasis on social justice and less on human rights under communism than had their predecessors, calling into question liberal capitalism both domestically and internationally.[30]

All in all, the 1960s provided increased opportunities for protest in general and saw a significant enlargement of the protest potential in the populace at large. Compared to Adenauer's "reign" in the 1950s, the governments of the 1960s suffered from significantly lower popularity. On the whole, they were unable to offer an interlocking policy package suited to its times and comparable to the one that had served as the foundation of Adenauer's success. The Grand Coalition and the Emergency Laws, along with the SPD's shift toward the political center, stirred sizable disenchantment with domestic democracy. At the same time, the recession and government attempts to counteract it opened space for protest by exposing weakness in a central pillar of the postwar order.

In foreign relations, furthermore, changes in the international arena opened space for the issues the peace movement promoted, lending it

---

28. Quoted in Alfred Grosser, *The Western Alliance: European-American Relations since 1945* (New York: Continuum, 1980), 238.

29. Cited in Grosser, *The Western Alliance,* 246.

30. Grosser, *The Western Alliance,* 245.

greater credibility than it had enjoyed during the cold war's height in the 1950s. Budding superpower détente, nuclear parity, and East-West arms control initiatives suggested new possibilities for reducing tensions in Europe, while the Berlin Wall and the Soviets' strengthened hold over Eastern Europe demonstrated that reunification was nowhere in sight. Since Adenauer and his conservative successors resisted corresponding changes in West German foreign policy, a new policy toward Eastern Europe (Ostpolitik) became the burning foreign policy issue of the decade. In addition, the Vietnam War set off passionate moral debates about German support for American "imperialism."

Thus across the board, West German governments of the 1960s saw their popularity decline from the heights Adenauer had enjoyed in the 1950s. The CDU/CSU lost the absolute majority it enjoyed in the Bundestag from 1957 to 1961, while the SPD's share of the vote rose gradually but steadily.[31] Finally, an increasingly restive populace gradually developed a political culture more open to extraparliamentary mobilization.

Although political space expanded for protest in general, conditions limited opportunity for peace protest specifically. Despite their growth, the yearly Easter Marches never reached the size of the antinuclear demonstrations of 1958. In particular, the 1960s peace movement suffered from the limited salience of peace issues over which it enjoyed a general monopoly. In the 1950s and the 1980s, peace movements opposed weapons policies of monumental importance and sustained salience. In contrast, the 1960s peace protest opposed nuclear weapons in principle but dealt with only one specific deployment proposal, of brief salience and modest significance, the Multilateral Nuclear Force.

The peace movement of the 1960s favored détente and a more conciliatory Ostpolitik, but, as the next section of this chapter will show, it had to share that demand with the SPD and the Protestant Church, although neither institution allied itself with the peace movement. Likewise, when the peace movement joined student protest against the Emergency Laws and the Vietnam War, it became submerged in this larger wave of protest, and the issue of peace became overshadowed by competing concerns. This indeterminate political opportunity structure limited peace mobilization per se without making it impossible, while at the same time it opened space for mobilization on other issues with which the issue of peace became intertwined.

---

31. Chandler, "Party System Transformations in the Federal Republic of Germany."

The Easter March Movement and the Extraparliamentary Opposition: Ideological Resources and Movement Composition

Protest in the 1960s took on a new tone as West Germany's protest potential changed shape and composition. As in the 1950s, the peace movement gathered together opposition to government policy. After the SPD's Godesberg Program and the DGB's Düsseldorf Program moderated the ideology and strategy of the official labor movement, however, the peace movement became a truly extraparliamentary force. It opposed not only the government but also all parties represented in parliament, including the SPD, although it shared some of the SPD's demands. As the labor movement became increasingly integrated into the West German economy and polity, moreover, the mantle of socialist opposition passed increasingly from the working class to the more radical elements in the new middle class. Whereas workers had contributed the numerical bulk of the 1950s movements, protest from the 1960s on increasingly mobilized the middle class. This new, critical intelligentsia was most concentrated among the youth at universities and high schools *(Gymnasia)* and among tertiary-sector and public-sector employees *(Angestellte* and *Beamte)*. Together with the "old left" remnants of the traditional labor movement and Protestants already active in the 1950s, it led the 1960s movements that changed the face of German politics.

Peace protest in the 1960s differed from the movements of both the 1950s and the 1980s. The latter two focused largely on concrete government weapons decisions (rearmament, NATO membership, and nuclear weapons in the 1950s; and the double-track decision in the 1980s), although they each united a wide range of opposition forces. In contrast, while the 1960s peace protest of course opposed nuclear weapons in principle, it had only one specific deployment decision to work with, the Multilateral Nuclear Force, whose salience was brief and only temporarily a high point of the campaign. The 1960s movement, however, fought proactively for policies like German Ostpolitik, disarmament, test-ban treaties, and nuclear nonproliferation—policies that later became government policy. At its high point late in the decade, the 1960s movement submerged foreign policy themes into a much broader critique of "the system" as a whole, in which questions of domestic democracy and Western imperialism overshadowed more specifically German foreign policy issues. These differences gave the 1960s movement a different dynamic from those of the 1950s and 1980s. Instead of starting with a splash and then petering out when the initial issue faded, the 1960s movement started small but grew continuously as it increasingly united the oppositional forces of the decade.

The 1960s movement began with the small, pacifist, antinuclear Easter March movement and ended with the tumultuous, broad-based Extraparliamentary Opposition movement (called the APO, short for *Ausserparlamentarische Opposition*), including the student movement of 1967/68. Although they partially overlapped chronologically, three phases of this process can be distinguished. In its earliest phase, the Easter March movement gathered together small numbers of protesters ethically motivated against nuclear weapons in general. The second phase began as the movement grew by incorporating a more diverse set of groups, which transformed the movement's unspecific opposition to nuclear weapons into much more concrete demands for foreign and security policies that reflected the issues of the period. As a sign of this change, the movement renamed itself Campaign for Disarmament. A further name change to Campaign for Democracy and Disarmament signified the third and final phase, in which the movement absorbed still further political currents by linking foreign policy issues to their domestic roots in the political and economic system. This broadening of themes reflected the student movement's and APO's critique of "the system," with its domestic political, economic, and foreign policy components.

As this multinamed "peace movement" went through these transformations, it increased steadily in both size (numbers of demonstrators, etc.) and variety of activists. Beginning with a few Christians and pacifists, it soon encompassed many more Protestant pastors and laypeople, Social Democrats and unionists at odds with their institutions' official policies, communists, and student groups. The movement's growth in size and diversity became inextricably intermingled with the growth of its ideological resources as well, as each group saw the overlap between its concerns and the peace issue.

Phases One and Two: From Ethical Pacifism to Concrete Foreign Policy Demands

The Easter March movement began in 1960 as a feeble continuation of the 1950s protest against nuclear weapons and recruited from antinuclear activists who did not hail from the traditional labor movement.[32] The movement originated with religiously motivated pacifists, led by

---

32. Two other strands of opposition left over from the 1950s survived into the 1960s, but they remained entirely marginal. One was the Munich-based Kommittee gegen

Hans-Konrad Tempel, a Hamburg teacher, SPD member, and Quaker. Other founding members came from conscientious objectors' organizations like the Verband der Kriegsdienstgegner and the Internationale der Kriegsdienstgegner, traditional pacifist groups like the Deutsche Friedens-Gesellschaft, and traditional socialist groups like the Naturfreundejugend. Along with members of these groups, the Central Committee (Zentraler Ausschuß) in 1960 had a considerable number of protestant pastors relative to its size.[33]

The first Easter March, modeled after the Campaign for Nuclear Disarmament (CND) marches in England, included people of various political opinions, social backgrounds, and ages, all united in their opposition to "the bomb" rather than to any specific policy or party. Its ideology was thus ethical-pacifist, rather than political. In its earliest stage, the Easter March movement was far from the critical and emancipatory claims of the later Extraparliamentary Opposition movement (APO) and was not even as political as the Kampf dem Atomtod of the 1950s.[34] In 1960 the movement remained explicitly nonpartisan and actively eschewed political demands, appealing instead to conscience and general humanitarianism. The turnout (one thousand participants) was small, reflecting not only organizational weakness and lack of publicity but also the absence of any tradition of protest not embedded in institutions. As of Easter 1960, the SPD's image as the parliamentary arm of the antinuclear campaign still lingered. (Herbert Wehner's Bundestag speech indicating SPD acceptance of NATO and nuclear weapons did not take place until June 1960.)

This initial phase proved of short duration. In order to grow, the movement had to expand ideologically and incorporate further social groups. By the 1961 march, the movement entered a second phase, which

---

Atomrüstung, which, although active until 1963, was of no political importance and dissolved in 1966. The other strand contained a number of communist-oriented groups supported by the illegal KPD, the most important of which was called the Aktionsgemeinschaft gegen atomare Aufrüstung. This group was dissolved in 1962, by which point its most prominent members had joined the Deutsche Friedensunion (DFU), which later joined the communist wing of the 1980s peace movement.

33. Otto, *Vom Ostermarsch zur APO.* Otto's book is the standard—and only comprehensive—empirical treatment of the subject. Guido Grünewald, "Zur Geschichte des Ostermarsches der Atomwaffengegner," *Blätter für deutsche und internationale Politik* 27, no. 3 (1982): 303–23, provides a good, much shorter overview.

34. Otto, *Vom Ostermarsch zur APO,* 70–74.

lasted through the mid-1960s. On the ideological level, the movement saw that its nonpolitical, ethical-pacifist approach was not sufficient. Over the next few years, it expanded the spectrum of its arguments, making policy demands with concrete reference to the political debates of the period. At the same time, it attracted mainstream Protestants (beyond its founding Quakers), along with independent socialists, dissident Social Democrats, and unionists.

In part, the movement rejuvenated themes of the 1950s, demanding a nuclear-free zone in Central Europe. More significantly, however, the movement began to push proactively for the German government to join international trends toward détente and arms control, trends that the government had so far resisted. In its support for the Test-Ban Treaty and nuclear nonproliferation, and in its opposition to the MLF, the movement drew on international trends in arms control and pressed the government to forswear access to nuclear weapons. In doing so, it took aim at the government's refusal to accept the European territorial and political results of World War II. The movement saw the government's eagerness to join the proposed NATO Multilateral Nuclear Force (thereby gaining access to nuclear weapons) as a strategy for revising the postwar status quo. Thus the 1964 Easter March concentrated on opposing the MLF and supporting a nuclear-free zone in Central Europe. During the 1965 election campaign, the movement called for détente and disarmament as the only possible ways to safeguard peace.[35]

The peace movement also played an avant-garde role in advocating a new policy toward Eastern Europe (Ostpolitik), the most controversial foreign policy issue of the day. To be sure, the governing CDU took steps toward relaxing Adenauer's rigid policies toward Eastern Europe, although its steps were small compared with the treaties later concluded with the East. Because of resistance from within the CDU/CSU and the rising threat of right-wing extremism, moreover, the government's policy departures seemed hesitant and halfhearted to those impatient for bolder and quicker steps. Thus during the mid-1960s, the peace movement gathered together the political forces intent on extraparliamentary pressure for arms control and disarmament and for change in Germany's Ostpolitik.

Protestant groups interested in a new Ostpolitik pushed for policy change both inside the church and through the peace movement. In addition to the hundreds of Protestant pastors who signed the movement's various *Aufrufe* (calls to action) before each march, the Protestant Kirchliche Bruderschaften belonged to the Easter March movement's Central Com-

---

35. Ibid., chaps. 5–7.

mittee.[36] Heirs to the Confessing Church of the Third Reich, the Bruder-schaften pushed for a bold new Ostpolitik as early as 1961, several years before the EKD officially advocated it as an institution. Drawing on the Stuttgart Declaration of Guilt and the Berlin-Weißensee synod meeting of the early postwar years, the Bruderschaften reiterated the linkage of spiri-tual redemption and progressive politics begun in the 1950s. Tying Chris-tian repentance to an acceptance of the political facts of postwar Ger-many, they decried the West German revanchist tendency to apply the "right to homeland" to the lost German territories, given that Germany had lost them through its own fault. They urged politicians to accept Ger-man borders, normalize relations with Eastern Europe, and accept the German Democratic Republic as a state.[37]

The peace movement joined in the call for arms control and a new Ostpolitik, thus apparently offering support from the extraparliamentary arena for the SPD's push for policy change in the Bundestag and in the Grand Coalition government. However, the movement stood for a much more radical application of these notions and vehemently opposed many of the SPD's concrete policies—for example, its acceptance of nuclear weapons on German soil and its support for the MLF proposal and the American war effort in Vietnam. The movement therefore grew rapidly as it attracted dissidents from the SPD and the unions, who rejected the SPD's post-Godesberg course, its "common foreign policy" with the CDU, and its participation in government with the CDU. For these dissi-dents the movement served as an outlet for their sentiments and a vehicle through which to pressure the SPD leadership on nuclear issues.

Indeed, although the SPD had officially committed itself to NATO and nuclear deterrence, a look at party convention debates shows ample antinuclear sentiment remaining in the SPD's rank and file. The rank and file expressed this sentiment through participation in the peace movement, in protest against the SPD's new course. Dissident Social Democrats reluc-tantly acquiesced to the SPD's commitment to national defense and NATO membership and concentrated their efforts on keeping the Bun-deswehr nonnuclear. Indeed, the SPD's leadership had anticipated rank-and-file resistance to the Godesberg Program, couching its new policy in Social Democratic rhetoric from the 1950s.[38] The program stressed that national defense had to be "appropriate" to Germany's geopolitical posi-

---

36. Ibid., 209.

37. Letter from the Arbeitskreis kirchlicher Bruderschaften to the synod of the EKD, *Kirchliches Jahrbuch* 88:32–33; "Besinnung und Gebet für den Frieden," letter to pastors from the Leitungsausschuss der kirchlichen Bruderschaften, *Kirchliches Jahrbuch* 88:81–83; "Tübinger Memorandum," *Kirchliches Jahrbuch* 89:75–78.

38. Wette, "Sozialdemokratische Sicherheitspolitik in historischer Perspektive," 37.

tion and consistent with German reunification. It called for including all of Germany in a zone of détente devoid of foreign troops, general disarmament, and the creation of an international order that would eventually replace national defense forces. Finally, it maintained that West Germany must neither produce nor deploy nuclear weapons.[39]

This understatement of the SPD's new commitment to national defense showed good tactical judgement on the leadership's part. The delegates at the party convention at Bad Godesberg showed their lingering commitment to many of the causes of the 1950s. Some even opposed the change in direction altogether. Above all, the party convention reasserted the SPD's traditional opposition to nuclear weapons for Germany. Whereas the initial draft of the Godesberg Program stated that nuclear weapons *should* not be produced or employed by Germany,[40] under delegate pressure the final draft was revised to read that nuclear weapons *may* not be produced or employed. Pressure against nuclear arms for the Bundeswehr continued at subsequent party conferences. Discussion at the 1960 convention revolved around whether the party's official security resolution clearly enough excluded nuclear weapons for the Bundeswehr.[41]

Over the years, the SPD's rank and file overwhelmingly supported arms control. What arms control meant in practice was, however, a matter of considerable debate, with party congress delegates often pushing for a more disarmament-oriented interpretation than the leadership. When NATO's Multilateral Nuclear Force (MLF) scheme came onto the West German political agenda, the SPD debated it in terms of nuclear nonproliferation. The party was united in support of nonproliferation in principle[42] but disagreed over whether German participation in the MLF furthered it in practice. The leadership supported the MLF on the grounds that it facilitated nonproliferation and represented both a "division of labor" and cooperation within NATO.[43] Most delegates, however, opposed the MLF because it would contradict the principles of arms control and nuclear nonproliferation.[44] Precisely such disagreement led to Social Democratic participation in the peace movement, which vehemently opposed the MLF.

---

39. Vorstand der SPD, *Protokoll der Verhandlungen* 1959:6, 17.
40. Vorstand der SPD, *Protokoll der Verhandlungen* 1958:528.
41. Vorstand der SPD, *Protokoll der Verhandlungen* 1960:128–82.
42. See, for example, Fritz Erler's speech "Vom vierten zum fünften Bundestag," in Vorstand der SPD, *Parteitag der Sozialdemokratischen Partei Deutschlands vom 23. bis 27. November 1964 in Karlsruhe: Protokoll der Verhandlungen und Anträge* (Bonn: Neuer Vorwärts-Verlag, 1964), 71–95, especially 88–90.
43. See the resolution of the SPD's executive committee *(Vorstand)* and Erler's speech, both in Vorstand der SPD, *Parteitag der SPD* 1964:954–56 and 213–17, respectively.
44. Vorstand der SPD, *Parteitag der SPD* 1964:221–29, 950–53.

Although it was to grow still further in a few more years, by the mid-1960s the peace movement had succeeded in uniting all extraparliamentary forces around a common set of foreign policy themes. Protestants, pacifists, middle-class professionals, students, and dissident Social Democrats and unionists had come together around a platform of nonnuclear defense and a new West German foreign policy toward the East. This expansion of themes propelled and reflected the movement's growth, both in turnout for its marches and rallies, and in the size and diversity of its activist core. In the process, the movement became the first instance of extraparliamentary opposition with a relatively broad base.

Phenomenal movement growth occurred from 1961 to 1967. The first Easter March in 1960 attracted only 1,000 participants. By 1962 the movement had begun to attract more attention and had started to address current foreign policy concerns. Nine thousand marched in 1961, and 23,000 attended the final rally.[45] In 1962 marchers numbered 15,000, with 50,000 at the final rally. In 1963 the numbers at the final rally stabilized at 50,000, but the number of marchers climbed to 23,000. Opposition to the MLF in 1964 brought an explosion of participation, with 100,000 participating in marches and rallies, and 8,000 signatures on the movement's *Aufruf*. By 1967 the movement had added the Vietnam War to its foreign policy concerns and had combined those concerns with highly controversial issues concerning domestic democracy. Participation in the movement grew yet again by half, with 150,000 people attending some eight hundred events. Moreover, the number of signatories to the *Aufrufe* for the yearly activities increased fivefold, from 3,000 in 1963 to 15,000 in 1967.[46]

Such growth reflected penetration of a broader social and political spectrum. A breakdown of the signatures of the 1963 and 1964 *Aufrufe* (calls for participation in the Easter March events) revealed the movement's penetration into unions, churches, and middle-class professional groups. In 1963, 600 of the 3,000 *Aufruf* signatures belonged to Protestant ministers. Of the 8,000 signatures in 1964, 452 came from union functionaries and members of factory councils *(Betriebsräte);* 183 from university professors; 529 from teachers; 280 from lawyers, judges, and artists; and 1,100 from clergy.[47] *Aufruf* signatories and members of the movement's executive councils were often prominent in their respective

---

45. The difference between participation in demonstrations/marches and participation in final rallies lies in the difference between the two forms of action. The marches took place on one or more days, and participants covered significant distances on foot. Thus marches were much more strenuous for participants than the final rallies, which took place in one central location and involved no walking.

46. Otto, *Vom Ostermarsch zur APO,* 100–147.

47. Ibid., 119.

professions, adding luster and appeal.[48] The social composition of the 1967 *Aufruf* signatories also revealed the strong participation of clergy and theologians, teachers, professors and scientists, union functionaries, representatives of youth and student organizations, and artists and literary figures, all in roughly equal proportions.[49] Movement conferences featured speeches by Social Democrats, FDP members, and unionists, showing support from dissidents within the SPD and DGB that opposed these institutions' official policy in the post-Godesberg era. Further support came from growing coverage by religious or socialist journals, for example, *Das Argument* and *Junge Kirche*.[50] While many of these organs boasted only small circulations, collectively they provided an important network of information and informal contacts, and their readership was a source of potential mobilization.

Phase Three: Toward a Comprehensive Critique of "the System"

In the mid-1960s, a series of controversies that polarized West German politics also gave the extraparliamentary opposition a new dimension. The student movement and dissident unionists catalyzed this shift in emphasis when they joined forces with the peace movement, forming the large and comprehensive Extraparliamentary Opposition movement (APO) of the late 1960s. This combining of forces doubled the ranks of the 1968 Easter March (to 300,000 from 150,000 in 1967).[51] Up to 1965 the peace movement had concentrated primarily on concerns relating to foreign policy and disarmament. Thereafter the focus shifted, on the domestic front, to the proposed Emergency Laws, the dominance of conservative tabloids in the print media, and university reform, while on the international front the focus shifted to imperialism and the Vietnam War. Under the influence of the broader APO, the peace movement's theoretical sophistication grew, as it now coupled its demand for détente with a critique of the "undemocratic" social and political structures that seemed to explain the government's "unpeaceful" policies. At the same time, the peace movement's earlier emphasis on disarmament and German foreign policy issues became

---

48. Helmut Gollwitzer, Heinz Kloppenburg, Heinrich Vogel, and Martin Niemöller were all prominent in the Protestant Church; Stefan Andres, Heinz Hilpert, Erich Kästner, and Gunter Anders were prominent cultural and literary figures.

49. Otto argues that although youth dominated public impressions of the marches and demonstrations, these figures show that the movement was never primarily a "youth" movement (*Vom Ostermarsch zur APO*, 148).

50. For additional examples, see Otto, *Vom Ostermarsch zur APO*, 119.

51. Grünewald, "Zur Geschichte des Ostermarsches," 314.

increasingly submerged in the APO's new focus on Vietnam and domestic democracy.

The APO as a whole developed a broad theoretical critique of "the system," based on its perceptions of structural contradictions in the political and economic systems. In foreign policy, the APO saw a contradiction between the government's proclaimed defense of freedom, on the one hand, and the repressive, "imperialist" consequences of anticommunism in the Third World, on the other.[52] The West German state under Adenauer had drawn considerable legitimacy from anticommunism—internationally as a member of the western "free world" and domestically through the contrast of its democratic order with the East German regime. With détente, consolidation of Eastern European socialism, and decolonization, however, anticommunism softened. Especially to a postwar generation unconcerned with a possible "domino effect," the American war effort in Vietnam (and German support for it) represented "imperialist" suppression of anticolonial liberation movements. In addition, visits to Germany by the Shah of Iran and Moise Tschombe of the Congo catalyzed student protest against West German support for other Western-oriented, but repressive, Third World governments.

Equally serious in the APO's eyes was the contradiction between the ideal of democracy and the fact of the Grand Coalition, raising the domestic-regime aspect of the German question—whether Germany could ever overcome its authoritarian past in domestic politics. First, the joint CDU/CSU–SPD government meant the absence of a true socialist alternative or indeed of any meaningful parliamentary opposition, and it suggested a system apparently blocked to reform of society or foreign policy.[53]

Second, the Grand Coalition raised fears of a rightward drift even farther than in the 1950s, past the boundaries of democracy and into the territory of authoritarianism. Stimulated by the neo-Nazi National-demokratische Partei Deutschland (NPD) winning seats in some *Land* parliaments and threatening entry into the Bundestag, Chancellor Kiesinger's Nazi background, and Finance Minister Franz Joseph Strauss's animosity toward the oppositional press—evident in the Spiegel Affair of 1962—the extraparliamentary opposition revived interest in "fascism." Indeed, as noted by Markovits and Gorski, the APO developed a massive critique of "the complacency and accommodation of the Bonn republic's institutions and political culture vis-à-vis the Nazi regime,"

---

52. Otto, *Vom Ostermarsch zur APO,* 146.
53. Ibid.

accusing West German society and politics of "continuing the Nazi regime's very essence without its worst excesses."[54]

Third, a crucial manifestation of this danger in the APO's eyes were the proposed Emergency Laws. The APO regarded them as a potentially authoritarian usurpation of power, which would enable the Grand Coalition and subsequent governments to undermine fundamental democratic freedoms. This concern was reinforced by the official reaction to the demonstrations of the late 1960s, in which harsh police measures against demonstrators enjoyed the support of local governments and seemed to represent a general suppression of political opposition. Etched into all politically active students' minds were the events of June 2, 1967. During a demonstration against the Iranian shah's visit to West Berlin, a policeman shot and killed a student named Benno Ohnesorg. Although contradicted by eyewitness accounts, the policeman pled self-defense and was subsequently acquitted in court. In the APO's eyes, the events of June 2 showed that the government was willing to use even physical violence against oppositional forces; and the APO considered those events a foretaste of the Emergency Laws in action.[55]

Finally, the APO took on a further pillar of the "growing fascism" in West Germany, the tabloid press empire owned by Axel Springer. Springer's domination of the print media made possible manipulation of public opinion in favor of "the establishment." The Springer press was openly hostile toward striking workers, détente, and East Germany; explicitly supported the Grand Coalition; and gave blanket approval to the forces of "law and order," including the Ohnesorg shooting. The student movement's hostility toward the Springer press grew even greater when its tabloids agitated their readers against the students. When a young man shot Rudi Dutschke, the students' most prominent leader, the APO held the Springer press responsible and organized a fiery but relatively unsuccessful blockade of all Springer tabloid deliveries.

As the events involving the APO indicate, the late 1960s saw an intensification of protest, as a broader set of actors organized much more frequent protest events around a wider range of themes. Whereas in the early and mid-1960s the peace movement gathered various oppositional tendencies into its occasional events, in the late 1960s the student movement, the unions, and the peace movement emerged as distinct and identifiable pillars of the APO. Each came to the APO's sometimes joint and sometimes parallel protest actions from its own perspective.

The student movement arose when the first postwar generation of

54. Markovits and Gorski, *The German Left*, 21.

55. Gerhard Bauss, *Die Studentenbewegung der sechziger Jahre in der Bundesrepublik und Westberlin* (Cologne: Pahl-Rugenstein, 1977), 144.

educated youth underwent a significant left-wing radicalization. Novel in German politics at that time was the breadth of the student movement's concerns. In the 1950s and early 1960s, the labor movement had protested against a number of developments that concerned labor interests, and the issue of peace drew a broad range of groups together in "single-issue" protest (albeit stemming from a variety of motivations) against government defense policy. The student movement, in contrast, was decidedly more versatile in the issues it pursued. In addition to university reforms directly affecting students' interests, the student movement took part in protest against the whole range of issues important in the 1960s, from the Emergency Laws, the Springer press, and neo-Nazism (in domestic politics), to "imperialism" in Vietnam and other Third World countries (in the international arena).

In addition to widening the range of protest issues, the student movement spearheaded a revival of left-wing theory. Within the loose network of numerous student groups, the Sozialistischer Deutscher Studentenbund (SDS) was the prime organizational and theoretical mover. Formerly the Social Democratic recruiting channel at the universities and part of the SPD's left wing, the SDS was expelled from the party in 1960 for its opposition to the Godesberg Program. Following its expulsion, the SDS revived and extended Marxist theory and restyled itself as the theoretical avant-garde for a socialist intelligentsia. It distanced itself from both the SPD and orthodox communists, aiming to draw not from the traditional labor movement but from middle-class academic circles.[56]

Reflecting the theoretical diversity of the student movement, two wings coexisted uneasily within the SDS. The traditionalists still considered the working class the revolutionary subject, even in advanced capitalist countries with highly integrated labor movements, and regardless of actual levels of class consciousness or class conflict. For them, alliances with the unions remained a chief goal, and the Bundestag could still provide the arena for advancing socialist goals, assuming strong alliances between parliamentary and extraparliamentary forces.

The theoretical innovators of the student movement and the SDS, however, were the antiauthoritarians, with their theoretical foundations in the critical theory of the Frankfurt School. According to Bauss, they were subjectively anticapitalist and socialist but were objectively radical democratic and decidedly anticommunist and anti-Soviet. Indeed, their emphasis on Third World liberation struggles like Vietnam and Cuba allowed identification with revolution, without easing their reservations toward socialism as it actually existed in Eastern Europe. Critical of the existing

---

56. Fichter and Lönnendonker, *Kleine Geschichte des SDS.*

system, they had no full-fledged alternative to offer. For the antiauthoritarians, the working class in advanced capitalism was too apolitical, too integrated, and too successfully manipulated to perceive its own interests, and it was therefore no longer capable of being a revolutionary subject. They were not sure who should take over this role, but in the meantime the self-appointed avant-garde could begin the struggle through consciousness-raising activities, without waiting for perfect objective revolutionary conditions. Political action did not have to orient itself toward specific goals; it could even be fun and directed toward self-liberation of the actors involved.[57]

Certain unions formed the second pillar of the extraparliamentary opposition of the late 1960s. Primarily involved in protest against the Emergency Laws, many unionists considered this legislation a potentially existential threat to labor's most fundamental interests and to their own organizational capacities to represent labor. The DGB, however, was by no means united in its opposition to the Emergency Laws. As on other occasions, the various unions' attitudes toward the legislation depended on how they viewed organized labor's role in the political system. The debate between activist and accommodationist unions continued, manifesting itself in controversy over the Emergency Laws, the unions' newly minted Düsseldorf Program outlining fundamental goals and strategies, and the unions' relationship to the SPD's post-Godesberg course.

The drafting of the new program (to replace the DGB's founding document of 1949) witnessed pronounced conflict between the accommodationists and the activists. The accommodationist unions, led by Georg Leber, viewed labor as an "integrative element" *(Ordnungsfaktor)* of advanced capitalism. Workers, they felt, were no longer simply proletarians in West Germany's free, democratic, and prosperous society. Rather than class conflict, they envisioned a politics of inclusion, a society of interest associations asserting themselves within the democratic framework. Labor's role in the new order was to gradually improve its members' standing, not to challenge the system in which it had become a full partner. To the activists, led by IG Metall's Otto Brenner, West Germany represented a genuine *Rechtsstaat* that unions were willing to defend, but it nonetheless placed a disproportionate burden on the working class. Although not revolutionary, the activists followed a modified Marxism and still thought in terms of class conflict. Since they viewed capital and labor as collectivities with fundamentally conflicting interests, they rejected the accommodationists' view that a "social partnership" between the two would most benefit the working class. The activists' and accom-

---

57. Bauss, *Die Studentenbewegung der sechziger Jahre,* chap. 9.

modationists' diverging views finally found a compromise, engineered by Ludwig Rosenberg and expressed in the DGB's Düsseldorf Program of 1963.

Conflict over the Emergency Laws during the 1960s both complicated the process of compromise within the DGB and reinforced the division between activist and accommodationist lines. For the accommodationists and Godesberg adherents in the SPD, support for the Emergency Laws allowed the SPD to highlight its new moderate image while working to eliminate some of the most severe measures. Unionists like Leber believed that if the harshest measures restricting strikes and other civil liberties were removed, the Emergency Laws would help West Germany defend its democratic order against political extremes. They also supported passage of modified emergency laws as a matter of pragmatism. Leber argued that the question was not whether but how the laws would be instituted in West Germany. Thus he wanted the unions to try to influence the content of the laws instead of rejecting them outright.

Activists like Brenner, however, compared the laws' intent and potential effects to the beginning of dictatorship in West Germany, especially for the unions, since their antistrike measures directly threatened labor's most powerful weapon. In support of a general strike if the laws passed, activists often pointed to the Kapp Putsch in 1920, when organized labor defended the Weimar democracy. They also likened the proposed laws to the Weimar constitution's Article 48, whose implementation helped destroy Germany's first democracy and facilitated the subsequent Nazi dictatorship. Moreover, as Markovits notes, activists saw the Emergency Laws as "ultimate expressions of a centralized, bureaucratized and dehumanized state whose prime concern was to uphold a mechanistic, technology-oriented and profit-dominated order, rather than the defense of its citizens' democratic rights."[58]

In a vote at the DGB's Hannover congress in 1962, 276 delegates rejected union support for the Emergency Laws, while 138 approved. Over the next six years until the legislation's final passage in 1968, activist unions like IG Metall, Chemie, and Druck und Papier conducted major activities against the Emergency Laws. The issue again dominated the Berlin congress in May 1966, and activist unions joined others in the Notstand der Demokratie demonstration, with its twenty thousand participants. But the unions' protest was mostly verbal and programmatic. After the Bundestag passed a modified version of the Emergency Laws in 1968 with the SPD's parliamentary support, even activist unions did nothing more than organize another meeting, this time in Dortmund. Organized

---

58. Markovits, *The Politics of the West German Trade Unions,* 99.

labor participated only minimally in the APO's march on Bonn, leaving the rest of the APO to its own devices.[59]

Merely one of three pillars of the broader APO, the peace movement was also active in the protest campaigns of the late 1960s, expanding its focus by linking these new issues to its traditional concerns. Called the *Kampagne für Abrüstung* (KfA, or Campaign for Disarmament) at this point, the movement made the qualitative leap to developing social criticism, in particular of the perceived underlying social and economic causes of "unpeaceful" government policies. In the concept of one leader, Arno Klönne, the KfA had become a movement against the social conditions and causes of war. In addition to opposing the Vietnam War, the arms race, and the militarization of society, the movement opposed the structural causes of these phenomena as well, including the "military-industrial complex" and deficits in domestic democracy. The KfA organized against the emergency legislation on the grounds that it provided for militarization in peacetime and would empower the government to suspend democratic rights in service of militarization for the second time in the twentieth century. The legislation would, moreover, hurt the chances of European détente and German reunification. In late 1966, the KfA helped organize much of the protest against the Emergency Laws, after it realized that these laws were part of the arms policy it opposed.[60] The KfA also joined the anti-Springer campaign after coming to two conclusions: first, that the Springer press's aggressive anticommunism hindered domestic democracy and détente in foreign policy; and, second, that securing peace depended on change in popular attitudes, which in turn required freedom of opinion and deconcentration of the media.[61]

By the 1968 Easter March, the KfA had adopted a range of concrete demands concerning the major themes of the period. With respect to the Vietnam War, the KfA demanded an end to West German monetary support for the United States (which amounted to cofinancing of the war), an end to support for South Vietnam's Ky government, and an official distance between West Germany and America's policy in Vietnam. In addition, the KfA demanded that West Germany renounce carrier systems for nuclear weapons, recognize East Germany, and break off diplomatic relations with the junta in Greece.[62]

---

59. Ibid., 93–100. Helga Grebing, "Gewerkschaften: Bewegung oder Dienstleistungs-organisation 1955 bis 1965," in *Geschichte der Gewerkschaften in der Bundesrepublik Deutschland,* ed. Hans-Otto Hemmer and Kurt Thomas Schmitz (Cologne: Bund-Verlag, 1990), 149–82.

60. Otto, *Vom Ostermarsch zur APO,* 154–66.

61. Bauss, *Die Studentenbewegung der sechziger Jahre,* 88.

62. Ibid., 199.

Organizational and Tactical Innovations

The peace movement and the larger APO made lasting organizational and tactical contributions to West Germany's political culture. Over time, the peace movement developed durable organizational structures fully independent of parties or any other established institutions, which endowed the movement with enough stability to launch regularly recurring protest for eight years. Indeed, the Easter March movement was founded in 1960 by veterans of the 1950s protest, who were sorely disappointed by the inconstancy of the SPD and DGB, and who were determined to attain organizational independence. This sustained, but fully extraparliamentary, protest was unprecedented in West German politics before the 1960s. In its final APO phase, the movement introduced new protest forms, permanently widening the repertoire of protest in German political culture.

Although now independent of established institutions, in its early phases the peace movement was not yet organized along the grassroots, antihierarchical principles commonly associated with movements from the late 1960s on. In its initial, Easter March phase, the movement suffered an organizational dilemma. On the one hand, it presented a protest opportunity to anyone who refused to accept the failure of the 1950s peace movement. On the other hand, the movement's pacifist and religious initiators were determined to protect the movement from communist dominance (either in fact or in its public image) and to protect the credibility of its protest against nuclear weapons on both sides of the Iron Curtain. For its first, small march in 1960, the movement therefore constituted special ad hoc committees with responsibility for organizing the separate pillars of the *Sternmarsch* (star march) that collectively converged like spokes to a wheel's center on the march's target, the newly stationed Honest John missiles in Bergen-Hohne. Proclaiming in 1961 that it was not a mass-membership organization but instead a loose union of like-minded citizens, the movement required people to participate as individuals rather than as identifiable subgroups. This provision kept communist visibility low without necessarily excluding communists as individual marchers. The requirement of individual participation also reflected the founders' religious and pacifist ethos of individual conscience and personal willingness to sacrifice.

As the movement's organizational capacities solidified, the effort to avoid communist infiltration resulted in a centralized and hierarchical (some said "authoritarian") leadership structure and style. The Central Committee (Zentralausschuß) assumed the national leadership of the movement and maintained tight control over its general political direction and over the projection of its image, including slogans, brochures, and speeches. It provided local march organizers with "required slogans" and "optional slogans," and it forbad the use of slogans not approved. Again to avoid communist penetration, the Central Committee expected local groups to choose only "unimpeachable" local march directors. The committee reserved the right to dissolve local groups and cancel local activities that strayed too far from the designated path.[63]

As the movement grew, the Central Committee faced certain challenges. Inherently controversial given the movement's rhetorical emphasis on conscience-driven individual participation, the committee's authority depended on voluntary obedience from regional and local groups. It also had to maintain movement cohesion in the face of considerable political diversity, and in particular it had to keep its "bourgeois" and "socialist" wings united. The committee addressed these problems through the inclusiveness of its composition and its consensus-generating procedures. In addition to its officers and prominent personalities who lent the movement prestige, integrity, and political autonomy, the committee assured horizontal integration by including representatives of its political constituencies, particularly socialists (but not communists), mainstream Protestants and Quakers, pacifists, and conscientious objectors.

The Central Committee also included representatives of the regional committees, which in turn represented the local committees, and thus assured vertical communication between the national leadership and local groups. Mirroring the Central Committee's functions at a lower level, the regional and local committees played important roles in practical organization and actual mobilization of participation and helped integrate the movement with the broader society and established institutions. Although they were directed by the fundamental decisions imparted from above and thus lent the movement only a limited grassroots quality, these committees displayed local initiative in organizing protest events and varied considerably among each other. To remain nonpartisan they refused to accept representatives of parties or other institutions in their official capacities, but they did solicit unionists, church functionaries, and dissident Social Democrats as individual participants and informal representatives of their institutions.

Inclusiveness of composition and vertically integrated territorial organization helped maintain the movement's cohesion and increase its mobilization. Movement cohesion got a second boost from the decision-making procedures adopted, which facilitated consensus formation within the movement despite its diversity. Decision making through majority rule raised the possibility of disgruntled minorities splitting off from the movement, so the movement decided against majority rule and

---

63. Otto, *Vom Ostermarsch zur APO*, 82.

instead committed itself to discussing issues until a compromise emerged. According to the movement's chronicler, the movement reached major decisions through internal "learning processes," as rethinking fundamental questions often led to higher levels of politicization and willingness to expand the range of political concerns the movement espoused.[64]

When the peace movement joined forces with the APO in the late 1960s, many of its organizational and tactical precepts changed in the course of interaction with the student movement and the SDS. Up to 1967, the peace movement (KfA) both provided the dominant organizational framework for extraparliamentary opposition and managed to keep itself strictly nonpartisan vis-à-vis both the Communist Party and the SPD. After 1967, this began to change. The movement lowered its guard toward communist groups as it grew alongside the broader APO mobilization. In 1968 the Central Committee admitted a number of student groups as new members, in an effort to integrate the growing student unrest and stabilize it organizationally. The committee eventually even admitted a few groups considered close to the Communist Party, since it had acquired so much size, strength, and reputation as an autonomous political actor that maintaining an infiltration-free image became a less pressing tactical concern. Through participation in SDS-sponsored events, moreover, regional and local committees were showing signs of autonomy by carrying placards with slogans unauthorized from above and were increasingly undermining prohibitions against communist participation anyway.[65]

As the Campaign for Disarmament joined forces with the SDS and the unions in the broader APO campaign, it lost both its relatively narrow focus on foreign policy issues and its dominant position in the extraparliamentary opposition. By participating in the protest against the Emergency Laws and the Springer press, the KfA joined a formal coalition with student groups for the democratization of social structures, however much it stressed their connection to peace and disarmament. By cooperating with the SDS and the unions, the peace movement had to decide whether to move away from its earlier status as a single-issue movement and toward cooperation in a unified socialist movement. The SDS demanded an explicit commitment to "socialist politics" and saw the fight against the Emergency Laws as part of a political and ideological crusade oriented toward the ultimate goal of a new revolutionary movement, into which it hoped to pull the unions and the KfA.

The SDS and KfA could agree on criticism of government policy and favored alternatives. They disagreed, however, on opposition and mobilization strategy. The SDS pushed for a strategy that went beyond extra-

---

64. Ibid., 76.
65. Ibid., 81.

parliamentary attempts to influence the Bundestag; it was instead antiparliamentary and proclaimed its desire to recover genuine popular representation from a parliament that had irrevocably lost this function. The SDS also wanted social criticism for its own sake, while the KfA understood itself as an umbrella movement and restricted social criticism to what was relevant for its disarmament goals. The KfA made the symbolic concession of changing its name from the Campaign for Disarmament (KfA) to the Campaign for Democracy and Disarmament (KfDA) in the hopes of keeping itself and the SDS together in a broader extraparliamentary opposition, but it also indicated thereby the limits to its willingness to change its basic structure and function.[66]

Although participation in the APO's campaigns seemed to expand the peace movement's reach, it resulted in its subordination to the SDS. Thus what seemed to be the high point of the Easter March movement's decade-long development in fact catalyzed its disintegration. The merging of the student movement/SDS with the peace movement (now called KfDA) was a disaster for the latter. The growth in the KfDA demonstration of 1968 was accompanied by a disproportionate influx of youth into the movement, which caused a generation gap among the protestors and shifted the balance of forces within the KfDA toward student and youth groups. Student tendencies toward an elitist "revolutionary" subculture deflected the peace movement from its more concrete formulations of foreign policy goals, while their antiauthoritarian criticism of the labor movement as "old left" and of unions as "counterrevolutionary organizations" destroyed the budding cooperation with the unions in the struggle against the Emergency Laws. Such developments led, moreover, to a break between the KfDA and the SDS over the question of violent confrontation with the state for the sake of exposing the "fascist" tendencies of "the establishment," since the KfDA had no intention of using such tactics. The passage of the emergency legislation greatly weakened the common ground between the KfDA and the unions, which largely withdrew from the APO. Much of the New Left abandoned the KfDA as well, leaving the field to the communist groups within it and robbing it of its umbrella character. Finally, the Soviet invasion of Czechoslovakia divided communists from other groups when the former refused to go along with the latter's "socialist critique" of the Soviet Union.

In its double confrontation with the SDS radicals and antiauthoritarian student movement, on the one hand, and communists, on the other, the peace movement had thus lost its power to integrate an autonomous

66. Ibid., 170, 171.

movement.[67] The decision to cancel the 1969 Easter March revealed the movement's loss of momentum, while the "official" resignation of the traditional KfDA factions from the movement provided the final coup de grâce. Although the KfDA continued a formal existence for some time, its confrontations with the SDS radicals and antiauthoritarian student movement and with communist forces cost it the ability to gather extraparliamentary groups and themes into its organizational fold.

In the final analysis, the peace movements of the 1950s and 1960s remained modest in size compared to their successor in the 1980s, but for very different reasons. Compared to the 1950s, the 1960s movement was favored by an international situation that lent more credibility to its message, a larger protest potential in the general political culture, and a government that was on the whole much more unpopular than the Adenauer government had been. Compared to the 1950s, however, the 1960s movement lacked a salient issue over which it enjoyed a monopoly, and, in the extraparliamentary arena, its concerns became overshadowed by more compelling issues. In terms of its composition, the 1960s movement again united the various political forces opposed to government defense policy and broader political developments. These forces drew on the frames of redemption, democratization, and the German question, but they redefined those frames in light of domestic and international developments. In addition to a new emphasis on arms control and détente, the movement also introduced the frame of imperialism as a basis for opposition to government policy. On the organizational front, the 1960s movement developed the capacity for ongoing mobilization independent of parties or other institutions.

Although the movement eventually disintegrated under the weight of factionalism, its new organizational forms provided the foundation for all future protest. During the 1960s, moreover, extraparliamentary political activity gradually acquired a "normal" and even "democratic" status, and it suffered less from the taint of subversiveness or disloyalty than it had in the 1950s. Furthermore, the 1960s movement helped "democratize" the political agenda more lastingly than had earlier movements, by contributing to ongoing discussion within the parties, churches, and unions on alternatives to the CDU's policy. The movement helped revive the SPD's left wing after it had been defeated because of the party's centrist strategy. The movement also influenced public opinion on foreign policy questions by questioning the CDU's "policy of strength," which helped make possible the upcoming Ostpolitik of the social-liberal coalition of the 1970s and the West German signature to the Nuclear Non-Proliferation Treaty.

---

67. Ibid., 173–76; Rolke, *Protestbewegungen in der Bundesrepublik*, 214–16; Legrand, "Friedensbewegungen in der Geschichte der Bundesrepublik," 28, 29.

Finally, the various movements of the 1960s stimulated interest in New Left variants of Marxism and radical democracy, which spread throughout the now permanent protest potential and became attached to new issues in the social movements of the 1970s and 1980s.[68]

---

68. Otto, *Vom Ostermarsch zur APO*, 178–79; Legrand, "Friedensbewegungen in der Geschichte der Bundesrepublik," 29.

CHAPTER 4

The 1970s: New Political Opportunities and a New Ideological Resource for the 1980s Movement

Social movement theory goes farther to explain the 1980s peace movement than earlier movements. Since 1945, increasing numbers of youth had been socialized under conditions of prosperity and peace and had undergone value change in comparison with their parents. And sure enough, younger generations participated in, and sympathized with, the 1980s peace movement to a greater degree than older generations.[1] In like manner, by the 1970s a perceived crisis of modernity had taken root on a large scale; in particular the ecology movement questioned the value of unlimited economic growth. With respect to resource mobilization, a number of resources were much more abundant than in earlier decades. During the 1970s a protest subculture had grown up, with its own organizational networks and communication structures. But how did value change, perceptions of modernization gone awry, and increased resources translate into a concrete movement?

If we designate the 1950s and 1960s as the period in which the "CDU State" was established and unraveled, the 1970s and early 1980s can analogously be called the period during which the "SPD State" rose and fell. This process of development and decline provided new opportunities and new ideological resources for the 1980s peace movement. Indeed, in the 1980s, expanded opportunities, ideological resources, and organizational

---

1. Sozialwissenschaftliches Institut Nowak und Sörgel [SINUS], "Sicherheitspolitik, Bündnispolitik, Friedensbewegung: Eine Untersuchung zur aktuellen politischen Stimmungslage im Spätherbst 1983," Munich, Oct. 1983.

capacities converged to produce West Germany's largest protest wave of any kind.

Launching the 1980s Peace Movement: The Expansion of Political Opportunities in the 1970s

In the 1970s, peace protest was virtually absent. There were no salient weapons decisions on the political agenda, and many of the peace movement's concerns had been institutionalized into mainstream politics and even into government policy. Indeed, in the golden age of East-West détente, former peace movement activists supported the government's approach to security and hoped for further positive developments. At the same time, however, other developments were paving the way for the upcoming peace movement of the 1980s. For one thing, the political opportunity structure for protest was expanding. A substantial political culture of protest evolved during the 1970s, as the "new social movements" exposed ever widening circles of people to firsthand experience of protest. The Social Democratic paradigm of politics, moreover, greeted with such enthusiasm in the early 1970s, began to crack as the decade progressed and opposition grew to government policies across the board. When NATO's 1979 decision to deploy nuclear missiles in Europe (if acceptable negotiation results proved unobtainable) finally presented a salient weapons decision, it fell onto very fertile soil, catalyzing the largest peace movement in German history. The 1980s peace movement proved the crowning glory of a sustained cycle of popular mobilization. It was able to tap that mobilization while for once enjoying a monopoly on the most compelling issue of the day.

To understand the greatly expanded political opportunities of the 1980s peace movement, we must first explore the rise and fall of the Social Democratic paradigm of politics. Like Adenauer's trio of parliamentary democracy, the social-market economy, and Western integration, the Social Democratic paradigm also encompassed domestic politics and foreign policy.

Domestic Politics in the 1970s

With the 1969 election, Willy Brandt became the first Social Democratic chancellor since the Weimar Republic, breaking the CDU's twenty-year monopoly on the office. The formation of the SPD's "social-liberal" coalition with the liberal Free Democrats (FDP) marked a turning point in West German history, and its designation as a *Machtwechsel* (change of power constellations) rather than a mere *Regierungswechsel* (change of government) showed that it was also widely viewed as such. To the left, Brandt's chancellorship raised hopes of significantly remaking domestic politics, the economic system, and foreign policy, and a broad reform euphoria swept large parts of the politically interested public.

Such euphoria was not to last, however, and by the mid-1970s disillusionment had set in. The resignations of Brandt and Foreign Minister Walter Scheel in 1974 and their replacement by Helmut Schmidt and Hans-Dietrich Genscher symbolized the end of high-flying hopes for change, introducing a much more pragmatic, measured, and somber approach. Already visible during the latter part of the Brandt government, the limits to reform tightened still further under Schmidt, as economic crisis and tensions within the social-liberal coalition narrowed the scope of feasible change. Schmidt's efforts to combat economic crisis repeatedly angered both his union constituencies and the more monetarist Free Democrats. At the same time, civil-rights and "new politics" issues alienated the New Left components of the original SPD/FDP electoral coalition.

Brandt's slogan "Dare more Democracy" became a trademark of his administration and a symbol of the expectations for reform he raised. His *Regierungserklärung* upon assuming office in 1969 (akin to a state-of-the-union message) functioned as a manifesto for a new beginning or, indeed, a new age. Proclaiming that West Germany was just beginning its democratic development, Brandt committed his government to a new understanding of democracy: whereas for the CDU/CSU democracy meant the organizational form of the state, for the SPD it represented a principle that penetrated all social existence.[2] Brandt entered office promising to liberalize politics and society, advance economic justice, and pursue a new Ostpolitik.

Liberalizing politics and society meant introducing more participation into political, social, and economic processes, as well as certain specific reforms. In politics, lowering the voting age to eighteen expanded participation in the electoral process. New laws governing political protest, moreover, relieved demonstrators of legal accountability for violence at demonstrations as long as they individually were not involved. Further reforms liberalized other aspects of criminal law as well. In the area of social self-determination, the Brandt government had a big impact, as it relaxed laws concerning homosexuality, divorce, and abortion. Educational reform consisted largely of plans to reorganize secondary and university education via the creation of *Gesamtschulen* and *Gesamt-*

2. Wolfgang Jäger, "Die Innenpolitik der sozial-liberalen Koalition 1969–74," in *Republik im Wandel 1969–74: Die Ära Brandt,* by Karl Dietrich Bracher, Wolfgang Jäger, and Werner Link (Stuttgart: Deutsche Verlags-Anstalt, 1986), 25.

hochschulen, which would replace the tracking system segregating students into academic or vocational training paths during adolescence. Billed as a path to social change, democracy, efficiency in education, and a new breed of self-confident citizens *(mündige Bürger)*, these educational reforms were partially stymied by strong resistance along partisan and ideological lines at the level of both the federal and the state governments. The Constitutional Court, moreover, had already set limits to expanded self-governance at the universities.

In economic matters, a new version of the Works Constitution Law, governing labor rights within individual plants, gave individual workers more voice over matters directly affecting them, improved union access to firms, and widened the rights of the works councils *(Betriebsräte)* in personnel and social policy questions. In addition, after a long struggle with the FDP and its business clientele, the codetermination law affecting large firms was widened to create apparent parity between capital and labor on supervisory boards, although certain provisions meant that codetermination still fell short of genuine labor-capital parity in labor's eyes. Tax reform adjusted a variety of tax rates and exemptions, but without significant redistributive effect in the final analysis. Reforms of the social insurance system assured all retirees a minimum standard of living irrespective of their incomes as active workers and improved health insurance benefits and provisions for the handicapped. The Schmidt government, however, abandoned expansion of vocational education and proposals for helping workers build financial assets as too ambitious given the economic difficulties of the mid- and late 1970s.[3]

While Brandt's accomplishments were not insignificant, they frequently fell short of their original promise even during his chancellorship. Constituting to some extent "sins of omission," they disappointed some of the most ardent Social Democratic voters. Bitter disillusionment with both the Brandt and Schmidt governments resulted from additional "sins of commission" regarding their policies on terrorism and political extremism more generally. Although right-wing extremism had briefly flared up in the 1960s, in the 1970s both conservatives and the Social-Democratic government viewed the radical left as the chief threat to domestic security. The radicals' methods ranged from terrorism to the "long march through the institutions" by radicals seeking civil-service jobs. The social-liberal coalition responded to both threats with fairly stringent measures. Terrorists murdered individuals prominent in "the system," burned public buildings, and hijacked airlines. Additional "revolutionary cells" used protest against nuclear power and other issues as the stage for violent confronta-

---

3. Ibid., 126–55.

tion with the police. The Brandt and Schmidt governments responded by expanding police authority to search apartments, check identity cards, and the like, while also restricting contact between terrorist suspects awaiting trial and defense attorneys suspected of facilitating their communication with compatriots outside prison.[4] To prevent communists and other far-left radicals from acquiring influence through civil-service positions (especially in the schools), the Brandt government passed the controversial Decree on Radicals *(Radikalenerlass,* more commonly called the *Berufsverbot),* which instantly became wildly unpopular with the left.[5]

Such, then, were some of the hopes, accomplishments, and disappointments concerning political and economic participation, education, and social policy. Economic policy followed a similar course. During the Grand Coalition, the SPD had established a new image of economic competence for itself, as Karl Schiller's application of Keynesian demand management helped overcome the 1966/67 recession. When Brandt entered office, the capacities of economic planning to achieve the "magic rectangle" of stable prices, full employment, positive balance of trade, and steady economic growth seemed unlimited. In trying to combat the economic crises of the 1970s, however, Schmidt found himself wedged between his union constituencies and his coalition partner, the FDP, and its business and industry clientele. In the end, tensions over economic policy between the unions and the FDP contributed to the fall of Schmidt's government.

Although Helmut Schmidt often received high marks for economic crisis management, the multiple economic crises of the 1970s generally did not prove as susceptible to Keynesian techniques as had the 1966/67 recession. The effective revaluation of the mark by almost 40 percent after the switch to floating exchange rates[6] eliminated the advantage for German exports that an undervalued currency had previously brought. Unions pursued large wage gains more aggressively, in part because of increased rank-and-file militancy (including wildcat strikes). Increased inflation following the two oil shocks (especially the second one) upset government efforts at stabilization, while the Bundesbank's restrictive monetary policies contributed to unemployment and slowed recovery from recessions. Private investment declined in response to "stop-go" Keynesian fiscal policies and lower profitability. By the late 1970s, mass unemployment remained stubbornly high, the result not only of conjunctural downturn

---

4. Ibid., 77–86; Wolfgang Jäger, "Die Innenpolitik der sozial-liberalen Koalition 1974–1982," in *Republik im Wandel 1974–1982: Die Ära Schmidt,* by Wolfgang Jäger and Werner Link (Stuttgart: Deutsche Verlags-Anstalt, 1987), 74–89.

5. Jäger, "Die Innenpolitik der sozial-liberalen Koalition 1969–74," 83–86.

6. Hennings, "West Germany," 494.

but also of structural causes like technological advances, capital export, and increased competition from newly industrialized countries.[7]

Gradually, the Social Democratic economic policy paradigm for sustaining economic growth lost credibility, as it proved unable to overcome the new challenges posed by the far more difficult economic environment after 1973. In no other policy field was the *Machbarkeit* euphoria of the Brandt period so destroyed.[8] In his attempts at crisis management, Schmidt found himself caught between the demands of the unions and the SPD left, on the one hand, and the FDP with its business clientele, on the other. Schmidt's policy of centrism failed to satisfy their competing demands. The FDP had moved decidedly to the right on economic issues during the 1970s. In pursuit of "more market," the FDP wanted to reduce the state's role in the economy, by cutting state spending and the deficit, and by reducing regulations and taxes on business. Schmidt himself supported periodic austerity even during economic downturns, cutting spending on education and social services, while also curbing active labor market programs and fiscal policy because of the growing deficit. These practices deeply alienated the unions and the SPD's left. Although the more traditional unions long defended Schmidt's policy as the lesser of two evils, by 1980 most unions had begun to attack Schmidt for spending cuts and "social dismantling." Prominent union leaders even spoke at a demonstration against spending cuts in November 1981. The left also pushed in vain for state "guidance" of investment and "structural policy." The social-liberal coalition's breakup in 1982 substantially resulted from the two parties' inability to agree on measures against the economic crisis.[9]

In his attempts to deal with the economic crises of the 1970s, Schmidt gradually estranged his traditional labor-based constituencies, who still clung to traditional social democratic notions of economic growth and redistribution. But these were not the only sources of increasing discontent with the Schmidt government. At the same time, another realm of "new politics" was gradually emerging. As we shall see in detail in chapter 5, extraparliamentary movements increasingly challenged the worth of economic growth and technological progress themselves, as well as concrete policies ranging from ecology and nuclear power to feminism and foreign policy. Many of these currents eventually joined forces to form the Green

---

7. Hennings, "West Germany"; Jäger, "Die Innenpolitik der sozial-liberalen Koalition 1969–74," 46–53, 107–16; Jäger, "Die Innenpolitik der sozial-liberalen Koalition 1974–82," 14–21, 193–201; Markovits, *The Politics of the West German Trade Unions,* 126–30.

8. Jäger, "Die Innenpolitik der sozial-liberalen Koalition 1974–82," 17.

9. Andrei Markovits, "The Vicissitudes of West German Social Democracy," *Studies in Political Economy* 19, (spring 1986), 83–112; Jäger, "Die Innenpolitik der sozial-liberalen Koalition 1974–82," 265–68.

Party in the late 1970s. Even before the formation of a rival party on the SPD's left, however, these extraparliamentary movements both expressed and fomented dissatisfaction with the Schmidt government.

Foreign Policy in the 1970s

In foreign policy, the 1970s were a decade of détente and Ostpolitik. The compatibility between Adenauer's policy of Western integration and his allies' interest in containment had been one secret of his success in the 1950s. With the development of East-West détente, however, Adenauer—and to a lesser extent his successors in the 1960s—found themselves caught in his "policy of strength," which hoped to effect reunification through unconditional Western integration and by refusing to recognize the political changes wrought by World War II. In contrast, Brandt's Ostpolitik accepted postwar realities and sought to establish a modus vivendi with Eastern Europe based on them.

Brandt and Foreign Minister Walter Scheel were the first to cross the rubicon of de facto (although not de jure) recognition of East German statehood and of the finality of Germany's postwar border with Poland. Brandt and Scheel sought cooperation with the DDR (East Germany) to lessen the human costs of German division, while transferring the long-term goal of national unity to an envisaged "European peace order," the establishment of which would overcome European and thereby German division. For all of these reasons, Brandt's Ostpolitik was in tune with the Western allies' interest in détente at the time, overcoming German isolation within NATO during the 1960s.[10] Indeed, West German Ostpolitik became the centerpiece of détente in the early 1970s; and later in the decade, Schmidt and Genscher took on a limited role as "interpreters" between the superpowers.[11]

In terms of concrete policy, Ostpolitik during the Brandt/Scheel government consisted mainly of a series of treaties with Eastern Europe, the *Ostverträge*. Each treaty resolved specific issues resulting from World War II, thereby laying the foundation for normalization of relations.[12] The treaty with the Soviet Union explicitly recognized postwar realities, including the existence of the DDR, the inviolability of the Oder-Neisse line as the German-Polish border, and the mutual renunciation of force. West

---

10. Haftendorn, *Sicherheit und Entspannung,* 53–55.

11. Hanrieder, *Germany, America, Europe,* 4; Werner Link, "Aussen- und Deutschlandpolitik in der Ära Brandt 1969–1974," in *Republik im Wandel 1969–74: Die Ära Brandt,* by Karl Dietrich Bracher, Wolfgang Jäger, and Werner Link (Stuttgart: Deutsche Verlags-Anstalt, 1986), 163–282, here 233.

12. Griffith, *The Ostpolitik of the Federal Republic of Germany,* chap. 5.

Germany implicitly recognized Soviet hegemony over Eastern Europe as well. The treaty with Poland again confirmed the sanctity of Polish-German borders, while Brandt's famous gesture of kneeling before the memorial to the Warsaw Ghetto symbolized the political and moral importance of acknowledging the past and making a new beginning. The four-power agreement on Berlin secured the "existing situation" by sanctioning the status quo without injuring the signers' diverging legal positions. Finally, the *Grundlagenvertrag* with the DDR established a new relationship between the two Germanies. Although the treaty did not grant the DDR full (de jure) recognition as a separate country, thus keeping unification an open possibility, it did establish relations "on the basis" of and "according to the principles" of international law, thus granting de facto recognition.[13] Taken together, as Grosser notes, the 1970–72 agreements contained important German concessions, like renouncing the lost eastern territories, but the concessions "were made in the interest of détente, of peace, and of personal relations with the population of the other German state."[14]

In addition to normalization of relations with Eastern Europe, Ostpolitik represented a new approach both to the German question and to security. Brandt's new Ostpolitik was a new *Deutschlandpolitik,* which adapted West German policy to existing realities without renouncing the goal of eventual reunification. The new approach acknowledged that East Germany belonged to the Soviet bloc, but it hoped to preserve national unity by increasing relations between the two German states. In order to reduce tensions and eventually draw the two closer together (thus getting to *Miteinander* via *geregeltes Nebeneinander*), inter-German exchange between groups, families, and ordinary citizens was to protect "national substance" and leave a chance for future self-determination. This was a strategy of overcoming the status quo by recognizing it, in the hopes that the German-German relationship could be indefinitely regulated until it was fully resolved in a European peace order.[15]

Brandt's new Ostpolitik put a novel slant on national security as well. On the one hand, Ostpolitik brought a new realism into security policy. Hanrieder maintains that social-liberal willingness to accept the territorial status quo confronted German security problems at their political roots, by working toward reconciliation with Eastern Europe on the basis of the status quo: "By recognizing the territorial and political realities stemming from the Second World War, the Germans meshed their security and East-

---

13. Link, "Aussen- und Deutschlandpolitik in der Ära Brandt 1969–1974," 179–225.

14. Grosser, *The Western Alliance,* 251–52.

15. Link, "Aussen- und Deutschlandpolitik in der Ära Brandt 1969–1974," 214–25.

ern policies . . . ,"[16] overcoming the contradictions that had existed between them in the Adenauer era. Moreover, Ostpolitik brought West German security policy into line with that of the other NATO allies. Brandt and Schmidt repeatedly emphasized that West German security and indeed Ostpolitik itself continued to depend on the NATO alliance. Schmidt also waged a continual battle to maintain defense spending, resisting pressure to finance domestic reforms by reducing defense allocations.[17]

On the other hand, Ostpolitik brought a more visionary and even utopian approach to security, a quality most clearly embodied in Brandt's talk of a European peace order and Egon Bahr's outlines for attaining it. Reminiscent of the SPD's security proposals of the 1950s, this concept departed significantly from previous emphasis on maintaining ties to the West and keeping a distance from the East. A European peace order, its proponents argued, would provide for West German security by helping to "secure peace" *(Friedenssicherung)*—that is, by reducing political tensions that could erupt into armed conflict—and would also perhaps eventually overcome German division.

Security problems stood at the center of this pan-European thinking, because a European peace order presupposed a "European security system" as a constituent part. Two possible models for constructing such a system existed in principle: either by improving the existing security alliances' relationship with each other or by gradually dissolving them and putting something else in their place. The SPD's thinking over the years moved between these two poles. Brandt felt that realism required focusing on the first model but not excluding a later transition to the second. Bahr, however, preferred the second model and advocated replacing both pacts with a security system of equal European states, guaranteed by both superpowers, who were not themselves members. Thus both alliances would be replaced by a new Central European security system composed of both Germanies, the Benelux, Poland, and Czechoslovakia. Bahr saw such a system as the optimal context for German reunification, although, as Enders argues, reunification was by no means as central to such schemes as it had been in the 1950s.[18] Bahr of course realized that neither superpower was likely to accept such loss of influence in Europe and that a security system that replaced existing alliances had little chance in the foreseeable future. In practice, Bahr and Brandt had to concentrate on détente and

---

16. Hanrieder, *Germany, America, Europe,* 21.

17. Link, "Aussen- und Deutschlandpolitik in der Ära Brandt 1969–1974," 233–37.

18. Thomas Enders, *Die SPD und die äußere Sicherheit: Zum Wandel der sicherheitspolitischen Konzeption der Partei in der Zeit der Regierungsverantwortung* (Melle: Verlag Ernst Knoth, 1987), 130.

arms control within the existing alliance system. Bahr noted, however, that agreements could perhaps be reached to continue the existing system at reduced military capacity, which could be a preliminary stage *(Vorstufe)* of a new order. Thus he held out hope for an eventual Central European security system despite certain superpower resistance.[19]

Such, then, was the partly realistic and partly visionary quality of Ostpolitik and the idea of a European peace order. Both faced highly visible limits, after Schmidt replaced Brandt as chancellor. One problem was the dramatic rise in superpower tensions, which set limits on Ostpolitik if Schmidt did not want to risk German-American tensions. By the later 1970s, displeasure over Soviet behavior took the gilt off détente in American eyes. This displeasure was provoked in part by the Soviet arms buildup outside of SALT I (Strategic Arms Limitations Talks) provisions and by Soviet (and proxy) involvement in armed conflicts in the Third World. In turn, President Carter's policy toward China and his support for dissidents in Eastern Europe, among other things, did little to ingratiate him to Soviet ruling elites. The Soviet invasion of Afghanistan and the declaration of martial law in Poland dealt the final death blows to détente in American eyes. Schmidt, however, balked at further endangering détente and arms control by criticizing Soviet policy. Continued Ostpolitik thus put West German diplomacy at odds with American policy.[20]

A second problem confronting Brandt's vision was the emergence of Eastern European limits to Ostpolitik during the 1970s, which illustrated the contradictions inherent in West Germany's goal of "change through rapprochement" in the East. The Polish government's crackdown on the Solidarity movement and declaration of martial law showed the limits of democratization and thus of "change" in Eastern Europe. Similarly, the East German regime set limits to "rapprochement" with a policy of *Abgrenzung,* measures designed to limit its citizens' contact with the West in order to ward off pressure for liberalization. Nonetheless, although Ostpolitik helped stabilize communist rule, Schmidt doggedly pursued economic, political, and cultural relations with Eastern Europe for the sake of détente.[21]

The third problem that posed limits to the more visionary aspects of Ostpolitik remained West German security. In accord with NATO's

19. Timothy Garton Ash, *In Europe's Name: Germany and the Divided Continent* (New York: Random House, 1993), 79–83; Link, "Aussen- und Deutschlandpolitik in der Ära Brandt 1969–1974," 169–73.

20. Werner Link, "Aussen- und Deutschlandpolitik in der Ära Schmidt 1974–1982," in *Republik im Wandel 1974–1982: Die Ära Schmidt,* by Wolfgang Jäger and Werner Link (Stuttgart: Deutsche Verlags-Anstalt, 1987), 275–432, here 310–13; Haftendorn, *Sicherheit und Entspannung,* 407.

21. Link, "Aussen- und Deutschlandpolitik in der Ära Schmidt 1974–1982," 353–63.

Harmel Report of 1967, the social-liberal coalition focused on détente and arms control as new pathways to increased security, while remaining willing to acquire additional arms to maintain military balance if need be. Haftendorn describes arms control as a "security partnership" between the superpowers, which aimed to reduce risk of military confrontation.[22] The Mutual and Balanced Force Reductions (MBFR) negotiations on conventional troop reductions in Vienna aimed at stabilizing the conventional military balance at a lower level, while the SALT negotiations aimed at nuclear control. The West German government even hoped that détente would allow European states to replace bloc confrontation with more cooperative, "bloc-overarching" *(blockübergreifend)* structures, one of which could be the Conference on Security and Cooperation in Europe (CSCE).[23]

Both processes proved disappointing. The CSCE did not create a new pan-European security system, although the CSCE conferences became a quasi-institutionalization of the East-West dialogue. At the MBFR talks, the two sides could not agree on how much military capacity actually existed on each side, and therefore they could not agree on what "parity" meant. The talks stagnated over the years, and by the early 1980s they were "consuming" détente rather than renewing it.[24]

Schmidt and the Double-Track Decision

NATO's double-track decision proved the final straw in this series of foreign policy disappointments, and it catalyzed the 1980s peace movement. As chancellor, Schmidt pursued a far less visionary security policy than Brandt's rhetoric conjured up. He aimed instead at negotiating an East-West balance at a lower level of military force. The biggest worry of the later 1970s was the regional European imbalance in medium-range nuclear missiles. Schmidt's main goal was to recreate a European balance of military force *(Gleichgewicht),* through arms control if possible but through arms measures if necessary. For Schmidt and others, there was no question that the European balance was threatened. After the Soviet Union had reached intercontinental parity with the United States, its traditional superiority in conventional forces was harder to counterbalance. In addition, neither SALT I nor SALT II covered the Soviets' increasing medium-range capability, which was nicely adequate for striking Western Europe. The Soviets were thus gradually undermining NATO's concept of

---

22. Haftendorn, *Sicherheit und Entspannung,* 189, 190.

23. Ibid., part 5.

24. Ibid., parts 5 and 6; Link, "Aussen- und Deutschlandpolitik in der Ära Schmidt 1974–1982," 297–305.

strategic unity by creating a purely regional threat. This situation worsened as the 1970s progressed, with arms control stagnating in all areas.[25] Thus a zone of diminished security was arising in Western Europe, potentially exposing the region, and particularly West Germany, to political black-mail. The persistent Soviet buildup of medium-range SS-20s increasingly intensified these concerns.

The Carter administration concluded that only new American medium-range missiles could assuage European concerns. Carter's first answer to the problem was the neutron bomb. Conceived as an instrument of "flexible response" that would counteract the East's conventional supe-riority and thereby raise the credibility of the West's deterrent posture, the neutron bomb stimulated a highly polemical discussion of deterrence in West Germany, laid to rest only after Carter canceled the entire project.

The double-track decision of December 12, 1979, represented NATO's second response to Schmidt's concerns after the debacle of the neutron bomb. Medium-range missiles would provide Europe-based "counterstrike" capacity, a variant of "flexible response," aimed at mili-tary installations rather than population centers. NATO argued that the new missiles would restore the credibility of deterrence and "recouple" America and Western Europe politically by linking the nuclear forces based on their respective soils in an unbroken chain of nuclear escalation. At the same time, medium-range missiles would help NATO control esca-lation and thus would contribute to stability in times of crisis.

Schmidt's main objective was to restore the balance of military power in Europe. One way to attain this restoration was through arms control, and NATO in fact decided to negotiate the fate of medium-range missiles with the Soviets, while still reserving the right to station any additional missiles necessary to redress the "Eurostrategic" imbalance. NATO's dou-ble-track decision thus followed a two-track strategy of arms control and weapons deployment, which corresponded to the Harmel Report's philos-ophy of pursuing détente while maintaining adequate defense capabilities. This novel approach of conducting negotiations before stationing new weapons reflected Schmidt's foreign policy line in general, as well as the practical fact that the new weapons would not be available until 1983.

The political climate for a new arms control venture, however, was anything but favorable. Détente and arms control lost all remaining momentum when the Soviets invaded Afghanistan, and Carter gave up hope for Senate ratification of SALT II. With the new Reagan administra-tion in office, Intermediate Range Nuclear Forces (INF) negotiations began after all in November 1981, but after many twists and turns, they

---

25. Link, "Aussen- und Deutschlandpolitik in der Ära Schmidt 1974–1982," 294–95.

ultimately failed to produce agreement. The United States presented its "zero option," in which NATO would cancel deployment of Pershing II and cruise missiles if the Soviets eliminated their SS-20s, SS-4s, and SS-5s. For their part, the Soviets called for ceilings on medium-range missiles and aircraft, which would prevent NATO from stationing any additional missiles. Each side rejected the other's proposal. Ambassador Paul Nitze and Soviet negotiator Juri Kvitsinsky's "walk in the woods" produced the next major proposal in the summer of 1982, which called for the superpowers to have equal numbers of intermediate nuclear missiles in Europe and which set other limits as well. The Soviet government rejected the proposal, and from NATO's perspective it violated the principle of parity in terms of both warheads and missile travel times. In March 1983, President Reagan proposed an interim agreement in which the United States agreed that it would station a small number of Pershing II and cruise missiles if the Soviets reduced their weapons to an equal number and that it would leave British and French weapons out of the equation. The Soviets rejected this idea, and NATO rejected the next Soviet offer on the grounds that it would grant the Soviets a monopoly of medium-range missiles and effectively decouple Western Europe from its American ally. In August 1983, Yuri Andropov repeated the Soviet offer to reduce its SS-20s to the number of British and French missiles already in existence, which again would have prevented any new American missiles and was correspondingly rejected by the NATO governments. This impasse characterized the INF negotiations on November 22, 1983, when the West German Bundestag conducted its scheduled vote on the missile issue, voting to deploy in the absence of acceptable negotiation results.[26]

Throughout the negotiations, the Soviets alternated between inducements not to deploy new Western missiles and threats should deployment take place. In West Germany, some decried Soviet statements as propagandistic attempts to beguile the public, while others greeted them as evidence of Soviet sincerity and willingness to negotiate. For example, the Soviets stressed that West Germany would itself become a target of Soviet nuclear counterattack should the West deploy medium-range missiles. In March 1982, Brezhnev announced that the Soviets would freeze their SS-20 deployments in the European parts of their territory, but he warned of countermeasures if American missiles were stationed. In January 1983, Andropov warned of dire consequences for peace in Europe if Western deployments took place. This transpired during the Bundestag election

---

26. Jeffrey Herf, *War by Other Means: Soviet Power, West German Resistance, and the Battle of the Euromissiles* (New York: Free Press, 1991), chaps. 9 and 10.

campaign of 1983, in which the Soviets made no secret of their wish for a Social Democratic victory.[27]

Political Opportunities for the 1980s Peace Movement:
A Reprise

NATO's double-track decision ended the period of calm that had befallen peace protest in the 1970s. Compared to other postwar decades, little *peace* protest took place during the 1970s. Under Brandt many peace movement positions found institutionalized representation in government policy. Enthusiasm for Ostpolitik and superpower détente temporarily led many to believe that foreign policy could be safely left to the government and that peace and disarmament would find suitable solutions at the international diplomatic level.[28] Peace activists even mobilized popular support for government policy, especially in the face of CDU opposition to the Ostpolitik treaties. Although interest in "peace policy" remained alive at the grassroots level, the hopes raised by Brandt and Bahr led to inaction by those who were satisfied with the government's performance for the time being. As a result mass peace protest did not occur for most of the 1970s.

As time went on, however, there were small exceptions to this rule. Activists grew disappointed with social-liberal defense policy and Ostpolitik. Many had expected détente to move beyond the formal Ostpolitik treaties, leading eventually to broad disarmament. They hoped that a new era of international cooperation would banish forever the ghost of the cold war past. Peace groups followed the Helsinki Conference on Security and Cooperation in Europe closely and found their own priorities mirrored in its Final Declaration. However, the continuation of "politics as usual," reflected in continued defense spending, gave such hopes pause.[29]

Although they lacked a concrete foreign policy issue salient enough to launch a mass campaign, isolated peace groups began to mobilize on behalf of détente and disarmament as disappointment over unfulfilled expectations mounted. The Komitee für Frieden, Abrüstung und Zusammenarbeit (KOFAZ), formed in 1974, contributed significantly to this early mobilization. Composed of members of long-standing pacifist groups, conscientious objectors, churches, unions, the SPD and FDP, remnants of the student movement, and communists, KOFAZ organized yearly demonstrations from 1976 on, supporting détente and reduced mil-

---

27. Ibid., chaps. 8–10.
28. See Legrand, "Friedensbewegungen in der Geschichte der Bundesrepublik," 19–35, on this point.
29. Knorr, *Geschichte der Friedensbewegung,* 146–75.

itary spending.[30] The 1976 demonstration, with the slogan "Stop the Arms Race," attracted forty thousand people; and sixty-eight thousand attended the 1977 activities.[31] In addition, organized opposition was growing against government suggestions to incorporate women into the army.

The brief flurry of opposition to the neutron bomb, moreover, as noted by Herf, proved "a microcosm and foreshadowing of the battle to come over the euromissiles" and "put the issue of nuclear weapons in the West German public eye for the first time since the 1950s."[32] Known officially as an Enhanced Radiation Weapon (ERW), the neutron bomb was intended as a short-range tactical weapon that could help overcome NATO conventional weakness in the European theater. Boutwell notes, however, that precisely because it was designed to "limit blast effects while increasing prompt radiation," many Europeans (along with the Soviet government) castigated it as the "ultimate capitalist weapon" that would "kill people while leaving property intact."[33] Egon Bahr, a foreign policy expert in the SPD, condemned it roundly, reflecting the attitude of much of his party. The issue blew over within less than a year when Carter canceled production of the ERW, but not without costing Schmidt much political capital at home.

In brief, although the 1970s saw a lull in peace protest on the whole, in the course of the social-liberal coalition many seeds for the 1980s movement were sown. NATO's double-track decision provided the spark that ignited protest unprecedented in scale or scope in West German history. The major components of positive political opportunity were all in place. The first component was the immense salience acquired by the weapons decision: as the next section of this chapter details, the weapons' advanced technology and changes in NATO's nuclear doctrine combined to make them seem more dangerous than older systems already in place. With nuclear issues largely dormant during the 1960s and 1970s, moreover, the proposed missiles acquired salience simply by forcing nuclear questions to the forefront of public consciousness for the first time in many years. As Joffe notes, "suddenly Western publics were again confronted with the murderous premises of their security."[34]

In keeping with the issue's salience, public opinion set the stage for potentially high mobilization. The ambiguity of survey data admittedly

---

30. Interview with a KOFAZ representative.

31. Knorr, *Geschichte der Friedensbewegung,* 168–70.

32. Herf, *War By Other Means,* 60.

33. Jeffrey Boutwell, *The German Nuclear Dilemma* (London: Brassey's, 1990), 66. See also his broader discussion in chaps. 2 and 3.

34. Josef Joffe, "Peace and Populism: Why the European Anti-Nuclear Movement Failed," *International Security* 11, no. 4 (spring 1987): 3–40, here 14.

made it difficult to ascertain just where the public stood. Although some registered a majority for the NATO decision,[35] this majority held only as long as both parts—the commitment to negotiation as well as intended deployments—were mentioned in the survey question. In contrast, a majority disapproved when surveys mentioned only the intended deployments.[36] This latter finding is consistent with the high levels of support registered for the movement in various surveys.

The percentage of avowed activists remained relatively small, rising from 6 percent of respondents in 1981 to 8 percent in 1983.[37] This figure, however, appears to capture only those who consistently participated over time. Seventeen percent of respondents in another survey reported participation in at least one peace movement activity, even *before* the movement's peak in the fall of 1983. The level of passive support for the movement, moreover, is equally striking; "sympathy" levels rose from 46 percent in 1981 to 61 percent by 1983. Although somewhat higher among the young, SPD or Green Party supporters, the better educated, and tertiary-sector employees, support for the movement transcended the usual age, educational, occupational, and even party cleavages. Fifty-six percent of CDU supporters were sympathizers of the movement despite their party's unrelenting hostility, along with 59 percent of those over 60 years of age and 65 percent of blue-collar workers.[38] This broad level of sympathy reflected Michael Howard's observation that "the doubts expressed by the peace movement differed in intensity but not in kind from the increasing worries of citizens, strategists, and governments."[39]

The second major component of positive political opportunity that was in place by the end of the 1970s was the credibility that the international environment lent to the peace movement's diagnostic frames. The 1970s had established détente, arms control, and Ostpolitik as the preferred currency of East-West relations, given the benefits in human contacts, trade, and security. The new missile decision came to symbolize dangers to détente and Ostpolitik, coinciding as it did with stagnant arms control talks and rising East-West tensions over Afghanistan and other matters. In the early 1980s, fear of war loomed larger across Europe than

---

35. Elisabeth Noelle-Neumann, "Drei Viertel gegen die Raketenstationierung?" *Frankfurter Allgemeine Zeitung,* 16 Sept. 1983, 11.

36. Karl-Heinz Reuband, "Die Friedensbewegung nach Stationierungsbeginn: Soziale Unterstützung in der Bevölkerung als Handlungspotential," *Vierteljahresschrift für Sicherheit und Frieden* 3, no. 3 (1985): 147–56, here 150.

37. Sozialwissenschaftliches Institut Nowak und Sörgel, "Sicherheitspolitik," 71.

38. Sozialwissenschaftliches Institut Nowak und Sörgel, "Sicherheitspolitik," 71.

39. Michael Howard, *The Causes of War* (Cambridge: Harvard University Press, 1983), 4–5; cited in Richard Eichenberg, *Public Opinion and National Security in Western Europe* (Ithaca: Cornell University Press, 1989), 10.

it had in the 1970s. In October 1981, 67 percent of German survey respondents thought that peace in Europe had become less secure in the past year.[40] The public still perceived a Soviet threat, although not as much as in the 1950s. While 59 percent of movement nonsupporters perceived a Soviet threat to West Germany, 30 percent of movement activists and a full 45 percent of sympathizers also did. But the preferred solution to this threat remained détente and arms control, clearly nonmilitary instruments of security. In 1983 the instruments considered most suitable for West German security included détente, arms control, and renunciation of force, which received very high levels of support (80–90 percent approval), while there was a decided lack of support for arms measures like the Strategic Defense Initiative (which received roughly 15 percent approval). Not surprisingly, 72 percent were against military defense of West Germany with nuclear weapons.[41]

Perceptions of American foreign policy also lent credibility to the peace movement's message. Confidence in American leadership, judgement, and even intentions dropped sharply, reaching new lows during the first Reagan administration.[42] Whereas America in the 1950s had been viewed primarily as friend and protector, some Germans now saw American policy as a threat to West Germany's very survival. In addition to its rejection of détente, the main cause was the bellicose rhetoric emanating from key political figures, such as Reagan's own references to the "evil [Soviet] empire" and the "age of Armageddon," his joke about "bombing Russia," reports of American planning for "protracted nuclear war," and T. K. Jones's remarks about surviving nuclear war "with enough shovels."[43] Along with American buildup of new nuclear systems, such as the MX missiles and the Strategic Defense Initiative (SDI), this rhetoric collided with the West German preference for nuclear parity. While West Germans as a whole were wary of experiments like withdrawal from NATO and unilateral disarmament (which received only 29–35 percent approval), 70–80 percent thought that the superpowers should be equally strong and that one side should not enjoy predominance.[44] But at the peace movement's height, according to Eichenberg, "about 60 percent of

---

40. Joffe, "Peace and Populism," 16; Hans Rattinger, "The Federal Republic of Germany," in *The Public and Atlantic Defense,* ed. Gregory Flynn and Hans Rattinger (London: Croom Helm, 1985), 123.
41. Sozialwissenschaftliches Institut Nowak und Sörgel, "Sicherheitspolitik," 9–35.
42. Eichenberg, *Public Opinion and National Security,* 95.
43. All these comments are cited in Müller and Risse-Kappen, "Origins of Estrangement," 81.
44. Sozialwissenschaftliches Institut Nowak und Sörgel, "Sicherheitspolitik," 9–35.

all Europeans believed that the United States was seeking superiority."[45] Finally, talk of actually using nuclear weapons further sapped confidence in American leadership. While support for deterrence in general remained high in West Germany (around 60 percent of all respondents), support for nuclear weapons dropped dramatically when survey questions mentioned their *use*. Thus, as Eichenberg notes, in the early 1980s "[t]alk of using nuclear weapons probably contributed as much to the eruption of public concern about INF as did deployment of the weapons themselves."[46]

The third component providing positive political opportunity at this time was the immense coverage that the media devoted to the issue, with much of the left-liberal media assuming a decidedly critical stance toward new missile deployments. The weekly news magazine *Der Spiegel,* for example, repeatedly ran critical stories, while its publisher, Rudolf Augstein, personally contributed signed articles and editorials condemning the NATO decision. Donsbach, Kepplinger, and Noelle-Neumann have observed that "[i]n 1981, *Der Spiegel* published so many negative statements that one can speak of a campaign against NATO's nuclear armament. . . . In many articles, *Der Spiegel* described the terrifying vision of a nuclear war as a consequence of NATO's armament . . . [giving] the impression that the armament was not necessary and a one-sided risk for the Federal Republic of Germany."[47] In addition to its own circulation of nearly one million copies for each weekly issue, *Der Spiegel* enjoyed further functions as an "opinion leader," because it served as a news source for additional media as well.

The fourth political opportunity component was the virtual monopoly that the peace movement enjoyed on opposition to the double-track decision until 1983, because all major parties supported the missile decision and a Social Democratic chancellor had instigated it. The emerging Green Party capitalized greatly on the missile issue and was helped into the Bundestag by peace movement supporters. The Green Party's rise occurred parallel to that of the peace movement, however, and did not detract from the movement's hold on the issue or co-opt its followers until well past its high point in 1983.

The fifth political opportunity component is found in the area of political culture, where a considerable protest potential susceptible to

---

45. Eichenberg, *Public Opinion and National Security,* 78 and chap. 3 passim.

46. Ibid., 111.

47. Wolfgang Donsbach, Hans Matthias Kepplinger, and Elisabeth Noelle-Neumann, "West Germans' Perceptions of NATO and the Warsaw Pact: Long-Term Content Analysis of *Der Spiegel* and Trends in Public Opinion," in *Debating National Security: The Public Dimension,* ed. Hans Rattinger and Don Munton (Frankfurt: Peter Lang, 1991), 239–68, here 243–50.

mobilization had been created by the "new social movements" of the 1970s. Both public acceptance of protest and actual participation in protest grew by leaps and bounds in the 1970s. The peace movement came toward the end of a long wave of mobilization around many "new politics" themes, in particular ecology and feminism. When it became salient in the early 1980s, however, peace took top priority as the protest issue of choice, easily outranking potential competitors. Antinuclear power mobilization, for example, had already enjoyed several peak phases, in particular in Brokdorf (1977) and Gorleben (1979). Its adherents were effectively siphoned off by the peace issue until later in the 1980s.[48]

Finally, the Schmidt government had already aroused opposition across a number of the political fronts in the 1970s—economic policy, civil rights, ecology, and so on. Indeed, the entire Social Democratic policy package, based on economic growth, social justice, and "peace politics," was under severe stress. The SPD's share of the vote in federal elections had already reached its high point in 1972, declining under Schmidt at the national level and in a number of state-level elections.[49] For the constituencies already disappointed by, and indeed mobilized against, a number of Social Democratic policies, it was not difficult to march against Schmidt's defense policy as well.

The double-track decision provided the spark that ignited protest unprecedented in scale or scope in West German history. The 1980s movement brought together the largest extraparliamentary coalition of political activists ever to launch sustained protest. It also spread farthest into the mainstream populace, in terms of both passive support and grassroots participation. The 1980s movement brought together a greater profusion of arguments against government defense policy than any of its predecessors. In part, this reflected the growth of a new ideological resource called *peace research.*

Peace Research: A New Ideological Resource for the 1980s Movement

Like any other social movement, the peace movement struggled to define the missile issue on its own terms and to change the prevailing political discourse on security and peace. Like previous peace movements, the 1980s movement brought many broader issues to the discussion of peace, ranging this time from religion to ecology and feminism, and thus expanded the missile issue beyond the range of military and political concerns discussed

---

48. Joppke, *Mobilizing against Nuclear Power,* 130; Rob Burns and Wilfried van der Will, *Protest and Democracy in West Germany* (New York: St. Martin's Press, 1988), chap. 5.
49. Chandler, "Party System Transformations in the Federal Republic of Germany."

by the government. Indeed, the ideological resources of the 1980s movement proved more diverse than ever before and reflected a larger and more varied coalition of core peace groups than ever before.

Unlike previous West German peace movements, the 1980s movement took advantage of an immense additional resource: access to "alternative" security policy arguments offered by "counterexperts." In the 1950s, peace protestors feared the effects of NATO membership on German reunification and decried the potential horrors of nuclear war. They did not, however, delve far into military strategy. In contrast, the 1980s peace movement used military-strategic arguments to a much greater extent and to much greater advantage. While the argumentation of individual protestors and groups ranged from the simplistic to the sophisticated, the movement as a whole could take credit for a relatively coherent (if highly controversial) view of concrete defense issues.

In its struggle to influence public opinion, the peace movement had to be able to counter the proponents of the double-track decision, in part by justifying opposition to the new missiles in terms of the arguments in their favor. In order to counter charges of ignorance in security matters, the movement challenged "the establishment" by debating the issue in the latter's terms, categories such as threat assessment, weapons technology, and deterrence strategy. Whereas in the 1950s the movement had been largely unable to debate the government in military-strategic terms, in the 1980s it had the capacity to do so.

The peace movement prided itself on its "counterexpertise" and explicitly aimed to create a "counterpublic" *(Gegenöffentlichkeit)* adhering to its views and to thereby break the government's hold on public opinion. In this area the movement's main resource was "critical peace research" *(Friedensforschung)*. Having begun their work in the early 1970s, by 1980 peace researchers had developed a comprehensive alternative strategic analysis. The peace movement adopted these arguments as its analytic foundation. "Critical" peace researchers also disseminated their ideas via the book market and discussion fora sponsored by movement groups.

Ironically, the social-liberal coalition itself launched and funded much of this peace research, thereby sowing the seeds for the critiques that would later be directed against its own policies. Chancellor Brandt and Federal President Gustav Heinemann initiated government support for peace research in 1969.[50] In 1970 and 1971, five new peace research insti-

---

50. Karl Kaiser, *Friedensforschung in der Bundesrepublik* (Göttingen: Vandenhoeck and Ruprecht, 1970), 11, 12.

tutes or foundations were founded,[51] among which the *Deutsche Gesellschaft für Friedens- und Konfliktforschung* allocated twenty-two million deutsche marks of largely government funds to peace research projects in the course of the 1970s. Each major church also had an associated peace research institute.[52] One branch of peace research grew especially rapidly in the 1970s, a radical version that dubbed itself critical peace research and found its way into the broader "critical" intelligentsia on the left through a variety of avenues. Peace research findings were published by a number of magazines and publishing houses, ranging from *Der Spiegel* and the SPD's monthly journal *Neue Gesellschaft* to paperback series from Rowohlt Verlag and Suhrkamp Verlag.[53]

Peace research was a science with a mission—discovering the causes of war and the conditions of peace.[54] Peace research was a politicized science dedicated to making war obsolete,[55] eliminating it as "politics by other means."[56] According to its proponents, critical peace research differed from the more traditional study of conflict and arms control, because it hoped to eliminate the power structures within society that cause war. Traditional study of conflict, critical peace researchers felt, tried to establish *rules* of conflict, accepting the existence of nuclear weapons and trying to tame the arms race by rationalizing the system of mutual threat. In contrast, critical peace research strove to get to the root of the arms race and to overcome the system altogether.[57] Critical peace research thus represented an attempt to rationalize state relations in an age of nuclear weapons, under the assumption that atomic weapons had fundamentally

---

51. The five institutes are the Deutsche Gesellschaft für Friedens- und Konfliktforschung, the Hessische Stiftung Friedens- und Konfliktforschung, the Max Planck Institut zur Erforschung der Lebensbedingungen der wissenschaftlich-technischen Welt, the private Berghof Stiftung für Konfliktforschung, and the Institut für Friedensforschung und Sicherheitspolitik an der Universität Hamburg—listed in Herf, *War By Other Means*, 84, 85.

52. These are the Protestant (EKD) Forschungsstätte der Evangelischen Studiengemeinschaft and the Catholic Katholischer Arbeitskreis Entwicklung und Frieden—listed in Hermann Pfister and Alfred Walter, *Friedensforschung in der Bundesrepublik Deutschland* (Waldkirch: Pädagogische Informationen, 1975), 61–67, 135–41.

53. Herf, *War By Other Means*, 85. See also his extended discussion of peace research in his chap. 6.

54. Johan Galtung, "Friedensforschung: Vergangenheitserfahrung und Zukunftsperspektiven," in *Strukturelle Gewalt* (Reinbek: Rowohlt, 1975), 37–60, here 41.

55. Ekkehard Krippendorff, "Staatliche Organisation und Krieg," in *Friedensforschung und Gesellschaftskritik*, ed. Dieter Senghaas (Munich: Carl Hanser Verlag, 1970), 23–39, here 27.

56. Dieter Senghaas, "Einleitung," in *Friedensforschung und Gesellschaftskritik*, ed. Dieter Senghaas (Munich: Carl Hanser Verlag, 1970), 14.

57. Ekkehard Krippendorff, "Einleitung," in *Friedensforschung* (Cologne: Kiepenheuer and Witsch, 1968), 15.

changed the relationship of war to politics.[58] Peace research, moreover, found the major causes of international conflict mostly in domestic political and economic structures, rather than in conflicts of interest between states or shifting balances of power.

In addition to general theoretical writings, many peace researchers wrote specific critiques of the double-track decision, which became the basis of the peace movement's military-strategic critique. The peace movement's argumentation was, however, by no means unified. Three major lines emerged: a left-wing social democratic line; a more radical critique by Moscow-oriented communists; and, finally, an even more radical, but different, critique centered around the Green Party. The left-wing social democratic version was perhaps the most complex and the most finely argued, and it was certainly closest to the view of the movement's nonactivist "sympathizers" in the broader public on several key points.

The Peace Movement's Critique of the Double-Track Decision: Soviet Intentions and the Military Balance

Although the peace movement was often called "soft on communism," it in fact (apart from its communist minority) professed to reject communism as a political system, which, however, did not keep some groups from wanting other sorts of radical change. Many peace movement moderates (Social Democrats and others) explicitly professed support for Western democratic values and the German political system. Communism was not compatible with democracy and therefore not acceptable, according to William Borm, an FDP parliamentarian and prominent member of the peace movement.[59] According to a representative of the Gustav-Heinemann-Initiative, the GHI regarded the Soviet Union as a totalitarian regime, whereas it fundamentally accepted Western values and the German political system.[60]

Peace movement moderates often criticized the Soviet and Eastern European political systems. For example, a booklet published by the Jungdemokraten viewed the Polish Solidarity movement as an outgrowth of defects in the communist system itself, ranging from misguided policies to the government's ideological obduracy.[61] Most of the peace movement

---

58. Gertrud Kuehnlein, *Die Entwicklung der kritischen Friedensforschung in der Bundesrepublik Deutschland* (Frankfurt: Haag and Herchen, 1978), 10–15.

59. William Borm, "Frieden ist machbar—wir mischen uns ein!" in *Frieden in Deutschland,* ed. Hans Pestalozzi et al. (Munich: Wilhelm Goldmann Verlag, 1982), 82–87, here 84.

60. Interview with a GHI representative.

61. Jungdemokraten, *Für Entspannung, Abrüstung, internationale Solidarität,* pamphlet (Bonn, Sept. 1982).

saw the Soviet Union as hegemonical and imperialist and wanted to keep West Germany free of Soviet influence. West Germany had to assert itself against Marxist-Leninist ideology and Soviet military power, according to Karsten Voigt, a prominent Social Democratic peace movement activist.[62] Peace movement moderates even felt that the Soviet SS-20s represented a means of pressuring Europe and that West Germany needed an adequate defensive capability.

These views notwithstanding, however, the entire peace movement viewed the Soviet Union as a defensive power. Here, of course, the movement differed from more conservative views, which held that the Soviets were fundamentally expansive, driven by traditional Russian imperialism and/or an inherently aggressive ideology. For the peace movement, the Soviet threat could easily be contained without additional weapons, since the USSR had neither interest in war nor the capacity to hold European territory.

According to a Jungdemokraten representative, the Soviet Union pursued no grand offensive goals but instead wanted to prevent war.[63] Or, as the prominent Social Democrat Erhard Eppler stressed, the Soviet government depended on Western Europe economically as a trading partner and politically as a brake on American policy. Since, Eppler argued, the Soviets would gain nothing from a European nuclear desert, which would extend to Moscow, a Soviet invasion of West Germany was unlikely.[64] Furthermore, the Soviets would not have the capacity to hold conquered territory because of fundamental weaknesses of the Soviet system. Eppler noted that the attractiveness of communist ideology was declining, Soviet industry was not internationally competitive, and the Soviets already had too much trouble with their Eastern European satellites to rule Western Europe.[65]

How then did the peace movement account for Soviet hegemony over Eastern Europe and the invasion of Afghanistan in 1979? The movement viewed the Soviets as conservative hegemons, anxious to preserve their own sphere but far from desiring expansion beyond it. As a superpower intervening in its sphere of influence, the USSR did not differ greatly from the United States, which also intervened in places like Central America. (Here, of course, the peace movement diverged from the more conservative

---

62. Karsten Voigt, "Dem Frieden dienen und die Abrüstung fördern," *Frankfurter Allgemeine Zeitung,* 9 Jan. 1985.

63. Interview with a Jungdemokraten representative.

64. Erhard Eppler, "Europa—Kriegsschauplatz oder Brücke zwischen Ost und West, Nord und Süd," in *Frieden in Deutschland,* ed. Hans Pestalozzi et al. (Munich: Wilhelm Goldmann Verlag, 1982), 68–76, here 73.

65. Erhard Eppler, "Deutschland—Vorfeld oder Schlachtfeld?" in *Frieden ohne Waffen?* ed. Josef Joffe (Hamburg: Zeit Verlag, 1981), 73–81, here 75.

view of American foreign policy. NATO supporters viewed the peace movement's tendency to "equate" superpower intervention as unfounded and close to blasphemy.) Just as the Soviet Union wanted the Polish Solidarity movement suppressed to maintain the communist regime, the invasion of Afghanistan also represented Soviet defense of its sphere of influence, to which Afghanistan had belonged since the early twentieth century. Social Democrat Erhard Eppler condemned the invasion of Afghanistan as a violation of international law but professed understanding for Soviet difficulties caused by the ineptness of Afghanistan's communist regime and the Moslem reaction within the USSR. According to Eppler, the Soviets used military force to assert their political interests, which did not qualitatively differ from American involvement in Vietnam.[66] The peace movement also regarded the Soviets as having special security needs derived from numerous invasions (including two at German hands), which explained Eastern Europe's satellite status and Soviet arms levels.[67]

When it came to considerations of the military balance, peace movement moderates sharply contradicted conservative assertions that Soviet superiority in weaponry required additional Western force levels. They admitted that Soviet SS-20s posed a military threat to West Germany,[68] but they denied that NATO needed to station Pershing II and cruise missiles in response. First, the Soviet SS-20s did not subject Europe to blackmail as NATO argued. The Soviet Union was too weak economically to blackmail Europe, and in any event, West Germany's NATO membership guaranteed German defense even without new missiles. American soldiers in West Germany prevented blackmail, regardless of arms levels, because any military intervention would pit the Soviets immediately against the Americans.[69] NATO thus did not need exact equality in soldiers or weapons with the Warsaw Pact to avoid blackmail. Given the risks of nuclear escalation, partial military superiorities could not be used for political blackmail.[70]

Second, whereas NATO argued that Soviet superiority in conven-

---

66. Ibid., 75.

67. Karl-Heinz Koppe, "Nato-Beschluß—Afghanistan—und wie geht es weiter?" *Neue Gesellschaft* 27, no. 3 (1980), 254–58, here 257. The Jungdemokraten attribute Soviet military strength to Western attempts to reverse the Russian Revolution. See Jungdemokraten Nordrhein-Westfalen, "Entwurf eines neuen Grundsatzprogramms der Jungdemokraten," *Tendenz* (periodical of the Jungdemokraten) 3 (Mar. 1984): 16.

68. Wolfgang Biermann, "'Nachrüstung' als Übergang von der Strategie der atomaren Abschreckung zur Strategie der Führbarkeit des Atomkrieges," *Neue Gesellschaft* 28, no. 5 (1981): 416–23.

69. Interviews with Liberale Demokraten, GHI, and IFIAS representatives.

70. Voigt, "Dem Frieden dienen und die Abrüstung fördern."

tional forces required strong nuclear forces to deter attack, the peace movement denied that the Soviets had either a conventional or a nuclear advantage over NATO, even without new missiles. The movement drew particularly on peace researcher Dieter Lutz's studies of the military balance.[71]

Lutz asserted that NATO's traditional means of assessing Soviet military capacities (e.g., comparisons of military spending levels, weapons systems, and troop deployments) painted a false picture of Soviet conventional superiority. His own comparisons of the two alliances suggested that if France was included in the calculation, NATO actually had more manpower than the Warsaw Pact. Furthermore, training of Warsaw Pact soldiers was relatively poor, especially in complicated weapons systems. Soviet divisions in Eastern Europe maintained high readiness, but Soviet divisions at home did not. While the Warsaw Pact had numerical superiority in tanks, many were too old to function well. NATO, in contrast, had good antitank defenses. After similar comparisons of air and sea power, Lutz refuted NATO's thesis of dangerous Warsaw Pact superiority in conventional areas. NATO had technological superiority in almost all types of conventional weaponry, which easily made up for nominal imbalances resulting from strictly numerical comparisons. Thus despite nominal Warsaw Pact superiority in some areas, it did not have the 300 percent superiority needed for an acceptable risk level for the attacker.[72]

In *Weltkrieg wider Willen?* Lutz made similar arguments about nuclear forces in Europe.[73] Arguing that the balance of medium-range nuclear weapons could only be judged in terms of the overall nuclear balance and broader strategic context, Lutz stressed the additional importance of qualitative factors, such as reliability, penetration of enemy defense, survivability in enemy first strikes, and so on. His comparisons of nuclear force levels revealed no strong Warsaw Pact advantage when qualitative factors were taken into account.

According to Lutz, NATO enjoyed numerical superiority in

71. Dieter Lutz's *Weltkrieg wider Willen? Die Nuklearwaffen in und für Europa* (Reinbek: Rowohlt, 1981) was his most important study for these purposes. By 1982, twenty thousand copies had been printed. Several peace movement groups used Lutz's studies in condensed versions as brochures. Lutz himself authored one, *Besitzt die Sowjetunion in der konventionellen Rüstung eine militärische Überlegenheit?* booklet of the Jungdemokraten, 6th ed. (Düsseldorf: Nordrhein-Westfalen Landesverband, n.d.).

72. Lutz, *Besitzt die Sowjetunion in der konventionellen Rüstung eine militärische Überlegenheit?* 14–80.

73. Dieter Lutz, *Weltkrieg wider Willen?* See also Dieter Lutz, *Das militärische Kräfteverhältnis im Bereich der euronuclearen Waffensystems* (Bonn: Jungdemokraten, n.d.). The booklet was originally an IFSH research report (Institut für Friedensforschung und Sicherheitspolitik-Forschungsbericht, no. 12), released in Oct. 1979.

battlefield nuclear weapons and rough parity in mid-range tactical nuclear forces. In both cases, NATO enjoyed an advantage when qualitative factors were considered. With regard to long-range tactical nuclear weapons (the area covered by the double-track decision), the Warsaw Pact enjoyed numerical superiority, but qualitative advantages of Western nuclear systems and bombers compensated almost completely for the purely numerical superiority of Warsaw Pact systems. No reason existed, therefore, to assume that NATO was militarily inferior. (Lutz included British and French forces in his assessment of the European nuclear military balance. This inclusion was highly controversial since NATO left these systems out of its comparisons. Lutz and others in the peace movement maintained, however, that the British and French forces would be available to NATO in emergencies.)

Across the board, then, Lutz denied the existence of a European "missile gap," an argument NATO used to justify the double-track decision. Moreover, he argued, the timing of the new missiles' development suggested that the Soviet SS-20s became a convenient excuse to station the new weapons. Pershing II development started in 1974, before American satellites discovered the SS-20 in 1975. Cruise missiles were tested successfully in 1976, with no corresponding Soviet systems yet in place. Thus, Lutz maintained, justifying the double-track decision as a reaction to Soviet SS-20s was a typical case of ex post facto rationalization.[74]

Several peace movement groups came independently to Lutz's conclusion that the military balance was not unfavorable to NATO. The left-wing Social Democratic group the Initiative für Frieden, internationalen Ausgleich und Sicherheit (IFIAS) reproduced documents from the American and West German defense departments that showed—on balance, if not in every category—that the United States generally enjoyed superiority or parity with the Soviet Union. An American chart showed that NATO had consistently outspent the Warsaw Pact since 1965, even excluding the costs of the Vietnam War. A German chart likewise showed American superiority or parity with the Soviet Union in all weapons categories except for five, including, admittedly, land-based medium-range missiles.[75] The Jungdemokraten too spoke of a "myth of threat" maintained by the government to give arms programs more appeal. When a new arms buildup was imminent (e.g., the double-track decision), reports abounded on Warsaw Pact strength. At the same time, the opposite was

---

74. Lutz, *Kräfteverhältnis*, 32.

75. U.S. Dept. of Defense, "U.S. Military Posture, FY 1984" and German Defense Dept., "Programm für Forschung, Entwicklung und Beschaffung" (1983), both reproduced in Initiative für Frieden, internationalen Ausgleich und Sicherheit [IFIAS], *Frieden und Abrüstung* 10, Bonn, 1985: 56–61.

maintained in other quarters. Thus in February 1980, U.S. Defense Minister Harold Brown told the Foreign Affairs Committee that American arms were neither inferior nor ineffective and that efficiency in weapons technology had to be considered when making numerical comparisons.[76]

The peace movement thus denied the existence of any serious missile gap and maintained that overall American-Soviet parity constituted a perfectly adequate answer to any nominal regional imbalance. As the Jungdemokraten noted, the Soviet Union had medium-range missiles for twenty years.[77] Moreover, the German government itself maintained that the principle of "equal security for all" governed Alliance relations. Since an attack against Europe would also be an attack against the United States, an aggressor would face retaliation by all NATO's means—including American intercontinental nuclear weapons.[78] As long as this principle governed Alliance defense, numerical regional imbalances generated by the SS-20s posed no grave threat, given the overall balance of nuclear and conventional forces. Parity weapon for weapon was not essential.

Karsten Voigt of the IFIAS expanded on this idea by emphasizing deterrence capacity. A stable military balance existed when both sides had equal capacity to defend their own alliance partners. Additional arms only made sense if the Warsaw Pact acquired new capabilities for military action that NATO could no longer deter. Imbalances with respect to individual weapons categories did not necessarily destroy the balance of deterrence capacity. Quoting Christoph Bertram to the effect that the balance necessary for deterrence still held despite the recent Soviet arms buildup, Voigt denied the need for further Western acquisitions.[79]

The Peace Movement's Critique of the Double-Track Decision: Deterrence, the Arms Race, and American Strategies

The new missiles' mere superfluity, however, would not have produced the fear of war or sense of personal threat and victimization *(Betroffenheit)* characteristic of the 1980s movement. Indeed, for the peace movement the proposed missiles were not merely redundant tools of a deterrence strategy that had assured European security, however tenuous, for the past thirty

---

,76. Jungdemokraten, *Für Entspannung, Abrüstung,* 5.

77. Jungdemokraten, *Tendenz: Zeitung der Deutschen Jungdemokraten* (Bonn, [early 1982]), 2.

78. Jungdemokraten, *Hier täuscht die Bundesregierung sich und/oder ihre Bürger,* pamphlet (Bonn, 1981), 3.

79. Karsten Voigt, "Erweiterung der Konzeption des militärischen Gleichgewichts," *Neue Gesellschaft* 27, no. 11 (1980): 956–63, here 957.

years. Instead, the new missiles posed a mortal threat. In important new ways, they were actually going to decrease European security by exacerbating the inherent dangers of deterrence, stimulating the arms race, facilitating aggressive new American/NATO strategies, and thus increasing the risks of catastrophic war on European soil.

Much of the peace movement's anxiety stemmed from its critical relationship to deterrence, absorbed largely from peace research critiques.[80] In the movement's eyes, deterrence had led inexorably to the arms race. The traditional concept of military balance considered equilibrium possible only when opposing sides enjoyed equality of force in every conceivable situation. With each side seeking balance in every sort of weapon, however, the arms race threatened to elude political control.[81] Even détente had not brought the arms race under control, especially since failure to ratify SALT II prevented negotiations on SALT III. Instead, arms levels were rising during a return to worldwide confrontation.[82]

In the movement's eyes, deterrence had acquired a dangerous new source of instability by the early 1980s, as qualitative improvements in weapons technology now undermined its very foundations, turning it on its head. New weapons technology encouraged a self-propelling dynamic that led to confrontation even in the absence of hostile intentions. On the one hand, deterrence's credibility depended on the high probability of nuclear weapons actually being used if deterrence failed. Thus selectively usable bombs with relatively little collateral damage would actually deter the potential adversary more than immensely destructive weapons. Since such "holocaust weapons" deter the user as much as the potential adver-

---

80. The most far-reaching critique of deterrence came from Dieter Senghaas, one of the earliest German peace researchers. See Dieter Senghaas, *Abschreckung und Frieden* (Frankfurt: Europaeische Verlagsanstalt, 1969). He argued that the world is suspended in a state of "organized peacelessness." Deterrence tries to prevent war through the "rational" manipulation of violence. However, this "rationality" turns out to be more apparent than real. Nuclear weapons are too destructive to be rationally integrated into a military strategy as instruments of actual war, in the Clausewitzian sense of "politics by other means." Instead, deterrence takes over the minds of those who purportedly manipulate it, so that they see the world only through its premises. Deterrence is not just a pattern of potential aggression and corresponding reaction; rather it largely consists of unilateral action that takes place regardless of an enemy's actual aggressiveness. The enemy can never prove its peaceful intentions even if they exist, since deterrence dismisses as deceit any enemy action that contradicts previous assumptions. Deterrence thus becomes a self-fulfilling, though pseudorational, policy. Deterrence destabilizes international relations in the long run, since it fuels the arms race and has failed to eliminate force.

81. Eppler, "Deutschland," 73–80, here 78, 79.

82. Wolfgang Biermann, "Positionen der SPD zur Friedenspolitik und zum Verhältnis von SPD und Friedensbewegung," in *Frieden in Deutschland,* ed. Hans Pestalozzi et al. (Munich: Wilhelm Goldmann Verlag, 1982), 92–101, here 93.

sary, less destructive weapons lower the threshold for use and therefore make them more effective deterrence instruments. So technological refinements during the 1970s that made weapons systems selectively usable, and thus better instruments of actual war, would seem to strengthen deterrence.

On the other hand, the peace movement argued, the lower the threshold of use, the greater the danger that a crisis situation would get out of control. If one side feared the selective use of nuclear weapons, it would be more willing to preclude this through preventive strikes. Selectively usable nuclear weapons like Pershing II, cruise missiles, Trident II, MX, or Midgetman thus in fact undermined the very foundations of deterrence. Such weapons were also being developed on the Warsaw Pact side. In Europe, these developments were manageable as long as détente and arms control between NATO and the Warsaw Pact were part of everyday political life. In the context of renewed superpower confrontation, however, refinements in deterrence that permitted limited nuclear war necessarily endangered the security of Europe.[83] Weapons that were supposed to deter could also be used for war fighting, thereby making catastrophic war more likely.

For the peace movement, this new instability became all the more serious in the context of new American/NATO war-fighting strategies. In the movement's eyes, the United States had turned away from détente and military balance as the foundation of defense policy.[84] Reagan in particular had adopted a "policy of strength," and American officials mused about the "wageability" of nuclear war. Carter's Presidential Directive 59 of 1980 meant that Soviet military centers would become the targets of American nuclear weapons (a war-fighting strategy), rather than cities or industrial centers (a deterrence strategy) as before. The failure to ratify SALT II was an early sign of this shift and was followed by a massive arms buildup.[85] The American move toward military supremacy was going to

---

83. Wolfgang Biermann, "Genfer INF-Verhandlungen und Friedensbewegung," *Neue Gesellschaft* 30, no. 9 (1983): 854–58, here 855–56. See also Alfred Mechtesheimer, *Rüstung und Frieden* (Munich: Wirtschaftsverlag Langen-Müller/Herbig, 1982); and Karsten Voigt, "Riskien neuer Waffentechnologien," *Neue Gesellschaft* 26, no. 2 (1979): 98–102, here 99–102.

84. Polls found evidence of the peace movement's tendency to "equate" the superpowers. Both movement supporters and nonsupporters agreed in their negative assessment of the Soviet Union's foreign policy methods. But activists, and to a lesser extent movement sympathizers, said that the United States also showed the same negative traits as the Soviet Union: it intervened in other countries' internal affairs, threatened world peace, saw war as an instrument of policy, and propelled the arms race forward. See Sozialwissenschaftliches Institut Nowak und Sörgel, "Sicherheitspolitik," 9–35.

85. Jungdemokraten, "Hier täuscht," 6, 8, 23, 25.

destabilize deterrence by upsetting the balance between the superpowers, launching a new cold war, and giving the Soviet Union free rein to arm as it liked.[86]

In the context of these changes in American policy, the double-track decision took on a sinister meaning for the peace movement. Although the United States initially was not keen to station new missiles in Europe, with Reagan's election the missiles became embedded in the new strategy of supremacy. Their technical capabilities rendered them useful instruments of actual war fighting. Because their quick flight time reduced the Soviets' warning and thus their ability to launch a second strike, the Pershing IIs had first-strike capability. The cruise missile's capacity to evade radar enhanced its military usefulness despite its slow flying speed. Both missiles had an important role in the new strategy, because their ability to destroy the military and economic centers of the Soviet Union gave the United States a chance to emerge victorious.[87]

For the peace movement, these changes in weapons technology and military strategy created a strong sense of victimization. Europe became the potential victim not of the "enemy," the Soviet Union, but of the supposed friend, America, and its military strategies.[88] An American victory in nuclear war would inevitably mean Europe's destruction, the movement argued. The double-track decision expressed an objective American interest in decoupling the risks of a nuclear war from its own territory, thereby acquiring a strategic advantage over the Soviets. The new medium-range missiles were theater nuclear forces for the United States, whereas they represented strategic weapons to the Soviet Union. The United States

---

86. Interview with GHI and IFIAS representatives.

87. Interview with a Liberale Demokraten representative. See also Dieter Lutz, *Das militärische Kräfteverhältnis im Bereich der euronuklearen Waffensysteme,* 11, for the technical qualities that give the Pershing II first-strike capability.

88. Although mildly expressed here, some of the peace movement's language took on a decidedly anti-American tone, going beyond criticism of contemporaneous American foreign policy to intense suspicions of American motives and wholesale condemnation of American politics and the American economic system. Some suggest that the anti-Americanism of the German peace movement outstripped that of any other European movement because of the unique complexity of the German-American relationship. As Markovits and Gorski observe: "Beyond the manifest level of German-American relations hovers a submerged iceberg of domination, submission, gratitude, jealousy, overprotection, fear of abandonment, friendship and rivalry which is much more pronounced in this relationship than in any other the United States has had in postwar Europe. Americanism and anti-Americanism have attained a qualitatively different meaning (both positive and negative) in the Federal Republic from elsewhere in Europe . . . [because of] perceptions in the Federal Republic that—at least until October 3, 1990—it suffered from a deficit in political sovereignty, especially vis-à-vis the United States." See Markovits and Gorski, *The German Left,* 26.

could inflict strategic damage to the Soviet Union through missiles based in Europe without the Soviets having any corresponding capability vis-à-vis the United States. Thus even without suggesting that NATO had aggressive intentions, the new missiles represented a new quality in NATO's deterrence strategy.[89]

This situation posed a grave threat to European security and even to its very survival. Land-based Pershing II and cruise missiles were vulnerable to Soviet attack and hence could not serve as second-strike weapons. Precisely because their only potential use was for first strikes, the missiles invited a Soviet preventive strike against them. American medium-range missiles in Europe put the Soviet Union in a situation akin to the one faced by the United States in the Cuban missile crisis. The double-track decision flew in the face of the agreement between Kennedy and Khrushchev not to station medium-range missiles in territories immediately adjacent to either superpower, in order to eliminate the possibility of surprise attacks.[90] Thus it was obvious that these missiles would become targets of a Soviet strike. Since the American reaction to Soviet missiles in Cuba had almost brought the world to World War III, the danger inherent in the proposed medium-range deployments was obvious.[91]

The peace movement viewed the new missiles as part of the larger "craziness" of deterrence, a system that could potentially fail spectacularly. Peace groups argued that although deterrence had worked in the past, there was no guarantee for its future performance. If deterrence failed, the new medium-range missiles were so deadly that military conflict could only lead to catastrophic destruction of both sides.[92] The overabundance of arms threatened to destroy what it was supposed to defend, while 10 percent of the weapons already in stock would suffice to deter.[93]

Thus prevention of war was Germany's main task and was much more worrisome than a possible Warsaw Pact attack.[94] However, in the age of deterrence, war prevention faced numerous difficulties that the new missiles would only exacerbate. The danger of an irrational decision was

---

89. Wolfgang Biermann, "Nachrüstung," 418–19.

90. Ibid., 423. See also Christoph Strässer, "Der Krefelder Appell," in *Frieden in Deutschland,* ed. Hans Pestalozzi et al. (Munich: Wilhelm Goldmann Verlag, 1982), 87–92, here 90.

91. Jungdemokraten, *Für Entspannung, Abrüstung,* 6.

92. Interview with a Liberale Demokraten representative.

93. Dieter Lattmann, "Die Formelsprache der Rüstungspolitiker: Pazifismus als Kampfwort," in *Frieden in Deutschland,* ed. Hans Pestalozzi et al. (Munich: Wilhelm Goldmann Verlag, 1982), 76–82.

94. Gerd Krell, "Die Entwicklung des Sicherheitsbegriffs," *Neue Gesellschaft* 26, no. 10 (Oct. 1979): 906–10, here 906.

always inherent in crisis situations.[95] If the new missiles were deployed, the Soviet Union would have to launch a preemptive strike against them in a crisis, and the United States would have to act even faster to prevent this preemptive strike. Europe faced unprecedented danger in times of crisis. In addition to the threat of aggressive intentions, Europe could now be destroyed through miscalculations on either side.[96]

The Peace Movement's Alternative Defense Proposals

The peace movement did not rest its case with a critique of the new missiles. On the contrary, it outlined a number of alternatives to NATO strategies for the defense of Europe. Although all of these alternatives departed considerably from NATO strategy, they nonetheless exhibited considerable variety. All called for eliminating nuclear weapons in Germany and abandoning nuclear deterrence. They also implied an eventual dissolution of NATO and the Warsaw Pact. The most moderate proposals suggested a zone of military disengagement in Central Europe and a neutral status for this zone, without necessarily eliminating conventional defense of East and West. More far-reaching alternatives suggested massive changes in conventional defense as well, ranging from strictly defensive weapons, to civilian resistance, to unilateral disarmament. Although none of the alternative proposals could claim to provide risk-free defense, all argued that the risks inherent in their approaches were smaller than the risks of continued reliance on nuclear deterrence in a bipolar world order.

Proposals for military disengagement of NATO and the Warsaw Pact harked back to similar proposals from the 1950s. Disengagement would rest on three key elements: reduction of conventional arms, elimination of nuclear weapons, and withdrawal of foreign troops from a designated zone running the length of the border between East and West. In principle, each European country could remain a member of its military alliance, and the alliances would not necessarily be required to restructure their armed forces beyond disengagement. In practice, however, disengagement would remove West Germany as the cornerstone of NATO in Europe.

According to its proponents, disengagement had numerous advantages. It would help the superpowers resolve conflicts of interests peacefully, would create a larger role for nonmilitary aspects of security policy, and would help end the arms race. The European states would escape from superpower attempts to wage nuclear war on European soil. Conventional

---

95. Karsten Voigt, "Von der Konfrontation zur Sicherheitspartnershaft," *Neue Gesellschaft* 29, no. 4 (1982): 310–15, here 314.

96. Wolfgang Biermann, "Nachrüstung," 416–22, here 418, 419. See also Jungdemokraten, *Tendenz*, 2.

war would remain a possibility, but nuclear-free zones would facilitate East-West reconciliation and thus reduce this risk. At the same time, each country could remain under the protection of its respective alliance and thus avoid utter defenselessness.[97]

In principle, military disengagement would not require German withdrawal from NATO, but disengagement would reduce the European role in deterrence strategy. Given the political dynamics of the cold war, neutralism would be the natural complement of disengagement. Whereas disengagement alone would change the politics of the two alliances but not the alliances themselves, neutralism would remove key members from their respective alliances and might well result in the alliances' very dissolution. Proponents of neutralism suggested a neutral belt encompassing, at a minimum, both Germanies, Sweden, Switzerland, Austria, and Yugoslavia, and potentially Europe from Portugal to Poland's eastern border. This zone would belong to neither military alliance and would be free of nuclear weapons. The military blocs would lose their opportunities for "nuclear contact" in Europe, much of their European territory, and potentially their reason for being. In contrast to more conservative opinion, proponents of neutralism denied that it would make Germany dependent on the Soviet Union and maintained instead that Germany would gain room to maneuver. In any event the risk of "Finlandization" was less serious than being trapped in a nuclear exchange.[98]

The notion of "strictly defensive defense" was conceived as an interim step toward general disarmament and nonviolent conflict resolution. In particular, it represented a political approach to security, rather than a military-technical one. Western renunciation of nuclear deterrence would reduce Soviet perceptions of hostile encirclement, thereby breaking the mutual perceptions of threat fueling the arms race. The Soviets would then presumably reduce their own nuclear arsenal, and Europe would be spared the threat of nuclear strikes. Europe would remain defended by conventional means, although renouncing tactical nuclear weapons would require changes in military strategy. The armed forces would be deployed in small, mobile units, relying primarily on weapons without offensive capabilities (e.g., antitank weapons rather than tanks, and planes designed to defend against incoming aircraft rather than bombers). They would be organized with a view toward nonviolent conflict prevention rather than defense oriented to worst-case scenarios, with its military-technical thinking and arms acquisitions. Although West Germany could switch to defensive defense unilaterally, other countries on both sides would probably fol-

---

97. Komitee für Grundrechte und Demokratie, *Frieden mit anderen Waffen: Fünf Vorschläge zu einer alternativen Sicherheitspolitik* (Reinbek: Rowohlt, 1981), 120–30.

98. Ibid., 131–57.

low suit. Indeed, defensive defense would loosen the military blocs, without presupposing their dissolution. Such efforts would be embedded in a multipronged foreign policy, including détente, economic cooperation with Eastern Europe, an ecology-oriented economy, and development aid aimed at improving the whole populace's standard of living.[99]

The notion of "civilian defense" assumed that a neutral Germany could not really defend itself by conventional means against an aggressor willing to use all available weapons but would only be able to wage a "protest war" against an irresistible force (similar to the Norwegians holding out for twenty-two days against the superior German army in 1940). However, reliance on nuclear deterrence meant the possibility of total destruction. The notion of civilian defense did not pretend to be riskless but hoped to offer an alternative to annihilation or capitulation. Civilian defense would consist of resistance against occupying forces, ranging from small-scale individual action to mass strikes, demonstrations, and sit-ins by masses of unarmed civilians, all aiming to undermine the morale of the occupiers. Civil disobedience and noncooperation would be the most important "weapons" of civilian defense, while demonstrations of humanity vis-à-vis the occupying forces would encourage the latter to rethink the occupation.[100]

The most radical alternative defense policy rested on the premise that war prevention required complete, unilateral disarmament. Admitting that getting rid of individual firearms would be unrealistic, proponents of disarmament concentrated on eliminating "only" nuclear, biological, chemical, and conventional weapons of mass destruction. Given their quantity, their place in NATO's military strategy, and the military's central position in mainstream politics, disarmament would never be possible without a massive popular movement on its behalf. Precisely such a movement would ensure that a disarmed Germany would not be left defenseless against its armed neighbors. Instead, disarmament in Germany would unleash a rethinking in the Eastern bloc, making it harder to justify high arms levels there. Unilateral disarmament would never be a national end in itself; rather it would be part of a multinational process of change. But, its proponents argued, one country had to begin, before it was too late.[101]

---

99. Ibid., 158–81.
100. Ibid., 182–204.
101. Ibid., 205–20.

CHAPTER 5

The 1980s: Strength and Diversity through Ideological Resources and Organizational Innovation

Ideological Resources and Movement Composition

The peace movement of the 1980s was by far the largest social movement West Germany had ever seen, and it reached into an incredibly wide array of social groups. In total, the peace movement's massive mobilization reflected two developments of the 1970s: the "greening" of the "sixty-eighter generation," and the development of extensive "middle-class radicalism." Political cooperation within the movement by Social Democrats, Free Democrats, Protestants, Catholics, and activists from the extra-parliamentary left represented an alliance between a "'post-Marxist' radical Left" and a "'post-material' reformist middle class."[1]

The entire peace movement made the military-strategic ideas outlined in chapter 4 the foundation of its minimal consensus. Each group within the movement, however, linked the missile issue to its own concerns as well. This issue overlap increased the salience of the missile question for the various groups and intensified the urgency of their participation. Radical Protestants focused as usual on the theme of redemption—on Germany's guilt from the Third Reich—and felt that new missiles contradicted repentance toward Eastern Europe. In the 1980s, however, Third World issues and religious socialism played a role as well. Catholic groups played an important role for the first time, drawing on doctrinal changes stemming from Vatican II and Pope John XXIII and on other developments within the church. For their part, Social Democrats contributed a number of secondary issues to the peace movement. Commitment to détente and

---

1. The terms come from Markovits and Gorski, *The German Left,* 79.

disarmament as instruments of peace, reconciliation with Eastern Europe through Ostpolitik, the conflict between defense spending and social programs, and the relationship of security policy to broad projects of social reform were the most important. Both the traditional communist and the independent socialist left linked foreign policy to issues of socialist transformation, viewing disengagement from the capitalist West and domestic taming of the military as preconditions for domestic reforms. The independent socialist left, moreover, brought the "new social movement" themes of the 1970s to bear on the missile question. The struggle against new missiles became part of a broader struggle against destruction of the environment, patriarchal social structures that oppressed women, and "imperialist" exploitation of the Third World. Finally, small groups in the movement explicitly raised the German question.

Social Democrats

Social Democratic participation was central to the 1980s peace movement. The struggle within the SPD, pitting Chancellor Schmidt's security policy against the views of his own left wing, contributed significantly to the Schmidt government's collapse and the SPD's return to the opposition benches. As the debate over the double-track decision intensified, Schmidt faced growing rebellion within his own party. In the 1960s, to be sure, Social Democratic dissidents had protested against the SPD's official support for the Vietnam War and the Multilateral Nuclear Force. The rank-and-file's wholesale abandonment of the double-track decision in the 1980s, however, had more lasting effects on the SPD's security policy.[2]

From the 1960s on, the SPD's official foreign policy facilitated subsequent peace protest. It established the interpretive frames of détente, Ostpolitik, and arms control as standards against which the double-track decision was later judged and found wanting. In particular, the SPD's defense policy became intertwined with its Ostpolitik. Even after its celebrated acceptance of NATO in 1959/60, the party continued to stress détente and arms control, not only as a complement to military defense but as central elements of "peace policy." In the 1960s and 1970s, a constituency grew up within the party around détente and Ostpolitik. In addition to peace research critiques of missiles, outlined in chapter 4, commitment to détente and Ostpolitik reinforced opposition to nuclear weapons. The SPD's stress on détente, arms control, and Ostpolitik in the 1960s and

---

2. This story is well told by Boutwell, *The German Nuclear Dilemma;* Herf, *War By Other Means;* Thomas Enders, *Die SPD und die äußere Sicherheit;* and Diane Rosolovsky, *West Germany's Foreign Policy: The Impact of the Social Democrats and the Greens* (New York: Greenwood Press, 1987).

1970s provided the party's left wing with principles to which it held party leadership, when it perceived the double-track decision to contradict these objectives. In the end, Schmidt ran into trouble because he seemed to emphasize military defense at the expense of détente.

As the dominant foreign policy topic within the SPD during the 1960s, Ostpolitik and détente became increasingly associated with the word *peace* in party discussion, particularly on the party's left. At the 1969 party convention, both the leadership and the delegates spoke of détente and arms control as crucial components of security policy, as had become customary during the 1960s. Now, in addition, they discussed détente as a contribution to a "lasting peace order" *(dauerhafte Friedensordnung)* as well. For many, all this meant was a normalization of relations between West Germany and the East European states. Parliamentary party leader Herbert Wehner spoke of a "compromise of interests" *(Interessenausgleich)* between West Germany and the Eastern European countries and of "coming to an understanding" *(Verständigung)* with them.[3] Others implied more when using the word *Friedensordnung.* Brandt hinted that turning Europe into a zone of détente and "peaceful neighborliness" could be a "precursor" *(Vorstufe)* to a lasting peace order that might go beyond mere détente.[4] The word *Friedenspolitik* also came increasingly into use. Literally meaning a policy that promoted peace, the term was often used synonymously with Ostpolitik. For example, after listing the concrete elements of his Ostpolitik (renunciation of force, normalization of relations, etc.), Brandt declared that German policy had to be Friedenspolitik.[5] Helmut Schmidt also referred to Brandt's policy as Friedenspolitik, and he noted that peace meant an inner harmony between domestic justice and nonviolent foreign relations. Thus Friedenspolitik was more than merely a rational, diplomatic effort toward security from external threats or reduced tensions.[6]

Although the importance of Germany's NATO membership received ample mention, over the years the connection between Ostpolitik and Friedenspolitik (or *Friedenssicherung,* "insuring continued peace") was continually driven home. Speaking to the 1970 convention, Wehner swore that the SPD would use its full power to keep German policy oriented toward *Friedenssicherung.* His version reflected the more limited goals of

---

3. Vorstand der SPD, *Außerordentlicher Parteitag der Sozialdemokratischen Partei Deutschlands vom 16. bis 18. April 1969 in der Stadthalle zu Bad Godesberg: Protokoll der Verhandlungen, Anträge* (Bonn: Neuer Vorwärts Verlag, 1969). See resolution A-273, pp. 489–92; and Wehner's remarks, pp. 151–56.

4. Ibid., 447.

5. Ibid., 447.

6. Ibid., 55.

Ostpolitik: cooperation and reconciliation with Eastern Europe, and a relationship with East Germany regulated by treaties.[7] Brandt too reinforced the notion of peace through compromise and détente, but he seemed to go further than Wehner. He hoped that his treaties would pave the way for reducing East-West confrontation in Europe, which in turn would facilitate mutual troop reductions and the eventual replacement of the military blocs with a European security system. Thus, he declared, "War would never again be launched from German soil" [Vom deutschen Boden darf nie wieder Krieg ausgehen], a phrase that later became a slogan of the peace movement.[8] As the 1970s progressed, German and NATO participation in the MBFR and CSCE talks was tied conceptually into this framework. As a party resolution put it, to make peace in Europe more secure and to overcome European division in the long run, it was necessary to reduce political tensions and military confrontation. Therefore West Germany was participating in the CSCE and MBFR talks.[9]

The SPD's rank and file concurred happily with Ostpolitik's general principles. From its inception, however, a minority pushed for a more far-reaching approach. Some hoped that détente would lead to reductions in military force or even eliminate the military blocs altogether, but neither hope was realized. As Helmut Hellwig noted, promotion of lasting peace would mean eliminating military and power blocs in Eastern and Western Europe and establishing instead a collective European security system.[10] Others linked détente to domestic policy goals. Disarmament and a demilitarized zone in Central Europe, Uwe Rüth noted at the 1970 party convention, could be coupled with reduced defense spending and money for domestic reforms.[11]

In the meantime, after 1968, criticism of the United States and of NATO became ever more vocal within the SPD. At the 1969 party conference, a few lone voices called NATO an instrument of imperialism, the leader of a worldwide alliance blocking social progress in the West and the

---

7. Vorstand der SPD, *Parteitag der Sozialdemokratischen Partei Deutschlands vom 11. bis 14. Mai in Saarbrücken: Protokoll der Verhandlungen, angenommene und überwiesene Anträge* (Bonn: Neuer Vorwärts Verlag, 1970), 92.

8. Ibid., 467–70.

9. See the Vorstand's proposed resolution in Vorstand der SPD, *Parteitag der Sozialdemokratischen Partei Deutschlands vom 10. bis 14. April 1973, Protokoll der Verhandlungen* (n.p., 1973), 1096–1103. For many of these themes see the Vorstand's proposed resolution A-233 in Vorstand der SPD, *Parteitag der Sozialdemokratischen Partei Deutschlands vom 11. bis 15. November 1975 in Rosengarten Mannheim: Protokoll der Verhandlungen* (Mannheim: Südwestdeutsche Verlagsanstalt, 1975), 1221–27; Brandt's speech in Vorstand der SPD, *Protokoll: Außerordentlicher Parteitag der SPD, Dortmund, Westfalenhalle, 18./19. Juni* (Bonn: Neuer Vorwärts-Verlag, 1976), 241.

10. Vorstand der SPD, *Außerordentlicher Parteitag der SPD*, 238.

11. Vorstand der SPD, *Parteitag der SPD* 1970:486.

Third World. How could NATO be an "alliance of freedom" when fascist Portugal belonged and Franco's Spain was being considered for member-ship?[12] Such criticism became a torrent at the 1970 convention. Debate raged over how strongly the SPD should condemn the United States's con-duct of the Vietnam War. No one really defended American policy, but the leadership—as head of an allied government—naturally could not permit the wholesale condemnation pushed by many delegates, who spoke of genocide by American imperialist interests under the guise of defending democracy.[13] Similarly, the SPD leadership had to plead against, as Hans Apel put it, using Greece's domestic order as a standard for NATO mem-bership.[14] Others felt that Greece under the military junta was a fascist regime and that its membership in NATO could not be squared with NATO's creed of defending freedom and democracy.[15]

The mid-1970s saw reduced treatment of foreign policy themes within the SPD, at least at party conventions. Not until the neutron bomb debate of 1977 did controversy return to social democratic discussion of foreign policy. In retrospect, the neutron bomb debate represented a mere prelude to the infinitely larger storm over the double-track decision of two years later, but it captured the major themes that were subsequently developed more forcefully.[16]

The SPD and the Double-Track Decision
The double-track decision dominated the discussion at SPD party conven-tions from 1979, when it emerged as an issue, to 1983, when the SPD majority rejected missile deployments. Until late 1982, opposition within the SPD to the double-track decision meant undermining the party's leader, Helmut Schmidt, and the SPD's hold on power. After 1982, the party's opposition status gave the antimissile forces freer rein. Both pro-ponents and opponents of the double-track decision within the SPD pro-fessed their continued adherence to détente and arms control. At its most basic level, debate over the NATO decision revolved around whether it contradicted these fundamental party principles.

At the 1979 party convention, the SPD's leadership defended the dou-ble-track decision in terms of détente and arms control. Brandt delicately fit the decision into the SPD's broader foreign policy principles as an

12. Vorstand der SPD, *Außerordentlicher Parteitag der SPD,* 116–18.
13. See, for example, Vorstand der SPD, *Parteitag der SPD* 1970:103.
14. Ibid., 109, 110.
15. Ibid., 120–24. For the debates on Vietnam and Greece at the 1970 convention, see ibid., 101–48.
16. The debate over the neutron bomb that took place at the 1977 party convention can be studied in Vorstand der SPD, *Parteitag der Sozialdemokratischen Partei Deutschlands vom 15. bis 19. November 1977 in Hamburg* (Bonn: Verlag Neuer Vorwärts, 1977), 258–86.

"interim measure." He noted the grave dangers still inherent in the international system and the need to guarantee "survival worthy of human dignity." While détente and military balance were still complementary components of security, the military balance had to be sought at the lowest possible level, since an arms race would inevitably lead to ruin. Détente and arms control were fundamental commitments for the SPD, to which the government would hold despite any necessary "interim decisions."[17] Egon Bahr reinforced a "policy as usual" atmosphere, noting that the 1980s would determine whether West Germany could build an indestructible peace in Europe on the foundation of détente. This would only work by gradually replacing security through deterrence with security through cooperation. Within this context, however, the SPD was willing to take arms measures.[18]

Schmidt fit the double-track decision into these principles more concretely and explicitly. Détente and defensive capabilities, he argued, remained the cornerstones of NATO. Détente had removed Central Europe from the center of international conflict, but NATO membership remained the only possible foundation for the balance of power and thereby for détente. In the 1980s Germany would contribute to Western defense through new disarmament efforts, but these presupposed equal security for both sides. Despite the superpower parity agreed on in SALT II, the Soviet Union was systematically creating an imbalance in the European theater through its SS-20s. Through the double-track decision, the West wanted to counter this imbalance—through negotiated reductions of SS-20s if possible, but through new medium-range systems if necessary. As Defense Minister Hans Apel made explicit, the double-track decision expressed the Harmel formula of security through détente and defense. It gave priority to negotiations over arms acquisitions, by making the latter dependent on failure of the former.[19]

Opponents of the double-track decision also argued their case in terms of détente and arms control, but they came to opposite conclusions—that the new missiles hindered arms control and thus threatened the very foundations of security and peace. Karsten Voigt laid out the classic arguments. Applauding the illustrious history of SPD détente policy, he called for a second phase of Ostpolitik, consisting of peace through

---

17. Vorstand der SPD, *Protokoll: Parteitag der Sozialdemokratischen Partei Deutschlands, vom 3. bis zum 10. Dezember 1979, Berlin* (Bonn: Neuer Vorwärts Verlag, 1979), 46, 47.

18. Ibid., 67. The last phrase is, however, a bit ambiguous: "Diese Stärke auszubauen, die Stärke unserer Friedens- und Entspannungspolitik, darin allerdings sind wir bereit aufzurüsten" [In order to expand this strength, the strength of our peace and détente policy, we are however willing to build up our arms].

19. Vorstand der SPD, *Protokoll: Parteitag der SPD* 1979:190–96, 253–57.

cooperation and arms control. The arms race and détente, he noted, could not parallel each other indefinitely; either arms control would come to pass or the arms race would cause new confrontation. Advances in weapons technology threatened the effectiveness of arms control and were currently undermining SALT II, whose passage was necessary for further agreements. Its failure would call into question the whole logic of the double-track decision. Arms control had to have political priority over new weapons technology, for the credibility of Germany's peace policy was more vital to security than the credibility of deterrence. The decision to station new weapons would have to be strictly provisional and would have to depend on negotiation results.[20]

At the 1979 conference, delegates' opinions were split roughly evenly. Many opponents of the NATO decision wanted to make ratification of SALT II a precondition for its passage.[21] Several made objections based on deterrence—on whether the new missiles invited preemptive strikes (destroying German territory) or made limited nuclear war more likely.[22] One of the most telling arguments came from Gerhard Schröder of the SPD's youth organization, the Jungsozialisten. He admitted he could not determine whether a military imbalance existed. He thought, however, that delegates should base their decisions not on military criteria alone but also on whether the Soviets could use their SS-20s to threaten West Germany politically, which he did not find plausible. Brandt's détente policy had been based on treaties that mandated inviolability of borders. In détente, security was guaranteed primarily by treaty and only secondarily by military aspects, whereas the double-track decision seemed to reverse these priorities and therefore represented a historical break with détente. Moreover, the United States had not always supported West German détente policy, but an INF negotiator was now able to determine the tempo of détente and disarmament policy.[23]

By the 1982 party convention, sentiment against the double-track decision had grown considerably. Delegates against it outstripped those in favor by roughly three to one. According to one delegate, moreover, proposed resolutions *(Anträge)* from the local party organizations ran against the double-track decision eight to one.[24] Concern over deteriorating superpower relations and Carter's withdrawal of SALT II from the Senate's ratification process heightened the debate's intensity. One woman

---

20. Ibid., 260–66.

21. Ibid., 270, 287.

22. Ibid., 282–83, 317.

23. Ibid., 305–6, 751–52.

24. Vorstand der SPD, *Protokoll: Parteitag der Sozialdemokratischen Partei Deutschlands, 19. bis 23. April 1982 in München* (Bonn: Neuer Vorwärts Verlag, 1982), 718.

maintained that nuclear war was becoming increasingly possible. She feared that without SALT II's passage, the new missiles would introduce a dangerous phase in the arms race, heightened by the superpowers' new policy of confrontation and military superiority. Because of the missiles' first-strike capabilities, she argued, Europe would be a launching pad and a target of retribution. Thus European "defense" could only mean suicide.[25] Another woman questioned deterrence altogether, saying that defense based on balance of power and military force had always fueled the arms race in the past and that military balance was a mythical notion.[26] Others felt that the United States no longer recognized the connection between détente and security policy and that superpower tensions would doom the Geneva negotiations.[27]

By the November 1983 party convention, much water had flowed under the SPD's bridges. Schmidt's government had fallen, and power had passed to the new CDU/FDP coalition. The SPD's new role as parliamentary opposition, coupled with the peace movement's growth in West Germany as a whole, allowed the release of even more pent-up opposition to the double-track decision within the party. Few new arguments were introduced, but events were striking. The executive committee *(Vorstand)* sponsored a resolution that opposed stationing the new medium-range missiles, whereas in the past the *Vorstand's* resolutions had always supported the Schmidt government and the double-track decision. Sentiment against the proposed missiles had grown so strong that only 14 out of 422 delegates[28] voted against the *Vorstand's* resolution (and thus in favor of deployments), with three abstentions.[29] Brandt and Hans-Jochen Vogel spoke in favor of the resolution and thus against the double-track decision as originally conceived by Schmidt. Both implicitly argued that arms control should have priority over stationing, noting that neither the United States nor the Soviet Union had taken the Geneva negotiations seriously enough.[30]

Social Democratic Groups in the Peace Movement
The SPD spectrum of the peace movement contained four subgroups: the SPD's moderate left, the FDP's left, certain unions, and the SPD's far left. Although there were several youth groups within this spectrum, many

---

25. Ibid., 319–20.
26. Ibid., 724.
27. Ibid., 328–42.
28. Vorstand der SPD, *Protokoll: Außerordentlicher Parteitag der Sozialdemokratischen Partei Deutschlands vom 18. bis 21. 1983 in Köln* (Bonn: Neuer Vorwärts Verlag, 1983), 118.
29. Ibid., 189.
30. Ibid., 120–37; 163–66.

groups' members fell into the 35–60 age bracket and were well established professionally, which made them older and much more established than peace movement activists in general. Academicians and the educated middle class were well represented. The members of these groups (whether the groups themselves had existed since 1969 or not) had supported the Brandt/Scheel coalition of 1969–74 and its major policy positions, from détente and Ostpolitik to the general reform orientation of "daring more democracy." Groups dedicated to détente and social reforms spearheaded social democratic peace activism, linking these causes to their opposition to the NATO decision.

The bulk of the SPD spectrum took moderate positions compared to other wings of the peace movement. The SPD's moderate left was represented by the Initiative für Frieden, internationalen Ausgleich und Sicherheit, or IFIAS (Initiative for Peace, International Compromise, and Security), and the Gustav-Heinemann-Initiative, or GHI. Founded in 1978, IFIAS was dedicated to defending détente, reforming NATO strategy, and furthering arms control. Its members included prominent Social Democrats like Johannes Rau and Heinrich Albertz; other well-placed Social Democrats from the party's executive committee *(Vorstand);* religious, academic, and cultural figures; and a number of peace researchers. Most IFIAS members had enthusiastically supported Brandt and détente, which formed the basis of their "foreign policy consciousness." IFIAS's founding stemmed from concern over superpower confrontation from 1976 on, the difficulties surrounding CSCE, the accelerated arms buildup, and the slow progress on SALT II. The IFIAS was founded as an attempt to save détente before it was too late.[31]

The Gustav-Heinemann-Initiative was also founded in 1978, to defend the tradition represented by Gustav Heinemann, the *Bundespräsident* of Germany under Brandt—in particular his concern for civil rights. The GHI illustrated the close links between progressive Protestantism and the SPD. GHI members were generally *linksliberal* (left-liberal) and came primarily from the SPD and the Protestant Church, but they included FDP-liberals, some Greens, civil servants, and teachers as well. The most prominent GHI members were Erhard Eppler, Helmut Gollwitzer, Petra Kelly, and William Borm. The average member was between 40 and 60 years in age.[32]

The social democratic spectrum encompassed the left wing of the FDP as well, represented by the Liberale Demokraten (Liberal Democrats) and the Jungdemokraten (Young Democrats). The Liberal Democrats formed as a breakaway party in November 1982, in response to the

---

31. Interview with an IFIAS leader.
32. Interview with a GHI representative.

FDP's switch from the social-liberal coalition to its present coalition with the Christian Democrats.[33] The party's main emphasis was on "social-liberal" issues, such as civil liberties, education, détente, and arms control. Members were generally well-educated professionals, such as lawyers and teachers, although some were students. Most Liberal Democrats entered the FDP between 1969 and 1974, during the first social-liberal coalition and the controversy over Ostpolitik, because the FDP supported a more cooperative stance toward the Eastern bloc early on.[34]

The Jungdemokraten (JUDOs) were the FDP's official youth organization until 1982 and left the FDP as a result of the coalition switch. The JUDOs also formed part of the left-liberal wing of the FDP and were concerned primarily with civil liberties and détente. They took particular offense at the discrepancy between the civil liberties set out in the Grundgesetz (Basic Law) and the limitations on their actual practice in German politics. Thoroughly caught up in the reform euphoria of the Brandt/Scheel period, which brought a large influx of new members, the JUDOs took the "Dare More Democracy" slogan seriously and pressed for change through parties and Parliament. As many desired reforms failed to materialize, the JUDOs became disillusioned with parties and turned more to grassroots politics and the citizens' initiatives of the 1970s. The JUDOs were interested in détente and disarmament from the mid-1960s on, spurred in part by contacts with youth organizations in the Eastern bloc that began around 1965, and they hoped that détente would include disarmament as well as economic and political cooperation.

The SPD spectrum also included the DGB-Jugend, the youth group of the German Confederation of Labor (DGB). The DGB as an institution distanced itself from the peace movement during its early stages and stressed its own yearly antiwar demonstrations. The DGB's executive committee forbad participation in the peace movement's first major demonstration in 1981 and castigated one of its members (Georg Benz) for speaking there. The DGB leadership's reluctance to participate was in part because of a communist presence in the organizational apparatus of the 1981 demonstration[35] and also because it did not want to embarrass the Schmidt government. Instead of participating in the budding peace movement, it sponsored its own petition, "Frieden durch Abrüstung" (Peace through disarmament),[36] which fared embarrassingly poorly in its quest

---

33. Following the coalition switch, the FDP lost some fifteen thousand members, some of whom founded the Liberal Democrats.

34. Interview with a Liberal Democrats staff member.

35. Jutta Roitsch, "Der Haß auf alles Kommunistische sitzt tief," *Frankfurter Rundschau,* 19 Nov. 1981.

36. For a text of the appeal, see *Sozialdemokratischer Pressedienst,* Oct. 1981.

for signatures.[37] By mid-1982, however, individual unions (like IG Metall) had moved closer to peace movement positions.[38] By late 1983, the Schmidt government had fallen, and the DGB's position had evolved so far that the executive committee called on its members to attend the large demonstrations in Bonn.[39] The DGB-Jugend, the unions' youth organization, began its formal affiliation with the peace movement in 1982. It had supported détente and Ostpolitik from the beginning and had participated in the Easter March Movement in the 1960s.

The largest component of the SPD spectrum was the SPD's own youth group, the Jungsozialisten (Young Socialists, commonly referred to as Jusos), who were a consistent organ of dissent within the SPD and the most radical group in the Social Democratic spectrum of the peace movement. In addition to the usual concern for détente and arms control, the Jusos brought more radical issues to bear on defense policy, including far-reaching desires for economic reform and highly critical attitudes toward the United States as the leading "imperialist" power.

Until the mid-1960s, the Jusos followed the changing course of SPD policy without complaint. They were part of the SPD's participation in the Paulskirche and Kampf dem Atomtod movements in the 1950s, but then they followed the SPD's reorientation in the Godesberg Program. Until 1965, they played a nonpolitical role within the party, performing campaign work and youth recruitment. On the foreign policy front, the Jusos's contacts with foreign organizations had a cold war flavor in keeping with the times. In the late 1960s, however, the Jusos became radicalized through the SPD's willingness to form the Grand Coalition with the "party of reaction," and through the student/extraparliamentary opposition. The extraparliamentary opposition brought the Jusos back to traditional social democratic themes: the need for social and economic reform within capitalism, and the conception of the SPD as a class party rather than a catch-all party. The SPD's acceptance of the Emergency Laws and Karl Schiller's economic policies seemed to strengthen the very system the party had previously wanted to change.[40]

---

37. Hugo Müller-Vogg, "Schwierigkeiten mit der Friedenspolitik," *Frankfurter Allgemeine Zeitung*, 17 Oct. 1981.

38. Hugo Müller-Vogg, "Der DGB im Sog der Friedensbewegung," *Frankfurter Allgemeine Zeitung*, 29 June 1982.

39. Ernst Breit, "Die Ansprüche der Friedensbewegung an die Gewerkschaften werden vermutlich immer größer sein als die friedenspolitischen Aktivitäten des DGB," *Solidarität* 34, no. 9 (Sept. 1983): 4–6.

40. Karlheinz Schonauer, *Die ungeliebten Kinder der Mutter SPD: Die Geschichte der Jusos von der braven Parteijugend zur innerparteilichen Opposition* (Hagen: Karlheinz Schonauer, 1982). See also Peter Arend, *Die innerparteiliche Entwicklung der SPD 1966–1975* (Bonn: Eichholz Verlag, 1975).

From the late 1960s on, the Jusos pursued relatively radical goals, demanding democratization of all areas of society and the gradual transition to a socialized economy.[41] After initial enthusiasm for Brandt's reform promises, the Jusos became increasingly critical of the Schmidt government. As the 1970s wore on, they became a conduit for peace movement ideas and other "new politics" themes into the SPD. The Jusos's stance toward the double-track decision showed how much they had internalized the SPD's key concepts during the 1970s: support for Ostpolitik, the link between détente and security, and the notions of a European peace order and collective security system.

At the same time, they subjected Ostpolitik to a very large set of expectations.[42] Maintaining that détente could stimulate domestic social change, the Jusos revived social democratic traditions of linking defense policy to labor movement goals. As early as 1969, the Jusos began to push for disarmament and a "collective security system." They observed that the "veto power" of the superpowers limited the range of social change possible within their respective blocs. The perception of threat on both sides, moreover, tended to cement the status quo by strengthening the "military-industrial complex" in each bloc.[43]

By 1973, the hope that détente could contribute to social change became inextricably intertwined with the idea that détente, disarmament, and a collective European security system could alone provide security. Security was defined exclusively as "securing peace," not as protecting against intentional military aggression. A socialist security policy had to overcome both the capitalist economic structures and the military bloc system that caused the current state of insecurity. Since nuclear defense could only lead to destruction, the Godesberg Program's call for disarmament was more relevant than ever.[44] The 1974 Jusos convention resolution succinctly expressed the linkage between peace and social change through a foreign policy of far-reaching détente: "Replacing NATO and the Warsaw Pact by . . . a European zone of détente and the withdrawal of all foreign troops from this zone, and thus a European peace order, are necessary presuppositions for the development and success of socialist democracy in

---

41. Markovits and Gorski, *The German Left*, 95.

42. For an overview of Juso security policy views, see Heidemarie Wieczorek-Zeul, "Jungsozialisten und Sicherheitspolitik," in *Jungsozialisten und Jungdemokraten zur Friedens- und Sicherheitspolitik,* ed. Reiner Steinweg (Frankfurt: Suhrkamp Verlag, 1977), 13–22.

43. Bundesvorstand der Jusos, ed., *Bundeskongreßbeschlüsse Jungsozialisten in der SPD 1969–1976* (N.p., n.d.), 13, 14.

44. Bundesvorstand der Jusos, ed., *Beschlüsse—ordentlicher Bundeskongreß der Jusos in der SPD in Bonn-Bad Godesberg, March 9–11, 1973* (N.p., n.d.), 13.

West Germany and Western Europe. Only through this process . . . [can] lasting peace in Europe be secured."[45]

In addition to their focus on détente, the Jusos developed a very critical attitude toward the United States and NATO. They considered NATO an imperialist military alliance of capitalists (although, they noted, Soviet behavior like the "intervention" in Czechoslovakia in 1968 also served to stabilize NATO), and they felt that the American presence in West Germany served capitalist interests in both countries.[46] The My-Lai massacre, symptomatic of America's conduct of the Vietnam War, showed how the "defense of democracy" was an excuse for an imperialist war.[47] Condemnation of NATO softness toward right-wing dictatorships like Greece, Turkey, Chile, and Iran occurred repeatedly throughout the 1970s.[48] The Jusos called for an "anti-imperialist" development aid for the Third World, which would not serve capitalist interests in either West Germany or the recipient country.[49]

Protestants

While the "guilt" issue and Ostpolitik were the most important Protestant contributions to West Germany's defense debate after the war, they were by no means the only ones. In the 1970s, Protestant discussion of peace issues ranged far and wide. Like in the SPD, discussion of Ostpolitik became linked to disarmament and the quest for an international peace order, foreshadowing peace movement treatment of these themes. Following its famous Ostpolitik missive of 1965, for example, the Protestant Church's Chamber for Public Responsibility issued a statement entitled "Germans' Tasks for Peace" in 1968. In addition to relating German historical guilt to the requisites of peace, it called for the church to work for a peaceful international order and questioned the role of deterrence. Deterrence, it maintained, helped keep peace between the superpowers and stabilized Europe militarily, but politically superpower confrontation sealed Europe's division and hindered détente. Even the present equilibrium was instable, for the arms race could make war possible again. The study also pointed to responsibilities for peace that spanned the East-West

---

45. Bundesvorstand der Jusos, ed., *Beschlüsse—ordentlicher Bundeskongreß der Jusos in der SPD in München, Jan. 25–27, 1974* (N.p., n.d.), 44, 45.

46. Ibid., 45.

47. Bundesvorstand der Jusos, *Bundeskongreßbeschlüsse Jungsozialisten in der SPD 1969–1976*, 16.

48. See, for example, ibid., 15, 83; Bundesvorstand der Jusos, *Beschlüsse . . . 1973*, 14–18.

49. Bundesvorstand der Jusos, *Bundeskongreßbeschlüsse Jungsozialisten in der SPD 1969–1976*, 31.

divide. Central European peoples shared a "community of danger" across the Iron Curtain, which made renunciation of force agreements and other forms of cooperation imperative.[50]

Debate also raged over "liberation theology" and Third World issues, and "Christian Socialism" met with renewed interest in the church. A second essay by the Chamber for Public Responsibility, published in 1969, bore the title "Christian Service for Peace" and linked peace to disarmament and overcoming Third World poverty. It no longer sufficed, it noted, to think of peace as the absence of war, for this did not solve conflicts of social justice. Industrial countries could not serve international justice if they primarily aimed at maintaining the world's current political and economic system. Given the destructiveness of modern warfare, the only possible goal of ethical political action was the settlement of opposing state interests, social justice, and protection of individual and state autonomy in the framework of an international peace order. This was only attainable if states gave up force in favor of nonmilitary means, putting international solidarity ahead of national interests.[51]

One Protestant group in the peace movement's national leadership particularly reflected the EKD's treatment of Ostpolitik. Founded in 1958, Aktion Sühnezeichen's mission was to do charitable work in countries that had suffered German aggression during the war, in order to both show "signs of repentance" (hence the group's name) and to contribute to reconciliation with these countries through service to their postwar populations. Aktion Sühnezeichen's original founders were members of the Bekennende Kirche's resistance to the Third Reich, and in the 1950s they actively fought rearmament and nuclear weapons. Supporters of Ostpolitik from the beginning, the group began consciousness-raising in the late 1970s as détente began to decline. Via this role, Aktion Sühnezeichen became one of the founding groups of the 1980s peace movement.

The EKD's treatment of the "guilt question," Ostpolitik, and conscientious objection were the most original Protestant contributions to German discussion of peace issues and were closely linked to Protestant participation in the peace movement. Further stimulus for participation, however, came from EKD discussion of the Third World and religious socialism. The Vietnam War met with considerable criticism in the EKD, and in the 1970s the question of an "antiracism" program created controversy. Left-leaning bodies within the church wanted to lend financial support to groups fighting oppression in the Third World (such as the South-West African People's Organization [SWAPO] in Namibia), while more conservative groups were against giving money to political groups, espe-

---

50. "Friedensaufgaben der Deutschen," *Kirchliches Jahrbuch* 95:114–23.
51. "Der Friedensdienst der Christen," *Kirchliches Jahrbuch* 96:71–82.

cially violent ones. Work in the world ecumenical movement brought the Third World to Protestant attention early on, as did broader public discussion of the Vietnam War and the "North-South problem." By the 1960s, the ecumenical movement was stressing the need to transform the world economic system, which in its view perpetrated "structural violence" on less-developed countries.

The "theology of revolution" and the removal of restrictions on Christian participation in revolution also found wide support in the ecumenical movement during this period.[52] In 1975, it called on Christians as individuals to renounce military defense and to make this known to their governments. One Protestant group active in the peace movement, Ohne Rüstung Leben (Live without Arms), or ORL, took up this call. ORL members in effect espoused unilateral disarmament and radical pacifism and professed themselves willing to live without any military defense at all. By the 1980s, ORL had 120 local chapters.[53]

Religious socialism became a controversial topic in the EKD when the student movement rediscovered Marxism, and it caused concern that the EKD was drifting too far to the left, especially when Protestant pastors began to join the Communist Party (DKP) and other communist groups. While many of those interested in the subject were students, prominent older theologians and laity were also deeply involved. Theologian Dorothee Sölle played a prominent role in renewing religious socialism. Her writings of the 1960s propagated dissolving the ties between Christian and bourgeois culture and opening dialogue between Christianity and Marxism.[54] Sölle later became one of the Protestant luminaries in the 1980s peace movement, giving speeches at both the 1981 Hamburg Kirchentag (the Protestant lay assembly that held one of the first public discussions on the missile issue) and at the peace movement's 1982 demonstration in Bonn.

Groups like the Protestant student association, the Evangelische Studentengemeinde (ESG), with its chapters at various universities, typified EKD involvement with such topics. The ESG was active both in the peace movement's national Coordinating Committee and as a local center of activity in university cities. The ESG's history exemplified the continuity of Protestant activism throughout the postwar period. It was associated

---

52. Gerta Scharffenorth, "Konflikte in der Evangelischen Kirche in Deutschland 1950 bis 1969 im Rahmen der historischen und ökumenischen Friedensdiskussion," in *Konflikte zwischen Wehrdienst und Friedensdiensten,* ed. Ulrich Duchrow and Gerta Scharffenorth (Stuttgart: Ernst Klett Verlag, 1970), 17–116, here 40, 41.

53. Pro Ökumene/Ohne Rüstung Leben, eds., *Ohne Rüstung leben* (Gütersloh: Gütersloher Verlagshaus Gerd Mohn, 1983).

54. Hermann Glaser, *Kulturgeschichte der Bundesrepublik Deutschland* (Munich: Karl Hanser Verlag, 1985), 297.

with the Bekennende Kirche during the Third Reich, and in the postwar period it often touched on the National Socialist past and its political consequences for the present. The ESG was active in the political debates of the 1950s, and from the 1960s on it worked with conscientious objectors' associations. The group studied peace research and "antimilitarism," and its work in the ecumenical movement led to discovery of Third World problems. The ESG became involved in the student movement of the late 1960s, which stimulated an interest in Marxism and reinforced the connection between Christian faith and its social and political implications. Its theological work in the 1970s and 1980s centered on a rediscovery of Karl Barth, religious socialism, and Third World theology. The ESG also became involved in new social movements, like the ecology and peace movements.[55]

Finally, the Aktionsgemeinschaft Dienst für den Frieden (AGDF) was an umbrella organization for a number of Protestant groups active in the above areas. Along with Aktion Sühnezeichen, AGDF was one of the initial mobilizers for the peace movement in the Protestant sphere. Its members included groups from several traditions. Aktion Sühnezeichen was itself a member of the AGDF, along with other Protestant groups active in Ostpolitik. Several groups reflected traditional Protestant pacifism, like the Quakers, the Brethren Service Commission in Geneva, and the Christlicher Friedensdienst, Deutscher Zweig. Still other groups came from the ecumenical movement and worked in underdeveloped nations, including Eirene-Internationaler Christlicher Friedensdienst, and the Ökumenische Förderergemeinschaft für soziale Dienst—Kinder in Not. Lastly, the experience of fascism provided the foundation for some of the groups, including Aktion Sühnezeichen and the Forschungsinstitut der Evangelischen Studiengemeinschaft's research project Der Beitrag von Theologie und Kirche zum Frieden.[56]

The Protestant Church as a whole remained divided as always. Its main statement on the missile issue was a *Denkschrift* released in 1981, which in 1982 was already in its fourth printing and sixty-thousandth copy.[57] On the one hand, the *Denkschrift* agreed that mutual deterrence served stability. The church confirmed the validity of the "Heidelberg Theses" of 1959—at present, peace in freedom was guaranteed neither through

55. Wolfgang Wiedenmann, "Evangelische Studentengemeinde—Kirche an der Hochschule?" in *Christen in der Demokratie,* ed. Heinrich Albertz and Joachim Thomsen (Wuppertal: Peter Hammer Verlag, 1978).

56. "Die Friedensdienste der Kirche der BRD und DDR," *Militärpolitik Dokumentation* 3, no. 11/12 (1979): 100–109.

57. Kirchenkanzelei der EKD, *Frieden Wahren, Fördern und Erneuern: Eine Denkschrift der Evangelischen Kirche in Deutschland* (Gütersloh: Gütersloher Verlagshaus Gerd Mohn, 1982).

nuclear deterrence nor without it. Because both options were risky and ultimately incalculable, Christians arrived at different opinions. Thus the church still recognized deterrence as compatible with Christianity.[58]

The *Denkschrift's* "yes and no" position angered Protestants close to the peace movement.[59] On the other hand, the rest of the *Denkschrift* in general held much closer to the movement's positions than to real support for the double-track decision. It continually stressed the need for an international peace order, arms control and disarmament, and the value of political contributions (confidence-building measures and cooperation) to peace and security. New weapons technology, it argued, had increased the danger of escalation. Thus the new weapons were problematic for deterrence, and deterrence as a concept was problematic. Today's task was to avert war, which was threatened by the high levels of arms between the blocs. Peace could not be solely or even primarily guaranteed by military force. An international peace order would mean renunciation of force between states, elimination of poverty, self-determination for all peoples, human rights, and environmental protection. Since such an order was not imminent, for the time being prevention of East-West war required détente and arms control, possible alternative approaches to defense, and calculated unilateral disarmament gestures to encourage arms negotiations.

Catholics in the 1980s Peace Movement

The 1980s peace movement saw the first significant, overt participation by Catholic groups in the history of postwar peace protest, although even then they remained fewer in number and were perhaps less visible than their Protestant counterparts. Until the early 1960s, Catholic participation lagged behind that of Protestants for several reasons: the two churches' differences in doctrine, their differing organizational structures, and the geographic distribution of their constituencies across West and East Germany. Catholic doctrine developed differently from Protestant doctrine in the postwar period, especially with respect to Catholic treatment of German guilt and its foreign policy consequences, the Catholic Church's relationship to conservative governments and parties, its treatment of Ostpolitik, and its relationship to conscientious objection.

During debates on rearmament and nuclear weapons in the 1950s, Catholic groups remained silent or supported the government's position, despite polling evidence of conservative (and therefore to some extent

---

58. Ibid., 58.

59. See, for example, Hans-Jürgen Benedict, "Auf dem Weg zur Friedenskirche?" in *Die neue Friedensbewegung,* ed. Reiner Steinweg (Frankfurt: Suhrkamp Verlag, 1982), 227–44, here 239.

Catholic) opposition to Adenauer's policies. Catholic dissidents existed but lacked specifically Catholic themes on which to mobilize a larger Catholic opposition. The Catholic Church's hierarchical structure and control of its lay associations, moreover, left little room for opposition groups to form and act within the church.

Starting in the 1960s, however, under the Papacy of John XXIII (1958–63) and the Second Vatican Council, Catholic political life changed on two fronts. Official doctrine began to stress new approaches to peace, and emphasis on democratization opened organizational avenues to dissenting Catholics. Catholic doctrine took a more skeptical view of nuclear weapons and deterrence, while German Catholics reevaluated the church's relationship to the Nazi past, the CDU, Ostpolitik, and conscientious objection. Compared to the 1950s, these developments opened space for Catholic participation in peace movements and other forms of dissidence. However, the continued conservatism of the German Catholic Church restricted the growth of left-wing Catholicism in comparison to its Protestant counterpart.

Changes Wrought by Vatican II and Pope John XXIII

Doctrinal change brought about by John XXIII and Vatican II coincided with the end of the Adenauer era in foreign and domestic policy. While neither the pope[60] nor the Second Vatican Council[61] condemned nuclear weapons altogether, they both undercut the assumptions of deterrence doctrine. Vatican II abandoned the static ethic of "just war" in which nuclear weapons could play a role, and it henceforth regarded deterrence as an "emergency ethic" valid only until superseded by something better.[62] Although the council did not condemn possession of nuclear weapons as instruments of deterrence altogether, it subjected their use to the *objective* ability to control their effects rather than to a subjective intention to do so, and it stated that the arms race and the so-called military balance neither constituted nor contributed to real peace.

The pope echoed these views and called for disarmament and negotiations as the preferred means of solving conflict. Whereas Pius XII had placed equal weight on just war and prevention of war, John XXIII altered the balance. He discussed no permissible uses of weapons whatsoever but rather concentrated entirely on ways to exclude war altogether. As later peace movements were to do, John XXIII spoke of the arms race (rather

---

60. In particular in his encyclical "Pacim in Terris" of April 1963.

61. In particular in "Gaudium et spes."

62. According to Walter Dirks, the council replaced the idea of just war by a historical process of arriving at true peace ("Abschied vom 'gerechten Krieg,' " *Frankfurter Hefte* 22, no. 7 (July 1967): 489–96.

than aggressive designs of the Soviet Union or conflict of interest between states) as a source of tension. Since exclusive focus on strategic balance in terms of military hardware *(Gleichgewichtsdenken)* led to arms acquisition, he noted, the potential for catastrophe was growing. The new pope stressed nonmilitary components of security, in particular development aid to poor nations, dramatically increasing Catholic awareness of Third World problems.[63] Pope Paul VI (1963–78) extended some of these themes. He labeled the arms race a danger to peace, since its inherent logic led to almost automatic escalation. Therefore, he called for an international order making the arms race unnecessary and, in the meantime, for gradual, balanced, but determined strategies of peace and disarmament.[64]

Vatican II and the popes of the 1960s and 1970s undercut earlier emphasis on just war doctrine and the position of nuclear weapons therein. Furthermore, they made justification of deterrence doctrine and arms acquisitions much more tenuous. They established de facto, if not as official doctrine, a position similar to the Protestant Church's "Heidelberg Theses": that Christian faith permitted both rejection of nuclear weapons and adherence to deterrence doctrine. John XXIII and the Second Vatican Council thus opened doctrinal space within the Catholic Church for arguments that the peace movement would later use.

Within German Catholicism, nonconformist thought gained ground in the 1960s and 1970s, including a reexamination of Catholicism's relationship to the Third Reich, new openness toward Brandt's Ostpolitik, and greater acceptance of conscientious objection. In the early 1960s, criticism grew of the church's behavior during the Third Reich. Stimulated by scholarly historical research and Rolf Hochhuth's popular novel *Der Stellvertreter* (The Deputy), this criticism reopened the "guilt question" and resulted in a process partially analogous to the Protestant *Stuttgarter Schuldbekenntnis* fifteen years earlier. Carl Amery, a prominent Catholic, extended this criticism to German Catholicism's relationship to the Adenauer era, attaining best-seller status along with Heinrich Böll.[65] Amery accused Catholicism of a new type of capitulation (to the forces of restoration) at the same time that documentary evidence questioning Catholic resistance to the Third Reich came to light. Amery was apparently not

---

63. Norbert Glatzel, "Neueste kirchliche Lehrverkündigungen zur Sicherheits- und Rüstungsdebatte ab 1945," in *Frieden in Sicherheit: Zur Weiterentwicklung der katholischen Friedensethik,* ed. Norbert Glatzel and Ernst Josef Nagel (Freiburg: Herder Verlag, 1981), 125–48, here 133–41.

64. Ibid., 141–46.

65. Walter Dirks, "Ein 'anderer' Katholizismus: Minderheiten im deutschen Corpus catholicorum," in *Bilanz des deutschen Katholizismus,* ed. Norbert Greinacher and Heinz-Theo Risse (Mainz: Matthias-Grünewald Verlag, 1966), 292–310.

alone in his sentiments; the societal response greeting his efforts revealed a latent Catholic alienation from the German hierarchy's previous course.[66]

Vatican II gave German Catholicism more opportunity to respond to changes in Ostpolitik as well. Catholic support for Ostpolitik was expressed in the *Bensberger Memorandum* of 1968, published by the Bensberger Kreis (Bensberg Circle).[67] Its preface mentions two sources of inspiration: the Protestant "Vertriebenendenkschrift" of 1965 (the "Essay on Refugees"), and Vatican II's call for a peace order. The *Memorandum* did not differ significantly in substance from the EKD's essay. Both stressed the crimes of the Third Reich in Eastern Europe and recognition of current German borders. Distinctions of authorship and reception between the two, however, reduced the *Memorandum's* impact among Catholics. While the EKD itself published the Protestant essay, the authors of the Catholic memorandum constituted a private Catholic "circle," initiated by the German Pax Christi and not by an official church body. Whereas the Rat der EKD, the highest EKD council, approved the Protestant essay, the German Catholic bishops did not take any particular position,[68] and as late as 1976 they failed to support political reconciliation with Eastern Europe.[69] Nonetheless, Catholic opinion had finally revealed its diversity.

Vatican II also opened German Catholicism to cautious recognition of conscientious objectors. The council gave the first Catholic theological justification of conscientious objection, stating reservedly that it "must be seen as justified."[70] Until 1968, the German Catholic Church had actively defamed conscientious objection because of its link to the Adenauer government.[71] Even after the Vatican Council relaxed its position on conscientious objection, the church initially still regarded it merely as an individual right. The church did not consider conscientious objection an equally valid alternative to military service until the 1970s.[72] Whereas the Protes-

---

66. Forster, "Der deutsche Katholizismus," 241–47.

67. Bensberger Kreis, *Ein Memorandum deutscher Katholiken zu den polnisch-deutschen Fragen* (Mainz: Matthias-Grünewald-Verlag, 1968).

68. Gottfried Erb, "Das 'Bensberger Memorandum'/Geschichte und erste Stellungnahmen," *Frankfurter Hefte* 23, no. 4 (Apr. 1968): 219–21.

69. Norbert Tholen, "Die Höhe des Glaubens und die Niederungen der Politik: Bischöfe schweigen zum Polenvertrag," *Frankfurter Hefte* 31, no. 5 (May 1976): 4, 5.

70. Scharffenorth, "Konflikte in der Evangelischen Kirche," 42.

71. The church, under pressure from the laity, did stand up for the individual's right to conscientious objector status in the 1950s rearmament debate, but only in cases where the war in question was objectively unjust, not for conscientious objection in principle. See Doering-Manteuffel, *Katholizismus und Wiederbewaffnung,* 236. The church further qualified its support by insisting that conscientious objectors should have to justify themselves before a panel, in contrast to the EKD position that the individual conscience can not be judged by others. See Kubbig, *Kirche und Kriegsdienstverweigerung,* 92, on this point.

72. Kubbig, *Kirche und Kriegsdienstverweigerung,* 91–99.

tant Church had an agency to advise conscientious objectors as early as 1955, the German Catholic Church did not establish one until 1968.[73] A survey of conscientious objectors in 1960 reflected this slowness on the German church's part. Although Catholics amount to almost half of the West German population, only 23 percent of applicants for conscientious objector status were Catholics,[74] who as late as 1981 were still underrepresented. Similarly, Catholics only constituted 34 percent of those who were "unwilling to serve in the army."[75]

Pope John XXIII and Vatican II introduced doctrinal changes that expanded ideological space within German Catholicism for critical attitudes toward the German past, Ostpolitik, and conscientious objection, all of which later typified the peace movement. This was part of a broader accommodation of various groups that had previously been labeled "nonconformist" and "left Catholic." Left Catholicism in the 1950s fought "restoration" of the social and political structures associated with the rise of fascism,[76] and it opposed the concept of "closed" Catholicism (Geschlossenheit), a Catholic front of tight organizations within a pluralist society. Whereas nonconformism in the 1950s consisted of small groups and journals of low circulation, the 1960s saw a push for democratization within German Catholicism.

Vatican II in particular introduced principles of democratization and pluralism within the church. While minority opinions thereafter still had difficulty within German Catholicism, they at least had a reference point within the worldwide Catholic Church. In addition, the SPD's Godesberg Program of 1959 made explicit overtures to both churches. Whereas in the 1950s the SPD's prewar contacts to the Catholic labor movement had been absorbed by the CDU or the German Union Federation (DGB),[77] the Godesberg Program made opening Catholicism to the whole society and exercising Catholic influence through multiple organs more attractive. German bishops stopped pressing Catholics to vote for the CDU, and the Catholic vote for the CDU indeed declined from 76 percent in 1953 to 61

---

73. Wolfgang von Eichborn, "Politisierung der Kriegsdienstverweigerung," in *Konflikte zwischen Wehrdienst und Friedensdiensten,* ed. U. Duchrow and Gerta Scharffenorth (Stuttgart: Ernst Klett Verlag, 1970), 147–77, here 160.

74. Doering-Manteuffel, *Katholizismus und Wiederbewaffnung,* 236.

75. Peter Nissen, "Prospects for a Realignment of the West German Party System" (paper presented at the conference "When Parties Fail: Paths of Alternative Political Action," University of California at Santa Barbara, 19–20 May 1982).

76. Stankowski, *Linkskatholizismus nach 1945,* 10.

77. Forster, "Der deutsche Katholizismus," 236, 237.

percent in 1961.[78] Karl Rahner's theological innovations, moreover, placed less emphasis on institutions and more on religious practice. Rahner's student Johann Baptist Metz introduced the postulate of the church as a socially critical institution in his "political theology." In the 1960s, these new ideas made their way into student groups at universities, reinforced by the papal encyclical "Humanae vitae."[79]

West German Catholic Dissidence since the 1960s

Such tendencies toward "critical Catholicism," however, were organizationally short-lived. The 1976 synodal meeting of German bishops failed to overcome the polarization between the institutional church and radical groups pushing for democratization. Attempts to reform the church from within failed to crack the "tough structures" of German Catholicism. Reform-minded Catholics ultimately remained a minority, however considerable. Symptomatic of this was the synod's refusal to question the ties still existing between German Catholicism and the CDU.[80]

In the mid-1970s critical forces suffered from malaise following their disappointing attempts at reform, but they were not squelched permanently. Other oppositional forces were also starting to make themselves felt. A movement of grassroots church communities *(Basisgemeinden)* began to take hold. Church communities focusing on new forms of Christian life (influenced by Bonhoeffer) existed within the Protestant Church throughout the postwar period. In contrast, because of the Catholic hierarchy's traditional dominance, self-determined grassroots movements started late within German Catholicism and arrived via models from Latin America and other European countries.

Although not necessarily in revolt against church authorities, these new groups looked for new forms of action. Centered around their perceptions of Christ's liberating message, grassroots communities mixed political questions with religious faith. They quoted biblical passages about God's creation during religious services at demonstration sites like Brokdorf (against nuclear power) or the Startbahn West (in opposition to enlargement of Frankfurt's airport). They were often involved in Third World groups and in new social movements, such as the ecology and then the peace movements. Although the grassroots movement remained

---

78. Willi Kreiterling, "Geschlossenheit als politische Dogma? Der Katholizismus in der organisierten pluralistischen Gesellschaft," in *Bilanz des deutschen Katholizismus,* ed. Norbert Greinacher and Heinz-Theo Risse (Mainz: Matthias-Grünewald Verlag, 1966), 311–27.

79. Klaus Kreppel, "Kritischer Katholizismus," in *Jenseits vom Nullpunkt?* ed. Rüdiger Weckerling (Stuttgart: Kreuz Verlag, 1972), 269–75.

80. Marianne Dirks, "Angst und Hoffnung—zur katholischen Synode," *Frankfurter Hefte* 31, no. 4 (Apr. 1976): 28–32.

restricted to three or four dozen groups as of 1982, many parishes adopted one political cause or another. The movement for self-help and lay initiative thus found a place in the larger church despite thwarting efforts of the hierarchy.[81]

Catholic discussion of security and disarmament in the 1980s reflected both doctrinal changes in world Catholicism and the growth of nonconformism within *German* Catholicism. Such discussion was restricted to marginal groups in the 1950s, although it raged in the Protestant Church. The changes of the 1960s made possible a more far-reaching Catholic discussion of these issues and greatly facilitated Catholic participation in subsequent peace protest, as they gave Catholics a point of reference within the church with which to justify their actions. Even as late as the 1980s, however, Catholic involvement was by no means as extensive as Protestant.[82] Whereas the Protestant Church's *Denkschrift* of 1981 sympathized a great deal with peace movement concerns, the Zentralkomitee der deutschen Katholiken, the umbrella organization of all German Catholic lay associations, expressed unreserved support for the double-track decision and new missiles.[83]

Catholic groups against the double-track decision, however, reflected the influence of Vatican II. The BDKJ (the Catholic youth organization) maintained that additional arms would reduce security as a general rule and that security policy could no longer be primarily military.[84] The German Pax Christi group made similar arguments. Founded after World War II to work for Franco-German reconciliation, Pax Christi became a major voice for alternative security ideas within the Catholic Church.

Next to Pax Christi, the Initiative Kirche von Unten (IKvU), literally the "Initiative for a Church from Below," was the only other Catholic group represented in the peace movement's Coordinating Committee. Founded in the early 1980s, the IKvU constituted the first broad alliance of oppositional Catholics for ten years. As of 1981, the IKvU consisted of fifty-six groups interested in political action and in internal church reform.[85] Its concerns ranged from the socioeconomic order to women in the church and homosexuality. Its goal was to renew the church in the

---

81. Thomas Seiterlich, "Basisgemeinden in der Bundesrepublik," *Frankfurter Hefte* 37, no. 9 (Sept. 1982): 35–42.

82. Ulrich Ruh, "Schwierigkeiten mit dem Frieden," *Herder Korrespondenz* 35, no. 2 (Feb. 1981): 53–55.

83. "Zur aktuellen Friedensdiskussion: Eine Stellungnahme des Zentralkomitees der deutschen Katholiken," *Herder Korrespondenz* 35, no. 12 (Dec. 1981): 624–30.

84. Hans-Otto Mühleisen, "Grundstrukturen der Friedensdiskussion in der katholischen Kirche," *Politische Studien* 33, no. 261 (Jan./Feb. 1982): 28–46, here 44.

85. Thomas Seiterich, "Gruppierungen innerkirchlicher Opposition," *Frankfurter Hefte* 36, no. 5 (May 1981): 10, 11.

sense of the Second Vatican Council, with special attention to grassroots groups outside of the church hierarchy. The IKvU conceived of the church as partisan in the tradition of Latin American "liberation theology," and it abjured the notion that the church should keep out of politics. Its intellectual origins also lay in the Bensberger Kreis, the author of the Catholic memorandum on Ostpolitik, and in Catholic work with Third World problems. The IKvU represented the "greening" of the Catholic Church in peace and security issues.[86] Although it was affected less than the EKD, the IKvU demonstrated that the Catholic Church was not spared the political turbulence of the 1970s altogether. The fact that the IKvU was not organized until the early 1980s, however, bore witness to the slowness of Catholic involvement in these themes.

The Extraparliamentary Left and the Greens

All the Social Democratic and religious groups discussed so far in this chapter derived from mainstream institutions (parties, unions, or churches) and based their participation in peace protest on principles established specifically by those institutions. In addition, many groups involved in the 1980s peace movement were based in the extraparliamentary left. Their participation reflected the ideological and organizational developments on the extraparliamentary left during the 1970s.

The Extraparliamentary Left of the 1970s
In the 1970s, the extraparliamentary left went through a number of transformations. Some parts maintained the antiauthoritarian impulse of the 1960s, while others took up various communist ideologies. As the 1970s progressed, the "new social movements" grew rapidly, tying notions of radical democracy to new issues like ecology, feminism, and the Third World. In doing so, the extraparliamentary left developed many of the issues that would later bring it into the peace movement.

After 1968 the extraparliamentary opposition (APO) declined and splintered. In the early 1970s, four strands within the left remained important. Many former protesters went through the institutional channels of the SPD/FDP coalition government from 1969 to 1974. The Brandt/Scheel government made a conscious effort to integrate APO activists into party politics, which their promises of reform made all the more attractive. For its part, the left considered work in parties, unions, and churches (its "march through the institutions") part of a double strategy. Work within institutions combined with simultaneous grassroots organizing *(Basisar-*

---

86. Interview with one of the Bonn representatives of the IKvU.

beit) would enable the left both to democratize decision making and to push for specific policy outcomes.[87]

Those remaining in the extraparliamentary arena went in three directions. One consisted of DKP (Deutsche Kommunistische Partei) membership and thus communism according to the Soviet model.[88] The DKP remained close to the Soviet Union and the East German SED, not having attained the independence characteristic of the Italian Communist Party. Active in universities and industries, the DKP had close links to youth and student groups.[89] The Maoist groups oriented toward the Chinese model formed a second important strand. Whereas the DKP-oriented groups were relatively few in number, the so-called K-Gruppen of Maoist persuasion proliferated rapidly. As neo-Stalinists, they abjured the changes in Soviet communism since Stalin's death and generally considered the USSR's foreign policy imperialist. Having generally failed to find a mass base elsewhere, some K-Gruppen became involved in the new social movements of the later 1970s and went over to the Greens upon their formation.[90]

The Sozialistisches Büro represented a third important current in the left—the "undogmatic new left." Founded in 1969, the Sozialistisches Büro stood in the tradition of West German protest movements and *undogmatic* socialism, as opposed to the dogmatic versions represented by the DKP and the various K-Gruppen.[91] The Sozialistisches Büro attracted veterans of past protest movements, former SDS members, and groups from the "new social movements" (see the next section of this chapter). The Sozialistisches Büro represented "pluralism on the left" and considered itself an umbrella organization for the undogmatic left.[92] Finally, a small anarchist movement went on to organized terrorism but also

87. This included work in citizens' initiatives. See Roland Roth, "Notizen zur politischen Geschichte der Bürgerinitiativen in der Bundesrepublik," in *Parlamentarisches Ritual und politische Alternativen,* ed. Roland Roth (Frankfurt: Campus Verlag, 1980), 74–97, here 83.

88. The former communist party, the KPD, was banned in 1956. Communists worked underground and refounded the party as the DKP in 1969 under much of the same leadership.

89. The SDAJ (Sozialistische Deutsche Arbeiterjugend), for example, was a youth group associated with the DKP. Groups close to the DKP on university campuses included the MSB Spartakus and the Sozialistischer Hochschulbund. See Gerd Langguth, *Protestbewegung—Entwicklung, Niedergang, Renaissance: Die Neue Linke seit 1968* (Cologne: Bibliothek Wissenschaft und Politik, 1983), 152–87.

90. Langguth, *Protestbewegung,* 60–123.

91. Roth, "Notizen," 81.

92. Langguth, *Protestbewegung,* 195–200. Uwe Schlicht, *Vom Burschenschaften bis zum Sponti: Studentische Opposition gestern und heute* (Berlin: Colloquium Verlag Otto Hess, 1980), 132.

blended into the squatters' movement to combat housing shortages, the struggle for youth centers free of state or other supervision, and the countercultural "Sponti" scene. Proponents of "direct democracy," these groups stressed grassroots organization rather than large, hierarchical structures, and they opposed parliamentarism and other state structures.[93]

New Social Movements

Although these four centers of left politics absorbed activists in the early 1970s, the new social movements represented the main development within the extraparliamentary left of that decade. They focused on "new politics" issues not represented by the major parties and popularized unconventional protest forms. The new movements flowed into the peace movement during the latter's height, bringing experienced activists into the movement and expanding its range of secondary issues. The most important new social movements were the ecology, women's, and "alternative" movements.

The ecology movement grew out of the citizens' initiatives movement, the *Bürgerinitiativbewegung*. Citizens' initiatives began as loosely organized groups to influence policy making on specific issues or to organize self-help. With time, however, many initiatives considered themselves concrete expressions of grassroots democracy as well, and a "social movement" identity emerged. Involvement in the initiatives brought the left back to contact with the populace after its excursion into splinter parties, while the initiatives themselves experienced a gradual politicization and broadening of their single-issue focus.[94]

The citizens' initiatives movement grew out of several converging trends. The APO had shown what unconventional action could accomplish and had encouraged political self-confidence among broad sectors of the population.[95] The APO, however, had concentrated on broad issues like the Vietnam War and had aimed at nothing short of capitalism's abolition. The initiatives, in contrast, turned to more mundane issues affecting the lives of average citizens. Reacting to problems growing out of rapid industrial growth, like pollution, noise, and destruction of natural landscapes,[96] the initiatives centered on city planning, highway systems, and so

---

93. Langguth, *Protestbewegung,* 210–33.

94. Andreas Buro, "Skizze zum gesellschaftlichen Hintergrund der gegenwärtigen Parlamentarismusdebatte," in *Parlamentarisches Ritual und politische Alternativen,* ed. Roland Roth (Frankfurt: Campus Verlag, 1980), 43–74, here 43, 44.

95. Roth, "Notizen," 78–79.

96. Karl-Werner Brand, *Neue soziale Bewegungen: Entstehung, Funktion und Perspektiven neuer Protestpotentiale* (Opladen: Westdeutscher Verlag, 1982), 60–61; Buro, "Skizze," 63.

on. This new focus coincided with concern for how policy was made. The early initiatives trusted the system's capacity for reform, but the policy-making process seemed to lack transparency because of domination by parties and large interest groups *(Verbände)*.[97] Finally, the general reform atmosphere of the Brandt government broadened the range of politically important themes, and the SPD's programmatic enthusiasm flowed into the initiatives.[98] Citizens' initiatives spread quickly as a form of political involvement. By 1973, surveys recorded that up to 12 percent of the populace had worked in an initiative, 34 percent were willing to do so in principle, 60 percent might consider it under certain circumstances, and 67 percent believed that initiatives influenced policy making. These percentages added up to several thousand initiatives, although exact figures are not available.[99] By 1973, the initiatives had formed an actual initiatives movement. The Bundesverband Bürgerinitiativen Umweltschutz (BBU), or National Association of Citizen Initiatives for Environmental Protection, became an initiatives umbrella organization.[100] The Club of Rome report, the government's environmental program of 1971, and public discussion of "quality-of-life" issues gave many initiatives a broader perspective. Continuing thematic expansion and network formation gradually transformed the initiatives into the ecology movement, which developed a critique of modern industrial systems and growth-oriented ideology. A major wing of the ecology movement subsequently concentrated on nuclear power, which led to a radicalization of protest and attracted radical groups previously alienated from the "bourgeois reformism" of the

---

97. Peter Mayer-Tasch, *Die Bürgerinitiativbewegung* (Reinbek: Rowohlt, 1976); Lutz Mez and Ulf Wolter, "Wer sind die Grünen?" in *Die Qual der Wahl*, ed. Lutz Mez and Ulf Wolter (Berlin: Olle and Wolter, 1980), 6–32; Joachim Dyllick, Lutz Mez, and Werner Sewing, "Gewerkschaften contra Bürgerinitiativen: Mißverständnisse oder Unvereinbarkeiten in der Atompolitik?" in *Die eigentliche Kernspaltung: Gewerkschaften und Bürgerinitiativen im Streit um die Atomkraft*, ed. Jörg Hallerback (Darmstadt: Luchterhand, 1978), 68–95.

98. The Jusos' proclaimed "double strategy" was supposed to tie local activity surrounding specific issues *(Basisarbeit)* with involvement in the party to create a single reform impulse (Roth, "Notizen," 83–85).

99. Mayer-Tasch, *Die Bürgerinitiativbewegung*, 13, 152; Horst Mewes maintains that there were fifty thousand initiatives by 1979, with perhaps 1.5 million members. See Horst Mewes, "The West German Green Party," *New German Critique* 28 (winter 1983): 51–85, here 53–54.

100. The BBU remained the moderate wing of the ecology movement. See Herbert Kitschelt, "Parlamentarismus und ökologische Opposition," in *Parlamentarisches Ritual und politische Alternativen*, ed. Roland Roth (Frankfurt: Campus Verlag, 1980), 97–120, here 97.

early initiatives.[101] At the same time, the critique of technology and technocracy mobilized people in liberal, conservative, and even reactionary camps, giving the movement a broad social base reaching into established parties and institutions.

The women's movement was a second major social movement of the 1970s. Despite provisions for gender equality embodied in the Basic Law, West German women on the whole adhered to traditional female roles well into the 1960s. The new women's movement of the 1970s emerged out of the extraparliamentary opposition of the late 1960s. At first the student movement paid little attention to gender issues. Attempts to establish a place for *women's* liberation began when female members of the Berlin SDS created the Aktionsrat zur Befreiung der Frau (Action Council for the Liberation of Women) because they resented their subordinate role within a movement that called itself antiauthoritarian. After otherwise radical men refused to undertake the personal "consciousness-raising" necessary to end exploitation in the "private sphere" as well as in society at large, independent women's groups were founded across Germany.

Ideologically, the movement split into reformist and radical factions. The campaign for abortion liberalization temporarily provided a unifying focus. After partial defeat in the abortion issue, many reform-minded women began their own "long march through the institutions" and established a striking presence within parties. In the 1980s, women and women's issues achieved particular prominence within the Greens. Feminists also promoted affirmative action and established commissions for women's affairs in politics, public administration, and academia. Still retaining the APO's distrust of formal organization, cooperation with parties, and partial reforms that left the capitalist/patriarchal order intact, more militant groups went in a separatist direction, dubbing themselves autonomous *(die Autonomen)*. Women took part in initiatives like "Women against Rape" and "Wages for Housework"; and feminist publications and women's cafés proliferated. Projects like shelters for battered women and other initiatives gave women organizational skills and political experience and contributed to the growth of a feminist "counterculture." Women's groups established themselves as identifiable, autonomous actors in the new social movements in general and in the peace movement in particular.[102]

---

101. Kitschelt, "Parlamentarismus und ökologische Opposition," 101; Joachim Raschke, "Ursachen und Perspektiven des Protests," in *Protest: Grüne, Bunte und Steuerrebellen,* ed. Detlef Murphy et al. (Reinbek: Rowohlt, 1979), 156–89, here 160.

102. Joyce Mushaben, "Feminism in Four Acts: The Changing Political Identity of Women in the Federal Republic of Germany," in *The Federal Republic of Germany at Forty,*

The last important new social movement of the 1970s was the "alternative" movement, the *Alternativbewegung.* The alternative movement inherited the countercultural values of the 1960s. Rebelling against such traditional virtues as order, industriousness, and hierarchy, along with the commercialization of social relationships, the alternative movement emphasized psychological needs and a lifestyle based on emotionality and creativity. Although these values permeated far beyond the immediate alternative movement, the latter attempted to practice alternative workplace and lifestyle models through self-organization and autonomous projects.

While the alternative movement decoupled itself from the socialist or social democratic reform projects of the 1960s and early 1970s, it retained a political character through its claim to "politicize daily life" *(Politisierung des Alltags),* although many simply concentrated on personal growth and meaningful forms of social life. Alternative movement projects included group living *(Wohngemeinschaften),* the squatters' movement *(Hausbesetzungen)* to combat housing shortages and real-estate speculation, and farming communes. A whole network of small artisanal and service firms sprang up, such as cafés, natural foods stores, auto repair, carpentry, schools, and counseling agencies, most of which tried to operate without organizational hierarchies. An alternative press network provided important information services, including multitudinous local newspapers and one national newspaper, the *Tageszeitung.*[103]

Groups from the Extraparliamentary Left in the 1980s Peace Movement

The new social movements constituted the bulk of the radical left in the second half of the 1970s. Focusing on new themes like feminism, ecology, and alternative lifestyles, they tied these to ideals of grassroots democracy. Although the new movements overlapped with radical political subcul-

---

ed. Peter Merkl (New York: New York University Press, 1989). This section of my text relies heavily on Mushaben's essay. See also Lottemi Doormann, "Die Frauenbewegung und die Linke," in *Die Linke: Bilanz und Perspektiven für die 80er Jahre,* ed. Hermann Gremliza and Heinrich Hannover (Hamburg: VSA-Verlag, 1980), 80–95; and Christoph Conti, *Abschied vom Bürgertum: Alternative Bewegungen von 1890 bis heute* (Reinbek: Rowohlt, 1984); and Brand, Büsser, and Rucht, *Aufbruch in eine andere Gesellschaft,* 123–54.

103. Brand, Büsser, and Rucht, *Aufbruch in eine andere Gesellschaft,* 154–79. See also Conti, *Abschied vom Bürgertum,* 150–92; and Lothar Kolenberger and Hanns-Albrecht Schwarz, *Die alternative Bewegung in West-Berlin,* F. G. S. Occasional Papers (Berlin: Freie Universität, 1982).

tures, they also drew the West German mainstream into involvement with these issues. They thus developed issues that provided avenues into expanded political activism, including peace movement participation.

The extraparliamentary left influenced the leadership, organization, and ideology of the 1980s peace movement. At the national level, the movement's Coordinating Committee contained many groups from the extraparliamentary left. The "new social movements" coalesced in the "independent" wing, while communist groups formed their own wing. Most groups found their way to peace protest by discovering an issue overlap, that is, links between their own themes and the broader focus on peace. The communist wing linked the double-track decision to traditional labor movement concerns and to détente. The independent wing found that activism in the peace movement would further feminism, ecology, and "alternative" social models, since NATO and nuclear weapons reinforced the structures against which they struggled.

The peace movement's communist wing contained groups oriented toward the West German Communist Party (DKP) and thus toward Soviet-style communism and the East German Communist Party (SED). They linked the struggle against the missiles to defense of détente and to working-class interests in social spending. Their positions generally mirrored the Soviet Union's foreign policy. They were also known for their *Bündnispolitik* within the peace movement, their attempts to build broad coalitions across the ideological spectrum and to devise strategies that encouraged maximum popular participation.

The Komitee für Frieden, Abrüstung und Zusammenarbeit (Committee for Peace, Disarmament, and Cooperation) was the leading group of this communist wing. KOFAZ was founded in 1974 by people from pacifist organizations, the Protestant Versöhnungsbund (Reconciliation League) and other religious groups working on peace issues,[104] unions, factory councils, the student movement,[105] and the left wing of the SPD and FDP. They shared a consensus that détente as a political process should find its complement in military measures, that is, disarmament. The group strongly supported the SPD's détente policy and participation in the CSCE process, but it felt that disarmament was never pursued consistently enough. KOFAZ organized yearly demonstrations starting in 1976, demanding more rigorous détente and reductions in arms spending. In the early 1980s, the group's participation in the peace movement was self-evi-

---

104. Martin Niemöller, one of the most prominent Protestant figures in the peace movements of the 1950s and 1960s, was a founding member.

105. Mechthild Jansen, a veteran of the university-based Sozialistischer Hochschulbund, was an active member of KOFAZ.

dent. Although the group was concerned about the new missiles' technical qualities and strategic implications, far more important to KOFAZ was the way the missiles showed, both symbolically and practically, that détente was not leading to far-reaching arms control as the group had wished.[106]

The Sozialistische Deutsche Arbeiterjugend (Socialist German Youth Workers), or SDAJ, was an explicitly Marxist youth organization striving for a socialist West Germany on the general model of the Eastern bloc. Founded in 1968 (along with the revived Communist Party itself), SDAJ members came from unions, the student movement, opponents of the Vietnam War, and groups demanding higher wages and youth leisure opportunities. The SDAJ subsequently focused on young workers' interests, pushing for more apprenticeship positions and youth recreation centers. The SDAJ was involved in foreign policy issues out of concern for the Soviet bloc and social spending. In the late 1960s it sympathized with Brandt's reform policies and organized strikes to support Ostpolitik. The SDAJ supported détente, peaceful coexistence, and arms control negotiations. Détente made possible East-West trade, which created jobs and reduced defamation of the left in domestic politics. Like KOFAZ, the SDAJ was disappointed that détente was not carried further and felt that social spending should have had priority over arms purchases. It opposed the double-track decision because the new missiles would expand American capacity to take military action against the Soviet Union.[107]

Although they were not explicitly Marxist, three further groups were commonly attributed to the communist (KOFAZ) spectrum because they generally sided with KOFAZ in meetings of the movement's Coordinating Committee.[108] The DFG-VK (Deutsche Friedensgesellschaft—Vereinigte Kriegsdienstgegner, "German Peace Society—United Conscientious Objectors") was the umbrella organization for conscientious objectors. With over 150 local chapters, it was one of the peace movement's largest mass organizations. Its geographical spread and relatively tight organizational structure gave the DFG-VK an important mobilizing function. As an umbrella association, the DFG-VK had members from the SPD leftward. The peace movement's different wings were reflected in miniature within the DFG-VK, which enabled the organization to be a bridge between the movement's communist, social democratic, and independent

---

106. Interview with a KOFAZ representative.
107. Interview with an SDAJ representative.
108. See, for example, Thomas Leif, *Die Strategische (Ohn-)Macht der Friedensbewegung: Kommunikations- und Entscheidungsstrukturen in den achtziger Jahren* (Opladen: Westdeutscher Verlag, 1990), 41–46.

wings. The DFG-VK was heir to two German pacifist traditions, bourgeois and radical.

The Deutsche Friedensgesellschaft (DFG) was founded in 1892 by Berta von Suttner and became the chief representative of bourgeois pacifism, working for international understanding, an international legal system, and domestic democratization. One "radical" wing adopted democratic socialism and propagated conscientious objection. After dissolution by the Nazis, the DFG was rebuilt after the war. Until 1968 it remained bourgeois-pacifist, oriented toward an international legal order and peaceful coexistence. The DFG was the first pacifist organization to take up contacts with the East German Peace Council (Friedensrat).

The DFG banded together in 1968 with the IdK, the Internationale der Kriegsdienstverweigerer (Conscientious Objectors' International). Founded in 1919, the IdK was originally a radically pacifist organization. Besides conscientious objection, the IdK worked in the 1950s for East-West understanding and disarmament. It was an active supporter of the anti-rearmament and the Kampf dem Atomtod campaigns and of the Easter March movement. The IdK was not known for pioneering theoretical work but brought a wide network of local conscientious objectors' groups into the fusion.

A third organization, the Verband der Kriegsdienstverweigerer (Association of Conscientious Objectors), or VK, joined the centripetal trend in 1974. The VK understood itself more as a conscientious objectors' pressure group or union than as a pacifist organization, and it had strong connections to the SPD's youth group (Jungsozialisten) and the union youth group (DGB-Jugend). In the 1980s, the DFG-VK still had two wings: a radical-pacifist, antimilitarist position; and a traditional bourgeois pacifism promoting international law and collective security systems.[109] The DFG-VK advised conscientious objectors and worked toward disarmament, coupling individual renunciation of force through conscientious objection with collective renunciation of force through disarmament.[110]

The Bundesschülervertretung (National Association of High School Students) was an umbrella group of high school student associations fighting against cuts in education spending and for students' rights. Work in the peace movement was also important for the organization, since students saw no point in merely studying for their individual futures when their very survival might be at stake. One avenue for involvement in the peace movement was through "peace education" *(Friedenserziehung)* in the

---

109. On the conflicts between these two wings, see also "Innerverbandliche 'Nullösung'?" *Graswurzelrevolution* 76 (June 1983): 34–37.

110. Interview with a DFG-VK representative.

schools, a movement in the 1970s to include peace-oriented projects in the curriculum. Schools took part in the unions' annual "antiwar days" *(Anti-Kriegstage)* and in the various anniversary observances of Hitler's assumption of power.[111]

The Vereinigung der Verfolgten des Naziregimes—Bund der Antifaschisten (Association of Those Persecuted by the Nazis—League of Antifascists), or VVN, was a small group that played a small role in peace movement proceedings. It was founded in 1946 by concentration camp survivors, and in its "oath of Buchenwald," it pledged to destroy Nazism at its roots and build a new world of freedom and peace. The VVN participated in the campaigns against remilitarization and nuclear weapons in the 1950s and 1960s. During the 1980s peace movement, the VVN argued against new medium-range missiles with the motto "The 55 million dead of World War II warn: Never again may a war be waged from German soil." In its brochures, the VVN drew a parallel between the Nazis' aggression and the aggressive military strategies of the "warmonger" Reagan administration that the new missiles were supposed to serve.[112]

The independent spectrum represented the new social movements in the 1980s peace movement. The ecology, women's, and "alternative" movements all found their place in this wing and brought their own special issues and flavor into the movement as a whole. New social movements got involved in the peace movement because of the military's impact on women, the environment, and social/economic structures. Opposition to the missiles became part of the struggle for these causes. In addition, groups embodying further themes of the extraparliamentary left in the 1970s found their place here. Groups dedicated to grassroots democracy, anarchism, independent socialism, and the Third World were all part of the independent spectrum. The Greens were an anomaly in this spectrum. By far the largest member, they were also the only party. The Greens lay both at the center and at the fringes of this wing. The Greens were its most vocal representatives, and yet the independents felt great ambivalence toward all parties, even one that emerged from their midst and represented their views far better than any other.

The ecology movement was represented in the peace movement's Coordinating Committee by the Bundesverband Bürgerinitiativen Umweltschutz (National Association of Citizens' Initiatives for Environmental Protection), or BBU, with over one thousand affiliated initiatives and over three hundred thousand individual members. The citizens' initia-

---

111. Interview with a member of the Bundesschülervertretung.

112. Präsidium der VVN—Bund der Antifascisten, eds., *Antifascistischer Jugenddienst—Informationen für Jugendpresse,* brochure, no. 2 (Frankfurt, 1984); and *Pershing II und Cruise Missiles—Stück für Stück in die USA zurück,* leaflet (Frankfurt, 1984).

tives contributed considerable manpower and organizational skill at the national and local levels, having earlier brought "new politics" themes and unconventional forms of political action into middle-class mainstream circles. New *Friedensinitiativen* (local peace groups) established in the course of the peace movement followed the example set by ecology-oriented citizens' initiatives in many cities. The BBU correspondingly played a significant role in the Coordinating Committee, and its best known leader, Jo Leinen, emerged as one of the peace movement's main spokespersons vis-à-vis the media and the federal government.

The ecology movement did not slide effortlessly into involvement with the peace movement.[113] On the contrary, the transition from ecology to peace required recognition of the relationship between the two. In the mid-1970s, antimilitarist themes were received with mistrust among the ecologists fighting nuclear power in the southwest German Kaiserstühl area.[114] Individual ecology activists pushed for cooperation with peace, women's, and Third World movements; but not until the double-track decision did nuclear war become pressing for most of the ecology movement.

Several developments moved the ecology movement toward consideration of defense issues. The antinuclear power movement provided one thematic link between ecology and peace, since the nuclear power industry could provide the materials needed for atomic weapons. The export of nuclear power plants to Brazil and Iran, with the accompanying danger of nuclear weapons proliferation, helped drive home the connection between all things nuclear. West Germany's budding plutonium industry through the *Schneller Brüter* technology and nuclear reprocessing plants provided another stimulus. A brochure entitled "Friedlich in den Atomkrieg" described West Germany's capacity to produce plutonium for nuclear weapons, suggesting that West Germany had both the technical capacities for nuclear weapons and a number of politicians who wanted them. The notion of West Germany possessing its own nuclear weapons was of course one of the left's ultimate horror visions.

In addition, several joint projects effected an alliance between, and

---

113. Petra Kelly, "Wie sich die Ökologiebewegung zur Friedensbewegung erweiterte, Variante A," and Jo Leinen, "Wie sich die Ökologiebewegung zur Friedensbewegung erweiterte, Variante B," both in *Prinzip Leben: Ökopax—die neue Kraft,* ed. Kelly and Leinen (Berlin: Olle and Wolter, 1982), 5–14 and 15–20, respectively.

114. Many of the more conservative elements (especially local winegrowers) of these antinuclear groups considered the peace issue a "leftist," and therefore suspect, cause. Leinen notes, however, that resistance also came from radicals who had belonged to the former K-Gruppen, who apparently did not want the Chinese nuclear potential to come under possible fire. See Leinen, "Wie sich die Ökologiebewegung zur Friedensbewegung erweiterte, Variante B," 18.

even a temporary merging of, the ecology and peace movements. Between 1978 and 1980, the BBU (environmental initiatives) and the DFG-VK (conscientious objectors) conducted various joint programs, notably the 1979 conference entitled "Ecology and Peace," which generated similar events by other peace and ecology groups and eventually a permanent study group in the BBU with that name. The Greens also tied these two themes together in their party program. Indeed, several of the most prominent BBU leaders, in particular Petra Kelly and Roland Vogt, were among the founders of the Greens. Many local citizens' initiatives also linked the two themes, protesting against local military activity, like noise from low-flying air force jets and the military's destruction of natural areas and farmland.[115] As Jo Leinen noted, it seemed halfhearted to protest against woodlands destruction for expansion of Frankfurt's airport while not fighting landscape destruction for expansion of military facilities.[116] People began to view the environmental impact of both military and industrial activity as springing from a common "mega-technological insanity" and the economic interests behind it.[117] Ecology movement activism in defense questions exploded with the birth of the 1980s peace movement. The BBU and the Greens were among the founding members of the alliance that formed its national core.

Women's groups played a prominent role in the peace movement from the beginning.[118] They generally joined the movement after linking women's questions with defense issues. Wars and defense policy, they argued, affected women as mothers, civilians, and reserve labor. As participants both in the women's movement itself and in other new social movements of the 1970s, women were well positioned for mobilization into the peace movement. They were heavily involved in the antinuclear power movement, often via women's groups. The feminist magazine *Courage*, for example, organized a conference in 1980 (Frauen gegen Atom und Militär), which brought out the links between women's opposition to nuclear

115. See, for example, the BBU's 1984 brochure entitled "Verkehrsplanung für den Krieg," on how the military influences civilian planning for transportation infrastructure, with corresponding environmental destruction. (Bundesverband Bürgerinitiativen Unweltschutz, "Verkehrsplanung für den Krieg?" brochure [Bonn, April 1984].)

116. Leinen, "Wie sich die Ökologiebewegung zur Friedensbewegung erweiterte, Variante B," 17.

117. As quoted in Kelly, "Wie sich die Ökologiebewegung zur Friedensbewegung erweiterte, Variante A," 9.

118. According to one observer, however, women's work in the movement has largely gone unnoticed in publications concerning the movement, as is usual with women's contributions to historical developments. Similarly, women's demands with respect to peace issues have received little attention in the press. See Edith Laudowicz, "Frauen und Friedensbewegung: Überlegungen zur aktuellen Diskussion," *Blätter für deutsche und internationale Politik* 27, no. 1 (1982): 74–88, here 74.

power and the military. Strongly influenced by the antinuclear power movement, the conference drew the connection between nuclear power and the effects of nuclear explosions. *Courage* articles often argued that both nuclear weapons and nuclear power reflected aggressive male drives and the will to dominate.[119]

From 1978 on, government proposals to integrate women into the army concretized "militarism" as a topic for women's groups. Indeed, one of their most distinctive protest forms was the *Verweigerungskampagne* (refusal campaign), in which women refused to cooperate with defense policy planning, even in civilian capacities like nursing. Proposals for "women in the army" led women to look more closely at "high politics," bringing them out of their previous focus on sexuality, violence against women, and consciousness raising. In the process, women made the leap to the peace movement. Other issues concerning women and the military emerged: whether a specifically female concept of peace exists; the relationship between increased defense spending and cuts in social spending, with its special impact on women; and foreign policy and women in the Third World.[120]

Although work in the peace movement has helped German feminism overcome its divisions to a certain extent, the distinction between socialist and radical feminism was evident in both movements. A group against women in the army (Frauen in die Bundeswehr—wir sagen Nein!) had a socialist stamp and was considered part of the KOFAZ (communist) spectrum of the peace movement, particularly since its chief spokesperson, Mechthild Jansen, was a KOFAZ member. In a letter to women in the peace movement, Jansen denied the importance of gender-specific issues, subsuming them instead under broader class ("societal") concerns. She also stressed the group's alliance with the labor movement. The group concentrated on the question of women in the army but also demanded liberal access to abortion and supported the labor unions' platform of a thirty-five-hour work week with no wage reductions.[121]

Although not communist, women's groups within the unions came at the question from a similar perspective. At DGB women's conferences, discussion revolved around the relationship between increased military spending and social spending cuts, particularly those affecting women (e.g., cuts in state funding of child care). Likewise, DGB women opposed the military's recruitment of women volunteers by offering them "career opportunities," taking advantage of female unemployment. This helped

---

119. Laudowicz, "Frauen und Friedensbewegung," 77.
120. Interview with a representative of Frauen gegen Krieg und Militarismus, Hamburg.
121. Cited in Leif, *Die strategische (Ohn-)Macht*, 43.

militarize society and would not improve women's occupational status. This position typified too the opposition to *drafting* women into the army. However, one noted feminist, Alice Schwarzer, argued that formal equality demanded equal access for women to positions in the armed forces, while she at the same time personally supported conscientious objection to military service.[122]

Other women's groups in the peace movement came from feminism's radical wing. Some attributed war to men's aggressive nature (whereas women, they argued, are by nature peaceful), thus using gender categories rather than historical explanations. Others argued against describing peace as the absence of actual fighting, for this definition masked the violence confronting women's everyday life within patriarchal structures.[123] The Anstiftung der Frauen für den Frieden (Association of Women for Peace) represented the radical feminist tendency within the peace movement's Coordinating Committee. As the group noted, women's emancipation would only come about via a demilitarization of society and a worldwide women's league against nuclear weapons and nuclear power. An essential goal was to fight violence against women by way of citizens' political involvement, not by depending on military blocs or parties.[124]

Another group conducted a study of the effects of war on women by inviting older women, who had directly experienced World War II, to join their study group. Rather than stressing capitalist economic systems, they looked more closely at patriarchal relationships and authoritarian state structures. They concluded that the state functionalized men as soldiers just as it did women as mothers of future soldiers. At the same time, societies at war exploited women with extra efficiency, forcing them to work in war-production industries at low wages while they also reared children under materially poor conditions. Since women constituted a large share of the civilian populace, their suffering at the hands of bombings and invading armies was correspondingly large. War was thus the worst form of institutionalized violence against women. Nuclear weapons had multiplied this tendency to an infinite degree and therefore required women's resistance at all levels.[125]

Antiauthoritarian, anarchist, and independent socialist impulses from the late 1960s found various roles in the peace movement. Indeed, several groups of the peace movement's Coordinating Committee came

---

122. Laudowicz, "Frauen und Friedensbewegung," 75–80.

123. Ibid., 80–84.

124. Cited in Leif, *Die strategische (Ohn-)Macht,* 38.

125. Edith Abel et al., *Bericht über das Projekt: Gewalterfahrungen von Frauen im Alltag—Zusammenhänge zwischen Sexismus und Militarismus* (Bonn: Fachbereich Frauen des Bildungswerks für Friedensarbeit, 1983).

from these traditions. The Komitee für Grundrechte und Demokratie (Committee for Basic Rights and Democracy), or KGD, was a relatively small organization, founded by intellectuals connected to the Sozialistisches Büro. Members tended to be "undogmatic" socialists or liberal reformers. Many were social scientists, like Wolf-Dieter Narr and Oskar Negt. Others were prominent figures from religious, literary, or other circles, like Heinrich Albertz, Walter Dirks, Ingeborg Drewitz, Helmut Gollwitzer, Robert Jungk, Horst-Eberhard Richter, and Dorothee Sölle, many of whom had been active in protest politics since the 1950s or 1960s.

The KGD was founded in 1980, in response to growing dangers to democratic rights in West Germany from economic crisis, the end of the 1970s reform policies, and general conservative tendencies. The KGD publicized violations of democratic rights, such as curtailments of the right to demonstrate, and cases involving the notorious *Berufsverbot,* the prohibition of radicals in public service. The KGD also sought to overcome structural inequalities for women, the elderly, prisoners, children, homosexuals, and so on. Although the KGD had only around eighty core members, its outreach was much greater. Its policy studies circulated to other political organizations, including parties, unions, professional organizations, and social movements. The KGD also held conferences on specific topics open to the entire left. Many of its reports were published in the Rowohlt publishing house's Rororo series, with a very large distribution.

Another area of concern was peace, largely due to the presence of veterans from previous peace protest. Klaus Vack, for example, worked in unions and in the Kampf dem Atomtod movement of the 1950s and thus represented the antimilitarist labor tradition. Others, like Helmut Gollwitzer and Heinrich Albertz, had long been active in Protestant peace protest. Still others, like Andreas Buro, come from the pacifist tradition and the conscientious objectors' movement. Active in the 1950s and 1960s, they turned to other questions in the 1970s, assuming that détente had put West German foreign policy on a better footing. They also realized that fighting "the bomb" required attacking the social processes behind it.

In the 1970s, activists worked in citizens' initiatives, parties, and social movements. After NATO's double-track decision, they returned to peace issues, hoping to use defense issues to mobilize grassroots participation and political consciousness. The KGD opposed the double-track decision for many reasons. It worried that the missiles would increase the militarization of society, encouraging people to think in militaristic categories of friend and enemy, which would inhibit "learning processes" furthering democratic development. The weapons decision could also lead the government to subordinate democratic rights to the requirements of deployment.[126]

The Föderation gewaltfreier Aktionsgruppen (Federation of Nonviolent Action Groups), or FöGA, was an umbrella organization of autonomous, grassroots groups dedicated to "libertarian socialism," or anarchism in the tradition of anarcho-syndicalism.[127] FöGA groups strove for a decentralized, nonhierarchical society that permitted self-determination of individuals and small social units. They envisioned "grassroots revolution" as a strategy for overcoming the multiple forms of power and violence in society, including the state and other instruments of rule. Self-organization of the oppressed in concrete areas like tenants' unions, factory groups, and environmental groups would lead people to unmask the "democratic" order and to overcome dominance by hierarchical structures. Other principles included nonviolent direct action (as opposed to working through parliaments), personal liberation, and alternatives to the current system, like food cooperatives, autonomous youth centers, communes, and so on.[128]

The oldest FöGA groups dated back to 1972. Many of their members were active in the student movement, in the citizens' initiatives, and as conscientious objectors. In the 1970s and 1980s, FöGA groups were heavily involved in the struggle against nuclear power—in their eyes the worst example of centralized technology and concentrated political and economic power—and also in other ecological causes. A typical article in *Graswurzelrevolution* discussed the connections between capitalist interests, government's links to these interests, and ecological destruction.[129]

FöGA groups also pursued antimilitarism, including "demilitarization of society," total unilateral disarmament, and the dissolution of military blocs. The double-track decision provided them with a concrete issue around which to articulate their broader positions. FöGA groups tied their critique of the NATO decision to the military's effects on social structures, in particular socialization of the citizenry to serve state interests.[130]

---

126. Interview with a KGD representative.
127. Interview with a FöGA representative. A drawing in the magazine *Graswurzelrevolution* (no. 7 [winter 1974]: 3) declares the magazine to be a "Zeitschrift für gewaltfreie libertär-sozialistische Gesellschaftsveränderung und Macht von unten" [Journal for nonviolent, libertarian-socialist change in society and grassroots power].
128. "Was heisst 'Graswurzelrevolution'?" *Graswurzelrevolution* 7 (winter 1974): 3–4. See also Andreas Kirchgäßner, "Diskussionsbeitrag: Was heisst 'Graswurzel'?" *Graswurzelrevolution* 34–35 (spring 1978): 16. For a criticism of parliamentary work, see "Bürgerinitiativen und Wahlen," *Graswurzelrevolution* 34–35 (spring 1978): 1.
129. For example, Bernd Clever, "Ökologie und strukturelle Gewalt," *Graswurzelrevolution* 16 (spring 1975): 3–4.
130. Interview with FöGA representative.

In this vein, a number of articles urged participation in the *Verweigerungskampagne,* a campaign calling on young men to abjure military service not just through conscientious objection but also through refusal to participate in anything that served the military, militaristic attitudes, or social structures supporting either. Training judges and attorneys for work in military courts, training personnel for medical service during large-scale crises, military propaganda at schools, and military recruitment were all targets of this campaign.[131]

FöGA groups were typical of the autonomous peace initiatives loosely organized in the Bundeskonferenz Unabhängiger Friedensgruppen (Conference of Independent Peace Groups), or BUF, and the Koordinationsstelle ziviler Ungehorsam (Coordinating Office of Civil Disobedience), or ZU.[132] Not linked to any party, most of these independent peace initiatives were of recent vintage, but the founding members passed through many of the stages of the radical left in the 1970s—the student movement, citizens' initiatives, the house-squatters movement, the K-Gruppen, conscientious objection, and the antinuclear power movement—from which they brought an emphasis on civil disobedience and blockades. This experience taught them that political goals could only be realized through direct confrontation with government institutions "from the streets," rather than through work in parties and unions. They therefore preferred civil disobedience and other radical protest forms and considered even demonstrations too tame. For BUF groups, the peace movement was a stage in their struggle against established political power and policies.[133]

The Bundeskongress entwicklungspolitischer Aktionsgruppen (National Congress of Development Aid Groups), or BUKO, is an umbrella association encompassing about 1,100 of West Germany's 3,000–4,000 groups interested in the Third World. West Germany's Third World movement supports "liberation struggles" by groups fighting Western "imperialism" and capitalist "exploitation" in the Third World. The movement's first interests were the Algerian War and South African apartheid. From 1965 on, the Vietnam War became the dominant internationalist theme for the entire extraparliamentary left. Protesters of all generations saw their positive images of American democracy destroyed, an especially poignant experience given the admiration for Kennedy. They

---

131. See, for example, Michael Lang, "Seid Sand im Getriebe!" *Graswurzelrevolution* 86 (June 1984): 16–17; and Ulrich Bröcklung, "Fünf vor Zwölf," *Graswurzelrevolution* 83 (Apr. 1984): 7–9.

132. The BUF was the successor to the Bundeskongreß der autonomen Friedensbewegung, or BAF.

133. Interview with a BUF representative.

also raised larger ideological questions, for they related the war to capitalist economic and strategic calculations.[134] Concern for Vietnam stimulated
rediscovery of classic internationalist texts.

Opposition to the Vietnam War laid the foundation for the Third
World movement of succeeding decades. It taught the necessity for action
outside of parties and parliaments and destroyed identification with "the
West" dating from the beginning of the cold war. The Third World became
the source of hope for revolutionary change after the SPD supported the
Emergency Laws and the United States in Vietnam. Brandt's Third World
policy initially showed promise, for he appointed left-leaning Erhard
Eppler to head the "development ministry," the Bundesministerium für
wirtschaftliche Zusammenarbeit (BMZ). Eppler, however, resigned after
the Schmidt government failed to raise the development aid budget as
promised. As events unfolded in the 1960s, the Third World movement
shifted from country to country—from Vietnam to Iran, the Congo,
Angola, and Mozambique—while in the 1970s and 1980s, Chile,
Argentina, Portugal, South Africa, and Central America underwent revolutions, putsches, and other crises. Church groups became involved in the
movement, gradually moving from humanitarian aid alone to more radically politicized views. In addition, Maoist K-Gruppen, Soviet-oriented
groups, and the undogmatic left struggled for influence within the Third
World movement.[135]

The peace movement stimulated the Third World movement to think
again about war and armed conflict. The majority of Third World groups
eventually joined the peace movement, but this did not happen automati-
cally. Long discussions were needed before Third World groups came to
realize the importance of the peace movement for their own work. Con-
versely, it also took time for the peace movement to realize that antiwar
and peace promotion included supporting liberation struggles. The Third
World movement eventually came to see the double-track decision
(together with the Rapid Deployment Force, the Host Nation Support
agreements, and strategies like the AirLand Battle 2000) as part of a
broader "imperialist" strategy to increase American/NATO capacity to
intervene in the Third World.[136]

The Greens represented an anomaly within the independent radical
left, for they were supported by groups and movements that ordinarily
detested parties. The Greens became the parliamentary representatives of

---

134. Werner Balsen and Karl Rössel, *Hoch die internationale Solidarität: Zur
Geschichte der Dritte Welt-Bewegung in der Bundesrepublik* (Cologne: Kölner Volksblatt Verlag, 1986), 123–30.

135. Ibid., 219.

136. Interview with a BUKO representative.

many who had left the SPD or FDP in the 1960s or 1970s. Founded in the late 1970s at the state *(Land)* level and as a federal party in early 1980, the Greens at last gave parliamentary expression to "new social movement" themes through representation in the Bundestag (starting in 1983) and in many of the state parliaments. The Greens represented three different aspects of the "new politics": its radical-democratic thrust, its social emancipatory character, and "new" issues like ecology, feminism, and peace that were previously neglected in German politics.

The ecology movement contributed the first issue around which the Greens formed, with people coming both from the citizens' initiatives and the antinuclear power wings. The Greens railed against industrial production techniques damaging to the environment and demanded concrete improvements, such as environmentally sensitive transportation with an emphasis on mass transit. Yet the Greens pursued more than a set of environmental policies, seeking an alternative society that would end exploitation of human labor and plunder of natural resources. Their quest for an "attainable utopia" of small, self-determined alternative projects rejected West Germany's traditional faith in economic growth, technology, and large-scale industry. A second pillar of Green politics was its critique of patriarchal culture and advocacy of women's equality. The Greens demanded legislation mandating equal educational and professional opportunities for women, paid parental leave and remuneration for child rearing, strict punishment for domestic violence, and full legalization of abortion.[137]

The Greens blamed social ills largely on growth-oriented industrial society, patriarchal culture, and the politics that undergirded them. Thus, in keeping with their maximalist policy demands (especially among party "fundamentalists"), the Greens felt that the political process itself had to undergo radical transformation. The Greens worried about the health of West German democracy as then constituted, fearful that the state cowed citizens and restricted popular participation through police surveillance, overbureaucratization, restrictions on protest forms (especially prosecution of nonviolent blockades as "coercion"), plans for computerized identity cards, and so on. In addition, the Greens wanted to move toward a much more decentralized, self-determined, grassroots form of politics. The Greens began with themselves, as an "antiparty party" different from conventional competitors. Within the party, the Greens initiated various pro

---

137. Die Grünen, *Das Bundesprogramm* (Bonn, 1980); Markovits and Gorski, *The German Left*, chaps. 4–6; Burns and van der Will, *Protest and Democracy in West Germany*, chap. 7.

cedures to put their democratic ideals into practice, including open meetings at all levels of the party, a "consensus principle" of decision making to protect minorities within the party, rotation of Bundestag seats among party members, and gender parity in leadership bodies and elected committees. Some of these practices had to be modified, however, when they proved unexpectedly controversial or disadvantageous.[138]

Opposition to the double-track decision rested on the same analysis as other Green positions, that is, on their fundamental critique of advanced industrial society. Historically, the same economic interests and the same technocratic attitudes toward nature that caused environmental destruction had also developed nuclear weapons that could destroy human life. As we will see in greater detail later in this chapter, for the Greens the pursuit of economic growth had pushed both superpowers into military and nuclear competition with each other, resulting in an arms race that threatened to destroy all life, with Europe but a battlefield between the two. Thus the German government's reliance on deterrence for military "security" was totally misguided. During the early 1980s, the Greens argued that Germany should withdraw from NATO, begin unilateral disarmament, and switch to nonmilitary defense.

Finally, the peace movement contained a small minority primarily concerned with the German question. Nationalism was not central to the movement's issues, nor was the movement as a whole strongly nationalist, but it did become a vehicle for nationalism to a limited extent, which of course had enormous potential implications for European politics at the time.[139] The movement, moreover, implicitly (and occasionally explicitly) linked pacifism with nationalism, because the security fears central to its identity formed the basis for a new facet of German identity. According to Verheyen, "It was nuclear *Angst* that led the Left to focus increasingly on a shared West German–East German 'peace interest.' . . . The new all-German consciousness . . . was generated by a desire to 'escape' from a Cold War that increased the chances of a conflict in which Germany would be the foremost casualty."[140] Or, in Diner's terms, for the peace movement America's perceived military decoupling from Europe, embodied in its talk of "limited nuclear war," implicitly reopened the German question by raising interest in a Central European zone of military engagement. If such

---

138. E. Gene Frankland and Donald Schoonmaker, *Between Protest and Power: The Green Party in Germany* (Boulder, Colo.: Westview Press, 1992), chaps. 5 and 7; Burns and van der Will, *Protest and Democracy in West Germany,* chap. 7.

139. Kim Holmes, *The West German Peace Movement and the National Question* (Cambridge, Mass.: Institute for Foreign Policy Analysis, 1984), 49.

140. Verheyen, *The German Question,* 178.

a zone were created, motivated first and foremost by security concerns, it would reopen the possibility of German reunification.[141]

Composed primarily of rather prominent individuals from different parts of the larger movement, this minority did not form an organized group, although it attracted a great deal of media attention. For some, nationalism was primarily a question of self-assertion against the super-powers, a search for protection of Germany from nuclear destruction, and a desire to escape becoming victims of American policy or superpower conflict. Within the Greens, for example, Rainer Trampert felt that the United States viewed Germany as a convenient "launching pad," through which America could shift the threat from its territory to Central Europe. Gerd Bastian, a former Bundeswehr general prominent in the Greens for a time, had always opposed the American military presence in West Germany and its influence on German politics. He particularly opposed the use of nuclear weapons in case of war, because they would destroy what they were supposed to defend. Precisely his commitment to defense of the "homeland" drove him from the army and into the peace movement. Similarly, Alfred Mechtersheimer, a former CDU parliamentarian who joined the Greens, hoped that the peace movement would help rid West Germany of American political and military influence.

The Greens' interest in neutralism and hopes of dissolving the military blocs derived primarily from their goal of severing German security links with the United States and escaping the "logic" of deterrence, although they realized that dissolution of the military blocs would help overcome the division of Europe and therefore of Germany as well. (When German unification under capitalist and western auspices finally became a reality in 1990, however, the Greens were distinctly unenthusiastic.) A number of Social Democrats held similar views. Social Democratic dissident Erhard Eppler, who in the 1950s had belonged to the neutralist Gesamtdeutsche Volkspartei, hoped that the peace movement would serve as a vehicle for national self-assertion against the superpowers, in particular against American influence on West Germany. Similarly, Heinrich Albertz saw in the peace movement a way to encourage West and East German withdrawal from the bloc system in Europe.

For some in the peace movement, however, nationalism included an active commitment to German reunification. On the left, the most committed were Herbert Ammon and Peter Brandt (Willy Brandt's son). Far removed from the anticommunist, right-wing nationalism of the Springer press and other West German conservatives, Brandt and Ammon hoped

---

141. Dan Diner, "Die 'nationale Frage' in der Friedensbewegung," in *Die neue Friedensbewegung: Analysen aus der Friedensforschung,* ed. Reiner Steinweg (Frankfurt: Suhrkamp Verlag, 1982), 86–112, here 91–92.

for an eventually neutralized German confederation via gradual withdrawal of both German states from their respective blocs, which would free the way for a national identity based on democratic socialism. For such thinkers, socialism had a much better chance in a unified Germany than in West Germany as then constituted. For Egon Bahr, an East-West "collective security" system would have both preserved peace and kept open the national option of eventual reunification as well.

Finally, a small number of right-wing patriots made common cause with the peace movement for opportunistic reasons. Looking to overcome the superpowers' "bipolar imperialism," Wolfgang Venohr in particular advocated a nationalist peace policy from the right. Similarly, historian Hellmut Diwald saw the United States as the most responsible for continuing German division. For both, association with the peace movement was a way to promote getting rid of foreign influences of all sorts.[142]

Conflicts within the Peace Movement over Political Questions

Constituting the core of the 1980s peace movement, the many groups described in the preceding sections of this chapter distributed themselves among four distinct wings—social democratic, communist, Green/independent, and Christian. Not surprisingly, this heterogeneity led to considerable conflict within the movement over various political positions and movement strategies, which led to the emergence of two main camps. The trademark of the first camp was its orientation toward traditional left politics. This "traditional" spectrum included DKP/Soviet-oriented communist groups like KOFAZ and the SDAJ; mainstream SPD/FDP groups (IFIAS, Jusos, Judos, Liberale Demokraten, etc.); and several Christian groups (Ohne Rüstung Leben, Aktion Sühnezeichen, Aktionsgemeinschaft Dienst für den Frieden, and Pax Christi). These groups oriented their protest toward influencing government decisions within West Germany's parliamentary structure. Their long-term goals did not require radical changes in existing political structures for their realization.

The second camp leaned toward a "new" understanding of politics, reflecting the antiauthoritarian impulses and new social movements of the 1960s and 1970s. This camp included the Greens and the independent spectrum—libertarian socialists (FöGA), independent peace groups (BUF), Third World Groups (BUKO), citizens' initiatives on ecology (BBU), independent socialists (KGD), and radical Christian groups like the Catholic IKvU, some local Pax Christi groups, ESG (Protestant university youth) chapters, and some member groups of the Protestant

---

142. Holmes, *The West German Peace Movement and the National Question.*

AGDF. These groups were oriented toward grassroots democracy and "alternative" approaches to economic and political organization, and their long-term goals, while often vague, generally required a substantial transformation of West Germany's political system.

Conflicts erupted frequently and intensely between the two camps, revolving around two clusters of issues: the sources of danger in the international system; and the movement's position toward the Soviet medium-range nuclear missiles targeted on Europe, the Polish Solidarity movement, and Eastern European peace movements. As heads of the "traditional" and "new" peace movement camps, respectively, KOFAZ and the Greens had significantly diverging views on the sources of danger in the international system. With its communist leanings, KOFAZ identified the United States as the sole important source of danger, consistently painting the United States as an aggressor with irredeemably militarist attitudes. The Pentagon, arms profiteers, and other militarists, noted KOFAZ, threatened to drag the world into a nuclear inferno. They sought to "roll back" communism in the East, using Europe as a pawn and keeping the United States out of danger. The United States refused to renounce first use of nuclear weapons, despite Soviet proposals that both sides do so.[143] Similarly, KOFAZ argued that the United States always initiated technical innovations in nuclear systems and was thus responsible for the arms race.[144]

According to KOFAZ, American military strategy, moreover, posed the fundamental threat to world peace. The United States considered military force the only viable approach to the Western economic crisis and Third World political instabilities. Reagan enthusiastically pushed the strategy of supremacy and had vastly accelerated the arms buildup. SALT II had still not been ratified, and strategists now considered "limited nuclear war" an option. The arms buildup was providing America with a first-strike capacity against the Soviet Union and increasing its capacities for worldwide intervention.[145]

In KOFAZ's eyes, the Soviet Union bore little responsibility for international tensions. On the contrary, it had always been a defensive power reacting to Western aggression and aimed at a balance of power and main-

---

143. Gerhard Kade, *Auseinandersetzung in den USA,* booklet of the Komitee für Frieden, Abrüstung und Zusammenarbeit [KOFAZ] (Cologne, [ca. 1983]), 3–4.

144. Gerhard Stuby, *Vom Gleichgewicht des Schreckens zur gleichen Sicherheit,* booklet of the Komitee für Frieden, Abrüstung und Zusammenarbeit [KOFAZ] (Cologne, n.d.), 14; Komitee für Frieden, Abrüstung und Zusammenarbeit [KOFAZ], "Diskussionspapier," in *Reader,* ed. Koordinationsausschuß der Friedensbewegung, large booklet (Bonn, 1984), 51–59, here 51.

145. Achim Maske, "Zur politischen Perspektive der Friedensbewegung," unpublished essay (photocopy), (Cologne, 1984), 1, 2.

tenance of parity. The West's concern with human rights and other Soviet domestic policies was, quite simply, misplaced. Instead, normal relations between states with different social systems meant not questioning the other system's legitimacy.[146]

In the 1980s, Europe emerged as both accomplice and victim of American policy in KOFAZ's eyes. NATO's intention to station new missiles was part of a strategy to win a war in Europe on all levels.[147] The double-track decision revealed the divergence between European and American interests. Europe bore the risks of harm to East-West relations,[148] while the United States tried to impose on Europe the economic costs of its recent military buildup.[149]

Having identified the causes of danger in the international system, KOFAZ adhered to traditional remedies, such as détente, coexistence, cooperation, and disarmament negotiations. Following demilitarization and the eventual dissolution of both military blocs, Europe would be transformed from a divided continent to a partnership, corresponding to the SPD's notion of "security partnership." In contrast to the Greens, KOFAZ was against West German withdrawal from NATO. NATO as a military alliance was a mere institution, whereas American aggressiveness and its instrumentalization of NATO for repression of the Third World was the real problem. West German withdrawal from NATO would only make sense when détente, cooperation, "security partnerships," and disarmament had progressed far enough to dissolve both military blocs.[150]

For the other camp, best represented by the Greens, industrial society was the root cause of international conflict. For decades modern war machines have driven technical "progress." Man's exploitative relationship to nature and fellow humans has brought humanity to the brink of self-extinction.[151] A more specific threat to peace lay in the phenomenon of *Feindbilder,* "images of the enemy" based as much on ideological misperceptions as on actual behavior.[152] For KOFAZ, the West manipulated public opinion through anticommunist *Feindbilder,* whereas the Soviet Union merely responded to objective threats posed by hostile capitalist powers. In contrast, the Greens saw *both* sides as simultaneously victims

---

146. Stuby, *Vom Gleichgewicht,* 13–32.

147. Komitee für Frieden, Abrüstung und Zusammenarbeit [KOFAZ], *Anmerkungen zur gegenwärtigen Diskussion,* brochure (Köln, n.d.), 1.

148. Maske, "Zur politischen Perspektive," 3.

149. Stuby, *Vom Gleichgewicht,* 27.

150. KOFAZ, "Diskussionspapier," 54.

151. Die Grünen, *Friedensmanifest,* brochure, (Bonn, 1983), 3, 4. The *Friedensmanifest* was passed at the Greens' convention in Oct. 1981.

152. This concept of *Feindbilder* can be traced back to Dieter Senghaas's work on deterrence as an "autistic" system based on misperceptions.

and perpetrators of *Feindbilder*. In their *Friedensmanifest*, the Greens maintained: "Construction of *Feindbilder* was always a 'tried and true' contribution to war preparations. The 'enemy' is blamed for everything bad in the world, in the country's own society, and in man himself. . . . The result was always mass murder for an allegedly just cause. Thus today the United States government sees Moscow-proxy 'terrorists' in all parts of the world, while the Soviet government suspects an agent of 'world imperialism' in every dissident."[153]

The Greens' insistence that both sides shared the blame for international tensions led to conflicts with the communist (KOFAZ) spectrum on many different points. The Greens stressed that *both* military blocs treated their allies as their own territorial property and intervened in their domestic politics.[154] Thus while the Greens and the KOFAZ spectrum shared a highly negative opinion of the United States, the Greens also saw the Soviet system as imperialist, particularly in Eastern Europe.[155] The Greens explicitly denied that the Soviet Union was a "bastion of peace," calling it instead a military-political-bureaucratic-industrial complex. The Soviets had engaged in a massive arms program, and their SS-20s increased the threat to Western Europe.

This last point did not, however, lead the Greens to the NATO position of returning fire with fire, or recreating a military balance. Instead, the Greens maintained that the real threat to peace lay not in any one side's weapons or strategies but in the deterrence game itself. Each side contributed to the arms race, as all measures led to countermeasures. Since the arms race was out of control, the Greens opposed all new weapons—the Pershing II and cruise missiles and the SS-20 alike.[156]

The Greens' alternative to this perceived madness was a nuclear-free, neutral, demilitarized Europe and a German withdrawal from NATO. Neutralism would allow Europe to escape from the "logic of bloc confrontation" and its "dynamic of self-destruction."[157] A first step would be a unilateral West German withdrawal from the double-track decision and the expulsion of all nuclear weapons from its soil. West German nonalign-

153. Die Grünen, *Friedensmanifest*, 2.

154. Ibid., 9.

155. See, for example, the Greens' translation of Edward P. Thompson's article "'Exterminismus' als letztes Stadium der Zivilization," in Die Grünen, *Entrüstet Euch* (Bonn, 1983), 30–51, here 31, 32.

156. Die Grünen, *Friedensmanifest*, 8. See also Thompson's much more sophisticated rendition of this argument on the "logic of the arms race" in his article in Die Grünen, *Entrüstet Euch*, 30–51.

157. Die Grünen, *Friedensmanifest*, 8–11. See also Rudolf Bahro, "Überlegungen zu einem Neuansatz der Friedensbewegung in Deutschland," in *Entrüstet Euch*, by Die Grünen, 52–73.

ment would not be simply a unilateral act of bravado; it would force changes in East Germany and Eastern Europe. The *Feindbild* of an aggressive West Germany, which Eastern European governments used to maintain domestic legitimacy and loyalty to the Warsaw Pact, would crumble. Two nonaligned German states would also help end German and European division.

Although KOFAZ also hoped for eventual dissolution of the military blocs, their vision varied significantly from that of the Greens. For KOFAZ, *governments* would negotiate simultaneous bloc dissolution after a long chain of détente, disarmament, and confidence-building measures. For the Greens, the *populace* would force withdrawal from alliances, unilaterally if necessary, as part of a grassroots effort for peace. In the meantime, the Greens supported "social defense" *(soziale Verteidigung),* defense by nonmilitary means (outlined in chapter 4).[158]

Disagreements between KOFAZ and the Greens over the Soviet role in the international system led to disputes over three related questions: the peace movement's position on the Soviet SS-21s and SS-23s, its response to the Polish Solidarity movement, and its relationship to the various Eastern European peace movements. These debates took place mostly at the peace movement's planning sessions and usually resulted in a confrontation between KOFAZ and the Greens. In each case, KOFAZ tried to shield the Soviet bloc from criticism, while the Greens extolled the virtues of grassroots efforts toward change.

KOFAZ defended the Soviet SS-21s, SS-22s, and SS-23s as "countermeasures," that is, reactions to NATO's new medium-range missiles. In light of NATO's aggressive strategies, advances in weapons technology, and refusal to abjure first use of nuclear weapons, what choice did the Soviet Union have but to restore "equal security" through whatever means necessary? Military factors being a reality, as witnessed in Nicaragua, Cuba, Vietnam, and Grenada, universal renunciation of military force still constituted an unaffordable luxury.[159] In contrast, the Greens saw the new Soviet missiles as one further unilateral heightening of the danger of war in Europe. The peace movement had to demand their unilateral withdrawal exactly as it demanded the withdrawal of the NATO missiles.[160]

The Polish declaration of martial law and banning of the independent union "Solidarity" posed a similar dilemma for the peace movement.

---

158. Die Grünen, *Friedensmanifest,* 11–13. See also Dieter Trautmann, "Soziale Verteidigung als Alternative zur militärischen Verteidigung," in *Entrüstet Euch,* by Die Grünen, 128–37.

159. KOFAZ, "Diskussionspapier," 52, 53.

160. Ursel Sieber, "Keine Mehrheit für 'Raus aus der NATO,'" *Tageszeitung,* 7 May 1984.

KOFAZ tried to block discussion of Solidarity to prevent criticism of a Soviet-bloc government,[161] and it later praised martial law for helping to maintain peace ("friedenssicherende Wirkung").[162] Within the peace movement, KOFAZ warned those criticizing martial law against "destructive debates" that would enable "establishment"-oriented anticommunism to paralyze the movement.[163] When the Greens and others did not, however, allow themselves to be deterred, KOFAZ demanded that the topic be excluded from discussion.[164]

The social democratic wing, also generally "traditional" in its orientation, reacted in accordance with its commitment to détente. It expressed regrets that martial law was crushing Solidarity, but it warned against instrumentalizing Polish domestic instability. Trying to break Poland out of the Warsaw Pact, for example, would violate principles that had helped maintain peace in Europe: respecting spheres of influence, nonintervention, and détente. Encouraging Polish domestic instability would only increase the chance of superpower intervention and conflict. The peace movement ought not adopt Poland as its central theme or let itself be distracted from its main task.[165]

The Greens declared their support for Solidarity and for the Czechoslovakian Charta '77 struggles for political/civil rights and identified with their principles of social justice, grassroots democracy, and nonviolence.[166] Petra Kelly compared Polish military rule with similar measures by Turkish and Chilean generals, implying that all military regimes were equally repressive. Martial law had proved that social change within the two blocs really was impossible. Détente, therefore, also had its limits because it was practiced only within these rigid bloc structures. If the peace movement wanted credibility, it had to demonstrate against attempts to thwart democratization not only in Turkey and Latin America but wherever they took place, including Poland. Stopping the medium-range mis-

161. "Quo vadis, Friedensbewegung," *Tageszeitung*, 10 Feb. 1982.

162. Georg Paul Hefty, "Die Überlebens-Parole eint nicht mehr," *Frankfurter Allgemeine Zeitung*, 8 Apr. 1982.

163. Rüdiger Schlaga and Hans-Joachim Spanger, "Die Friedensbewegung und der Warschauer Pakt: Ein Spannungsverhältnis," in *Die neue Friedensbewegung*, ed. Reiner Steinweg (Frankfurt: Suhrkamp Verlag, 1982), 54–86, here 66.

164. Karl-Heinz Janssen, "Ein klares Wort zu Polen," *Die Zeit*, 12 Feb. 1982. See also Rüdiger Schlaga, "Polen: Beginn vom Zerfall der Friedensbewegung?" *Graswurzelrevolution* 62 (May 1982): 25–26.

165. Christoph Strässer, "Jetzt wichtiger denn je: Frieden durch Abrüstung," *Blätter für deutsche und internationale Politik* 27, no. 2 (1982): 162–64. See also Erhard Eppler, "Polen wird zum Prüfstein einer europäisch konzipierten Friedenspolitik" (148–49) and Christian Götz, "Die Friedensbewegung darf sich nicht auseinanderdividieren lassen," (150–51) both in the same volume as Strässer.

166. Die Grünen, *Friedensmanifest*, 10.

siles was still the peace movement's most important goal, but it was much more than a single-issue movement. Notions like transforming ("overcoming") the alliance systems and nuclear free zones could make more space for movements like Solidarity, which strove for social and political emancipation in Eastern and Western Europe. The best support for civil rights movements in Eastern Europe was for Western European states to take concrete steps toward dissolution of bloc structures. The peace movement had therefore to strive for an independent European path from both superpowers.[167]

A third manifestation of this controversy arose in connection with the peace movement's relationship to Eastern European peace movements. Since KOFAZ considered the Soviet bloc pioneers in the quest for peace, the group viewed these governments as allies. The peace movement, therefore, could not simply support opposition groups from all countries regardless of their governments' policies. Likewise, the movement would fall prey to official anticommunism if it supported oppositional groups in Eastern Europe.[168] The Greens, however, repeatedly called for a *blockübergreifende Friedensbewegung,* an international peace movement that transcended the military blocs. Such a movement corresponded to the Greens' notion of nonalignment and also to their support for grassroots movements. According to this notion, peoples of both blocs would unite against their respective superpowers and free themselves from danger. Tactically, such cooperation across the Iron Curtain would undermine ideological support for arms measures on both sides, by reducing each sides' ability to accuse indigenous peace movements of serving the other side.[169]

Organizational Innovation

In the 1980s, the peace movement's organization and strategy differed significantly from that of the 1950s. In the 1950s, the movement required the SPD's and DGB's help to reach full mobilization capacity and disintegrated when they withdrew their support. In the 1980s, in contrast, the peace movement was able to mount the largest protests in West German history without depending on any mainstream institution, and it maintained its organization even after popular mobilization declined.

This capacity for autonomous organization in the 1980s reflected the evolution of the extraparliamentary left in the two preceding decades.

---

167. Petra Kelly, "Reagan als Schirmherr der polnischen Freiheit?" *Blätter für deutsche und internationale Politik* 27, no. 2 (1982):152–55.

168. KOFAZ, "Diskussionspapier," 56, 57.

169. Die Grünen, *Friedensmanifest,* 10.

During the 1960s and 1970s, the extraparliamentary left developed a wide range of organizations, protest networks, and communication structures, amounting to a veritable protest subculture. Some were formal organizations, like the DFG-VK for conscientious objectors or the socialist youth organization Die Falken. Many, however, were loose alliances of like-minded but autonomous groups, organized in federations whose journals or newsletters permitted exchange of ideas and information among member groups (e.g., the Federation of Nonviolent Action Groups with its journal *Grassroots Revolution*). The peace movement of the 1980s drew its organizational structure and its national leadership from groups like these and thus became a vast alliance of preexisting organizations and protest networks. This capacity for autonomous organization allowed the peace movement to flourish without depending on external allies like parties. Through its member organizations, moreover, the movement enjoyed considerable mobilization capacity at its core. It remained to build a national organization capable of effective cooperation while also encompassing the movement's diversity.

The West German political system's relative insulation from popular pressure, the initial absence of parliamentary allies, and the ideological predisposition against established politics made the extraparliamentary arena the obvious choice for the budding peace movement. Its combination of centralized and decentralized organization facilitated effective national action while also leaving space for autonomous grassroots involvement commensurate with the extraparliamentary left's ideology and the widespread popular opposition to the missiles. Coordination of peace movement activities took place at various levels, which did not, however, form any unified chain of leadership or command. The movement's structure also made it less dependent on charismatic leadership than it otherwise might have been. Although such leaders as Petra Kelly, Gert Bastian, and Jo Leinen were important for obtaining media coverage and reaching a broader public, the peace movement did not depend on them to develop an organizational structure or mobilize its core supporters. The organizational structure necessary to cohesive collective action had its sources in the national leadership's constituent groups, peace organizations based on professional affiliation, and local peace groups.

The movement's national collective leadership, the Coordinating Committee *(Koordinationsausschuß)*, performed multiple functions at the national level. First, it provided organizational services, planning most of the movement's mass demonstrations and serving as its mouthpiece vis-à-vis the government, the press, and the public. Second, only in the Coordinating Committee was the movement's entire ideological range represented. Indeed, the Coordinating Committee's growth reflected the growth of the movement itself in both size and ideological breadth. The first protest against the double-track decision took place at the Protestant Kirchentag (the national lay convention) in June 1981, organized by a small number of groups. Some of these continued their informal cooperation by forming the so-called Breakfast Club (Frühstücksrunde), which planned the first major national demonstration of October 1981. As the peace movement grew the Breakfast Club expanded, and it institutionalized itself as the movement's Coordinating Committee, whose membership stabilized at twenty-six groups representing the entire West German left.[170] The Coordinating Committee's groups had nationwide organization, generally predated the peace movement, and had an organizational life beyond that of the movement itself. The movement's mobilization of core activists at the national level was thus a question of bringing increasing numbers of groups into its circle, most of which are described earlier in this chapter.

Third, the Coordinating Committee performed mobilization functions for the peace movement at the national level. The movement did not have to mobilize its activists individually, because it could draw on the membership and organizational resources of the preexisting groups in the committee. These groups gave the peace movement a broad base in many areas of society: in churches, parties, universities, schools, unions, and the extraparliamentary left. Some groups, moreover, provided intellectual resources (with, e.g., professors and writers as members); others presided over well-organized mass memberships (like the conscientious objectors and the Young Socialists); and still others had considerable financial sums to contribute (like the Greens or the communist KOFAZ). Thus the Coordinating Committee and its Executive Committee overseeing daily operations *(Geschäftsführung)* provided the movement's national leadership, drawing its disparate strands together into a relatively cohesive, centrally coordinated, but nonhierarchical, structure.[171]

Although the Coordinating Committee gave the peace movement a certain degree of centralization, other organizational features gave it a decidedly decentralized character. This combination of centralized and decentralized structure provided multiple opportunities for participation by individuals and groups, ranging from the far left to the political center

---

170. Leif argues that the Coordinating Committee gave the peace movement a much more institutionalized national leadership than was true of other new social movements (*Die strategische (Ohn-)Macht*, 13).

171. Joyce Mushaben, "The Struggle Within: Conflict, Consensus, and Decision Making among National Coordinators and Grassroots Coordinators in the West German Peace Movement," in *Organizing for Change: Social Movement Organizations in Europe and the United States*, ed. Bert Klandermans (Greenwich, Conn.: JAI Press, 1989), 267–300.

and from the national to the local level. Many member groups of the committee were national organizations with local chapters of their own, which discussed the peace issue in the context of their own goals and identities. The movement thus thrived at the local level, independent of specific national coordination, while such organizations provided links when needed between national and local levels. The national association of conscientious objectors (DFG-VK), the umbrella organization of student associations (Vereinigte Deutsche Studentenschaften), and the umbrella organization of citizens' ecological initiatives (BBU) typified the national groups with local chapters involved in the peace movement.

For the first time in West German history, moreover, a significant number of peace groups formed around shared professional affiliations and operated independently not only of institutions like parties or churches but also of the Coordinating Committee itself. Some profession-based peace groups represented occupational sectors that would have to help repair the material and human damage in the event of nuclear war and therefore felt responsibility for averting war in the first place. Peace groups composed of health professionals, psychologists, teachers, social scientists, architects, and druggists fell into this category. Other peace groups were formed among occupational sectors whose work contributed directly or indirectly to the military, such as workers in the aerospace industry, the computer industry, or soldiers themselves. Still other peace groups arose among occupations related to culture and information, such as artists, journalists, athletes, and writers. Finally, some groups represented highly visible occupations whose members lent professional prestige to their groups' statements against the missiles, such as businesspeople, lawyers, and judges.[172]

Finally, numerous local peace groups shot up all over the country and enjoyed complete autonomy from both the Coordinating Committee and its member groups, although most of them did belong to regional and city-wide networks that often organized their own protests. Local peace initiatives *(Friedensinitiativen)* thus contributed greatly to the movement's grassroots, decentralized character. Most cities and larger towns had numerous local peace initiatives, groups founded specifically to oppose the double-track decision and with no organizational ties to any national organization whatsoever. They were of mixed ideological composition and often bore the name of a particular neighborhood of their city. Friedensinitiative Schoeneberg, Friedensinitiative Spandau, and Friedensinitiative Tempelhof were three examples in West Berlin. The number of

---

172. For the names of these groups see Ulrike Wasmuht, *Friedensbewegungen der 80er Jahre* (Giessen: Focus Verlag, 1987), 151.

local peace initiatives in all of West Germany reached an impressive total of four thousand to six thousand in 1983.

Survey work of local peace groups offers an interesting picture of the inner life of such groups.[173] While a small number formed in 1977–78 during the neutron bomb controversy, the double-track decision provided the catalyst for most (40 percent formed in 1981 alone). Most of these groups were extremely informal. Eighty-six percent labeled themselves "loose associations," abjuring the more formal German legal status of *eingetragener Verein*. Local peace groups were largely independent of other larger organizations (73 percent did not belong to any parent organization). Fiercely autonomous in spirit as well, only 5 percent wished for a unified, national organization, although most recognized the need for some nationwide coordination. Seventy-one percent of local groups, however, belonged to regional networks covering northern, western, and southern Germany; and 55 percent also belonged to citywide networks. Informality and independence accompanied small size and a high level of activity among these groups. Groups generally ranged from twenty to fifty members, small enough to allow a high level of individual participation. These groups were not simply a few activists with mailing lists. On the contrary, 42 percent met approximately weekly, and another 40 percent met two or three times a month. Because of their antihierarchical, grassroots orientation, one-third of the groups operated without any official hierarchy or officeholders, while many others had only two or three official positions.

At the national level, the peace movement put together the broadest and most durable coalition on the political center and left in West German history, reaching from various extraparliamentary extremes well into mainstream parties and churches. The movement's sheer heterogeneity, however, made cohesion difficult and conflict frequent. Fears that one wing might dominate the movement at the expense of the rest were heightened by the direct or indirect representation of three competing political parties in the movement as a whole and in the Coordinating Committee in particular: the Social Democrats, the DKP (Moscow-oriented communists), and the Greens. Conflict surrounded two organizational issues in particular: the legitimacy of the movement's decision-making structures, and its strategies and protest forms (in addition to conflicts over the movement's position on political issues like membership in NATO and events in Eastern Europe, discussed earlier in this chapter).

Several levels of decision-making authority evolved at the national level, which miraculously managed to plan national events without letting

---

173. Alice Cooper and Klaus Eichner, "The West German Peace Movement," in *International Peace Movements,* ed. Bert Klandermans (Greenwich, Conn.: JAI Press, 1992), 149–71.

controversial issues irrevocably split the heterogeneous movement. The peace movement's national organizational structures maintained a delicate balance between the need for effective planning and respect for grassroots democracy, although the tension between the two was never fully resolved. On the one hand, the ideal of grassroots democracy and an abhorrence of hierarchy pervaded most of the movement, leading to structures that allowed ultimate authority to flow upward from the "base" *(Basis)* to the Coordinating Committee and its Executive Committee *(Geschäfts-führung)* as the planning staff of the movement. The mechanism for allowing the base to determine the movement's goals and strategies was the series of "action conferences" *(Aktionskonferenzen)* in Cologne. Several hundred groups (around 250 in 1982) sent six hundred to fifteen hundred delegates to the seven action conferences between 1982 and 1985. On the other hand, from the perspective of grassroots democracy and self-determination, even the action conferences' legitimacy suffered from the charge that they disproportionately represented the Moscow-oriented communists and that the Coordinating Committee had preponderate influence because it circulated position papers in advance. Because of their sheer size and internal divisions, the conferences consistently threatened to slip into chaos or paralysis.[174]

The search for decision-making structures that combined legitimacy and efficiency was further complicated by the movement's need for a permanent organization to run daily operations, organize large events, and represent the movement to the broader public and the media. Parts of the movement deeply resented the domination of the Coordinating Committee and its Executive Committee and tried in particular to curb the influence of those who emerged as media darlings presuming to speak for the movement as a whole. Even within the Coordinating Committee some members complained that the Executive Committee was dominating the movement, because the latter prepared discussion materials for Coordinating Committee and action conference meetings, thereby setting the movement's agenda to a certain extent. Thus although authority formally flowed from the bottom up, via the action conferences, this design only partially mitigated tensions over the structures needed for effective action. Leif implies that these tensions had a basis in fact. According to his study, the Coordinating Committee structured and dominated action conference proceedings, which enjoyed a mere legitimating and acclamatory function. Stormy as they might be, the action conferences routinely adopted positions or plans already agreed on within the committee.[175]

In terms of the national movement, then, the Coordinating Commit-

---

174. Mushaben, "The Struggle Within."
175. Leif, *Die strategische (Ohn-)Macht,* 141.

tee was the locus of planning and political definition. Once the committee stabilized at twenty-six member groups, its composition was carefully balanced between five factions: religious groups, the independent (nonparty) left, Greens, Social Democrats, and Moscow-oriented communists. As noted previously in this chapter, conflicts arose between the factions over political positions (e.g., withdrawal from NATO and criticism of Eastern European socialist regimes), the danger of co-option by parties, and the movement's strategies and protest forms. These conflicts could have irrevocably split the Coordinating Committee and the movement, but they were held in check through the evolution of consensus mechanisms. Substantively, the movement agreed to a "minimal consensus" of opposition to the proposed missile deployments, while agreeing to disagree on controversial political questions and to allow a mix of strategies and participation modes that suited the various groups' self-images.

Procedurally, several conflict management strategies held dissension in check. First, the Coordinating Committee made decisions according to the "consensus principle." The committee discussed issues until it reached a consensus, rather than outvoting minority positions through majority rule. Second, in order to reach consensus, the committee tabled controversial subjects until a compromise could be hammered out by smaller working groups. These practices prevented factional defection and controlled rivalries, generating consensus within the Coordinating Committee, if not within the movement as a whole.[176] Similar strategies also operated at the local level. Serious conflicts were usually settled by forming subgroups, such as study groups. This allowed dissident members to express themselves without binding the group to their views.

The Collective Action Repertoire and Mobilization Strategies

Protest events are the centerpiece and expressive medium of social movements. This principle held true for the peace movement as well, which made its mark on politics in large part through multifaceted and frequent action. The peace movement's action repertoire spanned almost the entire spectrum of unconventional political action and protest forms. Indeed, the peace movement turned out to be particularly good at creatively varying its forms of action, which gave the varied groups opportunities to find appealing events. However, the search for new, unjaded, attention-grabbing but sustainable action led to conflict, as various movement cultures sought to express their political projects and identities.

The movement's various factions threw their support behind the par-

---

176. Ibid., chap. 7; Mushaben, "The Struggle Within."

ticular protest forms that best reflected their strategies for political or social transformation. As the movement gathered steam, conflict arose over which strategies would put the most effective pressure on the German government and would most likely move it to abandon missile deployments: massive demonstrations involving ever-widening circles of the populace, or escalation to nonviolent resistance (such as blockades of missile deployment sites) in order to raise the state's political costs of deployment. Additional controversies stemmed from other strategic dilemmas. Should protest be centralized to send a massive signal of public feeling, or would decentralized protest better raise consciousness by drawing connections to people's daily lives? Should the peace movement organize protest for its own sake to maintain momentum or engage only in clearly conceptualized protest tied to specific political positions? The peace movement developed no real consensus on these issues. Instead, it reached compromise by bundling various protest forms into a multifaceted package.[177]

As the movement progressed it moved through three partially overlapping phases: starting with public information campaigns and appeals, moving on to demonstrations, and subsequently adding nonviolent resistance. Each phase expressed a certain "logic" of mobilization, as well as the strength of various factions within the movement. Each phase also contained many different protest forms, amounting to a veritable smorgasbord of possibilities, from which groups could pick those most appealing to their own sensibilities. In addition to such nationally organized protest, local peace groups staged their own local or regional peace protest throughout the peace movement's life.

Nineteen eighty and the first half of 1981 marked the informational and appellative phase of the movement, which served to sensitize the public to the missile issue and to move discussion from security-elite circles to the public domain.[178] This phase emphasized disseminating information on the dangers of missile deployment and gathering signatures for petitions. The former helped create an interested public, while the latter provided the first major outlet for expression of public concern. Protestant churches were deeply involved in early efforts to inform the public and provide opportunities for expressive action. They organized the first of a series of annual "peace weeks" *(Friedenswochen)* in 1980, in which activities like prayer sessions, peace marches, lectures, discussions, films, school activities, plays, and music took place in 350 localities across West Ger-

---

177. Leif, *Die strategische (Ohn-)Macht,* 170–72.
178. This phase consisted of what Klandermans calls "consensus mobilization" ("The Formation and Mobilization of Consensus," 173–96).

many.[179] Organizational preparations both required and facilitated forming local alliances among groups that ordinarily did not work together, which paved the way for similar alliances at the national level later on. During this period the Krefelder Appell made the first major attempt to "let the masses be heard" in the form of a petition that garnered eight hundred thousand signatures in the first six months and later reached the two million level.[180]

A rally at the Hamburg Protestant Kirchentag (lay convention) in June 1981 initiated the movement's demonstration phase. Mass demonstrations took place during the years that sentiment against the missiles peaked, and the demonstrations were admirably suited to express this widespread opposition. In October 1981 came the first major mass demonstration in Bonn, with three hundred thousand participants. It was followed by a second, similar demonstration in Bonn in June 1982—on the occasion of President Reagan's visit to Germany—which attracted five hundred thousand. Besides expressing general nuclear anxiety, the 1982 demonstration raised for the first time additional issues like the Third World, the environment, and alternatives to NATO strategy.[181] Mass demonstrations peaked in October 1983—just prior to the November Bundestag decision on deployment—when two million to four million people participated in a week of activities.

Once the Bundestag voted to deploy the missiles, a certain resignation set in, and mass mobilization became much more difficult. At the same time, parts of the movement stepped up the resistance phase. Groups specializing in nonviolent civil disobedience established their presence at various centers of activity relating to the missiles or the military, with the aim of raising the costs of deployment through direct confrontation with the state. In November 1983 the Bundestag was "besieged" while the deployment decision was being made, as protestors tried to penetrate the cordon established around the Bundestag itself.[182] Permanent camps were established at missile sites like Mutlangen, where protestors tried to interfere physically with the missiles' stationing or to at least draw attention to their presence. Similarly, in 1984 protestors deployed themselves in the Fulda Gap area during NATO military maneuvers in order to impede their progress.

The 1980s movement represented the crowning glory of postwar

---

179. Aktion Sühnezeichen/Friedensdienste, *Frieden schaffen ohne Waffen* (Bornheim-Merten: Lamuv Verlag, 1981), 53.

180. Christoph Strässer, "Der Krefelder Appell," in *Frieden in Deutschland,* ed. Hans Pestalozzi et al. (Munich: Wilhelm Goldmann Verlag, 1982), 87–92.

181. Koordinationsausschuß der Friedensorganisationen, *Aufstehen! Für den Frieden: Friedensdemonstration anläßlich der NATO-Gipfelkonferenz in Bonn am 10.6.1982* (Bornheim-Merten: Lamuv Verlag, 1982).

182. Mushaben, "Grassroots and *Gewaltfreie Aktionen,*" 143.

peace protest. Most elements of political opportunity favored it, ranging from a salient issue over which it initially enjoyed a monopoly, to an international situation that lent credibility to its message, a high protest potential in the political culture at large, the dominance of its issue as the most compelling concern of the day, and a government already unpopular across a broad range of issues. The movement's varied ideological resources reflected the broad array of activists committed to its cause. In addition to the original frames of redemption and democratization, the movement emphasized détente, arms control, and Ostpolitik. It also used to its advantage the powerful military-strategic analysis offered by peace research. Through issue overlap, the movement was able to draw in activists from the social movements of the 1970s, including, among others, the ecology and feminist movements. Finally, the movement's organizational structure provided both the centralization and decentralization necessary to provide national leadership while still articulating the movement's diversity.

CHAPTER 6

Decline or Renewal? The Peace Movement from 1984 to 1989

By articulating the public's broad unease with nuclear weapons and deterrence, the peace movement of the early 1980s had an enormous impact on subsequent German politics, despite the Bundestag's vote in late 1983 to station the missiles the movement had fought so hard to prevent. The movement "democratized" security policy in several ways. First, it broke the monopoly of security policy elites on policy debate and decisions, as Risse-Kappen argues. Despite the continued dominance of economic and environmental issues, the movement raised the salience of security policy "from a third- to a second-rank issue in the public debate" and encouraged ongoing and substantial media coverage of security issues. The movement also broadened the "attentive public" for security policy discussion by engaging churches, unions, parties, and citizens' groups at both the national and grassroots levels.[1]

Second, the movement's hugely successful mobilization of the public, coupled with opinion surveys, revealed public wariness of nuclear weapons that in turn set new constraints on government policy making. Just as broad sectors of the public had opposed stationing new missiles in the early 1980s, they subsequently supported the arms control proposals of the later 1980s. According to Risse-Kappen, the German government's acceptance of the various arms control proposals represented public opinion's victory over conservative national security elites. Public opinion thus affected the general direction of security policy after 1983, by setting the

---

1. Thomas Risse-Kappen, "Anti-Nuclear and Pro-Detente? The Transformation of the West German Security Debate," in *Debating National Security: The Public Dimension,* ed. Hans Rattinger and Don Munton (Frankfurt: Peter Lang, 1991), 269–99, here 287.

overall range of policy options from which the government could choose without risking a legitimacy crisis and renewed large-scale popular mobilization.[2]

Third, many of the peace movement's positions became institutionalized in mainstream politics, as a result of substantial shifts in the party system to which the movement itself contributed. Opposition within the SPD to the double-track decision was one reason for the FDP's resignation from the social-liberal coalition in October 1982, which led to the SPD's fall from power and to the new conservative-liberal coalition under Helmut Kohl. Once in opposition, the Social Democrats shifted their defense policy considerably to the left. The Greens, moreover, won seats in the Bundestag for the first time in the 1983 election, and they used it as a platform for their radical defense proposals. Within the new government, the FDP insisted on continuity in foreign policy, in particular continuing Ostpolitik and supporting arms control measures. Finally, despite considerable resistance from its most conservative factions, even the CDU/CSU accepted limited arms control and continued Ostpolitik, which reflected popular attitudes even among the conservative electorate.

Ironically, however, after 1983 the peace movement became the victim of its own previous success. Despite its impact on German politics, the movement's capacity to mobilize the general public shrank rapidly under the impact of first defeat and then partial realization of its goals. Indeed, just as international and domestic politics became more friendly to arms control and disarmament, the peace movement itself lost internal cohesion and dynamism. Despite innovative work on alternative defense policies, the movement proved unable to generate new themes and strategies that could maintain the mobilization levels of the early 1980s. Without a common unifying goal, the movement's factions succumbed to divisive debate, robbing the movement of its former tenuous unity. In the end organizational unity suffered as well, as the movement's central structure dissolved and was replaced by a much looser coordinating network.

In comparison to the peace movement's flowering in the early 1980s, then, one can speak of 1983–89 as a period of relative decline, despite the ferment of ideas coming from the movement's core. Just as political opportunity, ideological resources, and organizational strength had all converged positively in the early 1980s, after 1983 these components deteriorated, contributing to the movement's relative decline.

---

2. Risse-Kappen, "Anti-Nuclear and Pro-Detente?" 291–93.

Political Opportunities after 1983

After 1983, the peace movement became the victim of its own success and of external forces, as political opportunities improved for its cause but deteriorated for the movement itself. The peace movement had blossomed in the early 1980s, blessed with a highly salient weapons issue and a virtual monopoly on opposition to the issue. In contrast, after 1983 the movement's capacity to mobilize the broad public declined. The double-track decision lost salience, and the movement lost its monopoly on antinuclear stances.

The aftermath of the double-track decision deprived the peace movement of a salient issue in two diametrically opposed ways, each of which robbed the movement of its capacity to mobilize the broad public. The movement met initial defeat in November 1983, when the Bundestag voted to station the Pershing II and cruise missiles according to the terms of the NATO decision. Whereas around 1,000,000 people had attended the giant "people's rallies" in four cities in October 1983, a year later only about 400,000 showed up for "human chains" symbolically linking military installations near three of the same cities. Similarly, the Easter Marches' attendance slipped from around 650,000 in 1983 to 450,000 in 1984.[3] Resignation set in as people lost their belief that extraparliamentary action could change security policy.

In the later 1980s the missile issue lost urgency for the opposite reason. "Institutional accommodation"[4] set in at multiple levels, as the superpowers, the German government, and the parties adopted arms control to varying degrees. Indeed, the movement saw its goals realized beyond its wildest dreams, as arms control agreements followed one another at a dizzying pace. After Gorbachev's rise to power in the former Soviet Union in 1985, he accepted the American "double-zero" option that previous Soviet leaders had vehemently rejected, the proposal to eliminate all Soviet and American medium-range missiles in Europe. It became the basis of the INF treaty, signed in December 1987, which eliminated the very missiles whose stationing the peace movement had fought so hard to prevent. Other arms control measures affecting more obscure nuclear weapons followed. In conjunction with the INF treaty, Chancellor Kohl agreed to give up the elderly Pershing Ia missiles stationed in Germany, despite efforts of conservatives within his own party to have them exempted, and he later

---

3. Leif, *Die strategische (Ohn-)Macht*, 3.

4. David Meyer, "Protest Cycles and Political Process: American Peace Movements in the Nuclear Age," *Political Research Quarterly* 46, no. 3 (Sept. 1993): 451–80, here 458.

agreed to remove rather than modernize shorter-range Lance missiles and nuclear artillery.[5]

These agreements took place during a pronounced thaw in East-West relations following Gorbachev's assumption of power in 1985. Whereas in the 1950s the peace movement ultimately fell victim to the intensification of the cold war, it now found its political space squeezed out by the waning of the cold war. Gorbachev launched a new era of détente with the West, following the frigid relations during the original INF negotiations and after the missiles' stationing. His image as a "man of peace" in Western Europe developed through enthusiasm for arms control and his references to "our common European home" stretching from the Urals to the Atlantic.[6] In the meantime, the peace movement's arch enemy, the "cold warrior" Ronald Reagan, significantly changed his image as well. He softened his rhetoric toward the Soviet Union during his second term in office and proved willing to conclude arms control agreements considered unthinkable only a few years earlier.

Public opinion responded to these changes in the atmospherics of East-West relations. In the early 1980s, support for arms control and fear of war had galvanized popular mobilization against the INF missiles. In the late 1980s, in contrast, Gorbachev's diplomacy, arms control, and improved superpower relations had put fears of war to rest. Public support for arms control remained very high. In 1987, 90 percent of the populace supported the "double-zero" solution incorporated into the INF treaty; and in 1988, 70 percent were against plans for modernizing short-range missiles based in Germany.[7] This time, however, support for arms control was coupled with a marked decline of fear. After Gorbachev took office, the public increasingly believed that the Soviets were serious about détente and arms control and that peace was more secure than before. By 1988, 66 percent felt confident about the future of peace in Europe, up from 38 percent in 1983, while the proportion that was "worried" fell from 55 percent to 21 percent.[8] Even supporters of conservative parties showed substantial trust in Gorbachev.[9] Peace seemed safe in the superpowers' hands, and trust in the arms control process revived.

The peace movement suffered a second, larger wave of demobilization as improving superpower relations and successful arms control robbed the

---

5. Bark and Gress, *A History of West Germany,* 2:481.

6. Herf, *War by Other Means,* 218–20.

7. *Politbarometer* (BPA), 2 June 1987; "Wenn das Gefühl der Bedrohung schwindet," *Frankfurter Allgemeine Zeitung* 22 July 1988.

8. "Neue Liebe zwischen Russen und Deutschen," *Stern,* 1 June 1989.

9. See, for example, "Affären wie in Kiel auch anderswo möglich? *Der Spiegel,* 2 Nov. 1987.

missile issue of its remaining urgency. Initial defeat had already reduced the movement's capacity for large-scale mobilization by a good half, from its high point of 1,000,000 at the 1983 mass demonstrations to under 500,000 in 1984 rallies. Between 1985 and 1989, however, mass mobilization declined precipitously once again, essentially reducing participation to a relatively hard core. In 1987 only around 100,000 participated in the June demonstration, while the 1988 and 1989 Easter Marches drew only around 80,000 each.[10]

The peace movement's political opportunities diminished dramatically as the missile issue lost salience, but this was not the movement's only problem. Equally serious, after 1983 the movement lost its former monopoly on antinuclear stances and alternative paths to peace. Here in particular the peace movement proved a victim of its own success, as certain movement positions found institutionalization in party platforms, in parliamentary representation, and even in government policy. The governing conservative-liberal coalition agreed to arms control proposals, especially under the liberal FDP's prodding. With its acceptance of the INF treaty, the Kohl government fulfilled the peace movement's earlier "minimal consensus." Government action thus co-opted the movement's most basic issue at the highest level of politics, contributing to popular demobilization. As the alliance of local Bonn peace groups (Friedensplenum) noted, people would not march in the streets for goals shared by both the peace movement and the FDP's Foreign Minister Genscher.[11]

Proposals for much more far-reaching changes in West Germany's defense policy, moreover, now found parliamentary representation by the SPD and the Greens, both of whom became official movement allies in the Bundestag. The electorally insignificant Communist Party (DKP) had supported the peace movement from the very beginning. In 1983, however, the Greens won seats in the Bundestag for the first time, based partly on peace movement support. In response to Green competition and pressure from its own membership, moreover, the SPD shifted its defense policy decidedly to the left. The party immediately forswore the double-track decision and developed security policies based on nonnuclear and strictly defensive postures. Whereas the movement had bitterly opposed the SPD's security policies under the Schmidt government, the movement now gained an official ally in the SPD. After prolonged controversy and soul-searching within the movement, Willy Brandt was invited to speak at the central demonstration in Bonn in 1983, and Oskar Lafontaine and

---

10. Leif, *Die strategische (Ohn-)Macht,* 3.
11. "Die Friedensbewegung in der Sinnkrise," *Tageszeitung,* 5 July 1989.

Hans-Jochen Vogel spoke at subsequent rallies.[12] From 1983 on, the SPD officially called on its members to take part in the peace movement's activities.[13] Prominent and ordinary Social Democrats joined events like human chains between symbolic locations, sometimes helping fill potentially embarrassing gaps.[14]

By 1983, then, the peace movement had three parties as allies. The parties competed for peace movement votes on the basis of quite different defense policies. Both the SPD and the Greens were innovating alternative defense proposals that stood in marked contrast to each other.

The Greens emphasized unilateral disarmament and West German withdrawal from NATO.[15] They considered the arms race and power politics inherently dangerous and morally reprehensible. Since they viewed NATO as inherently militaristic and thus incapable of significant reform, they advocated withdrawal from NATO and eventual dissolution of both blocs. Even before the Warsaw Pact's dissolution, the Greens demanded immediate steps toward unilateral disarmament, without waiting for arms control negotiations to bear fruit. They also rejected the SPD's proposal to switch to conventional defense, because such defense also relied on military force. Instead, the Greens based their security policy on the notion of "social defense" mentioned in chapter 4. Devoid of all military options, this strategy envisaged an occupied Germany engaging in passive resistance, which would eventually sour the occupiers on the experience and force them to withdraw.

Of the three parties allied with the peace movement, only the SPD gave extensive thought to West German military defense. Communists in the movement never mentioned *defense* (implying a potential threat from the Warsaw Pact), and the Greens rejected *military* defense. As both a party and a wing of the peace movement, in contrast, the SPD drew fire from conservatives and the movement, respectively. The SPD's post-1982 security policies contradicted fundamental NATO assumptions and led to concerns about the SPD's commitment to NATO, while the peace movement questioned the SPD's commitment to *alternatives* to NATO policy and thus to the movement itself.

---

12. "Lafontaine fordert einseitige Abrüstung," *Saarbrücker Zeitung*, 24 Oct. 1984; "Die Friedensdemonstranten fühlen sich mehr den je bestätigt," *Stuttgarter Zeitung*, 15 June 1987.

13. "SPD ruft zur Teilnahme an Friedensdemonstrationen auf," *Hannoversche Allgemeine*, 11 Sept. 1984; "SPD-Aufruf zur Beteiligung an den Ostermärschen," *PPP*, 1 Mar. 1987.

14. "Keine geschlossene Menschenkette," *Süddeutsche Zeitung*, 22 Oct. 1984.

15. Die Grünen, "Auflösung der Militärblöcke—Raus aus der NATO" (resolution on peace policy, Green Party Congress [Sindelfingen, 1983]); *Bundestagswahlprogramm* 1987; and *Friedenskonzept* (1987).

The SPD's defense policy shifted dramatically to the left after the party entered the opposition. From 1980 on, Social Democrats active in the peace movement had begun calling for a "second phase of Ostpolitik," in dissatisfied reaction to Schmidt's policies of nuclear deterrence and adherence to classical notions of balance of power. Worried by the decline of détente and aware of the voting potential of peace movement adherents, the younger generation of Social Democratic leaders around Karsten Voigt, Oskar Lafontaine, and Andreas von Bülow argued for a new security policy. In the "New Strategies" working group (Arbeitsgruppe "Neue Strategien"), they seized particularly on the ideas of Egon Bahr, the group's chairperson and the old visionary of Ostpolitik under Brandt in earlier years. Having recast his ideas in work for the Palme Commission in the early 1980s, Bahr popularized the notion of "common security" between East and West, arguing that European countries could no longer be secure "against" each other, but only "with" each other. Bahr's notion of common security revived the idea of a European peace order transcending the bloc system.[16]

Younger members of the "New Strategies" group weighed in with their own works. Andreas von Bülow urged adoption of a security policy based on a strictly nonprovocative defense posture (as opposed to NATO defense strategies based on plans of attack), termed a "structural incapacity to attack." Among other things, he called for an antitank belt along the German-German border, a corresponding reduction of tanks and aircraft capable of offensive operations, a nuclear-free zone in Central Europe, and removal of chemical weapons from the two Germanies.[17] Another rising star, Oskar Lafontaine, distanced himself sharply from NATO policy in a book entitled *Fear of the Friends,* in particular American friends. Peter Bender contributed significantly to revitalizing the notion of "Central Europe," implying that Germany's problems stemmed from Europe's division and superpower hegemony.[18]

The security policy resolution of the 1986 party congress at Nuremberg captured the evolution of the SPD's thinking in the 1980s.[19] It set the ultimate goal of a European peace order based on nonviolent conflict resolution and dissolution of the two blocs. Pending its realization, the Nuremberg resolution explicitly reaffirmed the SPD's support for military

16. Garton Ash, *In Europe's Name,* 312–19.

17. Jeffrey Boutwell, "Politics and Ideology of SPD Security Policies," in *The Silent Partner: West Germany and Arms Control,* ed. Barry Blechman and Cathleen Fischer (Cambridge, Mass.: Ballinger Publishing Company, 1988), 129–66.

18. Garton Ash, *In Europe's Name,* 316.

19. "'Unser Weg zu Abrüstung und Frieden' Beschluss zur Friedens- und Sicherheitspolitik der SPD, Parteitag in Nürnberg, 25.–29.8. 1986," in *Politik: Informationsdienst der SPD* 8 (Sept. 1986): 2–8.

defense, continuing NATO membership, and the West German army. The SPD, however, also advocated departures from traditional NATO policy. First, the party called for making NATO a strictly defensive alliance and for strengthening its "European pillar." Second, the SPD demanded replacement of deterrence by a "security partnership" with Eastern Europe and the Soviet Union, based on mutually negotiated security and eventual disarmament. For the medium term, the SPD recommended a purely defensive military strategy based on conventional weapons. This required a strategy of "structural nonattack capacity," in place of such NATO strategies as "AirLand Battle." Finally, the SPD called for substantial, but mutually negotiated, arms reductions. A "self-propelling dynamic" of détente was to replace a similar dynamic of the arms race. In this context, the SPD advocated a number of measures controversial at the time: a moratorium on new nuclear weapons and the Strategic Defense Initiative (SDI), removal of tactical nuclear and chemical weapons, and removal of medium-range missiles in both halves of Europe.

Framing the Issues: Factionalization along Ideological Lines

After 1983 the peace movement lost its capacity for mass mobilization for the reasons outlined in the preceding section of this chapter. In contrast to the 1950s and 1960s, however, defeat of the movement's original goals did not lead to its dissolution. Instead, the movement showed remarkable staying power. At the national level, the movement retained its core of activist groups and its organizational structure for most of the 1980s.

The peace movement opposed almost everything NATO did or proposed: strategies like AirLand Battle, the Strategic Defense Initiative, and modernization of short-range missiles to name a few. The movement launched campaigns against chemical weapons and defense spending. Gorbachev's arms control proposals enjoyed unanimous support. From 1984 to 1990, protest continued, even though mass mobilization had declined. In most years the core leadership organized rallies, while more radical parts of the movement continued acts of civil disobedience, like blockading missile sites. After the fall of the Berlin Wall, the movement proposed a "Federal Republic without an Army" (Bundesrepublik ohne Armee) and included East German routes in its 1990 Easter March.

This continued activism, however, could not hide the movement's loss of direction and focus. The real cost of initial defeat and, ironically, subsequent success was to the movement's internal cohesion and sense of direction. Initial defeat forced the movement to question its previous strategies. Successful arms control and relaxed East-West tensions, moreover, dealt two blows to the movement. First, they called the movement's analytic foundations into question. Ronald Reagan, the old "cold warrior" and the peace movement's archenemy, was a key player in the drama of the INF treaty. Similarly, NATO proved capable of disarmament (however limited), rather than inexorably pursuing the arms race. The movement had predicted damage to détente if the Pershing II and cruise missiles were stationed; yet East-West relations improved on all levels, including German-German relations, and the world was not plunged into war.

With the INF treaty, moreover, the peace movement lost the central issue that had held together the movement's disparate coalition. Loss of its minimal consensus starkly revealed the movement's lack of agreement on long-range tasks: alternatives to NATO's security policy, paths to further disarmament, and eradicating the ultimate causes of war. The absence of a concrete, common, compelling project allowed conflict over thematic emphasis and movement strategy to fragment the movement's Coordinating Committee along cleavage lines already manifest in the early 1980s, intensifying conflicts over the movement's goals, its strategy, and indeed its very identity. Fragmentation received further impetus from the party competition between the SPD and the Greens, which wormed its way into the movement's heart. In the end, this fragmentation fatally undermined the movement's organizational structures. The movement's core leadership ultimately proved unable to generate new consensus, disbanded, and was replaced by a much looser network.

Factional infighting intensified among the several camps that had already emerged within the movement. In many respects, each camp now went its separate way, leaving the movement with a profusion of ideas and strategies but no shared concept. In particular, the camps differed in their evaluations of NATO, the INF treaty and arms control in general, Gorbachev, and, most fundamentally, their suggestions for the movement's goals and strategy. The Coordinating Committee became a battleground for these contending views. Debate took place in two phases. The months between the defeat on the missiles in November 1983 and the resumption of arms control negotiations in 1985/86 were perhaps the darkest time for the peace movement, during which it pondered the reasons for its defeat and its outlook on the future. The resumption and successful conclusion of arms control negotiations, however, forced the movement to evaluate the contribution of arms control to peace, in comparison to alternative goals and strategies.

Up until late 1983 the movement as a whole directed its efforts primarily at preventing stationing of the new missiles. Even then, however, the movement had been under pressure from the "independent" spectrum of groups (drawn from the social movements) to broaden the range of its topics. In response, its national demonstrations in 1982 and 1983 had featured activities concerning women, the Third World, and ecology.[20] After 1983 the movement officially widened its goals. It now condemned arms in the East and in the West and demanded withdrawal of the Soviet "countermeasures" to the West's new missiles, the SS-22s and SS-23s stationed in East Germany and Czechoslovakia. It took a position against West Germany's plutonium industry because of its potential contribution to nuclear weapons, and it demanded reductions in arms spending.[21] Similarly, in 1985 the movement opposed European participation in the Strategic Defense Initiative, and NATO's "war-fighting" strategies like AirLand Battle. It demanded an end to "domestic militarization" measures, such as longer periods of compulsory military service and civil-military cooperation in the health system. Finally, it called for redirecting military spending toward the Third World, environmental protection, and job creation.[22]

Despite this considerable widening of the movement's official stance, fierce factional debate over the movement's direction raged within the Coordinating Committee. Divisions within the movement were so apparent that the Coordinating Committee called for a "grand consultation" *(Grosser Ratschlag)* in mid-1985 to discuss the movement's future goals. The contours of at least three camps emerged.

The "traditionalist" camp contained primarily social democratic and communist groups. Traditionalists worried about the newly stationed Western missiles in terms of their impact on East-West relations, on the arms race, and on the danger of war in Europe. They focused on promoting peace through political, rather than military, approaches to security. This approach meant attaining arms control through negotiations between the two blocs and eventually "overcoming the logic" of deterrence. It also meant opposing NATO's "war-fighting" strategies for "winning" a nuclear or conventional war against the Warsaw Pact and opposing German logistical support for American military efforts in the Third World.

Traditionalists argued that the movement had been on the right track despite its defeat. Since opposition merely to the new missiles no longer made sense, Social Democrats, such as Wolfgang Biermann, proposed expanding the movement's minimal consensus to appeal once again to the general public. The movement should continue to press for withdrawal of the new missiles and for arms control of other sorts. On a more political dimension, the movement should stress renewal of détente, solidarity with the Third World, and cooperation with peace movements in Western

---

20. Koordinationsausschuß der Friedensorganisationen, *Aufstehen!*

21. "Mehrheit für Volksbefragung," *Tageszeitung* 13 Feb. 1984.

22. Koordinationsausschuß der Friedensbewegung, *Rundbrief* 6 (Bonn, 1985): 2.

Europe and the United States.[23] The communist group KOFAZ and the conscientious objector association DFG-VK echoed these views. They warned against the nuclear dangers bringing the world ever closer to the abyss, and they took every opportunity to attack American policy. In focusing on the "militarization of space" through American plans for the Strategic Defense Initiative (SDI), they took up one of the main points on the Soviets' agenda at the time. They continued to oppose the Pershing II and cruise missiles, which made nuclear war "wageable" in Europe. Finally, they railed against weapons procurements needed for conventional "aggressive" military strategies like AirLand Battle.[24]

Most of the independent spectrum, including the movement's religious groups, concurred with the traditionalists on the need for "immediate measures" against the ongoing militarization that they perceived. They stressed removal of nuclear, biological, and chemical weapons and elimination of "aggressive" NATO strategies. In their long-term goals, however, these groups stepped back from primary focus on the dangers of weapons systems and military strategies. Instead, they pushed for a broader definition of peace and a broader definition of the peace movement's goals. As the Catholic IKvU argued, the peace movement's goal should be a world of peace and international justice, a world without exploitation or war. This vision presupposed far-reaching transformation of the social, economic, and international realms, as well as transformation of personal consciousness on the part of individuals, to be attained by "emancipatory pedagogy" and "liberating" political action.[25]

Pax Christi, another important Catholic group, argued along the same lines. It noted the movement's fixation on weapons systems and the military, understandable given the danger they presented. Pax Christi called, however, for other foci, like the connections between arms and social spending cuts, between arms export and Third World underdevelopment. It doubted that pressuring the government to undo the missiles' stationing through mass protests would be very effective. Instead, the movement should use thousands of local peace initiatives to relay to the public what true security policy involved: reordering of economic relation-

23. Wolfgang Biermann, untitled essay, in *Reader zur Strategie-Konferenz "Grosser Ratschlag" der Friedensbewegung* (Bonn, 1985, photocopy), 55–58.

24. Komitee für Frieden, Abrüstung und Zusammenarbeit [KOFAZ], "Für einen neuen Aufschwung der Friedensbewegung," in the *Rundbrief* of the KOFAZ, Feb. 1985, 1–5; Deutsche Friedensgesellschaft—Vereinigte Kriegsdienstgegner [DFG-VK], "Politische Friedenssicherung statt militärische Konfrontationspolitik," in *Reader zur Strategie-Konferenz*, 48–51.

25. Initiative Kirche von Unten [IKvU], "Diskussionsbeitrag zu den Perspektiven der Friedensbewegung," in *Reader zur Strategie-Konferenz*, 59–60.

ships on the basis of worldwide distributive justice, and sound ecological practices like energy conservation.[26]

One wing of the independent spectrum, represented by the Federation of Independent Peace Initiatives (BUF), consistently pushed for a more aggressive stance. These groups also urged the peace movement to move beyond its fixation on particular weapons systems. In BUF's eyes, the destructive power of various weapons was not the main issue. Instead, BUF groups focused on NATO military strategies that supported Western "imperialism." SDI and the AirLand Battle doctrine, BUF noted, served NATO's aggressive, war-fighting strategy against the East, as well as Western domination of the Third World. Although supposedly a response to the Warsaw Pact, such NATO strategies really helped secure American economic and technological supremacy, along with capitalist interests in the Third World. The peace movement could not simply focus on the danger of nuclear war for Europe; it also had to object to Western intervention in the Middle East or Central America. The peace movement should declare "no peace" with NATO, for the danger of war resulted not from one weapons system or another but from NATO as an alliance and its strategies and interests. The peace movement thus had to demand NATO's dissolution, not just its reform.[27]

The resumption of INF negotiations reopened this debate among the movement's factions. The movement, of course, supported the double-zero proposal to eliminate medium-range missiles on both sides, and also a "triple-zero" removal of smaller nuclear weapons. It attributed the successful conclusion of the INF treaty to the Soviets' "new thinking" under Gorbachev, rather than to any significant change in the West. The movement also agreed to prod the reluctant West German government to accede to the INF treaty. Finally, the movement agreed that the INF treaty represented real disarmament only if it also meant moving away from the "logic" of deterrence. The peace movement therefore had to fight against new Western arms in other areas that would compensate for the INF missiles in terms of deterrence and against Franco-German military cooperation that would bring West Germany indirect access to nuclear weapons.

The movement's various factions disagreed, however, on the significance of the INF treaty and the contribution of arms control to peace in principle. Traditionalist social democratic and communist groups saw the INF process as a possible step toward genuine disarmament, since they believed that negotiations could bring about disarmament given the

---

26. Karl-Heinz Koppe, "Eine politische Strategie zur Überwindung der militärischen Sicherheitsgesellschaft," in *Reader zur Strategie-Konferenz,* 67–70.

27. "Gegen Kriegsvorbereitung und Intervention," in *Reader zur Strategie-Konferenz,* 43–45.

genuine political will on both sides. They therefore threw their full weight behind renewed INF negotiations in the mid-1980s and argued that the peace movement's main task was to press the West German government to accede to the treaty. Gregor Witt of the DFG-VK, for example, saw proof that disarmament was truly possible. He hoped that the impending INF treaty would begin a disarmament process leading to complete elimination of nuclear weapons and would eventually allow political means of securing peace to replace traditional military means. Since NATO and West Germany had not yet fundamentally rethought their security policies, however, the peace movement still had work to do. Only an independent push for a nuclear-free, demilitarized Europe would make removal of the INF missiles a step toward real peace.[28] Achim Maske of the communist KOFAZ agreed with these views. He celebrated the peace movement's role in encouraging the Soviets' "new thinking" and desire for far-reaching disarmament, whereas NATO was still caught in deterrence thinking. The peace movement had to work with movements elsewhere to demilitarize the East-West relationship.[29]

The more radical parts of the independent spectrum greeted the INF agreement much more reservedly. The BUF and the Greens denied that the INF treaty was the beginning of a "disarmament dynamic," because NATO's service to capitalist interests rendered it inherently militaristic—"unreformable" and unwilling to cut its military force in real terms. The peace movement had not been able to prevent the missiles' original stationing at its high point and could not take credit for the INF treaty now. The treaty resulted, instead, from the Soviets' new policy. NATO had agreed to the treaty not because of any change of heart but because it had found alternative weapons for its war-fighting strategies. The INF treaty did not represent disarmament so much as redeployment. The peace movement should certainly not hope that parties, governments, or NATO could be trusted to bring peace and disarmament.[30]

Violent disagreement surrounded the movement's strategies as well, and again traditionalists and independents took opposing sides. The fundamental issue was whether popular pressure could ever change government policy. For traditionalists, changing government policy was admittedly difficult because it meant overcoming elite resistance, but it remained

---

28. Gregor Witt, "Null-Lösung—Anfang einer neuen Politik?" in the *Rundbrief* of the Koordinierungsausschuß der Friedensbewegung, May 1987, 3–6.

29. Achim Maske, "Vom Einstieg zum Ausstieg," in the *Rundbrief* of the Koordinierungsausschuß der Friedensbewegung, May 1987, 7–10.

30. BUF-Trägerkreis, "Ein Grund zum Feiern für die Friedensbewegung?" and Die Grünen, "Wer Null will darf nicht Null tun," both in the *Rundbrief* of the Koordinierungsausschuß der Friedensbewegung, May 1987, 10–13 and 17–19, respectively.

possible given sufficient extraparliamentary pressure. Social Democrat Wolfgang Biermann pointed to his own party's very visible rethinking of security policy in the mid-1980s and to change even in the conservative parties. To encourage this renewal, he argued, the peace movement needed to continue its realpolitik strategy of extraparliamentary pressure, despite the missiles' stationing. For starters, the movement needed a new common strategy that would keep local peace initiatives active.[31]

Similarly, communist groups argued that if the movement wanted to remain a factor in politics, it needed a strategy that would express the fears and longings of millions of people and increase the political pressure on the government. The peace movement had won a majority in popular opinion and had helped change the SPD's position, but it still had to change conservative circles as well. In order to stimulate even greater resistance to government policy, the movement had to adopt action forms that included as many people as possible and reached conservative sectors of the populace. Ruling out acts of violence both strategically and as a matter of principle, this approach meant using inclusive action forms that the whole populace could support, ranging from holding mass demonstrations to circulating petitions and sponsoring referenda, confronting parties with movement demands during campaigns, and conducting "information campaigns" that informed citizens and spoke to their daily concerns. The movement needed events both at locations that symbolized the military threat and in cities where broad participation was possible.[32]

The independents, however, maintained that mass action had already failed to prevent the missile stationing, and they called for "sharpening resistance" to government policy. They therefore pushed for confrontation with the state through actions that called its legitimacy and that of NATO into question, and they even condoned acts of violence performed by some of their members. In the independents' view, after the missiles' deployment a simple renewal of mass action against the missiles would bring about the movement's decline. Instead, it needed to turn discussion of new American "war-fighting" strategies into concrete action in order to qualitatively intensify resistance.

Given this fundamental division, the peace movement proved unable to agree on common strategies and protest forms after 1983. Instead, the movement followed a two-pronged approach by default. Each wing con-

---

31. Wolfgang Biermann, untitled essay in *Reader zur Strategie-Konferenz.*
32. DFG-VK, "Politische Friedenssicherung"; KOFAZ, "Für einen neuen Aufschwung der Friedensbewegung"; Komitee für Frieden, Abrüstung und Zusammenarbeit [KOFAZ], "Für das einheitliche Handeln der Friedensbewegung im Jahr 1986," in *Reader zur Aktionskonferenz der Friedensbewegung* (Bonn, Feb. 1986).

ducted its own actions, although they sometimes coordinated their events loosely with each other. Each faction, however, supported the other's endeavors at best halfheartedly, which reduced participation in both.[33]

Traditionalist religious, social democratic, and communist groups wanted mass actions to demonstrate that the struggle against stationing continued.[34] In 1984 they organized protest intended to demonstrate the movement's remaining strength without scaring potential participants. They conducted an unofficial referendum in conjunction with elections to the European parliament. Fifty-eight percent of those voting in the elections took part, of which 87 percent expressed their displeasure over the missiles' stationing.[35] Later that year, they planned a human chain from Bremerhaven in the North to Munich in the South, which again was intended to show the movement's strength, to give local initiatives an important role, to overcome passivity, and to attract previously inactive people through its local venue and its total innocuousness.[36]

Independent groups, however, wanted to turn the antimissile opposition into an anti-NATO or antimilitarist movement and focused increasingly on agitation against NATO's "preparations for war." They turned their efforts in 1984 to the Fulda region, the location of missile bases and NATO military maneuvers. They attempted to hinder NATO's practice maneuvers through having strolling activists impede troop movement, changing traffic signs, interfering with communication equipment, and blockading fuel and food supplies.[37] In a similar vein, the independents organized "refusal campaigns" to demonstrate "cancellation of loyalty" to the state. People signed statements indicating their refusal to take part in any "preparations for war," including military service, civilian defense, health service training for military casualties, or arms research.[38]

In 1986 the movement decided on action at the cruise missile stationing site in Hasselbach. Since the very diversity of protest forms in 1984 had resulted in disappointing turnout for the individual events—given the overall decline in mobilization—the movement now wanted to concentrate its fire. However, it proved unable to agree on a single protest form and remained divided over whether to blockade the missile sites. The local peace initiatives opposed blockades unanimously for fear that they would

---

33. Leif, *Die strategische (Ohn-)Macht,* 98.

34. "Grossaktion gegen Manöver bleibt umstritten," *Tageszeitung,* 7 May 1984.

35. "Fifty-eight percent gegen Raketen," *Tageszeitung* 19 June 1984.

36. ". . . um zu zeigen, dass die Friedensbewegung lebt und wächst," *Frankfurter Rundschau,* 25 Apr. 1984.

37. "Wird der 'Friedensherbst' zur Pleite?" *Mannheimer Morgen,* 17 Sept. 1984.

38. "Wenn Einigkeit zu teuer wird," *Deutsches Allgemeines Sonntagsblatt,* 1 Apr. 1984.

inhibit mobilization of the local, conservative, relatively rural populace,[39] but the movement's independent spectrum insisted on blockades. As a compromise the Coordinating Committee decided to have a mass demonstration at the missile site but to support civil disobedience carried out independently and to have the demonstration file past it as a gesture of recognition and support.[40]

Another problem for the peace movement's self-image was its relationship to parties. All groups agreed in principle on strict nonpartisanship and avoiding domination by parties. What this approach meant in practice, however, was a matter of constant debate, frequent rancor, and genuine dilemma. Parties sympathetic to the movement helped mobilize actual and potential activists and represented a channel of influence on parliamentary politics and, potentially, government policy. The chance to influence the parties also encouraged the movement to remain at least nominally united at the national level, despite disagreements that constantly threatened to splinter it. However, parties potentially threatened to dominate or co-opt the movement. While inviting SPD and Green representatives to speak at rallies enhanced the movement's public profile, for example, it also suggested that these parties were the movement's essential representatives and obscured the movement's broader perspectives.[41] Through their links to certain movement groups, moreover, the parties intensified divisions within the movement, since these groups tried to bring the movement into line with their respective parties' positions.

The Communist Party (DKP) and its affiliates in the movement posed the threat of dominance through alliance building. The DKP was not directly a member of the movement's Coordinating Committee, but several groups dominated by communists (most notably KOFAZ, itself an alliance dominated by communists) played key leadership roles in the committee. Ardent communists turned out in disproportionate numbers for each action conference as well, and in general they contributed to the movement's organizational base in vast disproportion to their numbers in the movement at large. Communist groups had always celebrated the movement as a broad coalition representing broad sectors of the population, a view that had a large measure of truth. Led by KOFAZ, communist groups exploited their organizational strength in attempts to bring the movement's positions into agreement with the DKP and the Soviet leadership. At the same time and with considerable success, they used appeals to the movement's unity to block criticism of Soviet policy, and they tried to

39. "Die 'Friedensbewegung' über die Blockadefrage zerstritten," *Frankfurter Allgemeine Zeitung,* 5 Aug. 1986.

40. "Friedensbewegung blockiert nur sich," *Tageszeitung,* 13 Aug. 1986.

41. "Offener Brief," *Tageszeitung,* 16 June 1987.

steer the movement toward support of Soviet arms control proposals and other policies.

For example, when the Soviets stationed SS-22s and SS-23s in Eastern Europe following NATO's deployment of the INF missiles, KOFAZ maintained that the danger of war would actually be greater without these "countermeasures." Such positions brought the communist groups into violent conflict with the Greens and other independent groups, who insisted that the movement's credibility depended on its autonomy to condemn all militarism.[42] Similarly, when the INF treaty was finally concluded, noncommunist groups thwarted communist suggestions that the peace movement and Gorbachev were triumphantly leading the world hand in hand into a "dynamic of disarmament," with the movement cast as the Soviets' supportive ally in future negotiations.[43]

The SPD posed a different kind of dilemma for the movement. On the one hand, it threatened to co-opt the peace movement's issues through its turnaround in defense policy. On the other hand, the SPD's innovative new policies further opened mainstream politics to alternative security ideas, put pressure on the other parties, and offered the movement the chance to widen its impact through fruitful exchange. Given the SPD's dominance and subsequent disavowal of the peace movement in the 1950s and its official support for the double-track decision under Schmidt, the peace movement remained highly suspicious of the party's motives. Social democratic and communist groups within the movement, however, pressed strongly for some inclusion of the SPD in movement activities. The ice was broken when Willy Brandt spoke at the movement's largest demonstration in 1983. In 1984 many prominent Social Democrats helped fill out the ranks of the incomplete human chain, while Oskar Lafontaine and Willy Brandt were invited to address various rallies.[44] Similarly, in 1987 Hans-Jochen Vogel was reluctantly permitted a five-minute "greeting" at the demonstration in support of the INF treaty, but he was met with eggs and hisses.[45]

A second effect of the SPD's new defense outlook was to bring intensified electoral competition into the heart of the movement. Competition for movement votes grew in the course of the 1980s, increasing the parties' rivalry within the movement as well. The Greens had gotten their

42. "Keine Mehrheit für 'Raus aus der NATO,' " *Tageszeitung,* 7 May 1984.
43. "Friedenskonferenz fehlt Orientierung," *Tageszeitung,* 30 Nov. 1987; "Je grösser die Ratlosigheit, desto länger der Text," *Frankfurter Rundschau,* 30 Nov. 1987.
44. "Kampfabstimmung in der Friedensbewegung," *Frankfurter Allgemeine Zeitung,* 3 Oct. 1984; "SPD-Prominenz als ungeliebte Glieder einer Kette," *Die Welt,* 23 Oct. 1984; "Lafontaine fordert einseitige Abrüstung," *Saarbrücker Zeitung,* 22 Oct. 1984.
45. "Der Friedensdemo fehlt das Feindbild," *Stuttgarter Nachtrichten,* 15 June 1987.

electoral start by wooing voters dissatisfied with the Schmidt government of the 1970s, including of course Schmidt's support for the double-track decision. Competition between the Greens and the SPD increased after 1983, as the SPD adopted left-wing positions in areas like nuclear energy and security policy and strove to win back its former voters. Indeed, the SPD's credibility as a true alternative to the conservative government grew with its innovative concepts of nonprovocative defense and security partnerships and thus offered a home to the movement's more moderate supporters. Competition between the SPD and the Greens for electoral support from the peace movement grew more vocal over time. While the Greens had always criticized Social Democratic policy, the SPD descended into the fray after 1983 as an opposition party with competition on its left. A key SPD spokesperson accused the Greens of "policy incompetence" in security issues, while the Greens labeled the SPD's new security policies a mere "half-peace."[46]

Such bitter exchanges poisoned the atmosphere within the movement and damaged its image in public perceptions. Moreover, the substantive differences between the two parties made the peace movement's task of arriving at new goals and strategies more difficult. Indeed, by 1983 three parties were competing for peace movement votes, although the DKP's vote remained marginal. Throughout the 1980s, the party-linked groups in the movement tried to bring it into line with their respective parties. In 1986, for example, communist groups hoped to concentrate on SDI, reflecting the Soviets' concern with that issue. Social democrats and the Greens, in contrast, wanted to avoid supporting the Soviet Union too one-sidedly. The SPD's general demand that the missiles be eliminated through negotiations struck the other groups as too modest. The Greens were still struggling to get the movement to adopt German withdrawal from NATO as a central demand, which communist and social democratic influence precluded. These diverse positions hindered the movement from arriving at a unifying goal.

---

46. Karsten Voigt accused the Greens of having no policy for German security after withdrawal from NATO. They call for unilateral disarmament but have no concept for reforming the reality of two highly armed military blocs. See Karsten Voigt, "Bekenntnisse zur Politikunfähigkeit, Anmerkungen zu sicherheitspolitischen Vorstellungen der Grünen," *Sozialdemokratischer Pressedienst,* 2 Dec. 1987; and "Zwischen Fundamentalismus und halbem Realismus, der SPD-Aussenpolitiker Karsten Voigt beschäftigt sich mit der Friedenspolitik der Grünen," *Tageszeitung,* 16 Oct. 1989. The Greens in turn accused the SPD of having no strategy for demilitarizing the East-West conflict and of supporting deterrence and the bloc system. See Die Grünen, *SPD-Sicherheitspolitik: Ein halber Frieden* (Bonn, 1986); Volker Böge, "Blockzersetzung statt Selbstbehauptung Europas," *Friedensjournal* (a periodical of the Komitee für Frieden, Abrüstung und Zusammenarbeit [KOFAZ]) 6 (1988):13–14.

Organizational Crisis: Restructuring of Movement Leadership

Organizational crisis played the final role in the relative decline of the peace movement in the late 1980s. The conflicts outlined above strained the movement's core leadership so severely that it finally disbanded and was replaced by a much looser coordinating network. As chapter 5 described, until 1989 the movement's leadership structure, the Coordinating Committee, was composed of thirty groups with links to churches, parties, unions, the new social movements, and other groupings on the left. The Coordinating Committee and its rotating Executive Committee ran the movement's daily business (finances, media, etc.) and steered its decision making by informally controlling the internal political agenda. Until 1984, the movement shared a minimal consensus in the struggle against the missiles, which facilitated cooperation among its various wings and helped contain the already rampant conflicts. That the Coordinating Committee had managed to contain these conflicts for so long was already a small miracle, accomplished by a delicate internal balance among wings, the adoption of democratic (almost parliamentary) procedures, the delaying of formal votes until compromise resolutions had been hammered out in working groups, and the use of action conferences open to the entire movement that legitimated, if somewhat tenuously, the Coordinating Committee's decisions vis-à-vis the movement's rank and file.

As first the stationing and then the removal of the missiles destroyed the minimal consensus as the basis for cooperation, the internal conflicts outlined above increasingly paralyzed the Coordinating Committee. Up to 1983, the common focus on preventing the new missiles facilitated cooperation based on "actionism," planning and execution of demonstrations and other protest. This common focus allowed the Coordinating Committee to put aside divisive issues in the name of organizational unity and effectiveness, while allowing groups to emphasize their favorite themes and protest forms as part of a broad panoply. Once the missiles became a moot question, old conflicts resurfaced without overarching compromises available to tame them. Although the INF treaty temporarily re-created a common focus, Coordinating Committee meetings increasingly consisted of fruitless searches for a new central agenda under which other projects could be subsumed. Mere opposition to various nuclear weapons was too narrow to inspire indefinitely, while other peace projects remained too diffuse to unite.

Conflicts over political issues and strategy both reflected and became embroiled in party competition within the Coordinating Committee. Shifting veto coalitions undermined its ability to formulate new approaches and strategies for the movement. The SPD squelched the Green demand for West German withdrawal from NATO, which would repel the SPD's moderate voters and much of the populace at large. Communist forces usually defeated Green initiatives to support the Solidarity movement in Poland or to condemn East German arrests of its peace activists. The SPD and Greens together vetoed communist proposals that too one-sidedly supported Soviet positions, while the SPD's focus on arms control negotiations seemed too meek for other groups—and so on.

In addition, conflicts arose over the Coordinating Committee's marked deficits in representing local peace initiatives and professionally-based peace groups, thereby excluding some of the most dynamic sectors of peace activism after 1983. Despite declining mass mobilization after 1984, the peace movement remained surprisingly vibrant at the local and sectoral level. Professionally-based peace groups of doctors, teachers, scientists, athletes, architects, attorneys, and so on flourished, representing the expansion of peace activism even further into mainstream society. These groups grew in popularity in the mid- and late 1980s despite the overall decline in participation.

Newly founded local peace groups, moreover, reflected the spread of peace movement activism into relatively conservative populations, especially where local military activity created a concrete sense of *Betroffenheit,* or direct disadvantage. To take a particularly striking example, local peace activism grew as cruise missiles were stationed in the traditionally conservative, rural Hunsrück region. Once deployments started, acts of resistance in surrounding villages increased. The government built six concrete bunkers for the missiles, which made the local populace feel vulnerable to "collateral damage" if the bunkers became targets of Soviet nuclear strikes. Residents erected ninety-six crosses to remind passersby of the local cruise missiles, and religious services were held each Sunday, rain or shine, in front of the bunkers.[47] Similarly, local peace groups flourished in other places where military installations directly affected people's lives, long after a broader fear of war had declined. The Easter Marches, which traditionally used multiple routes throughout West Germany, capitalized on local sensitivities to the military presence, such as public annoyance with low-flying military jets and their deafening roar, especially after the plane crashes at Ramstein and elsewhere.[48]

In the end, the question of representativeness was the final straw in the peace movement's organizational crisis, which eventually brought about the abandonment of the Coordinating Committee and the revamp-

---

47. "Das Kreuz da oben: Wie sich Menschen im Hunsrück gegen die Raketenstationierung wehren," *Die Zeit,* 28 Mar. 1986.

48. "Einäugige Marschierer," *Augsburger Allgemeine,* 5 Apr. 1988; "Mit Ostermarsch gegen Tiefflüge," *Frankfurter Rundschau,* 28 Mar. 1989.

ing of the movement's organizational structure. Although local peace groups were often tied into regional associations, these networks had neither seats nor votes in the Coordinating Committee, and there was also a lack of direct representation for the local groups in the committee. Professionally-based peace groups suffered the same lack of representation, as did women's peace groups. Indeed, the Coordinating Committee expanded only once in its entire career (when it took in four more groups in 1982), because an influx of new groups could have disturbed the finely-tuned balance between wings and might have upset internal operating procedures. The committee's strategy for consensus generation, which had long been contentious in the grassroots context of extraparliamentary politics, in the long run proved damaging to its legitimacy.

Dissatisfaction with the movement's national leadership structures simmered from the very beginning. Independent groups criticized the very formation of the Coordinating Committee, because a relatively small number of groups had instigated its formation from "above," in a closed circle insulated from the broader grassroots *Basis*. The Protestant Aktion Sühnezeichen proposed reforming the action conferences several times, in an attempt to reduce communist influence in the interest of representativeness.

Additional controversy surrounded the role and power of the Executive Committee, the *Geschäftsführung*. Since the Executive Committee attended to the movement's daily business, it gave interviews to the press and thus seemed to speak for the movement as a whole, which some groups felt violated the movement's grassroots constitution. The Executive Committee also prestructured the Coordinating Committee's meetings by drawing up proposals, which led to the criticism that the committee was blocking the movement by taking responsibility away from individual groups and was hindering the development of long-term perspectives because of its orientation toward planning protest events.

According to groups from the independent spectrum, the Coordinating Committee was too focused on "actionism" and compromises between the various factions, too tied into parties and other institutions, and too distant from the movement's grassroots. Such problems led to occasional proposals that the Coordinating Committee be relieved of its official responsibilities and be turned into a forum for discussion among groups that were much more loosely associated than before.[49] Despite these complaints, for a number of years no such action was undertaken.

By the late 1980s, however, cumulative stagnation in the Coordinating Committee led to renewed suggestions for disbanding. Its dissolution

---

49. Leif, *Die strategische (Ohn-)Macht,* 64–115.

began in 1989, when several church-oriented groups resigned. In particular, the Protestant Aktion Sühnezeichen/Friedensdienste (AS/F) dealt the committee a hard blow with its resignation, as the group had been a founding member and enjoyed considerable prestige, and since church-based groups had often performed a bridging function between the other wings. AS/F argued that the peace movement's future lay at the local and regional level, for which the committee had little relevance. Moreover, AS/F noted, multiple efforts to expand the committee to include new groups had been blocked in the interests of internal political equilibrium, but this robbed the committee of political weight and meaning.[50]

Other groups evidently also felt misgivings about continuing the Coordinating Committee's life. The committee was formally disbanded and was replaced by a network oriented toward grassroots peace groups. Whereas the committee had enjoyed a political mandate and decision-making powers, the Network (officially called the Netzwerk Friedenskooperative) was merely supposed to facilitate grassroots exchange and cooperation, along with meetings every three months to coordinate activities.[51] The Network had no official spokesperson, and peace projects now had to be financially and otherwise independent. The first Network meeting attracted around seventy groups, including groups formerly in the Coordinating Committee and groups that had been excluded, and it thus addressed the problems of representativeness. The Network has proven a durable organizational form, continuing even after German unification to serve its appointed function.

With declining political opportunities and reduced mobilization, ideological factionalization that undermined cohesion, and pressures for organizational reform, the peace movement declined after 1983, but it had not by any means drawn its last breath. The end of the 1980s turned out to be the end of the cold war as well, although the peace movement did not know it at the time. As the cold war drew to a close, the movement was still working on issues that had occupied it throughout the 1980s. Hoping that the INF treaty banning medium-range missiles in the East and in the West would pave the way for further disarmament, in 1988 and 1989 the peace movement resisted Western proposals to modernize short-range nuclear weapons in Germany. Such modernization, it argued, would further the arms race, whereas the peace movement hoped to eliminate the threat the arms race posed to humankind. In the fall of 1988 the movement also demonstrated against the construction of a military bunker at Linnich, which it viewed as a symbol of NATO's aggressive war-fighting strategies.

---

50. "Ausschuß der Friedensbewegung denkt über seine Zukunft nach," *Frankfurter Rundschau,* 1 July 1989.

51. "Ende einer Bewegungsäre amtlich," *Tageszeitung,* 3 Oct. 1989.

At the same time, the peace movement searched for consensus on a "positive peace policy," a comprehensive vision of a peaceful world that would permit enduring cooperation with unions and other social movements.[52]

These efforts proved the last hurrah of the peace movement during the cold war. The fall of the Berlin Wall in November of 1989, the collapse of the German Democratic Republic, and other developments in Eastern Europe and the Soviet Union spelled the end of the cold war roughly forty years after the birth of West Germany. These events took the peace movement by surprise as much as they did the rest of the world, confronting the movement with a very different situation.

---

52. "Auf der Suche nach einem neuen Profil," *Deutsches Allgemeines Sonntagsblatt,* 8 May 1988; "Kampagne gegen neue Nachrüstung," *Tageszeitung,* 22 Mar. 1989.

CHAPTER 7

The Peace Movement
since Unification

German unification, the dissolution of the Soviet bloc, and the (however uncertain) democratization of Eastern Europe have dramatically altered the world order, German domestic politics, and, of course, the environment in which German peace movements now work. Although unified Germany has overwhelmingly retained the governing institutions and formal procedures of the "old" Federal Republic, the absorption of the former German Democratic Republic has changed the tenor and dynamics of domestic politics. The unexpectedly large burden of restructuring the eastern German economy and providing for the citizens' welfare has put unprecedented strain on German federalism, fiscal policy, social policy, and industrial relations. The problems of unification have heightened conflict over resources and raised new issues (like immigration), which in turn have transformed the parameters of party competition.

In foreign policy, united Germany faces a new security and foreign policy situation. The end of the cold war, the collapse of the Warsaw Pact, and the Soviet Union's demise as a superpower have rendered the threat of military invasion almost nonexistent. Along with unification, this vastly diminished threat has released German foreign policy from many of the constraints that its exposed security position and German division had previously set. In search of a new foreign policy, Germany finds itself subjected to conflicting pressures in the international arena. On the one hand, it must assuage fears that unification has once again unleashed a resurgent, nationalistic, and aggressive nation, by assuring its neighbors that it will continue its multilateralist, nonmilitary policies of the past.

On the other hand, various crises around the world have led to calls for Germany to accept international responsibility commensurate with its new stature, which would mean an unprecedented willingness to use military force in contexts beyond national defense (though only in multilateral settings). For example, in January 1993, United Nations (UN) General Secretary Boutros Boutros-Ghali called for "comprehensive participation" by Germany in all UN operations.[1]

United Germany thus faces the necessity of defining a new foreign policy identity—its national interests and moral position in the new international constellation. No major political figure or party proposes a new German *Alleingang,* a single-minded pursuit of national interest regardless of its impact on other countries. Instead, the political class and attentive public are debating the extent to which Germany should become involved in conflicts beyond NATO's borders. The dominant governing party, the conservative CDU/CSU, seeks to "normalize" Germany's role in the world and its foreign policy identity, so that Germany will be no more constrained than any other power its size. Germany might acquire a seat on the UN Security Council, in this view, and would take part in both the decision-making and the policy-implementation processes of multilateral institutions, like any other member.

For the time being, however, German foreign policy is not yet normalized. Instead, it remains constrained by stiff domestic opposition to a greater German *military* role abroad, despite widespread support for non-military, diplomatic engagement. Postwar peace movements have left a highly visible imprint on politics, by setting firm constraints on foreign policy in the new, united Germany. Most of the political class and the broader public is marked by a "culture of reticence" toward the use of military force,[2] due in significant measure to the peace movement's influence. Disavowing both neutralism and the "power politics" of old, most Germans support multilateralism and a "politics of responsibility."[3] This aversion to the use of force has institutionalized itself firmly in the SPD and the Greens (which are quite likely to reenter the Bundestag in 1994), and it is visible in the FDP and even in the CDU/CSU. The public at large and the opposition parties in particular have firmly resisted expanding Germany's military role beyond the borders of NATO territory, or at least to anything more than participation in "blue-helmet" peacekeeping under UN auspices. Despite considerable discussion of the "out-of-area" question, the

---

1. "Governing Coalition Seeks German Involvement in UN 'Blue Helmet' Operations," *The Week in Germany,* 15 Jan. 1993; and "Rühe Calls for German Participation in UN Military Operations, 'Solidarity Pact' with Eastern Europe," *The Week in Germany,* 19 Feb. 1993.

2. Clay Clemens, "A Special Kind of Superpower? Germany and the Demilitarization of post-Cold War International Security," in *Germany in a New Era,* ed. Gary Geipel (Indianapolis: Hudson Institute, 1993), 199–240, here 209.

3. Harald Müller, "German Foreign Policy After Unification," in *The New Germany in the New Europe,* ed. Paul Stares (Washington: Brookings Institution Press, 1992), 126–73, here 131.

governing coalition has made only modest headway on the issue up to the time of this book's writing (summer 1994).

The peace movement may be currently quiet, but it is by no means "dead" or finished. Its potential political opportunities have changed significantly. The end of the cold war has dramatically changed the issues that earlier stimulated mobilization. With the military threat to Germany insignificant and the superpower rivalry largely eliminated, large-scale mobilization on the basis of perceived threat to life itself is now more difficult, although the Persian Gulf War proved that fear can sometimes resurface as a catalyst for mobilization. The current lack of Western involvement in large-scale military action, the remaining constraints on Germany's own participation in military ventures, and the multilateral context of the use of force offer few issues capable of generating mass mobilization.

Should Germany consider participation in combat missions in controversial trouble spots, however, mobilization on some scale is quite possible, reminiscent perhaps of the mobilization against the Emergency Laws in the 1960s. The peace movement has institutionalized itself quite effectively in the extraparliamentary arena and within the parties of the left. The requisite extraparliamentary organizational infrastructure and communication channels are still in place, as the Netzwerk Friedenskooperative created in 1989 is fully operational. The substantial antimilitarist factions in both the SPD and the Greens are well connected to the extraparliamentary networks. So far, the left both within and outside of these parties has maintained a watchful guard against realpolitik accommodations to the use of force by the SPD or the Greens.

Ideologically, however, the groups in the movement have trouble agreeing on a common "minimum consensus," although dissidence in the ideological ranks would not necessarily inhibit mobilization by the faithful. In the first years following reunification, the left has experienced unusual internal divisions over the use of force. During the cold war, condoning Western use of force was largely unthinkable for the left. Opposition to Western "imperialism" in the Third World went hand in hand with condemnation of the superpower arms race, although the left did accept the use of force by Third World "liberation" movements. In the left's view, deterrence threatened survival itself, the superpowers had a common "objective" interest in avoiding conflict that could escalate to nuclear catastrophe, and détente provided a peaceful adjudication of even the most intense ideological differences and power rivalries. In sum, the left considered pacifism a moral and existential imperative for the West.

In the "post-postwar" world, however, these ideological certainties have started to crack. In certain current conflicts (e.g., that in Bosnia), however, it is not clear that the warring parties can be brought to reason. Moreover, the conflicts are not embedded in larger superpower rivalries, and Western intervention would not necessarily serve "imperialist" Western interests. Regarding such conflicts, most on the left still say that force never solves problems, but a few now entertain notions of "just intervention" and think that a little force could sometimes go a long way to stop aggression, injustice, and massive civilian suffering. In their view, there could be situations where the use of force might be "just," in that the effects of force might not necessarily be disproportional to the gains achieved—especially if appliers of that force are multilateral bodies and if the United States and other major powers do not seem to be simply securing their own interests. In short, the use of "appropriate" levels of force might be justified to stop larger suffering, if done in service of justice, not "power politics." However, even these "dissidents" on the left are loathe to give the German government a blank check in the out-of-area question, and they would thus probably resist German participation in military activity beyond blue-helmet peacekeeping.

Paradoxically then, while the "culture of reticence" has put its stamp on much of the German body politic and currently constrains German foreign policy, the main "perpetrators" of that culture are engaged in considerable internal debate. These processes find illustration in the Gulf War, the Bosnia crisis, the situation in Somalia, and the out-of-area discussion more generally.

The "New" Germany in the "New" World Order

Germany now faces an entirely new, and much less threatening, security situation. Indeed, the hopes of the 1980s peace movement have largely been realized. The potentially existential threat once posed by confrontation between two nuclear-armed blocs has faded. Although both sides still have nuclear weapons, the dissolution of the Warsaw Pact has eliminated the bloc confrontation of the cold war, reduced the traditional role of nuclear deterrence in Western defense, and lowered German dependence on the United States for security. Indeed, as Linnenkamp writes, Germany now finds itself "encircled by friends, deprived of enemies."[4]

The collapse of communism and the Soviet withdrawal to Europe's periphery, moreover, has ended Europe's role as the symbolic battlefield in the East-West conflict and has softened Germany's former strategic dilem-

---

4. Hilmar Linnenkamp, "The Security Policy of the New Germany," in *The New Germany in the New Europe,* ed. Paul Stares (Washington: Brookings Institution Press, 1992), 93–125, here 94.

mas as a frontline state exposed to overwhelming military power.[5] Although both the United States and Russia still play essential roles in European security, neither maintains its earlier position as the benign or brutal pacifier of its respective sphere of influence.[6] While Germany remains firmly anchored in NATO, the collapse of the former Soviet Union may lessen the relevance of the American presence in Europe as well and has already reduced Germany's dependence on the United States for military security. Germany is actively pursuing advances in European integration, including the capacity of the European Union (EU) for common foreign and security policies. At the same time, Germany envisions the Conference on Security and Cooperation in Europe (CSCE) as a vehicle for integrating the former Warsaw Pact states into the Western economic, political, and security orbit.[7]

The political tensions that could have resulted in nuclear confrontation in Europe during the cold war have largely disappeared, although ethnic strife, increased immigration, and the threat of terrorism pose new challenges. Reductions in arms levels across Europe have resulted in a lower level of conventional military threat as well. Although significant levels of military capacity still exist, Europe has made major strides toward demilitarization. On the former Soviet side, the Treaty on Conventional Forces in Europe (CFE) reduced former Soviet European forces by two-thirds, thereby reversing forty years of conventional superiority over NATO. The Two Plus Four Treaty mandated withdrawal of all Soviet troops from eastern Germany by the end of 1994. In accordance with the CFE treaty, major portions of French and British troops will withdraw from their German bases, and the West has substantially reduced its nuclear arsenal as well. United Germany will also reduce its peacetime troop strength to 370,000 (a more than 40 percent reduction of the 495,000 for the former West German armed forces combined with 170,000 for the former East German army), and it will make substantial cuts in conventional weaponry.[8] As reported by Linnenkamp, united Germany also agreed to abide by both German states' earlier commitments to "renounce the manufacture, possession, and control of nuclear, biological, and chemical (NBC) weapons."[9]

---

5. Ronald Asmus, *German Unification and its Ramifications,* R-4021-A (Santa Monica: Rand, 1991), 37.

6. Linnenkamp, "The Security Policy of the New Germany," 104.

7. James Sperling, "German Security Policy After the Cold War: The Strategy of a Civilian Power in an Uncivil World," in *European Security without the Soviet Union,* ed. Stuart Croft and Phil Williams (London: Frank Cass, 1992), 77–98, here 86.

8. Linnenkamp, "The Security Policy of the New Germany," 95–110.

9. Linnenkamp, "The Security Policy of the New Germany," 98.

The Soviet threat and German division imposed severe restrictions on West Germany during the cold war. When these limits dissolved, various politicians, diplomats, academics, and commentators expressed concern that united Germany might embark on a newly assertive, unilateralist, and threatening foreign policy, reminiscent of German behavior prior to 1945.[10] Others, however, contend that Germany is still highly constrained and poses even less threat to its European neighbors than during the cold war. According to Sperling, Germany has assigned itself the role of a "civilian" power in Europe, because a military role has been "proscribed by history, conscience, treaty, and self-interest."[11]

Similarly, Müller argues, although the German government jumped at opportunities to realize unification (a goal of forty-five years), it did so through an "astonishing" web of consultations and mutual adjustment. More importantly, since unification, Germany has pursued a strategy of "self-containment by integration" by trying to bolster the integrative capacities of, and its own entanglement in, NATO, the EU, the West European Union (WEU), and the CSCE. Germany has also emphasized non-military instruments of diplomacy particularly strongly, such as economic assistance for Eastern Europe, arms control, and environmental agreements.[12]

Finally, Duffield stresses the continuity in approach between the foreign policies of united Germany and the former West Germany. Instead of demonstrating a new assertiveness or unilateralism, united Germany remains constrained, at the international level, by its integration into multilateral institutions at all levels. At the level of domestic politics, moreover, policy remains constrained by elites committed to multilateralism and accustomed to a narrow definition of security interests, by a political culture inclined toward antimilitarism and even pacifism, by constitutional constraints (until July 1994) on "out-of-area" military action whose amendment would require the support of all major parties, and by pressures for policy consensus emanating from coalition government.[13] Even if Germany acquired a desire for a more autonomous and adventuresome

---

10. One of the most notable examples was the "Chequers Pronouncement" resulting from discussions between politicians and bureaucrats under the aegis of then–British Prime Minister Margaret Thatcher. For discussions of these views see Andrei Markovits and Simon Reich, "Should Europe Fear the Germans?" in *From Bundesrepublik to Deutschland,* ed. Michael Huelshoff, Andrei Markovits, and Simon Reich (Ann Arbor: University of Michigan Press, 1993), 271–90, here 275–77.

11. Sperling, "German Security Policy," 78.

12. Müller, "German Foreign Policy after Unification," 129–30.

13. John Duffield, "German Security Policy after Unification: Sources of Continuity and Restraint," *Contemporary Security Policy* 15, no. 3 (Dec. 1994): 172–98.

foreign policy, its reduced troop levels and lack of independent national military and command structures would deter such ambitions.[14]

Nonthreatening as Germany may be, it still faces the problem of defining its new international identity, a subject of ongoing controversy in domestic politics. Although Germany's past still requires it to downplay its new power, Germany's allies have urged it to assume more international responsibility. Thus Germany's commitment to multilateralism and its desire to avoid international isolation have subjected it to calls for increased military involvement beyond its traditional NATO responsibilities, as the international institutions to which it belongs have become involved in military missions in troubled areas around the world.[15] To be sure, environmental security, migration, and economic stability have largely supplanted traditional military security as the dominant issues for the prosperous European countries and require corresponding nonmilitary instruments. However, other crises, in particular the Gulf War and Somalia, have demonstrated that defining Germany's global military role is an equally important key to its "new responsibility" and national identity.[16]

As the events of 1991–93 show, domestic German politics have become engulfed in waves of controversy over the "out-of-area" issue. Will German troops be deployed outside of traditional NATO territory, and, if so, under the aegis of which international institutions? The CDU/CSU desires a "normalization" of German foreign policy, so that Germany would participate in military missions under the mandate of various international institutions (e.g., the WEU and the UN) with the "same rights and duties" as any other Western nation. Most other parties and substantial portions of the populace, however, want a much more restricted role for the Bundeswehr. The out-of-area question has been debated in the context of specific international crises, including the Persian Gulf War, the Yugoslavia/Bosnia crisis, and Somalia, and in general terms in the context of proposals for amending provisions in the German constitution, or Basic Law (Grundgesetz), prohibiting troop deployments except in defense of NATO territory. In each case, debate over the merits of sending German troops to specific crisis areas has been embroiled in more fundamental debate over what the constitution allows and whether it should be amended.

Sending German troops on anything more than humanitarian mis-

---

14. Thomas-Durell Young, "The 'Normalization' of the Federal Republic of Germany's Defense Structures" (Strategic Studies Institute, US Army War College, 1 Sept. 1992).

15. Duffield, "German Security Policy after Unification."

16. Müller, "German Foreign Policy after Unification," 139.

sions beyond NATO territory would require reversing longstanding political practice and attitudes deeply ingrained in the German political "establishment" and in the populace at large. At the level of constitutional interpretation, Müller notes that after 1945 "West Germany's position on
engaging in military activities was based on an unequivocal interpretation
of ambiguous legal language."[17] The Basic Law allowed German participation in collective security systems but restricted the Bundeswehr's
involvement to defense activities. The UN, of course, also has collective
security functions, but the longstanding interpretation of the Basic Law's
language held that it did not legitimize missions conducted outside of
NATO territory. In the 1980s, this interpretation was confirmed both by
the SPD/FDP coalition shortly before its collapse and by the new Kohl
government soon after it assumed office.

Thanks in part to the peace movement's efforts since the 1950s, however, resistance to out-of-area troop deployments among political elites
and the public at large rests on more than customary constitutional interpretation. Instead, it constitutes a "culture of reticence" deeply ingrained
in Germany's broader political culture, stemming from the experience of
the Third Reich and forty years as a frontline state during the cold war.
Germany's waging of World War II under Hitler created profound reservations toward the role of power—in particular of military force—as a
"normal" instrument of policy, and, according to Schwarz, it turned Germany from a country "obsessed with power" into one "oblivious to
power."[18] West Germany's armed forces and NATO membership were
defined as contributions to containing potential Soviet expansion in
Europe, which in the 1950s was the only possible means of overcoming
domestic opposition to rearmament.

Although the legitimacy of the armed forces for this purpose gradually acquired general acceptance, Germans remained uncomfortable with
the idea that democracies might use military force to preserve stability and
uphold international law outside Europe. The focus on détente, arms control, Ostpolitik, and Germany's renunciation of force agreements reinforced these attitudes and fostered hopes that future conflicts could be
resolved through peaceful means. The cold war, moreover, limited West
Germany's view of military security to Central Europe. Given fresh memories of war and the potential for catastrophic destruction inherent in bloc
confrontation, West German security policy gave top priority to the prevention of war. Germany's primary worry concerning crises outside the
NATO area was that they might escalate to a broader confrontation

---

17. Ibid.
18. Hans-Peter Schwarz, *Die gezähmten Deutschen: Von der Machtbesessenheit zur
Machtvergessenheit* (Stuttgart: Deutsche-Verlags-Anstalt, 1985).

between the superpowers, which could spill over to a larger war on the central front. Chancellors from both major parties established a strict policy of German abstention from military involvement beyond the NATO area.[19]

These constitutional and political issues were at the heart of each specific debate of the out-of-area issue between 1991 and 1993. The first instance, the Gulf War, caught the German government rather unprepared for the demands that suddenly confronted it. Müller notes that German policy on the Persian Gulf was widely perceived as "lackluster, weak, pacifistic, and neutralist."[20] A torrent of criticism from abroad produced a debacle that left Germany diplomatically isolated. Apologists note that, like its allies, the German government condemned the Iraqi invasion of Kuwait, supported the UN Security Council resolutions, and contributed financial, logistical, and material support to the war effort. The Germans also sent fighter jets to help defend Turkey (a NATO alliance partner) against possible Iraqi attack, but only after objecting to this "provoked alliance obligation" and voicing suspicions that Turkey was manipulating NATO to serve its own ambitions in the region. Iraqi Scud missile attacks on Israel also occasioned a shift toward greater German involvement, given its historical legacy and the highly embarrassing revelations that German firms had illegally contributed to the Iraqi military buildup, including their possession of Scuds. Germany quickly sent humanitarian aid, Patriot air defense missiles, and antichemical warfare vehicles to Israel. Despite these contributions, even apologists admit that German policy suffered from major weaknesses, in particular an overall lack of commitment to the allied cause. In addition to criticisms coming from the public debate, the government itself offered only lukewarm support, with Kohl referring to the allies' "claim to our solidarity" rather than to the necessity or justice of the war.[21]

Scholars attribute Germany's hesitancy to several factors. First, Germany was in the final stages of unification when Iraq invaded Kuwait in August 1990. Politicians and bureaucrats were hard at work on the international treaties discussed earlier in this section and the internal unification treaty between the two Germanies. All of these efforts required reassuring the world—in particular the Soviets, who had not yet finalized

---

19. Karl Kaiser and Klaus Becher, "Germany and the Iraq Conflict," in *Western Europe and the Gulf*, ed. Nicole Gnesotto and John Roper (Paris: The Institute for Security Studies, Western European Union, 1992), 39–70, here 39–40; Ronald Asmus, *Germany after the Gulf War*, N-3391-AF (Santa Monica: Rand, 1992), 4–7; Duffield, "German Security Policy after Unification," 20–21.

20. Müller, "German Foreign Policy after Unification," 135.

21. Asmus, *Germany after the Gulf War*, 11–13.

the terms of troop withdrawal from East Germany—that united Germany would be nonmilitaristic and peaceful. Second, most politicians held that the Basic Law forbad a German military contribution to the allies' effort. Third, a German military contribution would have collided with the country's traditional definition of the Bundeswehr's purpose—to defend home territory and to deter rather than wage war. Finally, the German government quickly discovered the considerable public opposition to the Gulf War—at least prior to the actual Western attack during Operation Desert Storm—and the much higher opposition to any German military involvement at any point. Public opinion played a particularly strong role given the federal elections in December 1990 and the Hessen state elections in January 1991.[22]

As the government correctly anticipated, support of any sort for the allied war effort proved highly controversial. The Persian Gulf crisis became a salient issue soon after the Iraqi invasion of Kuwait. A poll taken in August 1990 revealed that Germans considered the gulf situation the second most salient issue, superseded only by German unification. Thirty-one percent feared that the gulf crisis potentially threatened the peace in Europe.[23] According to a poll taken on January 15, 1991, two days before Operation Desert Storm began, 79 percent favored further negotiations with Iraq even if it failed to obey the UN ultimatum demanding withdrawal from Kuwait, while only 16 percent favored attacking Iraq.[24] Polls taken in August 1990, October 1990, and January 1991 reveal that approximately 75 percent of Germans hoped to keep German troops out of the gulf conflict in particular and international conflicts in general. Rejecting a "world power" role, 40 percent named prosperous and neutral Switzerland as the model Germany should follow, followed by the neutral welfare state Sweden (29 percent). Only 6 percent saw the United States as a model.[25]

Once Operation Desert Storm began, public opinion exhibited both change and continuity. The allied military action against Iraq enjoyed higher levels of approval among the public than expected, but support for *German* participation in combat remained very low.[26] A poll of *western* Germans revealed that 66 percent considered military action necessary, including 52 percent of SPD voters and 47 percent of Green supporters;

22. Müller, "German Foreign Policy after Unification," 135–36; Kaiser and Becher, "Germany and the Iraq Conflict," 39–48.

23. "Angst vor einem Krieg am Golf," *Süddeutsche Zeitung,* 28 Aug. 1990.

24. "Was die Bundesbürger von einem Krieg am Golf halten," *Fernseh- und Hörfunkspiegel,* 16 Jan. 1990.

25. "Deutsche wollen sich bei internationalen Konflikten heraushalten," *Frankfurter Rundschau,* 4 Jan. 1991.

26. "ZDF-Politbarometer," *Fernseh- und Hörfunkspiegel,* 29 Jan. 1991.

and 57 percent agreed that the allies should not have waited any longer before attacking. Generational differences in these survey responses were slight.[27] Support for American action was also high, with 76 percent expressing approval for America's policy in the Gulf War.[28] Around half of western Germans supported sending German Luftwaffe jet fighters to Turkey, and nearly half even supported deploying the planes in the event of an Iraqi attack. Only one-fourth to one-third of *eastern* Germans approved of this measure, however,[29] and half of eastern Germans were *against* the military action as a whole.[30]

However, this relatively high level of support for Western military action against Iraq may well have represented an anomaly in German public opinion and should not necessarily be taken as a sign of more general willingness to join Western military missions. As Clemens argues, "German reluctance to sanction joint military action could be still greater in a challenge less egregious than that posed by Saddam, and where possible use of German-produced arms against Israel is not an issue."[31] Military aid to Turkey, moreover, represented a special case, as Turkey was a NATO ally on the margins of the conflict. Indeed, 62 percent rejected the participation of German soldiers in the allied effort against Iraq itself (75 percent in eastern Germany).[32] Men subject to the draft voted with their feet on the issue. Applications for conscientious objector status rose 169 percent in the first half of 1991[33] and doubled for 1991 as a whole.[34] Just as strikingly, the Gulf War did not change the public's general views on Germany's international role. In late January 1991, 74 percent remained opposed to a constitutional change permitting out-of-area troop deployments.[35]

War in the former Yugoslavia put German foreign policy to a second postunification test. Germany's recognition of Slovenia and Croatia constitutes the one case in which Germany has shown high profile and thus acted "assertively." Until mid-1991, German policy corresponded to

---

27. "Furcht vor Öl in Flammen," *Der Spiegel,* 28 Jan. 1991.

28. "Meinungsreport," *Fernseh- und Hörfunkspiegel,* 8 Feb. 1991.

29. Ibid.

30. "Politbarometer für Februar," *Fernseh- und Hörfunkspiegel,* 19 Feb. 1991.

31. Clay Clemens, "Opportunity or Obligation? Redefining Germany's Military Role outside of NATO," *Armed Forces and Society* 19, no. 2 (winter 1993): 231–51, here 247.

32. "Wie stehen die Deutschen zum Golfkrieg?" *Fernseh- und Hörfunkspiegel,* 11 Feb. 1991.

33. "Number of Conscientious Objectors Rose Sharply in 1991," *The Week in Germany,* 19 July 1991.

34. "Number of Conscientious Objectors doubled in 1991," *The Week in Germany,* 31 Jan. 1992.

35. "ZDF-Politbarometer," *Fernseh- und Hörfunkspiegel,* 29 Jan. 1991.

Western interests in keeping Yugoslavia intact, particularly because a forced breakup of Yugoslavia might encourage dissolution of the still-existing Soviet Union. By July, however, an emerging domestic consensus in favor of the seceding republics, an interest in discouraging violent resolution of ethnic conflict and territorial issues in Eastern Europe, and desires to demonstrate leadership after the Gulf War "debacle" moved the government to revise its policy. Germany began to press the EU to mediate and to recognize the seceding republics.

Germany adopted other multilateral approaches to ending the fighting as well. Genscher persuaded the CSCE to give pan-European legitimacy to the EU's attempts to mediate, brought the matter before the UN Security Council, and put Yugoslavia on the WEU agenda. Germany also hoped for European economic sanctions on Serbia, but the result was a suspension of arms deliveries and an oil embargo for all of Yugoslavia. As Serbia's aggression continued in the fall of 1991, Germany again took unilateral action, promising to recognize Slovenia and Croatia before Christmas. An unusual amount of German arm-twisting resulted in an EU-wide agreement on formal recognition.[36]

Despite its assertive diplomacy, however, the German government never entertained any notions of German military involvement in the Balkans, not even in a multilateral framework.[37] The German government supported, for example, the idea of a WEU peacekeeping mission, but it ruled out participation of German troops, because the constitution did not permit out-of-area deployments, and for historical reasons.[38] Klaus Kinkel, Genscher's successor as foreign minister, confirmed that the legacy of the past would prevent him too from sending German troops to Yugoslavia, although he would accept military intervention by others as a last resort.[39] Even one German destroyer and three German jets sent to monitor the embargo against Serbia, as part of a multinational observation action, caused controversy. While the Bundestag gave its consent, the SPD filed suit against the action before the Constitutional Court, arguing that the Basic Law allowed only defensive uses of the armed forces.[40] Concerned that the German pilots aboard the AWACS' planes might be indirectly involved in military activity if the UN Security Council decided to enforce the flight ban over Bosnia, the FDP later also asked the court to

---

36. Müller, "German Foreign Policy after Unification," 150–54.

37. Duffield, "German Security Policy After Unification."

38. "Bonn für europäische Friedenstruppe, aber ohne deutsche Soldaten," *Deutschland Nachrichten,* 20 Sept. 1991.

39. "Kinkel appelliert an Serbien: Gewalt in Bosnien beenden," *Deutschland Nachrichten,* 12 June 1992.

40. "Bundestag Approves German Monitoring of UN Embargo," *The Week in Germany,* 24 July 1992.

rule on the constitutionality of the issue.[41] The court decided against a restraining order blocking German AWACS' participation, because it would result in "significant foreign policy disadvantages" for Germany, but the court agreed that the issue fell within its jurisdiction in principle.[42]

Joining the UN mission in Somalia has constituted the largest and most visible German participation in out-of-area activity so far. In the second half of 1993 the government contributed to the UN mission some seventeen hundred soldiers, who established themselves in Belet Uen, a village about three hundred kilometers from Mogadishu. The government maintained that German soldiers were on a purely humanitarian mission, working in peaceful areas under the protection of armed infantry and using force only if necessary for self-defense.[43] The SPD maintained, however, that the German soldiers' lives were endangered and that the battles between Somali factions and UN forces demonstrated the military rather than humanitarian character of the UN mission. On these grounds, the SPD asked the Constitutional Court to block troop deployments to Somalia until the constitutionality of out-of-area military involvement in general had been resolved. The court ruled that this specific mission did not violate the Basic Law, but the court indicated that the ruling on the general question of out-of-area involvement might turn out differently.[44]

The Somalia mission was controversial almost from the start. First, it remained difficult to guarantee the safety of the Bundeswehr troops completely, given numerous incidents of UN soldiers coming under fire from armed bands.[45] Second, the specific purpose of the Bundeswehr's involvement went unfulfilled. The German soldiers were supposed to provide logistical support for an Indian brigade, which itself had the task of pacifying an area near Belet Uen and disarming the bands. The Indians never arrived in Belet Uen, however, having been deployed elsewhere due to changing circumstances. In the meantime the German soldiers occupied themselves with humanitarian projects concerning hospitals, water wells,

---

41. "Coalition Decides to Expand Participation in Bosnian Airdrop and Serbian Embargo; Agrees to Disagree in Awacs Conflict," *The Week in Germany*, 26 Mar. 1993.

42. "Germany to Participate in Military Enforcement of Bosnia Flight Ban," *The Week in Germany*, 9 Apr. 1993.

43. "Bundestag Approves Somalia Mission for German Armed Forces," *The Week in Germany*, 23 Apr. 1993; "Somalia-Einsatz der Bundeswehr nach Zusammenstössen in Mogadischu wieder umstritten," *Deutschland Nachrichten*, 11 June 1993.

44. "German Mission to Somalia Does Not Violate the Basic Law, Constitutional Court Says," *The Week in Germany*, 25 June 1993.

45. "Somalia-Einsatz der Bundeswehr nach Zusammenstössen in Mogadischu wieder umstritten," *Deutschland Nachrichten*, 11 June 1993; "Nach dem Mord in Phnom Penh nimmt die Debatte über deutsche Soldaten in Somalia an Heftigkeit zu," *Frankfurter Allgemeine Zeitung*, 16 Oct. 1993.

and schools, without, however, ever fulfilling their official mission.[46] Third, as violent conflict continued between Somalia's armed bands and the UN forces, the legitimacy and purpose of the UN mission in Somalia as a whole came increasingly under fire in Germany.

The Greens came out for a withdrawal of all UN armed forces from Somalia, while the SPD's Günter Verheugen maintained that the UN action in Somalia was undermining the very concept of blue-helmet peace-keeping missions.[47] Resistance to the Bundeswehr presence in Somalia surfaced in the FDP as well. FDP defense expert Jürgen Kippelin stated publicly that control over the Somali mission had escaped the UN. Since the French had decided to withdraw, he maintained, the Germans should too.[48] Even Helmut Kohl's chancellery stopped denying its discomfort with the developments in Somalia. Once the United States announced its withdrawal from Somalia, Defense Minister Volker Rühe felt that German forces had to follow, since they required American logistical services to survive in Belet Uen and would need American protection for their departure from Somalia. Foreign Minister Klaus Kinkel, however, did not want to announce a withdrawal until the UN had given its signal, in order to avoid the impression that the UN's mission was disintegrating.[49] In the end, the German government announced its withdrawal in a manner that fulfilled Kinkel's demands in terms of formal process and Rühe's demands in terms of actual policy.[50] Italy, Germany, and the United States all decided to pull out by March 31, 1994, leaving no large Western power in Somalia after that date.

Germany's involvement in Somalia paralleled, and intersected with, its debate on the out-of-area question more broadly. The discussion centered around whether to amend the Basic Law to give blanket approval to German troop deployments beyond the NATO area. Key questions included whether the Basic Law already permitted out-of-area military involvement, whether it should be amended to permit them, and whether Bundestag authorization for each specific mission should require merely a simple majority (giving the government relatively free rein) or a two-thirds majority (giving the SPD a de facto veto).

In their quest for "normalization" of German foreign policy, including a possible German seat on the UN Security Council, the conserva-

---

46. Wolfgang Lerch, "In Somalia bleibt viel zu tun," *Frankfurter Allgemeine Zeitung,* 14 Oct. 1993.

47. "SPD fordert Abzug der Bundeswehr," *Süddeutsche Zeitung,* 8 Oct. 1993.

48. "Forderungen nach Abzug aus Somalia," *Süddeutsche Zeitung,* 9 Oct. 1993.

49. "Kampf um einen geordneten Rückzug," *Süddeutsche Zeitung,* 16 Nov. 1993.

50. "Das Bundeswehr-Kontingent in Somalia wird verkleinert," *Frankfurter Allgemeine Zeitung,* 20 Nov. 1993.

tive-liberal coalition agreed that the government should enjoy greater lati-
tude in committing German troops to multilateral military engagements.
The CDU/CSU envisioned German participation in both peacekeeping
and combat (peace enforcement) missions, under the auspices of the UN,
or even of NATO or the WEU without a UN mandate. The FDP appeared
to agree with these proposals, although it sometimes insisted on a UN
mandate in all cases.[51] The governing parties also agreed that the constitution should be changed, or at least "clarified," to permit such deployments.
The CDU/CSU held that amendment was necessary for political, but not
necessarily legal, reasons. The FDP agreed with the SPD, however, that a
constitutional amendment was required for substantive legal reasons and
that a change in policy on out-of-area deployments could not be based on
the constitution as it stood.[52]

The SPD conducted a hot internal debate on the out-of-area issue for
some months before its November party congress in 1993. Far-reaching
agreement emerged that out-of-area Bundeswehr deployments should be
restricted to UN peacekeeping missions, and this position was incorporated into the resolution passed by the party congress. The resolution also
supported allowing German blue-helmet soldiers to use force (but only
"highly restricted" force) to defend themselves or their mission if needed,
thereby incorporating suggestions to this effect by Geschäftsführer Günter
Verheugen, the SPD's Präsidium, and the party's chair, Rudolf Scharping.[53] Scharping made clear, however, that he was against any participation in UN missions that explicitly intended to use force in the execution of
their tasks, such as the Gulf War, a sentiment overwhelmingly shared by
the party and echoed by the Präsidium.[54]

This position was not universally shared in the SPD, however, and
came under fire from two directions. Hans-Ulrich Klose, the leader of the
SPD's parliamentary group *(Fraktion),* courageously maintained that the
Bundeswehr should be allowed to participate in all UN missions under
UN direction, including those of a military nature. His position, however,
found little support beyond members of the Seeheimer Kreis, a conserva-

---

51. Duffield, "German Security Policy after Unification."

52. Müller, "German Foreign Policy after Unification," 139.

53. "Zwischen Parteitagsbeschluß und Kurswechsel," *Frankfurter Allgemeine Zeitung,*
18 Aug. 1993; "Verheugen: SPD muss ihre Haltung ändern," *Frankfurter Allgemeine Zeitung,*
9 Aug. 1993; "Zweifel in der SPD am Parteitagsbeschluß zu Blauhelmen," *Frankfurter Allgemeine Zeitung,* 10 Aug. 1993.

54. "SPD-Spitze für Teilnahme an UNO-Einsätzen 'ohne Vorbehalt,' " *Süddeutsche
Zeitung,* 10 Aug. 1993; "SPD-Führung hält an restriktivem Kurs bei UNO-Einsätzen der
Bundeswehr fest," *Süddeutsche Zeitung,* 25 Aug. 1993.

tive circle within the SPD.[55] However, at least one contingent within the party came out against participation even in peacekeeping missions. In Schleswig-Holstein, the rank-and-file delegates at the *Land*-level party convention rejected German participation in UN military actions and voted by a large majority for an international peace policy under UN auspices using exclusively nonmilitary means.[56]

In general the SPD insisted on parliamentary involvement in decisions concerning out-of-area deployments of any sort. Relatively early in the debate, foreign policy spokesperson Karsten Voigt proposed allowing a simple Bundestag majority to suffice for participation in peacekeeping missions, with a two-thirds majority required for any missions that were more risky militarily or politically.[57] This proposal echoed one made by the FDP chair, Foreign Minister Klaus Kinkel.[58] Party Chair Scharping, however, insisted on a two-thirds majority in the Bundestag for all deployments.[59]

The SPD's willingness to support Bundeswehr deployments in a peacekeeping context but hesitancy to go any further reflected attitudes in the broader public as of 1993. Horrified by the carnage in the former Yugoslavia, the number of Germans favoring Western intervention to end the war rose from 41 percent in July 1992[60] to 53 percent by the spring of 1993.[61] At the same time, at most one-third (and in some polls as few as 13 percent) were willing to let German troops participate in a Western or UN-directed military mission there, but as many as 45 percent were willing to allow Bundeswehr participation in blue-helmet peacekeeping forces.[62] Similarly, on the question of sending Bundeswehr troops to the UN mission in Somalia, as many as 80 percent of respondents thought that Bundeswehr soldiers should help with explicitly humanitarian tasks like repairing streets, drilling wells, or protecting food transports, while

---

55. "Klose: Die Bundeswehr soll an allen Massnahmen unter Kommando der Vereinten Nationen teilnehmen," *Süddeutsche Zeitung,* 24 Aug. 1993; "Zurück zur Politik," *Frankfurter Allgemeine Zeitung,* 18 Sept. 1993.

56. "SPD-Landesparteitag stimmt gegen Blauhelme," *Süddeutsche Zeitung,* 13 Sept. 1993.

57. "Der Streit um die Bundeswehreinsätze geht weiter," *Frankfurter Allgemeine Zeitung,* 27 July 1993.

58. "Zweiter Bundeswehrverband in Somalia," *Süddeutsche Zeitung,* 30 July 1993.

59. "SPD-Chef Scharping strebt Kompromiß über UNO-Einsätze der Bundeswehr an," *Süddeutsche Zeitung,* 14 Aug. 1993.

60. "Deutsche Soldaten nach Sarajevo: 73% sind dafür," *Bild am Sonntag,* 19 July 1992.

61. "Die Popularität der Regierung nimmt zu," *Süddeutsche Zeitung,* 24 Apr. 1993.

62. "Deutsche Soldaten nach Sarajevo: 73% sind dafür," *Bild am Sonntag,* 19 July 1992; Renate Köcher, "Breite Mehrheit für Blauhelm-Einsätze deutscher Soldaten," *Frankfurter Allgemeine Zeitung,* 11 Feb. 1993; "Die Popularität der Regierung nimmt zu," *Süddeutsche Zeitung,* 24 Apr. 1993.

around 60 percent expressed approval of the Bundeswehr mission in Somalia in general. However, only about 25 percent of western Germans and 15 percent of eastern Germans favored Bundeswehr participation in military action in Somalia.[63]

On the broader out-of-area question, support for allowing German troops to take part in UN military missions ranged from 12 to 27 percent from March 1991 to April 1993. Support for participation in UN peace-keeping efforts only generally hovered between 40 and 45 percent. Finally, anywhere from 25 to 40 percent wanted no change in the Basic Law at all, meaning that German troop deployment should be limited to NATO territory only. As usual, support for German involvement in any sort of international mission was significantly higher in western Germany than in eastern Germany.[64]

The Peace Movement Debates New Issues

Although unification dramatically changed the context in which it works, the peace movement has not remained idle in the debates over united Germany's foreign policy or its response to specific challenges. The Gulf War has provided the only opportunity for mobilization of any size so far, but the peace movement has contributed to each debate over foreign policy. While it by and large continues to oppose Western military involvement outside of NATO, the left finds itself involved in unaccustomed disputes within its own ranks over the use of force in the "new world order."

Despite polls indicating support for the effort against Iraq, significant discomfort with the Gulf War manifested itself in Germany. The streets remained quiet as long as the German government pressed for a diplomatic solution and the war against Iraq had not yet commenced. Demonstrations began when large-scale military action was imminent and the German government haltingly began to support the allied military efforts. Around 250,000 protestors demonstrated just before the beginning of Operation Desert Storm.[65] Spontaneous demonstrations took place in western Germany (but not much in the eastern states) on the night that the bombing of Baghdad began, and around 200,000 demonstrators came out

---

63. "Zur Hilfe verpflichtet," *Der Spiegel,* 26 Apr. 1993; "Infas-Umfrage zum Blauhelm-Einsatz der Bundeswehr in Somalia," *Fernseh- und Hörfunkspiegel,* 17 May 1993; "Emnid-Umfrage," *Fernseh- und Hörfunkspiegel,* 21 June 1993.

64. "Steuerlüge empört Mehrheit," *Der Spiegel,* 11 Mar. 1991; "FDP-Wähler wollen Schäuble," *Der Spiegel,* 29 June 1992; "Sollen deutsche Soldaten im ehemaligen Jugoslawien eingreifen?" *Fernseh- und Hörfunkspiegel,* 11 Feb. 1993.

65. "'Heiliger Georg, wir harren der letzten Ölung,'" *Tageszeitung,* 14 Jan. 1991.

on January 20–21.[66] The largest single demonstration, again drawing around 200,000 protestors, took place in Bonn on January 26.[67] These were the largest demonstrations since 1983. Another indication of protest against German involvement in the Gulf War was the rise in applications for conscientious objector status among draft-age men to 150,000 in 1991, double the number of the previous year, with most of the applications coming in the first six months. (All but 10,000 came from western Germany.)[68]

These large demonstrations put their stamp on the political landscape of the time. The peace movement's Netzwerk Friedenskooperative (the much looser successor organization to the Coordinating Committee of the 1980s) proved able to organize large demonstrations on short notice. The demonstrations' sponsors ranged from parties on the left— the Greens, the SPD, and the PDS (Party of Democratic Socialism, the successor to the former East German Communist Party)—to the unions, church groups, students, and peace and ecology groups. For the school children, who turned out in sizable numbers, the demonstrations were undoubtedly a socializing experience.

Like in earlier periods, mobilization against the Gulf War was catalyzed by a combination of fear and various moral and political arguments. Feelings of threat were based this time on ecology—not on the danger of direct nuclear annihilation like in earlier decades, but rather on the possible damage to the air and climate from burning oil fields. A diffuse moral outrage manifested itself in protest by school children and adults, who had assumed that the end of the cold war had opened the door to a truly peaceful world.

As the gulf crisis progressed, a more concise ideological stance that combined moral and political considerations into a multifaceted pacifist position developed. Many denied that the Gulf War was a morally persuasive cause. Most groups would have rejected the notion of "just war" in any event, and indeed some church groups issued a straightforward biblical denunciation of war.[69] Most protestors, however, objected primarily to the perceived hypocrisy of the West's motives. Virtually all peace groups condemned Iraq's invasion of Kuwait and its violation of international

---

66. "Bonn Cautions Antiwar Protestors against Anti-Americanism," *The Week in Germany,* 25 Jan. 1991.

67. "Two Hundred Thousand Protest War in Bonn," *The Week in Germany,* 1 Feb. 1991.

68. "Number of Conscientious Objectors Doubled in 1991," *The Week in Germany,* 31 Jan. 1992.

69. "Dieser Krieg schafft neues Unrecht und bedroht die Schöpfung," resolution of the Solidarische Kirche Westfalen und Lippe, *Frankfurter Rundschau,* 28 Jan. 1991.

law. But they asked why the UN and United States were determined to "prosecute" this violation, when they had let others pass. Why, indeed, were they combating this act of Iraqi aggression, when the West had armed Iraq in the first place and had condoned its war against Iran? The real motive for waging the Gulf War, the peace groups suspected, was the desire to safeguard access to the region's oil and to maintain the West's lavish lifestyle.[70] Or, as the "anti-imperialists" argued, the real issue was Western imperialism in the "north-south" conflict, not principles of international law. The widespread demonstration slogan "No Blood for Oil" reflected these assumptions.[71]

From the perspective of radical pacifism, the second moral problem with the Gulf War was the proportionality of means to ends. In the age of nuclear, biological, and chemical weapons, they argued, there was no such thing as a "just war." The death and destruction that any "high-tech" war wrought on civilians and, indeed, on the very fabric of society was simply too great to be justified by even the most laudable goal. This concern partly reflected Germany's own experience with bombing in World War II, which resulted in some people's identification with Iraq in the Gulf War.[72] In the peace groups' view, the fact that the West waged the Gulf War before exhausting all nonmilitary possibilities magnified the moral reprehensibility of the war still further. Instead the West should have given the UN sanctions against Iraq much longer to take effect (at least five years, in one peace researcher's opinion).[73]

In conjunction with their concern for proportionality of force to goals, peace groups feared the inexorable "logic" of military escalation. Just as earlier peace movements had feared that deterrence would inexorably result in eventual catastrophe, peace groups now worried that the Gulf War would escalate to horrific destructiveness. In particular, they feared that an Iraqi gas attack on Israel might be answered with American tactical nuclear weapons. Since both sides threatened to use weapons of mass destruction, both failed to meet moral standards.[74] Indeed, the West seemed to be one step "ahead" of the Iraqis from this point of view, for the United States had nuclear weapons at its disposal. As a prominent demon-

---

70. Andreas Buro, "Lieber Gartenzwerge als Soldaten," *Frankfurter Rundschau,* 30 Aug. 1990.

71. "Die Kinder des Friedens," *Die Zeit,* 25 Jan. 1991.

72. Ellis Huber, "Appel an alle: Krieg verhindern," *Volksblatt Berlin,* 12 Jan. 1991.

73. Johann Galtung, "Von schmutzigen Händen und der Suche nach geduldigen Menschen," *Frankfurter Rundschau,* 16 Oct. 1990.

74. Franz Alt, cited in Norbert Kostede, "Hoffen auf die heile Welt," *Die Zeit,* 19 Oct. 1990.

strator put it, he did not want the first crime, the invasion of Kuwait, to be answered by a second crime a thousand times greater.[75]

A "pragmatic" pacifism based on political judgments complemented these moral positions. Just as the peace movement had argued for "overcoming" rather than perfecting deterrence in the 1980s, peace groups now argued that war in the Persian Gulf would hinder resolution of the larger problems in the region. The only solution to the gulf conflict, in their view, was patient negotiations toward a broader Middle East solution involving Lebanon, the creation of a Palestinian state, and the Kurdish problem, in addition to the occupation of Kuwait.[76] The Gulf War, moreover, was one more hindrance to creating the "new world order" that peace groups envisioned. It would hinder disarmament, encourage the West to act as the world's police, and accustom people to military intervention instead of peaceful conflict resolution. Military measures would also hinder work on more fundamental problems like energy policy and north-south relations.[77] In the nuclear age, nonmilitary solutions were the only possible path.[78]

Further reasons for protest rested on ideological categories developed during previous peace movements. The connection between ecology and peace already established in the 1980s gained new prominence in protest against the Gulf War. Feelings of threat now rested on possible destruction of the environment, noted Till Bastian, former chair of the International Physicians for the Prevention of Nuclear War. The Gulf War demonstrated the indivisible connection between "peace policy" and ecology.[79] As futurologist Robert Jungk maintained, because of advances in military technology, war now would irreversibly damage the biological and ecological foundations of humanity. Whereas armed action against Hitler had made sense, ecological risks now ruled out analogous use of force.[80] Environmental groups gathered signatures for petitions requesting the German government to stop the "countdown to death" in the gulf.[81]

As they had in the 1980s, women's groups argued that war exacted an especially heavy price from women. Women stood above all for the civilian

75. Horst-Eberhard Richter, "Wo bleibt die Scham?" in *Frankfurter Rundschau,* 27 Nov. 1990.

76. Galtung, "Von schmutzigen Händen und der Suche nach geduldigen Menschen," *Frankfurter Rundschau,* 16 Oct. 1990.

77. Buro, "Lieber Gartenzwerge als Soldaten," *Frankfurter Rundschau,* 30 Aug. 1990.

78. Andreas Buro, "Diesen Konflikt kann man nicht mit Waffen lösen," *Berliner Zeitung,* 24 Jan. 1991.

79. "Friedenspolitik und Ökologie sind ein Thema," *Tageszeitung,* 8 Oct. 1990.

80. Robert Jungk, "Der Feind ist jetzt die Weltzerstörung," *Tageszeitung,* 14 Jan. 1991.

81. "Bundesregierung soll 'Countdown des Todes' am Golf stoppen," *Frankfurter Rundschau,* 9 Jan. 1991.

population, they maintained, and with every war the civilian share of total war dead had risen. By opposing the Gulf War, these women's groups expressed their sense of responsibility for the millions of war widows and orphans.[82] Similarly, those who had argued in the 1980s that détente provided an alternative to military confrontation in Europe now extended that notion to other regions. As the Social Democratic group IFIAS noted, no one granted Iraq the right to annex Kuwait. But given the vulnerability of today's civilization, war as a means of policy was not permissible even in pursuit of just goals. The success of détente and the end of the cold war enabled the world community to force compliance from an aggressor through political means and through economic boycott. Détente had kept the peace in Europe after 1968 and had contributed to the fall of dictatorships as well. It was the only alternative to war in the Middle East too.[83]

One new ideological category emerged from the East German "events" of 1989. Because unification was imposing massive adjustments on them, Eastern Germans began protest against the Gulf War later than many in the West, but they mounted an energetic, though different, protest in the end. As bombs began to fall on Iraq, churches revived the Protestant declaration of 1948 that "war is impermissible according to God's will," while local politicians declared their towns "war-free zones."[84] The peaceful revolution ending the communist regime in 1989 left its imprint on peace demonstrations in the East in 1991, for activists concluded that citizens can overthrow a repressive, violent regime by peaceful means. For many Easterners, their opposition to the Gulf War was an extension of the "no violence" maxim of 1989.[85] In his speech at the demonstration in Bonn, Gottfried Forck, a Protestant bishop of Berlin-Brandenburg who was active in the events of 1989, expressed his fellow Easterners' disappointment that their nonviolent revolution had not ushered in a new culture of nonviolence.[86] Easterners thought that the West should follow their nonviolent example, and they resented that Germany's financial contribution to the war diverted money from Eastern reconstruction. They also rejoiced in a bit of *Schadenfreude* that they could morally point their fingers in the "know-it-all" West's direction, reversing the usual flow.[87]

Finally, peace groups applied the "no war" lessons they drew from

82. "Frauenbündnis '90: Krieg ist keine Lösung," *Sozialdemokratischer Pressedienst,* 16 Jan. 1991.

83. "Nachdenken in der SPD," *Frankfurter Allgemeine Zeitung,* 25 Jan. 1991.

84. Günter Geschke, "Nicht alles war falsch," *Deutsches Allgemeines Sonntagsblatt,* 15 Feb. 1991.

85. Renate Rauch, "Die reagieren wie früher," *Die Zeit,* 1 Mar. 1991.

86. "Krieg ist kein brauchbares Mittel der Politik," *Evangelischer Pressedienst,* 29 Jan. 1991.

87. "Dem Westen Wege weisen," *Frankfurter Allgemeine Zeitung,* 7 Feb. 1991.

World War II to the Gulf War, just as they had applied them to nuclear questions after 1945. Germany has an enormous responsibility because of the two world wars, maintained Horst-Eberhard Richter at a demonstration in November 1990. Rather than expanding its military role, Germany should pursue its duty to help launch an antimilitarist peace policy. After Hitler and Auschwitz, unified Germany should become a moral force for overcoming the prevailing military and ecological irrationality.[88] Similarly, a group of five hundred professors appealed to the United States not to react to Saddam Hussein with war. Doing so would mean relapsing into thinking in categories of military power.[89]

Much of the left opposed the Gulf War, and for many of the same reasons that it had opposed military measures in the past. Whereas peace movements in the past had enjoyed the support of virtually the entire left, however, during the Gulf War the movement's usual milieu lost its "minimal consensus" on the ideological front. Indeed, the Gulf War occasioned an unprecedented split within the left. Despite fierce debates on various particulars, in the 1980s virtually the entire left had shared the peace movement's minimal-consensus opposition to NATO's double-track decision and American foreign policy. The Gulf War, in contrast, stimulated sharp debate within the left on the legitimacy of using force, German responsibility toward Israel, anti-Americanism, and "anti-imperialism." This debate revealed the extent to which the end of the cold war had upset previous ideological certainties. The debate created an ideological battlefront within the left, running through the Greens, the SPD, and the broader left milieu as a whole.

During the cold war, the worldview of both peace movements and the broader left rested in large part on the two-pronged motto "Nie wieder Krieg! Nie wieder Faschismus!" (Never again war! Never again fascism!). In the 1950s, the left's fear of renewed militarism led it to oppose remilitarization and nuclear weapons. Since the left considered capitalism the economic foundation of fascism, moreover, it tried to bring about economic reform. From the 1960s on, the left's opposition to nuclear deterrence and its support for détente continued unabated. The left, moreover, added anti-imperialism to its ideological roster, and it opposed virtually all use of force by the West, particularly by the United States. In contrast, the left supported armed struggle by Third World movements fighting against American forces or against regimes supported by the West (e.g., in Vietnam and Central America). Portraying Israel as America's imperialist "deputy" after the 1967 war, moreover, anti-imperialism extended to

88. Horst-Eberhard Richter, "Wo bleibt die Scham?" *Frankfurter Rundschau*, 27 Nov. 1990.

89. "Professoren-Appell an USA," *Frankfurter Rundschau*, 12 Dec. 1990.

demonstrative support for the Palestinian cause. Thus in the postwar period, the left claimed for itself a "higher" foreign policy morality based on anti-imperialism, anticapitalism, pacifism, and internationalism.

During the Gulf War, the internal coherence of this package came under fire within the left, unleashing vehement debate over the war itself and, indirectly, the continued viability of its postwar worldview. For the first time, parts of the left subjected the peace movement to unprecedented critique. Their questions involved the legitimacy of force and German responsibility to Israel. What, these critics asked, was the Gulf War really about—imperialist Western control over Middle East oil ("No Blood for Oil"), or the need to contain an expansionist dictator in some sense equivalent to Hitler? Would failing to resist Saddam Hussein repeat the mistakes of Western appeasement of Hitler in the late 1930s? What did German history teach about the use of force: was war categorically impermissible because of its victims, or was force sometimes necessary to defeat a dictator? What was Germany's responsibility to Israel, given that Iraqi Scud attacks and their potential use of poison gas had been made possible through technical help from German firms? Did history require Germany to protect Israel against threats to its very existence? Did "Never again fascism!" also require "Never again Auschwitz!"—even if the force needed to prevent a second holocaust violated the "Never again war!" tenet?

In the German context, the issue of using force in the gulf conflict rested on the comparability of Saddam Hussein with Hitler. Hans Magnus Enzensberger's widely cited essay in *Der Spiegel* represented the classic formulation of the Saddam Hussein–Hitler equation, by labeling Hussein the "historical double" of Hitler. Free from the usual constraints of self-preservation that "normal" dictators face, Enzensberger argued, Saddam Hussein was, like Hitler, an "enemy of the human race." Driven primarily by sheer aggressiveness, both Hussein and Hitler took on the entire world, accepting the destruction of their own people if need be. Just like the Germans' death wish during the Third Reich, the Arabs now hoped to die for Saddam Hussein in a collective orgy of destruction.[90]

Employing less demonic analytic categories, others pointed to the Iraqi Scud missile attacks on Israel, concrete manifestations of a potentially much larger threat to Israel's very existence. Although they only reluctantly gave up their opposition to war in principle, in their view defense of Israel, along with defense of human rights and international law more generally, justified use of force if no nonviolent alternative would suffice. Emphasizing Germany's historical responsibility to help defend

---

90. Hans Magnus Enzensberger, "Hitlers Wiedergänger," *Der Spiegel,* 4 Feb. 1991.

Israel, they pointedly criticized various faults of the peace movement, including its perceived misjudgments, naïveté, and anti-Americanism.

Several Jewish intellectuals with close ties to the German left played instrumental roles in stimulating this discussion. One prominent example was Wolf Biermann, an East German regime critic and songwriter, whose father had perished at the hands of the Nazis, and who had taken part in the peace movement's blockades of the Mutlangen missile site in the 1980s. Biermann agreed in principle that every war is unjust. Remembering, however, the appeasement of the Nazis in the 1930s, he too saw parallels between Saddam Hussein and Hitler: both had sworn openly to eradicate the Jews, and both were "nouveau riche" in terms of power and tyranny. In no uncertain terms, Biermann declared himself for the war against Iraq, hoping that it would destroy Iraq's capacity to build nuclear weapons for use against Israel. He considered it progress that Israel was armed to the teeth instead of passively waiting for allied troops to save them as in World War II. Moreover, Biermann maintained, he thanked the heavens that the Americans were willing to help defend Israel, even if for base motives like oil, just as Americans had helped save Germans from Hitler. Criticizing anti-American slogans, Biermann reminded the peace movement that Iraq was the aggressor in this case, and he called on the movement to adopt the moral imperative of using force to stop genocide.[91]

In like manner, Micha Brumlik, a Green representative to Frankfurt's city council, labeled Saddam Hussein an enemy who must be defeated, given his willingness to sacrifice his own people and his indifference to international law. He found it contradictory that the peace movement demanded a continued embargo as an alternative to war but was unwilling to enforce this embargo through military force. He also found the movement's slogan "No Blood for Oil" oversimplified, because it made the United States the main enemy and overlooked international law and Israel's security. A functioning "security order" depended on use of military force as an ultimate means of providing security for its members, so there were some armed interventions that were ultimately just.[92]

Similarly, a long-standing friend of the German left from the United States, Andrei Markovits, took the left to task for its decade-long anti-Israel stance, which he attributed to Germany's inability to identify with its own history. Only the left's tendency to heroize any Third World opponent of Israel and the United States could explain, in Markovits' view, its inability to recognize fascist traits in Iraq's Baath regime, from its charismatic leader to its use of violence against its own citizens. It took Scud attacks on Israel to crack the left's blindness to Israel's security

---

91. Wolf Biermann, "Kriegshetze, Friedenshetze," *Die Zeit*, 8 Feb. 1991.
92. "Keine Spaltung, sondern ein Lernprozeß," *Frankfurter Rundschau*, 25 Jan. 1991.

needs, and even now the majority of the left responded with mere lip service to Germany's historical responsibility to Israel. The peace movement by and large was prepared to accept Kuwait's annexation by Iraq as a lesser evil than the danger of global war that they attributed to America. Compared to other countries, moreover, the German angst concerning the Gulf War was vastly disproportional to the actual danger the country faced.[93]

Finally, Henryk Broder, who had earlier had close ties to the German left and was now a correspondent for the *Jerusalem Post,* took a number of leftist intellectuals to task for their remarks on the Gulf War and Israel. In the end of his article, he accused them, and a significant portion of the peace movement, of actually wanting Saddam Hussein to destroy Israel and thus to complete a job that the Nazis had left unfinished. Israel's destruction, he said, would enable the Germans to go about their business unburdened by the past.[94]

Although the peace movement's "silent majority" continued to oppose the Gulf War, a sizable number of non-Jewish intellectuals and political activists on the left made public their general agreement with the positions just described and their support (albeit often ambivalent) for the Gulf War. Udo Knapp of the Greens, for example, called the "Hitler analogy" correct, noted the danger of appeasement and the problem of Israeli security, and declared himself (in August 1990) in favor of military engagement if it became necessary. The superpowers and the UN had to defend democracy and human rights against people like Saddam Hussein, and Germans had to ask themselves whether to allow chemical weapons attacks on Israel. Joschka Fischer maintained that Green pacifism lacked credibility in avoiding the question of force-based sanctions. He also demanded solidarity with Israel and a clear position against anti-Americanism. Erhard Eppler, one of the earliest Social Democratic leaders to join the peace movement in the 1980s, now asked whether it would not be right to attack centers of Iraqi weapons production. It would cost some human life, but was it not necessary to stop crazed potentates when they threatened another people with genocide? Similarly, Ralf Fücks and Bernd Ulrich of the Greens argued that reducing the causes of the Gulf War to oil demonized the United States while whitewashing Saddam Hussein. Instead, they pointed to the West's concern with international law and the

---

93. Andrei Markovits, "Eine ernüchternde Erfahrung," *Die Zeit,* 15 Feb. 1991; and Markovits, "Die Linke gibt es nicht—und es gibt sie doch," *Frankfurter Rundschau,* 7 Mar. 1991.

94. Henryk Broder, "Unser Kampf," *Der Spiegel,* 29 Apr. 1991. See also Broder's essay by the same title in *Liebesgrüße aus Bagdad: Die 'edlen Seelen' der Friedensbewegung und der Krieg am Golf,* ed. Klaus Bittermann (Berlin: Edition Tiamat, 1991).

protection of Israel. Petra Kelly and Gert Bastian, two of the Greens'
founding leaders, criticized the peace movement's slogans as too short-
sighted, because one could not reduce the gulf conflict to "No Blood for
Oil." The movement's credibility had suffered greatly, moreover, because
of its incomprehensible silence concerning earlier crimes, like genocide in
Cambodia, the war in Afghanistan, the Iraqi invasion of Kuwait, and German arms exports that threatened Israeli security. Konrad Weiß, a leader
of the eastern German Bündnis '90/Die Grünen, called the Gulf War a
defeat for the peace movement, which had done nothing when Iraq gassed
Kurds and invaded Kuwait, and which had not taken Israeli fears seriously. The movement, moreover, lacked credible concepts for a nonviolent
solution to the conflict. It was ridiculous to direct protest against the West,
since Saddam Hussein was the aggressor. How did proponents of nonviolence plan to deal with a criminal armed with the worst weapons? How
could the movement demand defenselessness for those attacked while sit-
ting at a safe distance themselves? Willy Brandt signed a declaration of solidarity with the Western allies sponsored by the Atlantik-Brücke. Frankfurt School philosopher Jürgen Habermas approved of the gulf
intervention in principle, because help for Israel was absolutely necessary
and because Iraq's obvious violation of international law and UN resolutions justified limited use of force. For some, the war even had a special
legitimacy after the attack on Israel. Journalist Klaus Hartung maintained
that pacifism in the last analysis meant peace with dictators. Hessen's
Greens passed a resolution demanding German deliveries of Patriot
antimissile systems to Israel, although such shipments violated their general opposition to arms exports.[95]

These positions notwithstanding, many of the same critics also
expressed reservations about the Gulf War—revealing a profound ambivalence toward the Western effort—and avoided drawing general conclusions about the legitimacy of force. Joschka Fischer demanded solidarity
with Israel, said he was not a *Gesinnungspazifist,* and noted that Gandhi
would have been powerless against Auschwitz. In principle, however, he
shared the peace movement's goal of ending the war; and he noted the
hypocrisy of sending sons to die collecting the weapons that their fathers

---

95. "Dem Pazifismus 'gewaltfrei die Luft abdrehen,' " *Tageszeitung,* 30 Aug. 1990;
Norbert Kostede, "Hoffen auf die heile Welt," *Die Zeit,* 19 Oct. 1990; Konrad Weiss, "Die
Versäumnisse der Friedensbewegung," *Bild am Sonntag,* 27 Jan. 1991; "Fischer fordert Soli-
darität mit Israel," *Süddeutsche Zeitung,* 26 Jan. 1991; Ralf Fücks and Bernd Ulrich,
"Änderung der Parole," *Tageszeitung,* 23 Jan. 1991; Petra Kelly and Gert Bastian, "Ist die
Welt verrückt geworden? Die Friedensbewegung macht es sich zu leicht," *Die Zeit,* 8 Feb.
1991; Jürgen Habermas, "Wider die Logik des Kriegs," *Die Zeit,* 22 Feb. 1991; Klaus Hartung, "Zweites München für Hussein?" *Tageszeitung,* 29 Jan. 1991.

had sold to Iraq. While Ralf Fücks and Bernd Ulrich pointed out the West's reasons for military action, they also declared their general belief in antimilitarism, arguing that war could no longer be an instrument of policy given its political, ecological, social, and cultural "byproducts." Petra Kelly and Gert Bastian's rhetorical question "Has the world gone crazy?" concerned the continued use of war as an instrument of politics. Since other UN resolutions (such as the Palestinian question) had not been pursued with equal vigor, the West's disproportionate use of force gave the impression of a Christian war against an Arab country. War remained impermissible, including the Gulf War. Habermas also questioned the extent of Western force brought to bear against Iraq, noting that the Gulf War was justifiable only as a limited police action to fulfill the UN resolution, and that with every further day, its goals and means were looking less limited.

The Gulf War had raised a fundamental question: whether use of force is ever justifiable to contain an aggressive regime or to prevent genocide. The civil war in the former Yugoslavia occasioned further debate of the same basic issue, but in a very different context. The Bosnian Serbs' brutal pursuit of territorial gains, with the accompanying "ethnic cleansing," mass rapes, and detention camps, elicited the same horrified outcry within the peace movement as it did in the broader public. At the same time, the war confronted the peace movement with unaccustomed problems. In particular, the territorial conflicts there, rooted in national chauvinism, were not proving amenable to negotiated solutions between partners with a common interest in conflict resolution. Instead, the peace movement faced the dilemma of civil wars not defusable through "pacifist" instruments.

Demonstrations in Germany against the fighting—for example, before the Yugoslavian embassy in December 1991—attracted few participants. Despite widespread indignation, as one activist noted, the demonstrations lacked an "addressee," since neither Germany's NATO partners nor the German government itself had intervened militarily in the conflict.[96] Instead, the peace movement's activist core turned to practical help for opposition groups in Serbia, Croatia, and Bosnia and to help for the victims of the fighting. For example, in addition to financial help, the League for Social Defense (Bund für soziale Verteidigung) facilitated contact between peace groups in Belgrade and Zagreb by serving as a transfer point for fax and computer communications. The league also intended to help opposition radio stations and newspapers get the cassettes, paper,

---

96. "Es macht wenig Sinn, hier gegen die Kämpfe zu demonstrieren," *Rhein-Sieg-Anzeiger,* 8 Aug. 1992.

and other materials they needed. Various peace groups also helped settle refugees with German host families.[97]

The peace movement conducted wrenching debates over armed intervention in Bosnia—on whether its usual strict opposition to Western military intervention could be maintained—and again focused on the lessons of German history for present policy. The chief actors in the debate over Bosnia differed from those involved in the debate over the Gulf War. During the Gulf War, the debate centered in the broad left intellectual milieu as well as in the SPD and the Greens. In the case of Bosnia, in contrast, debate took place primarily among Green politicians in both eastern and western Germany. Prominent intellectuals like Wolf Biermann and Hans-Magnus Enzensberger contributed little to the public debate, while the SPD concerned itself primarily with the out-of-area question more broadly.

As during the Gulf War, debate focused on the lessons of German history, as well as the particulars of the Bosnian situation. Calls for military intervention in Bosnia came particularly from women within the western Greens and from human rights activists within the eastern Bündnis '90/Greens who had been active in the eastern German "events" of 1989. Claudia Roth and Helmut Lippelt opened the debate with calls for ending the war in the former Yugoslavia with outside military intervention if necessary. As Roth herself reported, she had traveled to the former Yugoslavia with clear pacifist convictions but had returned persuaded that international military intervention might be required to end the violence there. In her eyes, the situation in the former Yugoslavia had unambiguous elements of fascism, like concentration camps, "ethnic cleansing," and militarization of society. While attending an international women's conference against rape in Zagreb, prominent Green politician Waltraud Schoppe questioned whether peaceful solutions were still possible in Bosnia, while fellow Green Eva-Maria Quistorp demanded military intervention to end the mass rapes, detention camps, and slaughter. Bremen's environmental senator, Ralf Fücks, accused the peace movement of settling into its comfortable idyll while distant peoples attacked each other, and Daniel Cohn-Bendit echoed the call for military intervention. Eastern German peace and human rights activist Vera Wollenberger described the Bosnian conflict as genocide, while a commentator in the generally "Greenish" *Tageszeitung* accused fellow leftists of intentionally overlooking the true nature of the Serbian regime. The left, he noted, had always opposed invasions of small, underdeveloped countries by great powers (especially the United States), but did that mean that the left also had to

---

97. "Hass im Kriegsgebiet abbauen," *Frankfurter Rundschau*, 30 July 1992.

oppose military intervention when the Serbs fought a war of destruction against other peoples?[98]

Pragmatic considerations played a role as well in the calls for armed intervention. As one of the few "peace researchers" to call for intervention, Dieter Senghaas argued that strict application of "violence-poor" measures in the Yugoslavian case (such as the EC's attempts to negotiate a cease-fire) favored the aggressors. Because the Serbs were strongest on the ground, protracted negotiations let them extend and consolidate their holdings of Bosnian and Croatian territory. Although preferable in principle, negotiations could lose their "peace-policy innocence" in concrete application. Similarly, the arms embargo imposed on the entire former Yugoslavia benefited those who already had the most arms, the Serbs. The general embargo imposed on the rump-Yugoslavia was ineffective without military enforcement. So calls for embargoes were a great rhetorical escape but in reality a much less genuine alternative to military measures than often assumed. Finally, even UN peacekeeping troops could aggravate fighting, since their presence guaranteed that foreign troops would not intervene to stop it. Thus Senghaas not only supported armed intervention but advocated that it be used *early,* when the most could be accomplished with the least force. Veteran Green politician Lukas Beckmann also feared that failure to stop genocide against Bosnian Muslims could undermine the UN's credibility and chances for peaceful conflict resolution in the future. For *Tageszeitung* commentator Thomas Schmid, military intervention, at least to protect aid convoys to the people at risk of starvation, admittedly risked escalation of the Bosnian conflict, but nonintervention was letting the slaughter escalate unimpeded.[99]

In an "open letter to the peace movement," the eastern German Bündnis '90 (a party composed of former East German dissidents) called on the peace movement to revise its principles at the theoretical level. The peace movement would remain helpless in cases like Bosnia if its pacifism became ritualized. To revive its old strength, the movement should become a broad popular movement against human rights' violations wherever they occurred. The principle of intervention on behalf of human rights had to

---

98. "Es geht jetzt um das Wie einer Intervention: Die Grüne Europaabgeordnete Claudia Roth," *Tageszeitung,* 19 Aug. 1992; "Streit um Kampfeinsätze der Bundeswehr spaltet die SPD," *Die Welt,* 10 Aug. 1992; "Gefühl der Wut," *Der Spiegel,* 22 Feb. 1993; "'Ich verstehe nichts von Jugoslawien,'" *Tageszeitung,* 22 Feb. 1993; Ernst Köhler, "Publikumsbeschimpfung: Wer auf militärisches Eingreifen verzichtet handelt verantwortungslos," *Tageszeitung,* 25 Sept. 1992.

99. Dieter Senghaas, "Wie Gewaltfreiheit den Aggressor begünstigt," *Frankfurter Allgemeine Zeitung,* 7 July 1993; "Die Sorge um die Glaubwürdigkeit der Vereinten Nationen," *Frankfurter Allgemeine Zeitung,* 14 May 1993; Thomas Schmid, "Blockierte Debatte," *Tageszeitung,* 22 Feb. 1993.

complement the principle of nonviolence.[100] Explicitly drawing on the "doctrine of '89," Bündnis '90 leader Gerd Poppe later pled for a "concept of intervention" based on military means where necessary to end grave violations of human rights. For Bosnia, he suggested providing military security for aid convoys, enforcing the embargo, and liberating detention camps—all difficult efforts to undertake without armed force.[101]

All these considerations resulted in calls for armed intervention in Bosnia, although not without ambivalence on the part of some. Claudia Roth preferred to speak of "police intervention against criminals" rather than a return to military solutions. When her *Tageszeitung* interviewer pointed out that this approach would in effect break with the principled pacifism of a large majority of her party, Roth admitted her "complete dividedness" on the issue, but she still argued that one could not fight fascist structures without force.[102] In an event rare among Green politicians, Eva Quistorp cited NATO General Secretary Manfred Wörner on the feasibility of selective attacks in support of her call for armed force in Bosnia.[103]

This challenge to the left's traditional principle of nonviolence put the rest of the left on the defensive. The challenge was answered largely by other Green politicians. Those against armed intervention denied that the former Yugoslavia contained "fascist elements" necessitating the use of military force against them. Jürgen Trittin, Niedersachsen's minister for federal and European affairs, argued that the regimes in the former Yugoslavia were not really like Nazi Germany, because the killing was being done by paramilitary bands under no formal control (despite help from Serbia), and because the detention camps were not organized like the Nazi concentration camps.[104] Frieder Wolf, Green delegate to the European Parliament, argued along similar lines. Wolf admitted that force might be required when "crimes against humanity" reached the proportions of those prosecuted in the Nuremberg trials or those perpetrated in the siege of Stalingrad. He denied, however, that such extreme cases were the rule (and apparently they were not in the former Yugoslavia), and he wanted to avoid defining normal conditions as extreme cases. Remaining abstract, Wolf conceded the occasional necessity of force in principle but

100. "Plädoyer für eine Erneuerung: Offener Brief der Bürgerbewegung 'Bündnis '90' an die Friedensbewegung," *Tageszeitung*, 29 Aug. 1992.

101. " 'Ich verstehe nichts von Jugoslawien,' " *Tageszeitung*, 22 Feb. 1993.

102. "Es geht jetzt um das Wie einer Intervention," *Tageszeitung*, 19 Aug. 1992.

103. "Ratlose Friedensbewegung," *Berliner Zeitung*, 22 Feb. 1993.

104. Jürgen Trittin, "Grüne Aussenpolitik jenseits von Pazifismus und Bellizismus," *Frankfurter Rundschau*, 23 Sept. 1992.

denied its applicability to the Bosnian conflict or to any other "normal" cases.[105]

Others raised pragmatic objections to the use of force. The German military itself warned against armed strikes. On the basis of examples like Vietnam and Afghanistan, they warned that even limited military action like protecting aid convoys was hardly feasible and that massive intervention had no chance of success.[106] In a similar vein, Social Democrat Egon Bahr warned that military protection for aid convoys made the UN Security Council dependent on the warring parties and could escalate the fighting.[107] According to Frieder Wolf, military intervention in Bosnia lacked popular legitimacy because it lacked any definable military goal. He advocated instead "drying out" the conflict by controlling land transport of war goods, weapons smuggling, and so on, without, however, supporting force to do so.[108] Finally, Trittin in essence accused people like Claudia Roth of calling for military intervention while disguising it as "police action." He deemed it impossible to differentiate military intervention "in the classic sense" (abhorrent to all adherents of the peace movement) from suggestions for such "policelike measures" as trying to disarm bands. He argued that implementation of suggestions for "police action" really meant massive military intervention, whose consequence would be increased civilian suffering.[109]

Most peace movement adherents remained true to pacifist solutions to conflicts, including the Bosnian conflict. Horst-Eberhard Richter reaffirmed the eternal truth of two oft-cited tenets: that military force was never a suitable means for solving political problems and that arms exports always aggravated conflicts. He admitted that most leaders in the former Yugoslavia were still resisting reason and humanity, but he believed that at some point the brutality there would "suffocate on its own animosity toward life."[110] Trittin supported de-escalation as a general foreign policy principle (without specifying concrete methods), rather than temporary escalation to gain control of the situation. Long-standing pacifist Andreas Buro elaborated a sizable catalog of nonviolent approaches to the Bosnian conflict, including television transmissions against war propaganda and partnerships between cities, professional

105. Frieder Wolf, "Ein nüchterner Pazifismus ist immer noch angesagt," *Tageszeitung,* 22 Aug. 1992.

106. "Militärs bremsen Politiker," *Frankfurter Rundschau,* 12 Aug. 1992.

107. "UN-Beschluss skeptisch beurteilt," *Frankfurter Rundschau,* 17 Aug. 1992.

108. Frieder Wolf, "Ein nüchterner Pazifismus ist immer noch angesagt," *Tageszeitung,* 22 Aug. 1992.

109. "Grüne Aussenpolitik aus dem Bauch," *Tageszeitung,* 20 Aug. 1992.

110. Horst-Eberhard Richter, "Warum schweigt die Friedensbewegung?" *Frankfurter Rundschau,* 20 Aug. 1992.

associations, and churches in Europe and the former Yugoslavia. With respect to human rights, he advocated dissolving detention camps (without force, however), making population exchanges, and assigning responsibility for abuses. To encourage de-escalation, he suggested using UN blue-helmet troops to enforce the embargo and calling on people to desert from the army.[111]

Virtually all peace researchers (with the notable exception of Dieter Senghaas) likewise opposed military intervention in the former Yugoslavia. Alfred Mechtersheimer condemned "selling out" the peace movement by supporting military intervention in the Bosnian conflict. He suggested applying the peace movement's resistance forms from the 1980s to the Balkans—for example, a nonviolent blockade of the war area by the peace movement and Greenpeace.[112] Theodor Ebert recommended that the peace movement prepare for the "conflict after next" by teaching nonviolent action in the schools and starting a "civil peace service." For the people in Bosnia, Ebert recommended "long-distance" study of German exercises in nonviolence and capitulation to Serbian demands in the meantime, for capitulation would at least stop the fighting and render detention camps unnecessary. Clearly on the defensive at a conference on military intervention, Erik Krippendorff admitted that "peace professors" had the privilege of steadfast adherence to principle and that he understood nothing about Yugoslavia, while Uli Albrecht argued that peace research could not be expected to bless military concepts.[113]

The challenge mounted to the traditional pacifism of the peace movement, the Greens, and the Social Democratic left was clearly substantial. Supporters of the use of force in urgent cases, however, remained a minority within the left, according to accounts of the debate.[114] The intensity of both the debate and of pacifism in the Greens was on display at the party convention and at two previous meetings of the Greens' Länderrat, the council that represents the *Land*-level Green parties and that constitutes the second-highest decision-making body of the party. In March 1993, the Länderrat rejected proposals to support intervention by the Bundeswehr in Bosnia, arguing that the Greens had to remain consistently pacifist. If they supported military intervention in Bosnia, they would hardly be able to deny it to similar wars elsewhere. Since every intervention could escalate, no matter how limited the initial goals, lasting peace could not be

111. Andreas Buro, "Es gibt nicht den Generalschlüssel zum Frieden," *Frankfurter Rundschau*, 12 Sept. 1992.

112. Alfred Mechtersheimer, "Blockiert das Kriegsgebiet!" *Frieden 2000*, 9 Aug. 1992.

113. " 'Ich verstehe nichts von Jugoslawien,' " *Tageszeitung*, 22 Feb. 1993; "Frieden schaffen mit Waffen?" *Tagesspiegel*, 22 Feb. 1993.

114. " 'Ich verstehe nichts von Jugoslawien,' " *Tageszeitung*, 22 Feb. 1993.

imposed from the outside without agreement by the warring parties. In a resolution passed by twenty votes to six, the Greens spoke out against any change in the Basic Law that would permit out-of-area activity. Instead, the resolution proposed organization of a "peace service" for humanitarian, civilian missions under the auspices of the UN.[115]

In June 1993, however, the Länderrat decided that the UN had to secure the survival of Bosnia's Muslim populace with armed force if necessary—for example, by protecting humanitarian aid convoys, liberating detention camps, and guaranteeing people's safety in declared protection zones. The Greens still held "without deviation" to the principle of nonviolence, the Länderrat declared, but they were now establishing the protection of human rights as equally valid. Although the Länderrat passed this resolution with a bare majority, it rejected one calling for far-reaching UN military intervention.[116]

By the national party convention in November 1993, the pendulum had swung back to the Greens' traditional pacifism. With a 90 percent majority, the convention rejected all proposals suggesting military intervention in cases of severe violations of human rights like those occurring in Bosnia. The delegates instead voted for a "civilianization of foreign policy," a strategy of conflict prevention and coercive measures under the threshold of military action. Peacekeeping measures in conflict zones and comprehensive economic embargoes enforced by the UN in the manner of "customs police" would be acceptable, but the Greens remained strictly opposed to military "peace-creating" measures. German soldiers, they agreed, could serve as blue-helmet forces if the UN charter was corrected to exclude military measures and if the Bundeswehr was abolished.[117]

Despite the challenges posed by the Gulf War and the former Yugoslavia, the Social Democratic left also remained faithful on the whole to pacifist principles. The party convention of November 1993 agreed, with many dissenting votes, to accept German participation in UN blue-helmet peacekeeping operations, assuming a corresponding amendment to the Basic Law. The party granted these blue-helmet troops the right to defend themselves and their mission with force if necessary, which included implementing blockades. The party rejected, however, German participation in UN military missions or military "adventures."[118]

---

115. "Pazifismus trotz aller Nöte," *Frankfurter Rundschau,* 22 Mar. 1993.

116. "Länderrat der Grünen rüttelt am Grundsatz Gewaltfreiheit," *Frankfurter Rundschau,* 14 June 1993.

117. "Grüne lehnen jeden Militäreinsatz ab, Pazifisten setzen sich durch," *Süddeutsche Zeitung,* 11 Oct. 1993.

118. "Die SPD weiter gegen Kampfeinsätze," *Frankfurter Allgemeine Zeitung,* 19 Nov. 1993.

Thus most of the Green, Social Democratic, and extraparliamentary left remained opposed to military intervention under virtually all circumstances. Even German participation in UN blue-helmet peacekeeping forces remained highly controversial. Although the Social Democrats (reluctantly) approved, as did the east German Greens in Bündnis '90, the peace movement's core issued a strong statement warning that the Bundeswehr was sliding down a slippery slope to a warlike escalation policy. The path to a policy of military intervention, it argued, was being paved with participation in blue-helmet and "humanitarian" missions. The peace movement, including the Social Democrats' own youth group (Jusos), planned several demonstrations against German participation in UN peacekeeping missions in conjunction with the Social Democratic party convention that approved this policy change, in order to strengthen the hand of those Social Democrats who remained opposed.[119]

While the government promoted "normalizing" German foreign policy and fulfilling "international responsibility" by taking part in all categories of UN missions, including operations like the Gulf War, the broad left proved deeply reluctant to allow German participation in UN missions, fearing that such steps would revive the militarist "power politics" of the past. At worst the historically ugly German militarism could reassert itself, while at the very least Germany would join the circle of rich, industrialized countries that misused the UN in service of their own interests. On this point, the left's "antimilitarism" and "anti-imperialism" converged. Thus while the left supported the notion of collective security in principle, it worried that the UN as currently constituted provided a vehicle for traditional, if disguised, power politics on the part of rich, powerful nations. Whereas *Machtpolitik* had earlier played itself out in diplomacy and wars between nations, it was now being transferred to the level of multilateral institutions. A truly peaceful world order would require that the major powers stay out of conflicts around the world.

Peace researchers such as Erik Krippendorff warned against Germany's acquiring a capacity for worldwide intervention,[120] and pacifists such as Andreas Buro argued that the government's desire for German participation in UN missions was just a front for the real goal, a relegitimation of the Bundeswehr and expanded German hegemony. For the Greens' Jürgen Trittin, the UN as currently structured was not democratic but instead enforced international law arbitrarily, and thus its decisions corresponded to the interests of the dominant powers, like in the Gulf

---

119. "Friedensgruppen wollen die 'Petersburger Wende' aufhalten," *Frankfurter Allgemeine Zeitung,* 19 Sept. 1992.

120. " 'Ich verstehe nichts von Jugoslawien,' " *Tageszeitung,* 22 Feb. 1993.

War.[121] For many Greens, the UN still represented the basic consensus of rich countries.[122] As the Gulf War showed, the United States had hitched the UN to its wagon. To become the top world authority, the UN had to rid itself of American dominance and democratize its structures.[123] For the SPD too, the Gulf War had demonstrated conclusively that a stable world "peace order" was attainable neither through national "power politics" nor through the UN in its current form.[124]

While the German left could not accept large-scale German participation in UN missions as currently constituted, it did see the need for an international organization that could provide collective security and quell the many regional wars around the world. Many in the SPD and Greens espoused reform of the UN, both in its structure and in its methods of conflict resolution. To the efforts of a reformed UN, they indicated, they would be happy to contribute German personnel. The SPD's Heide Wieczorek-Zeul, for example, maintained that the SPD would support sending troops to the UN if it became a world police with permanently available troops, for this would enable it to counter misuse of power by a single state or a small group of states.[125] Her colleague Karsten Voigt agreed that if the UN became a world police, Germany would have to contribute, in order to prevent powerful states from deciding alone whether and how aggressors should be combated.[126] The Greens' Ludger Vollmer recommended a new foreign policy based on an "ecological-solidaristic world economy" regulated by democratically legitimated international sanctions, which would come to the aid of threatened peoples. The only other alternative, he noted, would be a return to nation-state power politics or the dominance of a global hegemon. This world community would rest on a fully reformed and democratized UN, to which countries would transfer their national sovereignty and abolish their own armies.[127] At the very least, argued the participants of a peace movement conference, the major powers' veto power in the UN Security Council, which currently allows them

121. "Grüne Aussenpolitik jenseits von Pazifismus und Bellizismus," *Frankfurter Rundschau*, 23 Sept. 1992.

122. "Grüne Aussenpolitik aus dem Bauch," *Tageszeitung*, 20 Oct. 1992.

123. Fritz Vilmar, "Die UN müssen zur Friedensmacht werden," *Frankfurter Rundschau*, 2 Sept. 1992.

124. "SPD-Streit um Aussenpolitik dauert an," *Frankfurter Allgemeine Zeitung*, 15 May 1991.

125. "Der politische Druck auf die SPD wird stärker," *Süddeutsche Zeitung*, 7 Aug. 1992.

126. "SPD nennt Bedingungen für Eingreiftruppe," *Tageszeitung*, 7 Aug. 1992.

127. Ludger Volmer, "Bosnien und der Pazifismus," *Tageszeitung*, 5 Sept. 1992.

to block decisions by the majority, should be abolished and should be replaced by a qualified majority voting system.[128]

At the time of this book's writing, most of the left prefers to keep German troops out of military missions and only reluctantly condones participation in blue-helmet peacekeeping endeavors, until reforms prevent an "imperialist" abuse of the UN by the Western powers. Historians often speak of a German "special path" to modernity, inextricably linked to the militarism of the Wilhelminian era and the Third Reich. The peace movement, in contrast, hopes that Germany has learned the lessons of the past and will henceforth pursue a *Sonderweg* dedicated to peace. The SPD's Herta Däubler-Gmelin, for example, wants Germany to get a seat on the UN Security Council in order to help peaceful coexistence and avoidance of conflict, rather than military missions, become the norm.[129] Similarly, in the discussion of foreign policy at the SPD's party convention in 1991, some members maintained that because of the world wars, Germany had neither the moral nor the political right to participate in UN military actions. Instead, Germany should oppose the Western tendency to look for military solutions to world conflicts.[130] The SPD's traditional "peace policy" *(Friedenspolitik)* defines its view of German responsibility. Instead of traditional military approaches to security, Germany should concentrate on arms reduction, avoiding ecological disasters, and eradicating the causes of underdevelopment and military conflict.[131] As one member of the Greens' executive committee *(Vorstand)* argued, the Greens should try to move Germany toward a "political pacifism" for the post–cold war era, replacing the prevailing military logic with a civilian one. Otherwise, Germany faces entrapment in the dominant logic of other interests.[132]

Fittingly, just as this book went to press, Germany's Constitutional Court handed down its opinion on the permissibility of out-of-area missions for the Bundeswehr, in response to the suit brought by both the SPD and the FDP. The court ruled that the Bundeswehr can indeed be deployed outside NATO territory, setting the stage for possible departure from (West) Germany's forty-year-old tradition of foreign policy restraint but also for continued controversy over actual out-of-area deployments.

---

128. "Gewalt-Ursachen beseitigen, statt Gewalt anwenden," *Frankfurter Rundschau,* 21 June 1993.

129. "Verraten und verkauft," *Berliner Zeitung,* 10 Aug. 1992.

130. Eckhard Fuhr, "Ortsverein und Weltfrieden," *Frankfurter Allgemeine Zeitung,* 11 May 1991.

131. "Die UNO muss das Zentrum einer neuen Weltordnung sein," *Frankfurter Rundschau,* 27 May 1991.

132. Ludger Volmer, "Bosnien und der Pazifismus," *Tageszeitung,* 5 Sept. 1992.

The court ruled that the Bundeswehr can be deployed outside NATO territory as long as the deployments take place in the context of multilateral collective security alliances and as long as they receive approval (in principle in advance) by a simple majority in the Bundestag.[133] The ruling represented virtually the most permissive possible interpretation of the relevant Basic Law articles. It provided, according to one commentator, a legal framework for German participation in UN blue-helmet missions, military missions ordered by the UN Security Council, and military assistance for allies all over the world. The ruling thus made possible the end of a forty-year tradition of restraint in German foreign policy. It also set the stage for renewed controversy over *political* (as opposed to legal) issues. Germany will now have to decide the concrete content of the catchphrases that have made the rounds since unification: "assuming responsibility," "return to normality," and the "capacity for international action." For whom and with what military means should Germany "assume responsibility?" What constitutes "normality"—the American invasion of Grenada, the Falklands war?[134] Or, as the irrepressible *Der Spiegel* posed the question, "Frieden schaffen mit deutschen Waffen?"[135]

Many assume that Germany will indeed adopt a more active international role, including involvement in military missions. Such a role is indicated by the Bundeswehr's out-of-area deployments so far, calls from the United States and the UN for Germany to do so, and other government actions.[136] Unless the government restricts itself to the most innocuous UN humanitarian relief and blue-helmet peacekeeping operations, the subject of foreign military missions is likely to remain controversial in German politics for the foreseeable future. Indeed, this became visible in the immediate reactions to the court's ruling. Foreign Minister Kinkel felt compelled to emphasize that Germany would retain its "culture of reticence," would "never pursue an interventionist policy," and in the future would be "saying 'no' more often than 'yes.'"[137] *Der Spiegel,* however, attributed this "reticence" on Kinkel's part to expediency rather than true

---

133. "Karlsruhe erlaubt UNO-Kampfeinsätze der Bundeswehr," *Süddeutsche Zeitung,* 13 July 1994; "Bundestag muss Entsendung der Bundeswehr zustimmen," *Süddeutsche Zeitung,* 13 July 1994.

134. Heribert Prantl, "Wir können—aber: sollen wir," *Süddeutsche Zeitung,* 13 July 1994.

135. The phrase means "Create peace with German weapons?" and represents a play on words alluding to the earlier peace movement slogan "Frieden schaffen ohne Waffen," as well as Kohl's "Frieden schaffen mit immer weniger Waffen." See "Nun siegt mal schön," *Der Spiegel,* 18 July 1994, 23.

136. Dieter Schröder, "Germans to the Front," *Süddeutsche Zeitung,* 23 July 1994.

137. "Court Rules German Constitution Allows Sending Troops Abroad," *Washington Post,* 13 July 1994.

conviction, calculating that the CDU and FDP wanted to avoid discussion of foreign policy interests, goals, and principles before the federal election scheduled for October 1994. Kohl and Kinkel did not really desire continued reticence, *Der Spiegel* concluded. The Germans would not in future play the "world police," but they did want to be "deputy sheriff."[138]

Only one week after the court handed down its decision, dissension emerged within the governing coalition over how decisions about out-of-area deployments would be made. Hermann Solms, head of the FDP's *Fraktion* in the Bundestag, demanded an *Entsendegesetz*, a law regulating how and in which cases action had to be taken and when the Bundestag had to give its approval. Defense Minister Volker Rühe of the CDU, in contrast, declined to "establish abstract norms" ahead of time, preferring to deliberate on each concrete situation as it arose.[139] Even though foreign deployments only require approval by a simple Bundestag majority, at the very least each deployment will be potentially subject to very heated parliamentary debate.

For the foreseeable future, the substantial pacifist strand in Germany's political culture will remain pitted against a second powerful strand running through much of the political elite, namely, the commitment to multilateralism, to being a "reliable ally," and to "normalizing" German foreign policy. Given these competing strands, broad consensus on German participation in combat missions may well remain elusive. To be sure, in a speech potentially reminiscent of Herbert Wehner's historic 1960 speech declaring the SPD's loyalty to NATO, the SPD's chair, Rudolf Scharping, maintained that his party approved of all Bundeswehr deployments within the resolutions of international bodies, and he spoke of the need for consensus between the major parties over Germany's basic principles in foreign policy.

As its first relevant act after the court ruling, moreover, the Bundestag approved by a four-fifths majority (thus clearly including the SPD) German participation in the UN's enforcement of the embargo against Yugoslavia and in the UN's AWACS surveillance of the no-fly zone over Bosnia, including the use of force if necessary.[140] Supported by all parties in the Bundestag, the government also sent one air force plane to the UN relief effort in Rwanda.[141] This unanimity notwithstanding, the SPD's high-ranking (Bundesgeschäftsführer) Günter Verheugen denied that Ger-

---

138. "Nun siegt mal schön," *Der Spiegel*, 18 July 1994.

139. "Dissens in der Bonner Koalition," *Süddeutsche Zeitung*, 18 July 1994.

140. "Bundestag billigt mit grosser Mehrheit Einsätze der Bundeswehr in der Adria und in AWACS-Flugzeugen," *Süddeutsche Zeitung*, 23 July 1994.

141. "Bundesluftwaffe beteiligt sich an den Hilfsmassnahmen für Flüchtlinge aus Ruanda," *Süddeutsche Zeitung*, 18 July 1994.

man participation in an ad hoc coalition like the Persian Gulf War of 1991 would be legal in the future, even in terms of the Constitutional Court's ruling, and argued that it would in any event have to be prevented on political grounds. Expanding NATO's or the WEU's role to measures outside alliance territory would likewise be illegal without renegotiating the relevant treaties.[142] According to the DGB's chair, Dieter Schulte, the unions would also oppose any Bundeswehr missions that went beyond humanitarian relief efforts.[143]

Thus the peace movement will undoubtedly have new issues to deal with, though they may not be as salient as those in the 1980s. Still, Germany is likely to see considerable resistance to Bundeswehr combat missions abroad. Germany's protest culture is so well developed that organizational capacity for protest on a broad range of issues remains, as does the peace movement's own coordinating body, the Netzwerk Friedenskooperative. So ideological developments may well hold the key to future peace movement action. Time will tell whether aversion to force retains dominance over a possible push in the opposite direction, accepting German participation in missions requiring force to reverse suffering and injustice.

---

142. "SPD: Kriege wie am Golf bleiben tabu," *Süddeutsche Zeitung*, 15 July 1994.
143. "DGB-Chef Schulte gegen Bundeswehr-Kampfeinsätze," *Süddeutsche Zeitung*, 20 July 1994.

CHAPTER 8

Conclusion

Peace movements accompanied virtually all phases of West German politics and foreign policy over the four decades of the postwar period and are
likely to have a continued voice in the politics and policy of united Germany as well. They articulated, but also helped consolidate and broaden,
popular unease with military force and nuclear deterrence, which waxed
and waned across the entire postwar period despite widespread
identification with the West. Although relatively ineffectual at first, peace
movements contributed to cultural norms and electoral patterns that
increasingly constrained policy options, and they now inhibit German
participation in military missions abroad even under multilateral auspices.

Had the cold war ever turned into actual war on the European continent, serendipity alone would have determined most individual West Germans' chances of survival. Had deterrence ever failed, all Germans would
have been equally threatened, regardless of class, gender, age, or political
leanings. Yet peace movements were able to mobilize only certain people at
certain times against this potential threat. In this book, we therefore have
sought to understand the ebb and flow of peace protest since 1945, the
composition of movement activism, and differences in organizational
structure and strategy.

Several theories of social movements shed considerable light on these
issues but also leave certain questions unanswered. Theories of value
change and crises of modernization delineate the broad structural conditions of the "new" social movements since the mid-1960s and help explain
the swelling of the social movement ranks across the board over time.
Resource mobilization theory points to the importance of strong organization, effective strategies, and other resources. None of these theories,
however, adequately explains the ebb and flow of peace protest specifically
or the composition of its core activists within the broad demographic variables suggested by the theories.

Thus we have examined German peace protest through the lens of the political process model and its three components: political opportunities, ideological resources, and organization. While these three components have served to analyze a range of social movements, I have argued in this book that they take on a unique configuration in German peace movements, different from their configuration in certain citizenship movements, like the women's movement or the American Civil Rights movement. Our understanding of the political process of German peace movements rests partly on conceptualizing them as "public-goods" movements, which pursue goods equally enjoyed by all, and which lack "natural" constituencies based on predefined categories like gender or race. The three categories of political opportunities, ideological resources, and organization help us understand the varying fortunes and constituencies of peace movements over time: their moderate size in the 1950s and 1960s, their virtual absence in the 1970s, their enormous size in the early 1980s, their waning in the later 1980s, and their modest presence in the united Germany of the 1990s so far.

A movement's political opportunity structure consists of the elements in its broader environment that facilitate or hinder its emergence and success. While citizenship movements often prosper when political and economic developments enhance the power resources of their constituent base, German peace movements rose and fell in part based on the "career" of their issue—the salience of defense issues over time, the extent to which the international system enhanced the credibility of the movement's message, and whether the movement monopolized opposition to official policy or saw its positions institutionalized in conventional politics. Peace movement mobilization also varied with the size of the protest potential in general, the extent to which peace took priority over other potentially competing concerns, and the extent to which the government's policy package was already in disarray.

The salience of defense issues contributed greatly to the peace movement's capacity to mobilize the public. The two biggest movements were in the 1950s and 1980s. In each case, a decision to acquire nuclear weapons was on the active agenda. In each case, the public saw the issue as definitive for West Germany's broader foreign policy—in the 1950s because nuclear weapons were linked with Western military integration and the chances for German reunification, and in the 1980s because they were linked to the future of détente in Europe. In the 1980s, moreover, many Germans viewed the nuclear issue as definitive for their very survival. The policy cycle of these issues also explains the longevity of the peace movements of each decade. The series of salient issues in the 1950s— rearmament, NATO membership, and nuclear weapons—provided an unusually long issue cycle stretching the length of the decade, and the peace movement remained mobilized for most of that time. In contrast, the time span in the 1980s from the initial proposal of the double-track decision to the government's final decision was much shorter, and the movement was of correspondingly briefer duration.

In the 1960s, nuclear issues enjoyed only brief and moderate salience in the form of the debate over the proposed Multilateral Nuclear Force. The movement initially lacked any issue that could attract a popular following. It grew only when it found in Ostpolitik an issue relevant to the German populace and definitive for foreign policy more broadly. The movement's capacity to mobilize on the basis of Ostpolitik remained limited, however, by the SPD's own pursuit of the issue. Vietnam became a highly salient moral issue for the German student movement and served to mobilize Germany's academic youth. But the peace movement remained smaller than in the 1950s or 1980s even in its "Vietnam phase," since the issues it monopolized were neither survival issues nor definitive for German foreign policy as a whole.

Even with a salient defense issue, the peace movement's mobilization capacity depended on the credibility of its positions in relation to the international situation of the time. This credibility in turn depended on popular definitions of friend and foe, the relative weight of the populace's fear of war compared to its fear of the Soviets, and the presence or absence of established alternatives to security based primarily on military means. In the 1950s, the peace movement's positions suffered from limited credibility. On the one hand, discussion of rearmament and nuclear weapons recalled painful experiences with World War II, and in the cold war context, Western military integration would plausibly deepen national division. On the other hand, these considerations were outweighed by many things. A large majority perceived an active Soviet threat, reinforced by the continual stream of East German refugees, the Soviet suppression of the Hungarian and Polish revolts, and the multiple Berlin crises. The United States, in contrast, enjoyed a positive image as a model democracy, guarantor of German economic recovery, and provider of military security. Thus although the populace was uneasy with rearmament and nuclear weapons, at the height of the cold war the peace movement could not meet popular security needs through proposals for military disengagement, German neutralization, and East-West détente.

In the 1960s and especially in the 1970s, in contrast, popular attitudes changed significantly. Despite continued ideological differences between East and West, opposing alliances, and plenty of military hardware on both sides, the popular perception of Soviet threat declined somewhat. Détente and Ostpolitik demonstrated, moreover, that alternatives to unadulterated military confrontation existed, which had the added benefits

of promoting trade and German-German contacts as well. Détente, Ostpolitik, and arms control suggested that even ideological and military
rivals shared a common interest in peace. German governments insisted on
the divisibility of détente, pursuing peace in Europe regardless of superpower conflicts elsewhere. In the meantime, America's image had worsened dramatically. The Vietnam War had tarnished its image in the 1960s,
and during the 1970s and 1980s Europeans questioned the soundness of
American judgment and leadership. This culminated in concerns that Germany might fall victim to American military adventurism, following President Reagan's loose rhetoric about "limited nuclear war" and other such
utterances in the early 1980s. Given these developments, the peace movement succeeded much more resoundingly in establishing the credibility of
its message than it ever had before.

The question of the movement's monopoly on opposition to government policy is complicated. On the one hand, when a defense issue is
highly salient, party involvement in the peace movement does not necessarily reduce popular mobilization. Indeed, in the 1950s the SPD's involvement actually increased mobilization by contributing organizational and
personnel resources at a time when peace groups lacked the necessary
cohesion and other resources on their own. Rather than reducing mobilization, moreover, SPD involvement in the 1950s reflected the pressure of
its own rather pacifist rank and file, although dependence on SPD involvement did ultimately cause the peace movement to collapse when the SPD
withdrew. Similarly, in the early 1980s, the Greens' electoral breakthrough
was made possible by the high popular mobilization around peace, ecology, and other "new politics" issues. In the short run, the Greens' success
did not reduce peace movement mobilization, which indeed reached its
highest level ever in the fall of 1983.

On the other hand, the institutionalization of peace movement positions in conventional politics, especially in policy, undoubtedly served to
demobilize its participants in the long run. Peace protest was virtually
nonexistent in the first half of the 1970s, as the Brandt government pursued détente, Ostpolitik, and arms control with unparalleled zeal. The
peace movement reached a second low point in the late 1980s, as many of
its positions became institutionalized in the INF treaty and other superpower negotiations, and its views achieved parliamentary representation
via the Greens and the SPD. At the same time, one of the movement's
major accomplishments was the SPD's adoption of movement positions
into its official party platform after 1983, and peace movement support
was instrumental to the Greens' electoral success. In the late 1950s and
1960s, the SPD had dropped peace movement positions in its search for
electoral success through competition with the CDU at the center of the

political spectrum, a strategy facilitated by the absence of serious competition on its left. In the 1980s, in contrast, the strength of the peace movement's mobilization and the rise of the Greens on the party's left contributed to the SPD's pursuit of an electoral majority "to the left of the Union" and its adoption of movement positions.

Peace movement fortunes varied significantly with the levels of protest potential in the political culture at large, the position of peace in the cycle of protest taking place at the time, and the solidity of the government's policy package. The 1950s movement suffered greatly from the general lack of popular mobilization, as the populace turned its attention to private life and economic recovery after the trauma of the Third Reich, traditional subcultural cleavages partially reasserted themselves and reestablished distance between various parts of the populace, and extraparliamentary mobilization suffered from the taint of Nazism. Starting in the mid-1960s, in contrast, the populace became much more willing to mobilize around a growing array of issues, as a new generation entered politics, subcultures lost distinctiveness during economic and social change, and extraparliamentary protest gradually won democratic legitimacy. Extraparliamentary mobilization reached new heights in the 1970s with the new social movements, of which the peace movement of the early 1980s proved the crowning glory. The 1980s peace movement profited from a second advantage compared to its predecessors. Coming at the end of a long cycle of protest, during which competing concerns (e.g., ecology and feminism) had already enjoyed peaks of mobilization, the salience of the peace movement's issue served to squeeze out any competitors for popular attention. In the 1960s, in contrast, peace issues competed with other more salient issues, like the Emergency Laws and Vietnam, which took priority during the high point of extraparliamentary protest during that decade.

Finally, German peace movements were most successful when the government's policy package was in the most disarray across the board. In the 1950s, Adenauer's combination of parliamentary democracy, economic recovery, and Western integration proved an integrated and hugely successful policy package, richly rewarded by the voters. The peace movement of that decade, opposing one element of an otherwise successful package, was clearly swimming against the tide. In the 1960s and particularly by the 1980s, however, governments were enjoying much less overall success. In the 1960s Adenauer's package was slowly dissolving, under the pressures of economic recession and the changing international arena. Similarly, by the early 1980s, the Social Democratic package was in disarray, as the Brandt and Schmidt governments had violated their promise to "dare more democracy," severe recessions brought cuts in social spending and ended all promise of economic reform, ecological considerations undermined consensus on industrial growth, and détente and Ostpolitik were stagnating. In these two periods, the peace movement was able to tap into growing popular frustration with politics in general as well as with foreign policy in particular.

Analysis of political opportunities contributes enormously to our understanding of the ebb and flow of German peace protest since 1945. In comparison with the 1980s, the peace movements of the 1950s and 1960s were modest in size and limited in impact, but for very different reasons. On the "plus" side, the 1950s movement enjoyed a series of highly salient issues, with no serious competition from other issues for the attention of extraparliamentary mobilization. Otherwise, however, political opportunities worked against the peace movement. The cold war limited the credibility of its positions, the political culture had a low protest potential in general, and Adenauer's policy package reigned supreme. In the 1960s, the peace movement faced an almost diametrically opposed set of political opportunities and likewise remained modest in size. The international transition to détente and arms control enhanced the credibility of the peace movement's message, popular willingness to engage in extraparliamentary opposition grew by leaps and bounds, and the conservatives' policy package was under assault on many fronts. The peace movement lacked, however, salient issues with which to mobilize a broad following; and other, more compelling, issues dominated the extraparliamentary opposition by the end of the decade. In the 1970s, with the institutionalization of many movement demands in government policy itself, the movement lacked salient issues altogether, and the left turned to the concerns of the new social movements.

Only in the 1980s did all aspects of political opportunity converge positively, setting the stage for the biggest peace movement of German history. Defense issues were once again highly salient, new nuclear weapons were perceived to threaten détente, arms control was perceived as an alternative to arms acquisition, protest potential was high, the issue of peace took priority over possible competitors, and the Schmidt government was unpopular across many policy fronts. After 1983, however, declining salience and institutionalization of movement positions again contributed to greatly reduced mobilization.

Political opportunities are not sufficient in themselves to launch a protest movement, no matter how favorable. Social movements begin only when people decide to take part, stimulated by a change in consciousness. Many scholars have sought reasons for *individual* participation in social movements. Some, following Inglehart, argue that unconsciously held postmaterial values increased readiness to support new social movements in the 1970s and 1980s. Others, following Habermas, maintain that people participate in protest after perceiving a crisis of modernity, in particular the negative side effects of industrialization. Still others have looked at individual motivation, ranging from cost-benefit analyses and the draw of group solidarity to feelings of personal efficacy and belief in group success.

Whatever might shape individual motivation, it is not the only level at which the decision to participate is made. This study focused on the *groups* that composed the peace movement's core leadership over the decades. These groups provided ideological resources and shaped the movement's "cognitive identity." Local units of these groups, moreover, served as recruiting grounds for many (though by no means all) participants in peace protest.

Insofar as the decision to participate in protest is made at a conscious level, people often arrive at this decision through discussion within groups to which they already belong. In the case of the peace movement, more-over, many groups made the decision to participate in the movement en bloc (though individuals were of course free to desist). Most groups pre-dated the movement and had an identity distinct from the movement. Very few of the groups, moreover, were "peace groups" with peace as their main concern. Nonetheless, a great many joined the peace movement at various times, especially in phases of high mobilization. Each group's written words—pamphlets, journals, statements, and so on—reflected its consensus on why it, as a group, was participating in the peace movement, quite often at the temporary expense of its usual concerns. These written words presupposed a "cognitive" process (through intensive discussion) on the part of the groups, in which they worked out and committed to paper the reasons for their participation.

At the movement's core, these groups engaged in ideological self-definition with respect to peace issues. At the same time, they shed light on why they joined the movement and thus on the movement's composition at the national level. Unlike movements based on race, gender, or sexual preference, peace movements were public-goods movements with no "natural" constituency that could be identified a priori. Unlike citizenship movements, their main concern was not gaining equality or some other right for the group in question. Instead, groups with varying identities had to decide for themselves why to fight for a public good like peace and thus whether to join the movement. They did so from a broad variety of vantage points, with most groups revealing quite group-specific reasons for participating.

Which groups became involved while others did not? As we have seen, the groups that became involved in peace protest generally had available interpretive frames that invited such participation. Groups found their way to the peace movement, with greater or lesser ease, when they found thematic links between their customary concerns and the promotion of peace. Usually the "interpretive frames" used to justify participation in the peace movement came from contexts larger than the groups themselves. Interpretive frames often came from institutional settings, in which case groups drawn from these institutions explicitly linked the frames with participation in the peace movement of the day. In addition, extraparliamentary groups came to the peace movement when they discovered "issue overlap" between their own concerns and the issue of peace.

As groups joined the peace movement, they contributed to the production of meaning by and for the movement as a whole, simultaneously helping the movement frame the peace issue for public consumption. As groups discovered links between peace and their own concerns, they expanded the movement's ideological foundations. In addition to its horror of war and concern for survival, the movement acquired a multifaceted and richly textured set of ideological resources. In the process, narrowly defined defense issues became much broader, as various groups within the movement linked them to questions of morality, social reform, or the biological foundations of life.

Over the decades the peace movement's ideological resources shifted and expanded, reflecting the changing composition of the movement over time. Some ideological frames and sources of participation remained constant. Drawing on their church's confession of guilt for its role in the Third Reich, Protestants launched the frame of redemption in the 1950s, and they justified their participation in peace movements across more than four decades on the basis of this frame. In the 1950s, Protestant peace activists argued that historical guilt morally precluded rearmament or nuclear weapons. In the 1960s, Protestants in the peace movement continued their call for redemption, linking it now to their church's call for a new Ostpolitik. In the 1980s, Protestants maintained their commitment to détente, Ostpolitik, and an international "peace order"—themes that their church had launched—and rejected the double-track decision on the grounds that new missiles would violate these principles. They also drew on themes associated with Christian socialism and the ecumenical movement. In contrast, in the 1950s Catholics had no interpretive frames from within their own church that they could have linked to peace issues, and the participation of Catholic groups in peace protest was negligible. Not until the 1980s were Catholics able to draw on doctrinal changes within their own church that served to justify peace protest—changes initiated by Vatican II and the popes of the 1960s.

Like Protestants, Social Democrats in the peace movement drew primarily on frames from their own institution. In the 1950s, Social Democrats, unionists, and communists launched the frame of democratization.

They worried about the dangers a new army might pose to the fledgling democracy, given their previous experience with the military under authoritarian regimes; and they argued that rearmament would impede the social reforms they sought by binding Germany's economic order more tightly to the capitalist West. Together with Protestants and assorted neutralists, the Social Democrats also introduced the frame of the German national question, maintaining that Western military integration would preclude reunification. In the 1960s, the German question was redefined in terms of Ostpolitik for the SPD as a party, as well as for Social Democrats in the movement. The SPD took up the cause of arms control as well, which Social Democrats in the movement used to justify their opposition to the proposed Multilateral Nuclear Force. In the 1980s and beyond, Social Democrats' commitment to détente, arms control, Ostpolitik, and an international peace order formed the basis of their participation in the peace movement. They drew on interpretive frames based on their party's official policy and the rhetoric of top party leaders, while radicalizing these frames in ways unintended by the party leadership.

Starting in the late 1960s, the extraparliamentary left took part in peace movements based on ideological frames from its own midst as well as on issue overlap between the cause of peace and other concerns. As part of the broader extraparliamentary opposition of the 1960s, the student movement appropriated the frame of democratization, which it coupled with a renewed anticapitalism and a utopian vision of radical democracy. The APO also launched the interpretive frame of "imperialism" (and the anti-Americanism linked thereto) during its opposition to the Vietnam War and to the German government's support of the American effort. Both of these themes reappeared in the "independent" spectrum of the 1980s peace movement. Third World groups, among others, based opposition to the double-track decision on their struggle against American "imperialism" in various parts of the world. Self-described "grassroots revolution" groups, again among others, linked defense issues of the 1980s to their hopes for far-reaching social transformation and democratization. On a more concrete level, groups from the social movements of the 1970s joined the 1980s peace movement when they discovered the issue overlap between peace and their own concerns. Ecology groups joined when they discovered the threat that nuclear weapons posed to the environment. Women's groups joined when they realized that the military reinforced the patriarchal structures and values they were fighting in other sectors of society. The Greens emerged from the social movements of the 1970s, incorporated most of their themes into their party platform, and played an important role in the peace movement of the 1980s.

Organization constitutes the final element of the political process approach, which argues that movements can not emerge, let alone survive, without adequate organization. The trajectory of West German peace movements supports this claim. Whereas citizenship movements based on race or gender depend on an adequate organizational infrastructure within their natural constituency, West German peace movements faced a different problem. While alliances with parties enlarged their mobilization potential and provided other resources, they left the movement woefully dependent on the parties involved for both initial mobilization and continued survival, as the 1950s movement amply demonstrated. The key to the peace movement's capacity for independent mobilization and survival lay in the growth of dense networks of autonomous extraparliamentary groups and the development of communication structures between them, in the groups' experience with protest forms and strategies, and so on. During the 1960s and 1970s, such networks of autonomous groups developed, based in the new social movements and with links to dissident groups within parties, churches, and unions. The first such networks made it possible for the 1960s movement to chart an independent course. The vast profusion of such networks in the 1970s made possible the enormous peace movement of the 1980s, which temporarily drew them into its political coalition and organizational fold.

The three elements of the political process approach—political opportunities, collective consciousness and ideological resources, and organization—have proved exceedingly useful for analyzing (West) German peace movements since 1945. Others have applied them usefully to movements involving issues ranging from civil rights and feminism to ecology and peace and occurring in diverse geographical locations. The political process approach has a number of advantages. Its analytic categories are flexible enough to encompass the diversity of social movements in the real world and still allow comparison of movements to one another. The political process approach maintains that all movements need favorable political opportunities, adequate levels of consciousness or ideological articulation, and adequate levels of organization. These analytic categories, however, can be filled with the actual content appropriate to each individual movement and sensitive to each national setting. Each study of one or more movements (including, I hope, this one), moreover, contributes to understanding both the immense diversity among social movements and the patterns that recur.

Although many different elements contribute to the peculiarities of each social movement, I have suggested that some of the German peace movement's traits resulted from its character as a public-goods movement, pursuing not new rights or status for a disadvantaged group but a good shared equally by all or none. Thus the movement's political opportunities involved circumstances that raised the salience of the movement's issue and the credibility of its message, rather than the power resources of its actors. The movement's ideology linked many different issues to the question of peace, rather than focusing on issues of equality or rights. The movement's organizational requirements involved the organizational infrastructure of a protest potential in the society at large rather than a specific constituency defined by race or gender. This discussion of the public-good quality of the German peace movement, however, remains suggestive. Subsequent research might profit from further exploring the extent to which the logic of citizenship movements and public-good movements differ.

Judging from the German case, peace movements have multiple, and often powerful, effects on the societies that give birth to them. On the level of public opinion, German peace movements may not have swayed ardent defenders of deterrence or reduced the public's loyalty to NATO, but they did articulate a broad current of unease with Germany's position in cold war Europe and with the nuclear weapons intended for its defense. Peace movements undoubtedly helped convert latent discomfort into more defined opposition to nuclear deterrence and related policies, by showing individuals that many of their fellow citizens shared their feelings, and by creating a common "identity" based on this discomfort. For activists, moreover, the movement provided the transforming experience of intense political participation. On the level of party politics and policy, the peace movement helped create an identifiable constituency for disarmament and continued détente. Given the evolution of the party system in the 1970s and 1980s, which resulted in the rise of the Greens, the peace movement had a definite effect on voting patterns and party platforms, recommitting the left to the policies it supported. At the policy level, the peace movement was never able to force the government to adopt "unrealistic" policies in terms of Germany's NATO obligations or the international situation. The movement did, however, help tip the balance of pressures to which policymakers were subject, contributing to the constraints on policy options by building an identifiable constituency for "peace." Since the movement helped create enduring cultural norms regarding the use of military force, for the foreseeable future the movement's legacy will continue to help shape the politics and policy of united Germany.

Bibliography

Primary Sources: Interviews, Documents, Essays by Political Figures, and Newspaper Articles

Interviews with Representatives of:

Aktion Sühnezeichen/Friedensdienste
Aktionsgemeinschaft Dienst für den Frieden
Antimilitaristische Gruppe Bonn
Bundeskonferenz unabhängiger Friedensgruppen
Bundeskongress entwicklungspolitischer Aktionsgruppen
Bundesschülervertretung
Bundesverband Bürgerinitiativen Umweltschutz
Demokratische Sozialisten
Deutsche Friedensgesellschaft-Vereinigte Kriegsdienstverweigerer
DGB-Jugend
Die Grünen
Evangelische Studentengemeinde
Föderation gewaltfreier Aktionsgruppen
Frauen gegen Krieg und Militarismus
Gustav-Heinemann-Initiative
Initiative für Frieden, internationalen Ausgleich und Sicherheit
Initiative Kirche von Unten
Jungdemokraten
Jungsozialisten
Komitee für Frieden, Abrüstung und Zusammenarbeit
Komitee für Grundrechte und Demokratie
Liberale Demokraten
Ohne Rüstung Leben
Pax Christi
SJD-Die Falken
Sozialistische Deutsche Arbeiterjugend
Vereinigte Deutsche Studentenschaften

Documents and Writings by Political Figures and Groups

Abel, Edith, et al. *Bericht über das Projekt: Gewalterfahrungen von Frauen im All-tag—Zusammenhänge zwischen Sexismus und Militarismus.* Bonn: Fachbe-reich Frauen des Bildungswerks für Friedensarbeit, 1983.

Aktion Sühnezeichen/Friedensdienste, Frieden schaffen ohne Waffen. Bornheim-Merten: Lamuv Verlag, 1981.

"Anfrage an die Synode der Evangelischen Kirche in Deutschland." In *Kirchliches Jahrbuch für die Evangelische Kirche in Deutschland, 1958,* ed. Joachim Beck-mann, 85:30–33. Gütersloh: Gütersloher Verlagshaus Gerd Mohn, 1959.

Asmussen, Probst Hans. Open letter dated 14 Mar. 1958. In *Kirchliches Jahrbuch für die Evangelische Kirche in Deutschland, 1958,* ed. Joachim Beckmann, 85:34–36. Gütersloh: Gütersloher Verlagshaus Gerd Mohn, 1959.

Bahr, Egon. "Wandel durch Annäherung: Rede zur Deutschlandpolitik in Tutzing am 15. Juli 1963." In *Sozialdemokratie, Krieg und Frieden,* ed. Christoph But-terwegge and Heinz-Gerd Hofschen, 325–27. Heilbronn: Distel Verlag, 1984.

Bahro, Rudolf. "Überlegungen zu einem Neuansatz der Friedensbewegung in Deutschland." In *Entrüstet Euch,* by Die Grünen. (Bonn, 1983): 52–73.

Bensberger Kreis. *Ein Memorandum deutscher Katholiken zu den polnisch-deutschen Fragen.* Mainz: Matthias-Grünewald-Verlag, 1968.

"Beschluss der Synode der Evangelischen Kirche der Union." In *Kirchliches Jahrbuch für die Evangelische Kirche in Deutschland, 1957,* ed. Joachim Beck-mann, 84:95. Gütersloh: C. Bertelsmann Verlag, 1958.

"Beschluss des Reichbruderrates in Frankfurt a.M. zur Kirchenleitung." In *Kirch-liches Jahrbuch für die Evangelische Kirche in Deutschland, 1945–1948,* ed. Joachim Beckmann, 72–75:2–4. Gütersloh: C. Bertelsmann Verlag, 1950.

"Besinnung und Gebet für den Frieden." Letter to pastors from the Leitungsaus-schuss der kirchlichen Bruderschaften. In *Kirchliches Jahrbuch für die Evange-lische Kirche in Deutschland, 1961,* ed. Gottfried Niemeier, 88:81–83. Güters-loh: Gütersloher Verlagshaus Gerd Mohn, 1962.

Biermann, Wolf. "Kriegshetze, Friedenshetze." *Die Zeit,* 8 Feb. 1991.

Biermann, Wolfgang. "Genfer INF-Verhandlungen und Friedensbewegung." *Neue Gesellschaft* 30, no. 9 (1983): 854–58.

———. "'Nachrüstung' als Übergang von der Strategie der atomaren Abschreck-ung zur Strategie der Führbarkeit des Atomkrieges." *Neue Gesellschaft* 28, no. 5 (1981): 416–23.

———. "Positionen der SPD zur Friedenspolitik und zum Verhältnis von SPD und Friedensbewegung." In *Frieden in Deutschland,* ed. Hans Pestalozzi et al., 92–101. Munich: Wilhelm Goldmann Verlag, 1982.

———. Untitled essay. In *Reader zur Strategie-Konferenz "Grosser Ratschlag" der Friedensbewegung,* 55–58. Bonn, 1985.

Bittermann, Klaus, ed. *Liebesgrüße aus Bagdad: Die 'edlen Seelen' der Friedensbe-wegung und der Krieg am Golf.* Berlin: Edition Tiamat, 1991.

Böge, Volker. "Blockzersetzung statt Selbstbehauptung Europas." *Friedensjournal* 6 (1988): 13–14.

Breit, Ernst. "Die Ansprüche der Friedensbewegung an die Gewerkschaften werden vermutlich immer größer sein als die friedenspolitischen Aktivitäten des DGB." *Solidarität* 34, no. 9 (Sept. 1983): 4–6.

Bröcklung, Ulrich. "Fünf vor Zwölf." *Graswurzelrevolution* 83 (Apr. 1984): 7–9.

Broder, Henryk. "Unser Kampf." *Der Spiegel* 29 (April 1991).

BUF-Trägerkreis. "Ein Grund zum Feiern für die Friedensbewegung?" In the *Rundbrief* of the Koordinierungsausschuss der Friedensbewegung (Bonn, May 1987): 10–13.

Bundesverband Bürgerinitiativen Unweltschutz, "Verkehrsplanung für den Krieg?", brochure (Bonn, April 1984).

Bundesvorstand der Jusos, ed. *Beschlüsse—ordentlicher Bundeskongreß der Jusos in der SPD in Bonn-Bad Godesberg, March 9–11, 1973.* N.p., n.d.

———. *Beschlüsse—ordentlicher Bundeskongreß der Jusos in der SPD in München, Jan. 25–27, 1974.* N.p., n.d.

———. *Bundeskongreßbeschlüsse Jungsozialisten in der SPD 1969–1976.* N.p., n.d.

"Bürgerinitiativen und Wahlen." *Graswurzelrevolution* 34–35 (spring 1978): 1.

Buro, Andreas. "Diesen Konflikt kann man nicht mit Waffen lösen." *Berliner Zeitung,* 24 Jan. 1991.

———. "Es gibt nicht den Generalschlüssel zum Frieden." *Frankfurter Rundschau,* 12 Sept. 1992.

———. "Lieber Gartenzwerge als Soldaten." *Frankfurter Rundschau,* 30 Aug. 1990.

Clever, Bernd. "Ökologie und strukturelle Gewalt." *Graswurzelrevolution* 16 (spring 1975): 3–4.

"Das Wort zum Frieden." In *Kirchliches Jahrbuch für die Evangelische Kirche in Deutschland, 1950,* ed. Joachim Beckmann, 77:7–10. Gütersloh: C. Bertelsmann Verlag, 1951.

"Der Friedensdienst der Christen." In *Kirchliches Jahrbuch für die Evangelische Kirche in Deutschland,* 1969, ed. Gottfried Niemeier, 96:71–82. Gütersloh: Gütersloher Verlagshaus Gerd Mohn, 1971.

"Der Rat der EKD zur Frage der Wiederaufrüstung." In *Kirchliches Jahrbuch für die Evangelische Kirche in Deutschland, 1950,* ed. Joachim Beckmann, 77:165–66. Gütersloh: C. Bertelsmann Verlag, 1951.

Deutsch, Julius. "Alte Reichswehr oder Neues Volksheer?" *Neue Gesellschaft* 2, no. 3 (May/June 1955): 48–50.

Deutsche Friedensgesellschaft—Vereinigte Kriegsdienstgegner [DFG-VK]. "Politische Friedenssicherung statt militärische Konfrontationspolitik." In *Reader zur Strategie-Konferenz "Grosser Ratschlag" der Friedensbewegung,* 48–51. Bonn, 1985.

"Die Friedensdienste der Kirche der BRD und DDR." *Militärpolitik Dokumentation* 3, no. 11/12 (1979): 100–109.

Die Grünen, "Auflösung der Militärblöcke—Raus aus der NATO." Resolution on peace policy, Green Party Congress. Sindelfingen, 1983.

———. *Bundestagswahlprogramm 1987.* Bonn, 1986.

———. *Das Bundesprogramm.* Bonn, 1980.

————. *Entrüstet Euch.* Bonn, 1983.

————. *Friedenskonzept.* Bonn, 1987.

————. *Friedensmanifest.* Brochure. Bonn, 1983.

————. *SPD-Sicherheitspolitik: Ein halber Frieden.* Bonn, 1986.

————. "Wer Null will darf nicht Null tun." In the *Rundbrief* of the Koordinierungsausschuss der Friedensbewegung, 17–19. Bonn, May 1987.

"Die Lage der Vertriebenen und das Verhältnis des deutschen Volkes zu seinen östlichen Nachbarn." In *Kirchliches Jahrbuch für die Evangelische Kirche in Deutschland, 1965,* ed. Gottfried Niemeier, 92:48–61. Gütersloh: Gütersloher Verlagshaus Gerd Mohn, 1967.

"Dieser Krieg schafft neues Unrecht und bedroht die Schöpfung." Resolution of the Solidarische Kirche Westfalen und Lippe. *Frankfurter Rundschau,* 28 Jan. 1991.

Dirks, Marianne. "Angst und Hoffnung—zur katholischen Synode." *Frankfurter Hefte* 31, no. 4 (Apr. 1976): 28–32.

Dirks, Walter. "Abschied vom 'gerechten Krieg.' " *Frankfurter Hefte* 22, no. 7 (July 1967): 489–96.

————. "Die Gefahr der Gleichschaltung." *Frankfurter Hefte* 13, no. 6 (June 1959): 379–91.

————. "Ein 'anderer' Katholizismus: Minderheiten im deutschen Corpus catholicorum." In *Bilanz des deutschen Katholizismus,* ed. Norbert Greinacher and Heinz-Theo Risse, 292–310. Mainz: Matthias-Grünewald Verlag, 1966.

"Entschliessung der evangelischen Delegierten." In *Kirchliches Jahrbuch für die Evangelische Kirche in Deutschland, 1950,* ed. Joachim Beckmann, 77:190–91. Gütersloh: C. Bertelsmann Verlag, 1951.

Enzensberger, Hans Magnus. "Hitlers Wiedergänger." *Der Spiegel* 4 (Feb. 1991).

Eppler, Erhard. "Deutschland—Vorfeld oder Schlachtfeld?" In *Frieden ohne Waffen?* ed. Josef Joffe, 73–81. Hamburg: Zeit Verlag, 1981.

————. "Europa—Kriegsschauplatz oder Brücke zwischen Ost und West, Nord und Süd." In *Frieden in Deutschland,* ed. Hans Pestalozzi et al., 68–76. Munich: Wilhelm Goldmann Verlag, 1982.

————. "Polen wird zum Prüfstein einer europäisch konzipierten Friedenspolitik." *Blätter für deutsche und internationale Politik* 27, no. 2 (1982): 148–49.

"Erklärung der Kirchenleitung der Evangelischen Kirche im Rheinland." In *Kirchliches Jahrbuch für die Evangelische Kirche in Deutschland, 1957,* ed. Joachim Beckmann, 84:89. Gütersloh: C. Bertelsmann Verlag, 1958.

"Erklärung der 'Kirchlich-Theologischen Arbeitsgemeinschaft.' " In *Kirchliches Jahrbuch für die Evangelische Kirche in Deutschland, 1950,* ed. Joachim Beckmann, 77:161–62. Gütersloh: C. Bertelsmann Verlag, 1951.

"Erklärung des Konvents der Kirchlichen Bruderschaft im Rheinland zur atomaren Bewaffnung." In *Kirchliches Jahrbuch für die Evangelische Kirche in Deutschland, 1957,* ed. Joachim Beckmann, 84:86–87. Gütersloh: C. Bertelsmann Verlag, 1958.

"Erklärung des Rates der Evangelischen Kirche in Deutschland gegenüber den Vertretern des ökumenischen Rates der Kirchen." In *Kirchliches Jahrbuch für die Evangelische Kirche in Deutschland, 1945–1948,* ed. Joachim Beckmann, 72–75:26–27. Gütersloh: C. Bertelsmann Verlag, 1950.

Erler, Fritz. "Möglichkeiten einer Politik der Disengagement." *Neue Gesellschaft* 5, no. 6 (1958): 435–41.

"Fragen an die Entschliessung 'Wehrbeitrag und christliches Gewissen.' " In *Kirchliches Jahrbuch für die Evangelische Kirche in Deutschland, 1952,* ed. Joachim Beckmann, 79:18–21. Gütersloh: C. Bertelsmann Verlag, 1953.

"Frauenbündnis '90: Krieg ist keine Lösung." *Sozialdemokratischer Pressedienst,* 16 Jan. 1991.

"Friedensaufgaben der Deutschen." In *Kirchliches Jahrbuch für die Evangelische Kirche in Deutschland,* 1968, ed. Gottfried Niemeier, 95:114–23. Gütersloh: Gütersloher Verlagshaus Gerd Mohn, 1970.

"Friedenspolitik und Ökologie sind ein Thema." *Tageszeitung,* 8 Oct. 1990.

Fücks, Ralf, and Bernd Ulrich. "Änderung der Parole." *Tageszeitung,* 23 Jan. 1991.

Galtung, Johann. "Von schmutzigen Händen und der Suche nach geduldigen Menschen." *Frankfurter Rundschau,* 16 Oct. 1990.

"Gegen Kriegsvorbereitung und Intervention." In *Reader zur Strategie-Konferenz "Grosser Ratschlag" der Friedensbewegung,* 43–45. Bonn, 1985.

"Gewalt-Ursachen beseitigen, statt Gewalt anwenden." *Frankfurter Rundschau,* 21 June 1993.

Götz, Christian. "Die Friedensbewegung darf sich nicht auseinanderdividieren lassen." *Blätter für deutsche und internationale Politik* 27, no. 2 (1982): 150–51.

Gundlach, Gustav. "Die Lehre Pius XII vom modernen Krieg." *Stimmen der Zeit,* April 1959. Reprinted in *Kann der atomarer Verteidgungskrieg ein gerechter Krieg sein?* ed. Karl Forster, 105–34. Munich: Karl Zink Verlag, 1960.

Habermas, Jürgen. "Wider die Logik des Kriegs." *Die Zeit,* 22 Feb. 1991.

"Handreichung an die Gemeinden zur Wiederaufrüstung." In *Kirchliches Jahrbuch für die Evangelische Kirche in Deutschland, 1950,* ed. Joachim Beckmann, 77:169–74. Gütersloh: C. Bertelsmann Verlag, 1951.

Heinemann, Gustav. *Deutsche Sicherheit.* Pamphlet. In *Kirchliches Jahrbuch für die Evangelische Kirche in Deutschland, 1950,* ed. Joachim Beckmann, 77:179–86. Gütersloh: C. Bertelsmann Verlag, 1951.

Henkel, Willi. "Ein Leitbild und seine Möglichkeiten." *Neue Gesellschaft* 2, no. 2 (Mar./Apr. 1955): 61–62.

Initiative für Frieden, internationalen Ausgleich und Sicherheit [IFIAS]. *Frieden und Abrüstung* 10. Bonn, 1985.

Initiative Kirche von Unten [IKvU]. "Diskussionsbeitrag zu den Perspektiven der Friedensbewegung." In *Reader zur Strategie-Konferenz "Grosser Ratschlag" der Friedensbewegung,* 59–60. Bonn, 1985.

Jungdemokraten Nordrhein-Westfalen. "Entwurf eines neuen Grundsatzprogramms der Jungdemokraten." *Tendenz* 3, March 1984.

———. *Für Entspannung, Abrüstung, internationale Solidarität.* Pamphlet. Bonn, Sept. 1982.

―――. *Hier täuscht die Bundesregierung sich und/oder ihre Bürger.* Pamphlet. Bonn, 1981.

―――. *Tendenz: Zeitung der Deutschen Jungdemokraten.* Bonn [early 1982].

Jungk, Robert. "Der Feind ist jetzt die Weltzerstörung." *Tageszeitung,* 14 Jan. 1991.

Kade, Gerhard. *Auseinandersetzung in den USA.* Booklet of the Komitee für Frieden, Abrüstung und Zusammenarbeit [KOFAZ]. Cologne [ca. 1983].

Kelly, Petra. "Reagan als Schirmherr der polnischen Freiheit?" *Blätter für deutsche und internationale Politik* 27, no. 2 (1982): 152–55.

Kelly, Petra, and Gert Bastian. "Ist die Welt verrückt geworden? Die Friedensbewegung macht es sich zu leicht." *Die Zeit,* 8 Feb. 1991.

Kirchenkanzlei der EKD. *Frieden wahren, fördern und erneuern: Eine Denkschrift der Evangelischen Kirche in Deutschland.* Gütersloh: Gütersloher Verlagshaus Gerd Mohn, 1981.

Kirchgäßner, Andreas. "Diskussionsbeitrag: Was heisst 'Graswurzel'?" *Graswurzelrevolution* 34–35 (spring 1978): 16.

Kirchliches Jahrbuch für die Evangelische Kirche in Deutschland, 1945–1960, ed. Joachim Beckmann, vols. 72–87. Gütersloh: C. Bertelsmann Verlag.

Kirchliches Jahrbuch für die Evangelische Kirche in Deutschland, 1961–1977, ed. Gottfried Niemeier, vols. 88–104. Gütersloh: Gütersloher Verlag Gerd Mohn.

Komitee für Frieden, Abrüstung und Zusammenarbeit [KOFAZ]. "Anmerkungen zur gegenwärtigen Diskussion." Brochure. Cologne, n.d.

Komitee für Frieden, Abrüstung und Zusammenarbeit [KOFAZ]. "Diskussionspapier." In *Reader,* ed. Koordinationsausschuß der Friedensbewegung, 51–59. Large booklet. Bonn, 1984.

―――. "Für das einheitliche Handeln der Friedensbewegung im Jahr 1986." In *Reader zur Aktionskonferenz der Friedensbewegung.* Bonn, Feb. 1986.

―――. "Für einen neuen Aufschwung der Friedensbewegung." In the *Rundbrief* of the Komitee für Frieden, Abrüstung und Zusammenarbeit [KOFAZ], Feb. 1985, 1–5.

Kogon, Eugon. "Das Gespenst der deutschen Remilitarisierung." *Frankfurter Hefte* 5, no. 1 (Jan. 1950): 2–3.

―――. "Zehn politische Argumente gegen die atomare Bewaffnung der Bundeswehr." *Frankfurter Hefte* 13, no. 6 (June 1958): 377–79.

"Können Christen mit Kommunisten zusammenarbeiten." *Herder Korrespondenz* 3, no. 6 (Mar. 1949): 279–81.

Koordinationsausschuß der Friedensbewegung. *Rundbrief 6.* Bonn, 1985.

Koordinationsausschuß der Friedensorganisationen, ed. *Aufstehen! Für den Frieden: Friedensdemonstration anläßlich der NATO-Gipfelkonferenz in Bonn am 10.6.1982.* Bornheim-Merten: Lamuv Verlag, 1982.

Koppe, Karl-Heinz. "Eine politische Strategie zur Überwindung der militärischen Sicherheitsgesellschaft." In *Reader zur Strategie-Konferenz "Grosser Ratschlag" der Friedensbewegung,* 67–70. Bonn, 1985.

―――. "Nato-Beschluß—Afghanistan—und wie geht es weiter?" *Neue Gesellschaft* 27, no. 3 (1980): 254–58.

Krell, Gerd. "Die Entwicklung des Sicherheitsbegriffs." *Neue Gesellschaft* 26, no. 10 (Oct. 1979): 906–10.

"Krieg ist kein brauchbares Mittel der Politik." *Evangelischer Pressedienst*, 29 Jan. 1991.

Krumpelt, Ihno. "Braucht Westdeutschland taktische A-Waffen?" *Neue Gesellschaft* 5, no. 1 (1958): 42–47.

"Kundgebung der Synode der EKD." In *Kirchliches Jahrbuch für die Evangelische Kirche in Deutschland, 1952*, ed. Joachim Beckmann, 79:83–85. Gütersloh: C. Bertelsmann Verlag, 1953.

Lang, Michael. "Seid Sand im Getriebe!" *Graswurzelrevolution* 86 (June 1984): 16–17.

Langenbach, Hans Joachim. "Sozialdemokratie und Wehrpolitik." *Neue Gesellschaft* 2, no. 1 (Jan./Feb. 1955): 38–43.

Lutz, Dieter. *Besitzt die Sovietunion in der konventionellen Rüstung eine militärische Überlegenheit?* Booklet of the Jungdemokraten. 6th ed. Düsseldorf: Nordrhein-Westfalen Landesverband, n.d.

———. *Das militärische Kräfteverhältnis im Bereich der euronuclearen Waffensystems.* Bonn: Jungdemokraten, n.d.

———. *Weltkrieg wider Willen? Die Nuklearwaffen in und für Europa.* Reinbek: Rowohlt, 1981.

Markovits, Andrei. "Die Linke gibt es nicht—und es gibt sie doch." *Frankfurter Rundschau*, 7 Mar. 1991.

———. "Eine ernüchternde Erfahrung." *Die Zeit*, 15 Feb. 1991.

Maske, Achim. "Vom Einstieg zum Ausstieg." In the *Rundbrief* of the Koordinierungsausschuss der Friedensbewegung. Bonn, May 1987, 7–10.

———. "Zur politischen Perspektive der Friedensbewegung." Unpublished essay. Photocopy. Cologne, 1984.

Mechtersheimer, Alfred. "Blockiert das Kriegsgebiet!" *Frieden 2000*, 9 Aug. 1992.

Münster, Clemens. "Atomare Verteidigung und christliche Verantwortung." In *Kann der atomare Verteidigungskrieg ein gerechter Krieg sein?*, ed. Karl Forster, 73–105. Munich: Karl Zink Verlag, 1960.

———. "Verantwortlich für Kernwaffen." In *Atomare Kampfmittel und christliche Ethik: Diskussionsbeiträge deutscher Katholiken*, 59–76. Munich: Kösel Verlag, 1960.

Niemöller, Martin. "Zur gegenwärtigen Aufgabe der evangelischen Christenheit, Predigt über 1. Joh. 4, 9–14." In *Kirchliches Jahrbuch für die Evangelische Kirche in Deutschland, 1945–1948*, ed. Joachim Beckmann, 72–75:29–42. Gütersloh: C. Bertelsmann Verlag, 1950.

Ollenhauer, Erich. "Stuttgart—Parteitag der Klärung." *Neue Gesellschaft* 5, no. 3 (1958): 167–71.

Peters, Karl. "Probleme der Atomrüstung." In *Atomare Kampfmittel und christliche Ethik: Diskussionsbeiträge deutscher Katholiken*, 40–59. Munich: Kösel Verlag, 1960.

Picht, Werner. "Staatsbürger in Uniform?" *Neue Gesellschaft* 2, no. 2 (Mar./Apr. 1955): 53–61.

"Plädoyer für eine Erneuerung: Offner Brief der Bürgerbewegung 'Bündnis '90' an die Friedensbewegung." *Tageszeitung,* 29 Aug. 1992.

Politbarometer (BPA), 2 June 1987.

Präses der Evangelischen Kirche von Westfalen. Speech at the Männertag in Dortmund, 23 Sept. 1951. In *Kirchliches Jahrbuch für die Evangelische Kirche in Deutschland, 1951,* ed. Joachim Beckmann, 78:159–70. Gütersloh: C. Bertelsmann Verlag, 1952.

Präsidium der VVN—Bund der Antifascisten, eds. *Antifascistischer Jugenddienst—Informationen für Jugendpresse.* No. 2, Frankfurt, 1984.

Präsidium der VVN—Bund der Antifascisten, eds. *Pershing II und Cruise Missiles—Stück für Stück in die USA zurück.* Leaflet. Frankfurt, 1984.

Pro Ökumene/Ohne Rüstung Leben, eds. *Ohne Rüstung leben.* Gütersloh: Gütersloher Verlagshaus Gerd Mohn, 1983.

Rantzau, Johann Albrecht von. "Zweiseitige Pakte und deutsche Mittellage." *Neue Gesellschaft* 2, no. 1 (Jan./Feb. 1955): 10–15.

"Ratschlag zur gesetzlichen Regelung des Schutzes der Kriegsdienstverweigerer." In *Kirchliches Jahrbuch für die Evangelische Kirche in Deutschland, 1955,* ed. Joachim Beckmann, 82:72–77. Gütersloh: C. Bertelsmann Verlag, 1956.

Reader zur Strategie-Konferenz "Grosser Ratschlag" der Friedensbewegung, ed. Koordinierungsausschuss der Friedensbewegung. Bonn, 1985.

Richter, Horst-Eberhard. "Warum schweigt die Friedensbewegung?" *Frankfurter Rundschau,* 20 Aug. 1992.

———. "Wo bleibt die Scham?" *Frankfurter Rundschau,* 27 Nov. 1990.

"Rundschreiben des Evangelischen Oberkirchenrat in Stuttgart." In *Kirchliches Jahrbuch für die Evangelische Kirche in Deutschland, 1959,* ed. Joachim Beckmann, 86:94. Gütersloh: Gütersloher Verlagshaus Gerd Mohn, 1960.

Senghaas, Dieter. "Wie Gewaltfreiheit den Aggressor begünstigt." *Frankfurter Allgemeine Zeitung,* 7 July 1993.

"Stellungnahme des Theologischen Konvents der Bekenntnisgemeinschaft der Evangelisch-lutherischen Landeskirche Hannovers zu der Flugschrift 'An die Gewehre? Nein.' " In *Kirchliches Jahrbuch für die Evangelische Kirche in Deutschland, 1950,* ed. Joachim Beckmann, 77:196–210. Gütersloh: C. Bertelsmann Verlag, 1951.

Strässer, Christoph. "Jetzt wichtiger denn je: Frieden durch Abrüstung." *Blätter für deutsche und internationale Politik* 27, no. 2 (1982): 162–64.

Stuby, Gerhard. *Vom Gleichgewicht des Schreckens zur gleichen Sicherheit.* Booklet of the Komitee für Frieden, Abrüstung und Zusammenarbeit [KOFAZ]. Cologne, n.d.

Thompson, Edward. "'Exterminismus' als letztes Stadium der Zivilization." In *Entrüstet Euch,* by Die Grünen, 30–51. Bonn, 1983.

Trautmann, Dieter. "Soziale Verteidigung als Alternative zur militärischen Verteidigung." In *Entrüstet Euch,* by Die Grünen, 128–37. Bonn, 1983.

Trittin, Jürgen. "Grüne Aussenpolitik jenseits von Pazifismus und Bellizismus." *Frankfurter Rundschau,* 23 Sept. 1992.

"Tübinger Memorandum." In *Kirchliches Jahrbuch für die Evangelische Kirche in*

Deutschland, 1962, ed. Gottfried Niemeier, 89:75–78. Gütersloh: Gütersloher Verlagshaus Gerd Mohn, 1964.

" 'Unser Weg zu Abrüstung und Frieden.' Beschluss zur Friedens- und Sicherheitspolitik der SPD, Parteitag in Nürnberg, 25.–29.8. 1986." In *Politik: Informationsdienst der SPD* 8 (Sept. 1986): 2–8.

Vilmar, Fritz. "Die UN müssen zur Friedensmacht werden." *Frankfurter Rundschau,* 2 Sept. 1992.

Voigt, Karsten. "Bekenntnisse zur Politikunfähigkeit, Anmerkungen zu sicherheitspolitischen Vorstellungen der Grünen." *Sozialdemokratischer Pressedienst,* Dec. 2, 1987.

———. "Dem Frieden dienen und die Abrüstung fördern." *Frankfurter Allgemeine Zeitung,* Jan. 9, 1985.

———. "Erweiterung der Konzeption des militärischen Gleichgewichts." *Neue Gesellschaft* 27, no. 11 (1980): 956–63.

———. "Riskien neuer Waffentechnologien." *Neue Gesellschaft* 26, no. 2 (1979): 98–102.

———. "Von der Konfrontation zur Sicherheitspartnershaft." *Neue Gesellschaft* 29, no. 4 (1982): 310–15.

Vorstand der SPD. *Außerordentlicher Parteitag der Sozialdemokratischen Partei Deutschlands vom 16. bis 18. April 1969 in der Stadthalle zu Bad Godesberg: Protokoll der Verhandlungen, Anträge.* Bonn: Neuer Vorwärts Verlag, 1969.

———. *Parteitag der Sozialdemokratischen Partei Deutschlands vom 11. bis 14. Mai in Saarbrücken: Protokoll der Verhandlungen, angenommene und überwiesene Anträge.* Bonn: Neuer Vorwärts Verlag, 1970.

———. *Parteitag der Sozialdemokratischen Partei Deutschlands vom 10. bis 14. April 1973, Protokoll der Verhandlungen.* N.p., 1973.

———. *Parteitag der Sozialdemokratischen Partei Deutschlands vom 11. bis 15. November 1975 in Rosengarten Mannheim: Protokoll der Verhandlungen.* Mannheim: Südwestdeutsche Verlagsanstalt, 1975.

———. *Parteitag der Sozialdemokratischen Partei Deutschlands vom 15. bis 19. November 1977 in Hamburg.* Bonn: Verlag Neuer Vorwärts, 1977.

———. *Parteitag der Sozialdemokratischen Partei Deutschlands vom 23. bis 27. November 1964 in Karlsruhe: Protokoll der Verhandlungen und Anträge.* Bonn: Neuer Vorwärts-Verlag, 1964.

———. *Protokoll: Außerordentlicher Parteitag der Sozialdemokratischen Partei Deutschlands vom 18. bis 21. 1983 in Köln.* Bonn: Neuer Vorwärts Verlag, 1983.

———. *Protokoll: Außerordentlicher Parteitag der SPD, Dortmund, Westfalenhalle, 18./19. Juni.* Bonn: Neuer Vorwärts-Verlag, 1976.

———. *Protokoll der Verhandlungen des Parteitages der Sozialdemokratischen Partei Deutschlands.* N.p., 1956.

———. *Protokoll der Verhandlungen und Anträge vom Parteitag der Sozialdemokratischen Partei Deutschlands in Hannover, 21. bis 25. November 1960.* Bonn: Neuer Vorwärts-Verlag, 1960.

———. *Protokoll der Verhandlungen und Anträge vom Parteitag der*

Sozialdemokratischen Partei Deutschlands in Köln vom 26. bis 30. Mai 1962.
Bonn: Neuer Vorwärts-Verlag, 1962.

———. *Protokoll der Verhandlungen des Parteitags der Sozialdemokratischen Partei Deutschlands vom 18. bis 23. Mai in Stuttgart.* Hannover-Bonn: Neuer Vorwärtsverlag, 1958.

———. *Protokoll der Verhandlungen des Parteitages der Sozialdemokratischen Partei Deutschlands vom 20. bis 24. Juli, 1954 in Berlin.* N.p., 1954.

———. *Protokoll: Parteitag der Sozialdemokratischen Partei Deutschlands vom 3. bis zum 10. Dezember 1979, Berlin.* Bonn: Neuer Vorwärts Verlag, 1979.

———. *Protokoll: Parteitag der Sozialdemokratischen Partei Deutschlands, 19. bis 23. April 1982 in München.* Bonn: Neuer Vorwärts Verlag, 1982.

———, ed. *Deutschlandplan der SPD—Kommentare, Argumente, Begründungen.* Booklet. Bonn: N.p., Apr. 1959.

"Was haben wir Christen in Westdeutschland heute für die Erhaltung des Friedens zu tun?" In *Kirchliches Jahrbuch für die Evangelische Kirche in Deutschland, 1953,* ed. Joachim Beckmann, 80:34–38. Gütersloh: C. Bertelsmann Verlag, 1954.

"Was heisst 'graswurzelrevolution'?" *Graswurzelrevolution* 7 (winter 1974): 3–4.

"Wehrbeitrag und christliches Gewissen." In *Kirchliches Jahrbuch für die Evangelische Kirche in Deutschland, 1952,* ed. Joachim Beckmann, 79:14–17. Gütersloh: C. Bertelsmann Verlag, 1953.

Weiss, Konrad. "Die Versäumnisse der Friedensbewegung." *Bild am Sonntag,* 27 Jan. 1991.

Witt, Gregor. "Null-Lösung—Anfang einer neuen Politik?" In the *Rundbrief* of the Koordinierungsausschuss der Friedensbewegung, May 1987, 3–6.

Wolf, Frieder. "Ein nüchterner Pazifismus ist immer noch angesagt." *Tageszeitung,* 22 Aug. 1992.

"Wort an die Pfarrer." In *Kirchliches Jahrbuch für die Evangelische Kirche in Deutschland 1945–1948,* ed. Joachim Beckmann, 72–75:4–7. Gütersloh: C. Bertelsmann Verlag, 1950.

"Wort der Evangelischen Kirche in Deutschland zum Frieden." In *Kirchliches Jahrbuch für die Evangelische Kirche in Deutschland, 1945–1948,* ed. Joachim Beckmann, 72–75:185–86. Gütersloh: C. Bertelsmann Verlag, 1950.

"Wort der Synode der EKiD an die Gemeinden in Ost und West, Espelkamp, 11.3.1955." In *Kirchliches Jahrbuch für die Evangelische Kirche in Deutschland, 1955,* ed. Joachim Beckmann, 82:47–49. Gütersloh: C. Bertelsmann Verlag, 1956.

"Wort des Rates der EKiD und der Kirchenkonferenz 'Um die Wiedervereinigung des deutschen Volkes,' 2.2.1955." In *Kirchliches Jahrbuch für die Evangelische Kirche in Deutschland, 1955,* ed. Joachim Beckmann, 82:15. Gütersloh: C. Bertelsmann Verlag, 1956.

Wünsch, Georg. "Deutschland und Europa." *Neue Gesellschaft* 2, no. 3 (May/June 1955): 51–54.

"Zur aktuellen Friedensdiskussion: Eine Stellungnahme des Zentralkomitees der deutschen Katholiken." *Herder Korrespondenz* 35, no. 12 (Dec. 1981): 624–30.

Newspaper Articles

"Affären wie in Kiel auch anderswo möglich?" *Der Spiegel*, 2 Nov. 1987.

"Angst vor einem Krieg am Golf." *Süddeutsche Zeitung*, 28 Aug. 1990.

"Auf der Suche nach einem neuen Profil." *Deutsches Allgemeines Sonntagsblatt*, 8 May 1988.

"Ausschuß der Friedensbewegung denkt über seine Zukunft nach." *Frankfurter Rundschau*, 1 July 1989.

"Bonn Cautions Antiwar Protestors against Anti-Americanism." *The Week in Germany*, 25 Jan. 1991.

"Bonn für europäische Friedenstruppe, aber ohne deutsche Soldaten." *Deutschland Nachrichten*, 20 Sept. 1991.

"Bundesluftwaffe beteiligt sich an den Hilfsmassnahmen für Flüchtlinge aus Ruanda." *Süddeutsche Zeitung*, 18 July 1994.

"Bundesregierung soll 'Countdown des Todes' am Golf stoppen." *Frankfurter Rundschau*, 9 Jan. 1991.

"Bundestag Approves German Monitoring of UN Embargo." *The Week in Germany*, 24 July 1992.

"Bundestag Approves Somalia Mission for German Armed Forces." *The Week in Germany*, 23 Apr. 1993.

"Bundestag billigt mit grosser Mehrheit Einsätze der Bundeswehr in der Adria und in AWACS-Flugzeugen." *Süddeutsche Zeitung*, 23 July 1994.

"Bundestag muss Entsendung der Bundeswehr zustimmen." *Süddeutsche Zeitung*, 13 July 1994.

"Coalition Decides to Expand Participation in Bosnian Airdrop and Serbian Embargo; Agrees to Disagree in Awacs Conflict." *The Week in Germany*, 26 Mar. 1993.

"Court Rules German Constitution Allows Sending Troops Abroad." *Washington Post*, 13 July 1994.

"Das Bundeswehr-Kontingent in Somalia wird verkleinert." *Frankfurter Allgemeine Zeitung*, 20 Nov. 1993.

"Das Kreuz da oben: Wie sich Menschen im Hunsrück gegen die Raketenstationierung wehren." *Die Zeit*, 28 Mar. 1986.

"Dem Pazifismus 'gewaltfrei die Luft abdrehen.' " *Tageszeitung*, 30 Aug. 1990.

"Dem Westen Wege weisen." *Frankfurter Allgemeine Zeitung*, 7 Feb. 1991.

"Der Friedensdemo fehlt das Feindbild." *Stuttgarter Nachrichten*, 15 June 1987.

"Der politische Druck auf die SPD wird stärker." *Süddeutsche Zeitung*, 7 Aug. 1992.

"Der Streit um die Bundeswehreinsätze geht weiter." *Frankfurter Allgemeine Zeitung*, 27 July 1993.

"Deutsche Soldaten nach Sarajevo: 73% sind dafür." *Bild am Sonntag*, 19 July 1992.

"Deutsche wollen sich bei internationalen Konflikten heraushalten." *Frankfurter Rundschau*, 4 Jan. 1991.

"DGB-Chef Schulte gegen Bundeswehr-Kampfeinsätze." *Süddeutsche Zeitung*, 20 July 1994.

"Die Friedensbewegung in der Sinnkrise." *Tageszeitung*, 5 July 1989.

"Die 'Friedensbewegung' über die Blockadefrage zerstritten." *Frankfurter Allgemeine Zeitung*, 5 Aug. 1986.

"Die Friedensdemonstranten fühlen sich mehr den je bestätigt." *Stuttgarter Zeitung*, 15 June 1987.

"Die Kinder des Friedens." *Die Zeit*, 25 Jan. 1991.

"Die Popularität der Regierung nimmt zu." *Süddeutsche Zeitung*, 24 Apr. 1993.

"Die Sorge um die Glaubwürdigkeit der Vereinten Nationen." *Frankfurter Allgemeine Zeitung*, 14 May 1993.

"Die SPD weiter gegen Kampfeinsätze." *Frankfurter Allgemeine Zeitung*, 19 Nov. 1993.

"Die UNO muss das Zentrum einer neuen Weltordnung sein." *Frankfurter Rundschau*, 27 May 1991.

"Dissens in der Bonner Koalition." *Süddeutsche Zeitung*, 18 July 1994.

"Einäugige Marschierer." *Augsburger Allgemeine*, 5 Apr. 1988.

"Emnid-Umfrage." *Fernseh- und Hörfunkspiegel*, 21 June 1993.

"Ende einer Bewegungsära amtlich." *Tageszeitung*, 3 Oct. 1989.

"Es geht jetzt um das Wie einer Intervention: Die Grüne Europaabgeordnete Claudia Roth." *Tageszeitung*, 19 Aug. 1992.

"Es macht wenig Sinn, hier gegen die Kämpfe zu demonstrieren." *Rhein-Sieg-Anzeiger*, 8 Aug. 1992.

"FDP-Wähler wollen Schäuble." *Der Spiegel*, 29 June 1992.

"Fifty-eight percent gegen Raketen." *Tageszeitung*, 19 June 1984.

"Fischer fordert Solidarität mit Israel." *Süddeutsche Zeitung*, 26 Jan. 1991.

"Forderungen nach Abzug aus Somalia." *Süddeutsche Zeitung*, 9 Oct. 1993.

"Friedensbewegung blockiert nur sich." *Tageszeitung*, 13 Aug. 1986.

"Friedensgruppen wollen die 'Petersburger Wende' aufhalten." *Frankfurter Allgemeine Zeitung*, 19 Sept. 1992.

"Friedenskonferenz fehlt Orientierung." *Tageszeitung*, 30 Nov. 1987.

Fuhr, Eckhard. "Ortsverein und Weltfrieden." *Frankfurter Allgemeine Zeitung*, 11 May 1991.

"Furcht vor Öl in Flammen." *Der Spiegel*, 28 Jan. 1991.

"Gefühl der Wut." *Der Spiegel*, 22 Feb. 1993.

"German Mission to Somalia Does Not Violate the Basic Law, Constitutional Court Says." *The Week in Germany*, 25 June 1993.

"Germany to Participate in Military Enforcement of Bosnia Flight Ban." *The Week in Germany*, 9 Apr. 1993.

Geschke, Günter. "Nicht alles war falsch." *Deutsches Allgemeines Sonntagsblatt*, 15 Feb. 1991.

"Governing Coalition Seeks German Involvement in UN 'Blue Helmet' Operations." *The Week in Germany*, 15 Jan. 1993.

"Grossaktion gegen Manöver bleibt umstritten." *Tageszeitung*, 7 May 1984.

"Grüne Aussenpolitik aus dem Bauch." *Tageszeitung*, 20 Aug. 1992.

"Grüne Aussenpolitik jenseits von Pazifismus und Bellizismus." *Frankfurter Rundschau,* 23 Sept. 1992.

"Grüne lehnen jeden Militäreinsatz ab, Pazifisten setzen sich durch." *Süddeutsche Zeitung,* 11 Oct. 1993.

Hartung, Klaus. "Zweites München für Hussein?" *Tageszeitung,* 29 Jan. 1991.

"Hass im Kriegsgebiet abbauen." *Frankfurter Rundschau,* 30 July 1992.

Hefty, Georg Paul. "Die Überlebens-Parole eint nicht mehr." *Frankfurter Allgemeine Zeitung,* 8 Apr. 1982.

" 'Heiliger Georg, wir harren der letzten Ölung.' " *Tageszeitung,* 14 Jan. 1991.

Huber, Ellis. "Appel an alle: Krieg verhindern." *Volksblatt Berlin,* 12 Jan. 1991.

" 'Ich verstehe nichts von Jugoslawien.' " *Tageszeitung,* 22 Feb. 1993.

"Infas-Umfrage zum Blauhelm-Einsatz der Bundeswehr in Somalia." *Fernseh- und Hörfunkspiegel,* 17 May 1993.

Janssen, Karl-Heinz. "Ein klares Wort zu Polen." *Die Zeit,* 12 Feb. 1982.

"Je grosser die Ratlosigheit, desto länger der Text." *Frankfurter Rundschau,* 30 Nov. 1987.

"Kampagne gegen neue Nachrüstung." *Tageszeitung,* 22 Mar. 1989.

"Kampf um einen geordneten Rückzug." *Süddeutsche Zeitung,* 16 Nov. 1993.

"Kampfabstimmung in der Friedensbewegung." *Frankfurter Allgemeine Zeitung,* 3 Oct. 1984.

"Karlsruhe erlaubt UNO-Kampfeinsätze der Bundeswehr." *Süddeutsche Zeitung,* 13 July 1994.

"Keine geschlossene Menschenkette." *Süddeutsche Zeitung,* 22 Oct. 1984.

"Keine Mehrheit für 'Raus aus der NATO.' " *Tageszeitung,* 7 May 1984.

"Keine Spaltung, sondern ein Lernprozeß." *Frankfurter Rundschau,* 25 Jan. 1991.

"Kinkel appelliert an Serbien: Gewalt in Bosnien beenden." *Deutschland Nachrichten,* 12 June 1992.

"Klose: Die Bundeswehr soll an allen Massnahmen unter Kommando der Vereinten Nationen teilnehmen." *Süddeutsche Zeitung,* 24 Aug. 1993.

Köcher, Renate. "Breite Mehrheit für Blauhelm-Einsätze deutscher Soldaten." *Frankfurter Allgemeine Zeitung,* 11 Feb. 1993.

Köhler, Ernst. "Publikumsbeschimpfung: Wer auf militärisches Eingreifen verzichtet handelt verantwortungslos." *Tageszeitung,* 25 Sept. 1992.

Kostede, Norbert. "Hoffen auf die heile Welt." *Die Zeit,* 19 Oct. 1990.

"Lafontaine fordert einseitige Abrüstung." *Saarbrücker Zeitung,* 24 Oct. 1984.

"Länderrat der Grünen rüttelt am Grundsatz Gewaltfreiheit." *Frankfurter Rundschau,* 14 June 1993.

Lerch, Wolfgang. "In Somalia bleibt viel zu tun." *Frankfurter Allgemeine Zeitung,* 14 Oct. 1993.

"Mehrheit für Volksbefragung." *Tageszeitung,* 13 Feb. 1984.

"Meinungsreport." *Fernseh- und Hörfunkspiegel,* 8 Feb. 1991.

"Militärs bremsen Politiker." *Frankfurter Rundschau,* 12 Aug. 1992.

"Mit Ostermarsch gegen Tiefflüge." *Frankfurter Rundschau,* 28 Mar. 1989.

Müller-Vogg, Hugo. "Schwierigkeiten mit der Friedenspolitik." *Frankfurter Allgemeine Zeitung,* 17 Oct. 1981.

———. "Der DGB im Sog der Friedensbewegung." *Frankfurter Allgemeine Zeitung*, 29 June 1982.

"Nach dem Mord in Phnom Penh nimmt die Debatte über deutsche Soldaten in Somalia an Heftigkeit zu." *Frankfurter Allgemeine Zeitung*, 16 Oct. 1993.

"Nachdenken in der SPD." *Frankfurter Allgemeine Zeitung*, 25 Jan. 1991.

"Neue Liebe zwischen Russen und Deutschen." *Stern*, 1 June 1989.

"Number of Conscientious Objectors Doubled in 1991." *The Week in Germany*, 31 Jan. 1992.

"Number of Conscientious Objectors Rose Sharply in 1991." *The Week in Germany*, 19 July 1991.

"Nun siegt mal schön." *Der Spiegel*, 18 July 1994.

"Offener Brief." *Tageszeitung*, 16 June 1987.

"Pazifismus trotz aller Nöte." *Frankfurter Rundschau*, 22 Mar. 1993.

"Politbarometer für Februar." *Fernseh- und Hörfunkspiegel*, 19 Feb. 1991.

Prantl, Heribert. "Wir können—aber: sollen wir." *Süddeutsche Zeitung*, 13 July 1994.

"Professoren-Appell an USA." *Frankfurter Rundschau*, 12 Dec. 1990.

"Quo vadis, Friedensbewegung." *Tageszeitung*, 10 Feb. 1982.

"Ratlose Friedensbewegung." *Berliner Zeitung*, 22 Feb. 1993.

Rauch, Renate. "Die reagieren wie früher." *Die Zeit*, 1 Mar. 1991.

Roitsch, Jutta. "Der Haß auf alles Kommunistische sitzt tief." *Frankfurter Rundschau*, 19 Nov. 1981.

"Rühe Calls for German Participation in UN Military Operations, 'Solidarity Pact' with Eastern Europe." *The Week in Germany*, 19 Feb. 1993.

Schmid, Thomas. "Blockierte Debatte." *Tageszeitung*, 22 Feb. 1993.

Schröder, Dieter. "Germans to the Front." *Süddeutsche Zeitung*, 23 July 1994.

Sieber, Ursel. "Keine Mehrheit für 'Raus aus der NATO.' " *Tageszeitung*, 7 May 1984.

"Sollen deutsche Soldaten im ehemaligen Jugoslawien eingreifen?" *Fernseh- und Hörfunkspiegel*, 11 Feb. 1993.

"Somalia-Einsatz der Bundeswehr nach Zusammenstössen in Mogadischu wieder umstritten." *Deutschland Nachrichten*, 11 June 1993.

"SPD: Kriege wie am Golf bleiben tabu." *Süddeutsche Zeitung*, 15 July 1994.

"SPD fordert Abzug der Bundeswehr." *Süddeutsche Zeitung*, 8 Oct. 1993.

"SPD nennt Bedingungen für Eingreiftruppe." *Tageszeitung*, 7 Aug. 1992.

"SPD ruft zur Teilnahme an Friedensdemonstrationen auf." *Hannoversche Allgemeine*, 11 Sept. 1984.

"SPD-Aufruf zur Beteiligung an den Ostermärschen." *PPP*, 1 Mar. 1987.

"SPD-Chef Scharping strebt Kompromiß über UNO-Einsätze der Bundeswehr an." *Süddeutsche Zeitung*, 14 Aug. 1993.

"SPD-Führung hält an restriktivem Kurs bei UNO-Einsätzen der Bundeswehr fest." *Süddeutsche Zeitung*, 25 Aug. 1993.

"SPD-Landesparteitag stimmt gegen Blauhelme." *Süddeutsche Zeitung*, 13 Sept. 1993.

"SPD-Prominenz als ungeliebte Glieder einer Kette." *Die Welt*, 23 Oct. 1984.

"SPD-Spitze für Teilnahme an UNO-Einsätzen 'ohne Vorbehalt.' " *Süddeutsche Zeitung*, 10 Aug. 1993.

"SPD-Streit um Aussenpolitik dauert an." *Frankfurter Allgemeine Zeitung*, 15 May 1991.

"Steuerlüge empört Mehrheit." *Der Spiegel*, 11 Mar. 1991.

"Streit um Kampfeinsätze der Bundeswehr spaltet die SPD." *Die Welt*, 10 Aug. 1992.

"Two Hundred Thousand Protest War in Bonn." *The Week in Germany*, 1 Feb. 1991.

". . . um zu zeigen, dass die Friedensbewegung lebt und wächst." *Frankfurter Rundschau*, 25 Apr. 1984.

"UN-Beschluss skeptisch beurteilt." *Frankfurter Rundschau*, 17 Aug. 1992.

"Verheugen: SPD muss ihre Haltung ändern." *Frankfurter Allgemeine Zeitung*, 9 Aug. 1993.

Volmer, Ludger. "Bosnien und der Pazifismus." *Tageszeitung*, 5 Sept. 1992.

"Verraten und verkauft." *Berliner Zeitung*, 10 Aug. 1992.

"Was die Bundesbürger von einem Krieg am Golf halten." *Fernseh- und Hörfunkspiegel*, 16 Jan. 1990.

"Wenn das Gefühl der Bedrohung schwindet." *Frankfurter Allgemeine Zeitung*, 22 July 1988.

"Wenn Einigkeit zu teuer wird." *Deutsches Allgemeines Sonntagsblatt*, 1 Apr. 1984.

"Wie stehen die Deutschen zum Golfkrieg?" *Fernseh- und Hörfunkspiegel*, 11 Feb. 1991.

"Wird der 'Friedensherbst' zur Pleite?" *Mannheimer Morgen*, 17 Sept. 1984.

"ZDF-Politbarometer." *Fernseh- und Hörfunkspiegel*, 29 Jan. 1991.

"Zur Hilfe verpflichtet." *Der Spiegel*, 26 Apr. 1993.

"Zurück zur Politik." *Frankfurter Allgemeine Zeitung*, 18 Sept. 1993.

"Zweifel in der SPD am Parteitagsbeschluß zu Blauhelmen." *Frankfurter Allgemeine Zeitung*, 10 Aug. 1993.

"Zweiter Bundeswehrverband in Somalia." *Süddeutsche Zeitung*, 30 July 1993.

"Zwischen Fundamentalismus und halbem Realismus, der SPD-Aussenpolitiker Karsten Voigt beschäftigt sich mit der Friedenspolitik der Grünen." *Tageszeitung*, 16 Oct. 1989.

"Zwischen Parteitagsbeschluß und Kurswechsel." *Frankfurter Allgemeine Zeitung*, 18 Aug. 1993.

Secondary Sources: Books and Academic Articles

Almond, Gabriel, and Sidney Verba. *The Civic Culture: Political Attitudes and Democracy in Five Nations*. Boston: Little, Brown and Company, 1965.

Arend, Peter. *Die innerparteiliche Entwicklung der SPD 1966–1975*. Bonn: Eichholz Verlag, 1975.

Asmus, Ronald. *German Unification and Its Ramifications*. R-4021-A. Santa Monica: Rand, 1991.

———. *Germany after the Gulf War*. N-3391-AF. Santa Monica: Rand, 1992.

Baker, Kendall, Russell Dalton, and Kai Hildebrandt. *Germany Transformed: Political Culture and the New Politics.* Cambridge, Mass.: Harvard University Press, 1981.

Balsen, Werner, and Karl Rössel. *Hoch die internationale Solidarität: Zur Geschichte der Dritte Welt-Bewegung in der Bundesrepublik.* Cologne: Kölner Volksblatt Verlag, 1986.

Baring, Arnulf. *Aussenpolitik in Adenauers Kanzlerdemokratie: Bonns Beitrag zur Europäischen Verteidigungsgemeinschaft.* Munich: Oldenbourg Verlag, 1969.

Bark, Dennis, and David Gress. *A History of West Germany.* Vols. 1 and 2. Oxford: Blackwell, 1989.

Barnes, Samuel, Max Kaase, et al. *Political Action: Mass Participation in Five Western Democracies.* Beverly Hills, Calif.: Sage Publications, 1979.

Bauss, Gerhard. *Die Studentenbewegung der sechziger Jahre in der Bundesrepublik und Westberlin.* Cologne: Pahl-Rugenstein, 1977.

Benedict, Hans-Jürgen. "Auf dem Weg zur Friedenskirche?" In *Die neue Friedensbewegung,* ed. Reiner Steinweg, 227–44. Frankfurt: Suhrkamp Verlag, 1982.

Borm, William. "Frieden ist machbar—wir mischen uns ein!" In *Frieden in Deutschland,* ed. Hans Pestalozzi et al., 82–87. Munich: Wilhelm Goldmann Verlag, 1982.

Boutwell, Jeffrey. *The German Nuclear Dilemma.* London: Brassey's, 1990.

———. "Politics and Ideology of SPD Security Policies." In *The Silent Partner: West Germany and Arms Control,* ed. Barry Blechman and Cathleen Fischer, 129–66. Cambridge, Mass.: Ballinger Publishing Company, 1988.

Brand, Karl-Werner. *Neue soziale Bewegungen: Entstehung, Funktion und Perspektive neuer Protestpotentiale.* Opladen: Westdeutscher Verlag, 1982.

Brand, Karl-Werner, Detlef Büsser, and Dieter Rucht. *Aufbruch in eine andere Gesellschaft: Neue Soziale Bewegungen in der Bundesrepublik.* Frankfurt: Campus Verlag, 1983.

Braunthal, Gerard. "West German Unions and Disarmament." *Political Science Quarterly* 73, no. 1 (1958): 82–99.

Brinton, Crane. *The Anatomy of Revolution.* New York: Knopf, 1965.

Brockett, Charles. "The Structure of Political Opportunities and Peasant Mobilization in Central America." *Comparative Politics* 23, no. 3 (1991): 253–74.

Burns, Rob, and Wilfried van der Will. *Protest and Democracy in West Germany.* New York: St. Martin's Press, 1988.

Buro, Andreas. "Skizze zum gesellschaftlichen Hintergrund der gegenwärtigen Parlamentarismusdebatte." In *Parlamentarisches Ritual und politische Alternativen,* ed. Roland Roth, 43–74. Frankfurt: Campus Verlag, 1980.

Butterwegge, Christoph, and Heinz-Gerd Hofschen. *Sozialdemokratie, Krieg und Frieden: Die Stellung der SPD zur Friedensfrage von den Anfängen bis zur Gegenwart.* Heilbronn: Distel Verlag, 1984.

Chandler, William. "Party System Transformations in the Federal Republic of Germany." In *Parties and Party Systems in Liberal Democracies,* ed. Steven Wolinetz, 59–83. New York: Routledge, 1988.

Childs, David. *From Schumacher to Brandt: The Story of German Socialism 1945–1965.* Oxford: Pergamon Press, 1966.

Cioc, Marc. *Pax Atomica: The Nuclear Defense Debate in West Germany during the Adenauer Era.* New York: Columbia University Press, 1988.

Clemens, Clay. "Opportunity or Obligation? Redefining Germany's Military Role outside of NATO." *Armed Forces and Society* 19, no. 2 (winter 1993): 231–51.

———. "A Special Kind of Superpower? Germany and the Demilitarization of post-Cold War International Security." In *Germany in a New Era,* ed. Gary Geipel, 199–240. Indianapolis: Hudson Institute, 1993.

Conti, Christoph. *Abschied vom Bürgertum: Alternative Bewegungen von 1890 bis heute.* Reinbek: Rowohlt, 1984.

Conway, John. "The German Church Struggle: Its Making and Meaning." In *The Church Confronts the Nazis: Barmen Then and Now,* ed. Hubert Locke, 93–145. New York: Edwin Mellen Press, 1984.

Cooper, Alice, and Klaus Eichner. "The West German Peace Movement." In *International Peace Movements,* ed. Bert Klandermans, 149–171. Greenwich, Conn.: JAI Press, 1992.

Costain, Anne. *Inviting Women's Rebellion: A Political Process Interpretation of the Women's Movement.* Baltimore: Johns Hopkins University Press, 1992.

Craig, Gordon. *The Germans.* New York: Oxford University Press, 1978.

Dalton, Russell. *Citizen Politics in Western Democracies: Public Opinion and Political Parties in the United States, Great Britain, West Germany, and France.* Chatham, N.J.: Chatham House Publishers, 1988.

Dalton, Russell, and Manfred Kuechler, eds. *Challenging the Political Order: New Social and Political Movements in Western Democracies.* Oxford: Polity Press, 1990.

Deutsch, Karl, and Lewis Edinger. *Germany Rejoins the Powers.* Stanford: Stanford University Press, 1959.

Dietzfelbinger, Eckart. *Die westdeutsche Friedensbewegung 1948–1955: Die Protestaktionen gegen die Remilitarisierung der Bundesrepublik Deutschland.* Cologne: Pahl-Rugenstein, 1984.

Diner, Dan. "Die 'nationale Frage' in der Friedensbewegung." In *Die neue Friedensbewegung: Analysen aus der Friedensforschung,* ed. Reiner Steinweg, 86–112. Frankfurt: Suhrkamp Verlag, 1982.

Doering-Manteuffel, Anselm. *Katholizismus und Wiederbewaffnung: Die Haltung der deutschen Katholiken gegenüber der Wehrfrage 1948–1955.* Mainz: Matthias-Grünewald-Verlag, 1981.

Dohse, Rainer. *Der Dritte Weg: Neutralitätsbestrebungen in Westdeutschland zwischen 1945 und 1955.* Hamburg: Holsten Verlag, 1974.

Donsbach, Wolfgang, Hans Matthias Kepplinger, and Elisabeth Noelle-Neumann. "West Germans' Perceptions of NATO and the Warsaw Pact: Long-Term Content Analysis of *Der Spiegel,* and Trends in Public Opinion." In *Debating National Security: The Public Dimension,* ed. Hans Rattinger and Don Munton, 239–68. Frankfurt: Peter Lang, 1991.

Doormann, Lottemi. "Die Frauenbewegung und die Linke." In *Die Linke: Bilanz und Perspektiven für die 80er Jahre,* ed. Hermann Gremliza and Heinrich Hannover, 80–95. Hamburg: VSA-Verlag, 1980.

Downs, Anthony. "Up and Down with Ecology—the 'Issue-Attention Cycle.' " *Public Interest* 28 (summer 1972): 38–50.

Drummond, Gordon. *The German Social Democrats in Opposition, 1949–1960: The Case Against Rearmament.* Norman, Okla.: University of Oklahoma Press, 1982.

Duffield, John. "German Security Policy after Unification: Sources of Continuity and Restraint." *Contemporary Security Policy* 15, no. 3 (Dec. 1994): 172–98.

Dyllick, Joachim, Lutz Mez, and Werner Sewing. "Gewerkschaften contra Bürgerinitiativen: Mißverständnisse oder Unvereinbarkeiten in der Atompolitik?" In *Die eigentliche Kernspaltung: Gewerkschaften und Bürgerinitiativen im Streit um die Atomkraft,* ed. Jörg Hallerback, 68–95. Darmstadt: Luchterhand, 1978.

Edinger, Lewis. *Kurt Schumacher: A Study in Personality and Political Behavior.* Stanford: Stanford University Press, 1965.

Eichborn, Wolfgang von. "Politisierung der Kriegsdienstverweigerung." In *Konflikte zwischen Wehrdienst und Friedensdiensten,* ed. U. Duchrow and Gerta Scharffenorth, 147–77. Stuttgart: Ernst Klett Verlag, 1970.

Eichenberg, Richard. *Public Opinion and National Security in Western Europe.* Ithaca: Cornell University Press, 1989.

Enders, Thomas. *Die SPD und die äußere Sicherheit: Zum Wandel der sicherheitspolitischen Konzeption der Partei in der Zeit der Regierungsverantwortung.* Melle: Verlag Ernst Knoth, 1987.

Erb, Gottfried. "Das 'Bensberger Memorandum'/Geschichte und erste Stellungnahmen." *Frankfurter Hefte* 23, no. 4 (Apr. 1968): 219–21.

Ericksen, Robert P. "The Barmen Synod and Its Declaration: A Historical Synopsis." In *The Church Confronts the Nazis: Barmen Then and Now,* ed. Hubert Locke, 27–93. New York: Edwin Mellen Press, 1984.

Eyerman, Ron, and Andrew Jamison. *Social Movements: A Cognitive Approach.* University Park: Pennsylvania State University Press, 1991.

Feld, Werner. "Aufrüstung und europäisch-amerikanische Spannungen—bricht die Allianz zusammen?" *Journal für Sozialforschung* 3 (1984): 293–312.

Fichter, Tilman, and Siegward Lönnendonker. *Kleine Geschichte des SDS.* Berlin: Rotbuch Verlag, 1977.

Finkel, Steven, Edward Muller, and Karl-Dieter Opp. "Personal Influence, Collective Rationality, and Mass Political Action." *American Political Science Review* 83, no. 3 (Sept. 1989): 885–903.

Fireman, Bruce, and William Gamson. "Utilitarian Logic in the Resource Mobilization Perspective." In *The Dynamics of Social Movements,* ed. Mayer Zald and John McCarthy, 8–45. Cambridge: Winthrop Publishers, 1979.

Forster, Karl. "Der deutsche Katholizismus in der Bundesrepublik Deutschland." In *Der soziale und politische Katholizismus: Entwicklungslinien in Deutschland 1803–1963,* ed. Anton Rauscher, 209–64. Munich: Gunter Olzog Verlag, 1981.

Frankland, E. Gene, and Donald Schoonmaker. *Between Protest and Power: The Green Party in Germany.* Boulder, Colo.: Westview Press, 1992.

Freeman, Jo. "Resource Mobilization and Strategy: A Model for Analyzing Social Movement Organization Actions." In *The Dynamics of Social Movements,* ed. Mayer Zald and John McCarthy, 167–90. Cambridge: Winthrop Publishers, 1979.

Galtung, Johan. "Friedensforschung: Vergangenheitserfahrung und Zukunftsperspektiven." In *Strukturelle Gewalt,* ed. Johan Galtung, 37–60. Reinbek: Rowohlt, 1975.

Gamson, William, and David Meyer. "The Framing of Political Opportunity." Paper presented at the annual meeting of the American Sociological Association, Pittsburgh, Pa., Aug. 1992.

Garton Ash, Timothy. *In Europe's Name: Germany and the Divided Continent.* New York: Random House, 1993.

Glaser, Hermann. *Kulturgeschichte der Bundesrepublik Deutschland.* Munich: Karl Hanser Verlag, 1985.

Glatzel, Norbert. "Neueste kirchliche Lehrverkündigungen zur Sicherheits- und Rüstungsdebatte ab 1945." In *Frieden in Sicherheit: Zur Weiterentwicklung der katholischen Friedensethik,* ed. Norbert Glatzel and Ernst Josef Nagel, 125–48. Freiburg: Herder Verlag, 1981.

Goeckel, Robert. *The Lutheran Church and the East German State: Political Conflict and Change under Ulbricht and Honecker.* Ithaca: Cornell University Press, 1990.

Graf, William. *The German Left since 1945: Socialism and Social Democracy in the German Federal Republic.* New York: Oleander Press, 1976.

Grebing, Helga. "Die Parteien." In *Die Bundesrepublik Deutschland: Geschichte in drei Bänden.,* vol. 1, *Politik,* ed. Wolfgang Benz, 126–91. Frankfurt: Fischer Taschenbuch Verlag, 1983.

———. "Gewerkschaften: Bewegung oder Dienstleistungsorganisation 1955 bis 1965." In *Geschichte der Gewerkschaften in der Bundesrepublik Deutschland,* ed. Hans-Otto Hemmer and Kurt Thomas Schmitz, 149–82. Cologne: Bund-Verlag, 1990.

Griffith, William. *The Ostpolitik of the Federal Republic of Germany.* Cambridge: MIT Press, 1978.

Grosser, Alfred. *The Western Alliance: European-American Relations since 1945.* New York: Continuum, 1980.

Grünewald, Guido. "Zur Geschichte des Ostermarsches der Atomwaffengegner." *Blätter für deutsche und internationale Politik* 27, no. 3 (1982): 303–23.

Gurr, Ted. *Why Men Rebel.* Princeton: Princeton University Press, 1969.

Habermas, Jürgen. *Legitimation Crisis.* London: Heinemann, 1976.

———. *The Theory of Communicative Action.* Vol. 2. Boston: Beacon Press, 1987.

Haftendorn, Helga. *Sicherheit und Entspannung: Zur Außenpolitik der Bundesrepublik Deutschland 1955–1982.* Baden-Baden: Nomos Verlagsgesellschaft, 1986.

Hanrieder, Wolfram. *Germany, America, Europe.* New Haven: Yale University Press, 1990.

Hanrieder, Wolfram, and Graeme Auton. *The Foreign Policies of West Germany, France, and Britain.* Englewood Cliffs, N.J.: Prentice Hall, 1980.

Hennings, Klaus Hinrich. "West Germany." In *The European Economy,* ed. Andreas Boltho, 472–501. New York: Oxford University Press, 1982.

Herf, Jeffrey. *War by Other Means: Soviet Power, West German Resistance, and the Battle of the Euromissiles.* New York: Free Press, 1991.

Holmes, Kim. *The West German Peace Movement and the National Question.* Cambridge, Mass.: Institute for Foreign Policy Analysis, 1984.

Honecker, Martin. "Kontroversen um den Frieden in der evangelischen Kirche und Theologie." *Politische Studien* 33, no. 261 (Jan./Feb. 1982): 17–25.

Howard, Michael. *The Causes of War.* Cambridge: Harvard University Press, 1983.

Hürten, Heinz. "Zur Haltung des deutschen Katholizismus gegenüber der Sicherheits- und Bündnispolitik der Bundesrepublik Deutschland 1948–1960." In *Katholizismus im politischen System der Bundesrepublik 1949–1963,* ed. Albrecht Langner, 83–102. Paderborn: Ferdinand Schöningh, 1978.

Hütter, Joachim. *SPD und nationale Sicherheit: Internationale und innenpolitische Determinanten des Wandels der sozialdemokratischen Sicherheitspolitik 1959–1961.* Meisenheim am Glan: Verlag Anton Hain, 1975.

Infratest. *Politischer Protest in der sozialwissenschaftlichen Literatur.* Stuttgart: Kohlhammer, 1978.

Inglehart, Ronald. *Culture Shifts.* Princeton: Princeton University Press, 1990.

———. "Generational Change and the Future of the Atlantic Alliance." *PS* 17 (summer 1984): 525–35.

———. *The Silent Revolution: Changing Values and Political Styles among Western Publics.* Princeton: Princeton University Press, 1977.

———. "The Silent Revolution in Europe: Intergenerational Change in Post-Industrial Societies." *American Political Science Review* 65 (1971): 991–1017.

"Innerverbandliche 'Nullösung'?" *Graswurzelrevolution* 76 (June 1983): 34–37.

Irving, R. E. M. *The Christian Democratic Parties of Western Europe.* London: Allen and Unwin, 1979.

Jäger, Wolfgang. "Die Innenpolitik der sozial-liberalen Koalition 1969–74." In *Republik im Wandel 1969–74: Die Ära Brandt,* by Karl Dietrich Bracher, Wolfgang Jäger, and Werner Link, 15–162. Stuttgart: Deutsche Verlags-Anstalt, 1986.

———. "Die Innenpolitik der sozial-liberalen Koalition 1974–1982." In *Republik im Wandel 1974–1982: Die Ära Schmidt,* by Wolfgang Jäger and Werner Link, 9–273. Stuttgart: Deutsche Verlags-Anstalt, 1987.

Jochmann, Werner. "Zur politischen Orientierung der deutschen Protestanten nach 1945." In *Christen in der Demokratie,* ed. Heinrich Albertz and Joachim Thomsen, 175–95. Wuppertal: Peter Hammer Verlag, 1978.

Joffe, Josef. "Peace and Populism: Why the European Anti-Nuclear Movement Failed." *International Security* 11, no. 4 (spring 1987): 3–40.

Joppke, Christian. *Mobilizing against Nuclear Energy: A Comparison of West Germany and the United States.* Berkeley: University of California Press, 1993.

Kaase, Max, and Alan Marsh. "Political Action Repertory: Changes Over Time and a New Typology." In *Political Action: Mass Participation in Five Western Democracies,* by Samuel Barnes, Max Kaase, et al., 137–66. Beverly Hills, Calif.: Sage Publications, 1979.

Kaiser, Karl. *Friedensforschung in der Bundesrepublik.* Göttingen: Vandenhoeck and Ruprecht, 1970.

Kaiser, Karl, and Klaus Becher. "Germany and the Iraq Conflict." In *Western Europe and the Gulf,* ed. Nicole Gnesotto and John Roper, 39–70. Paris: The Institute for Security Studies, Western European Union, 1992.

Katzenstein, Peter. *Policy and Politics in West Germany.* Philadelphia, Pa.: Temple University Press, 1987.

Kelleher, Catherine. *Germany and the Politics of Nuclear Weapons.* New York: Columbia University Press, 1975.

Kelly, Petra. "Wie sich die Ökologiebewegung zur Friedensbewegung erweiterte, Variante A." In *Prinzip Leben: Ökopax—die neue Kraft,* ed. Petra Kelly and Jo Leinen, 5–14. Berlin: Olle and Wolter, 1982.

Kitschelt, Herbert. "Parlamentarismus und ökologische Opposition." In *Parlamentarisches Ritual und politische Alternativen,* ed. Roland Roth, 97–120. Frankfurt: Campus Verlag, 1980.

———. "Political Opportunity Structures and Political Protest: Anti-Nuclear Movements in Four Democracies." *British Journal of Political Science* 16 (1986): 57–85.

Klandermans, Bert. "The Formation and Mobilization of Consensus." In *From Structure to Action: Comparing Social Movement Research Across Cultures,* ed. Bert Klandermans, Hanspeter Kriesi, and Sidney Tarrow, 173–96. Greenwich, Conn.: JAI Press, 1988.

Klandermans, Bert, Hanspeter Kriesi, and Sidney Tarrow, eds. *From Structure to Action: Comparing Social Movement Research across Cultures.* Greenwich, Conn.: JAI Press, 1988.

Klein, Ethel. "The Diffusion of Consciousness in the United States and Western Europe." In *The Women's Movements in the United States and Western Europe,* ed. Mary Katzenstein and Carol Mueller, 23–43. Philadelphia, Pa.: Temple University Press, 1987.

Klessmann, Christoph. *Die doppelte Staatsgründung.* Göttingen: Vandenhoeck and Ruprecht, 1982.

———. *Zwei Staaten, Eine Nation: Deutsche Geschichte 1955–1970.* Göttingen: Vandenhoeck and Ruprecht, 1988.

Knorr, Lorenz. *Geschichte der Friedensbewegung in der Bundesrepublik.* Cologne: Pahl-Rugenstein, 1983.

Kolenberger, Lothar, and Hanns-Albrecht Schwarz. *Die alternative Bewegung in West-Berlin.* F. G. S. Occasional Papers. Berlin: Freie Universität, 1982.

Komitee für Grundrechte und Demokratie. *Frieden mit anderen Waffen: Fünf Vorschläge zu einer alternativen Sicherheitspolitik.* Reinbek: Rowohlt, 1981.

Köpper, Ernst-Dieter. *Gewerkschaften und Aussenpolitik.* Frankfurt: Campus Verlag, 1982.

Kornhauser, W. *The Politics of Mass Society.* New York: Free Press, 1976.

Kraiker, Gerhard. *Politischer Katholizismus in der BRD: Eine ideologiekritische Analyse.* Stuttgart: Verlag W. Kohlhammer, 1972.

Krause, Fritz. *Antimilitaristische Opposition in der BRD 1949–1955.* Frankfurt: Verlag Marxistische Blätter, 1971.

Kreile, Michael. "West Germany: The Dynamics of Expansion." In *Between Power and Plenty: Foreign Economic Policy of Advanced Industrial States,* ed. Peter Katzenstein, 191–224. Madison: University of Wisconsin Press, 1986.

Kreiterling, Willi. "Geschlossenheit als politische Dogma? Der Katholizismus in der organisierten pluralistischen Gesellschaft." In *Bilanz des deutschen Katholizismus,* ed. Norbert Greinacher and Heinz-Theo Risse, 311–27. Mainz: Matthias-Grünewald Verlag, 1966.

Kreppel, Klaus. "Kritischer Katholizismus." In *Jenseits vom Nullpunkt?* ed. Rüdiger Weckerling, 269–75. Stuttgart: Kreuz Verlag, 1972.

Krippendorff, Ekkehard. "Einleitung." In *Friedensforschung,* 1–23. Cologne: Kiepenheuer and Witsch, 1968.

———. "Staatliche Organisation und Krieg." In *Friedensforschung und Gesellschaftskritik,* ed. Dieter Senghaas, 23–39. Munich: Carl Hanser Verlag, 1970.

Kubbig, Bernd. *Kirche und Kriegsdienstverweigerung in der BRD.* Stuttgart: Verlag W. Kohlhammer, 1974.

Kuehnlein, Gertrud. *Die Entwicklung der kritischen Friedensforschung in der Bundesrepublik Deutschland.* Frankfurt: Haag and Herchen, 1978.

Kupisch, Karl. *Kirchengeschichte,* vol. 5, *Das Zeitalter der Revolutionen und Weltkriege.* Stuttgart: Verlag W. Kohlhammer, 1975.

———. *Zwischen Idealismus und Massendemokratie: Eine Geschichte der evangelischen Kirche in Deutschland von 1815–1945.* Berlin: Lettner Verlag, 1955.

Langguth, Gerd. *Protestbewegung—Entwicklung, Niedergang, Renaissance: Die Neue Linke seit 1968.* Cologne: Bibliothek Wissenschaft und Politik, 1983.

Lattmann, Dieter. "Die Formelsprache der Rüstungspolitiker: Pazifismus als Kampfwort." In *Frieden in Deutschland,* ed. Hans Pestalozzi et al., 76–82. Munich: Wilhelm Goldmann Verlag, 1982.

Laudowicz, Edith. "Frauen und Friedensbewegung: Überlegungen zur aktuellen Diskussion." *Blätter für deutsche und internationale Politik* 27, no. 1 (1982): 74–88.

Legrand, Hans-Josef. "Friedensbewegungen in der Geschichte der Bundesrepublik Deutschland: Ein Überblick zur Entwicklung bis Ende der siebziger Jahre." In *Friedensbewegungen: Entwicklung und Folgen in der Bundesrepublik Deutschland, Europa, und den USA,* ed. Josef Janning, Hans-Josef Legrand, and Helmut Zander, 19–35. Cologne: Verlag Wissenschaft und Politik, 1987.

Lehmann, Reinhold. "Abrüstung, die tödliche Verschwendung." In *Kirche in der*

Gesellschaft: Der katholische Beitrag 1978/79, ed. Jürgen Wichmann, 19–33. Munich: Günter Olzog Verlag, 1978.

Leif, Thomas. *Die Strategische (Ohn-)Macht der Friedensbewegung: Kommunikations- und Entscheidungsstrukturen in den achtziger Jahren.* Opladen: Westdeutscher Verlag, 1990.

Leinen, Jo. "Wie sich die Ökologiebewegung zur Friedensbewegung erweiterte, Variante B." In *Prinzip Leben: Ökopax—die neue Kraft,* ed. Petra Kelly and Jo Leinen, 15–20. Berlin: Olle and Wolter, 1982.

Link, Werner. "Aussen- und Deutschlandpolitik in der Ära Brandt 1969–1974." In *Republik im Wandel 1969–74: Die Ära Brandt,* by Karl Dietrich Bracher, Wolfgang Jäger, and Werner Link, 163–282. Stuttgart: Deutsche Verlags-Anstalt, 1986.

———. "Aussen- und Deutschlandpolitik in der Ära Schmidt 1974–1982." In *Republik im Wandel 1974–1982: Die Ära Schmidt,* by Wolfgang Jäger and Werner Link, 275–432. Stuttgart: Deutsche Verlags-Anstalt, 1987.

Linnenkamp, Hilmar. "The Security Policy of the New Germany." In *The New Germany in the New Europe,* ed. Paul Stares, 93–125. Washington: Brookings Institution Press, 1992.

Locke, Hubert, ed. *The Church Confronts the Nazis: Barmen Then and Now.* New York: Edwin Mellen Press, 1984.

Löwke, Udo. *Für den Fall, daß . . .: Die Haltung der SPD zur Wehrfrage 1949–1953.* Hannover: Verlag für Literatur und Zeitgeschehen, 1969.

Maier, Charles. "The Politics of Productivity: Foundations of American International Economic Policy after World War II." In *Between Power and Plenty: Foreign Economic Policy of Advanced Industrial States,* ed. Peter Katzenstein, 23–50. Madison: University of Wisconsin Press, 1986.

Markovits, Andrei. *The Politics of the West German Trade Unions.* Cambridge: Cambridge University Press, 1986.

———. "The Vicissitudes of West German Social Democracy." *Studies in Political Economy* 19 (spring 1986): 83–112.

Markovits, Andrei, and Philip Gorski. *The German Left: Red, Green, and Beyond.* New York: Oxford University Press, 1993.

Markovits, Andrei, and Simon Reich. "Should Europe Fear the Germans?" In *From Bundesrepublik to Deutschland,* ed. Michael Huelshoff, Andrei Markovits, and Simon Reich, 271–90. Ann Arbor: University of Michigan Press, 1993.

Marsh, Alan, and Max Kaase. "Measuring Political Action." In *Political Action: Mass Participation in Five Western Democracies,* by Samuel Barnes, Max Kaase, et al., 57–96. Beverly Hills, Calif.: Sage Publications, 1979.

Marx, Gary. "External Efforts to Damage or Facilitate Social Movements: Some Patterns, Explanations, Outcomes, and Complications." In *The Dynamics of Social Movements,* ed. Mayer Zald and John McCarthy, 94–125. Cambridge: Winthrop Publishers, 1979.

Mayer-Tasch, Peter. *Die Bürgerinitiativbewegung.* Reinbek: Rowohlt, 1976.

McAdam, Doug. "Micromobilization Contexts and Recruitment to Activism." In

From Structure to Action: Comparing Social Movement Research across Cultures, ed. Bert Klandermans, Hanspeter Kriesi, and Sidney Tarrow, 125–55. Greenwich, Conn.: JAI Press, 1988.

———. *Political Process and the Development of Black Insurgency 1930–1970.* Chicago: University of Chicago Press, 1982.

McCarthy, John, and Mayer Zald. "Resource Mobilization and Social Movements: A Partial Theory." In *Social Movements in an Organizational Society,* ed. Mayer Zald and John McCarthy, 15–49. New Brunswick, N.J.: Transaction Books, 1987.

Mechtesheimer, Alfred. *Rüstung und Frieden.* Munich: Wirtschaftsverlag Langen-Müller/Herbig, 1982.

Merritt, Anna, and Richard Merritt, eds. *Public Opinion in Semisovereign Germany: The HICOG Surveys, 1949–1955.* Urbana: University of Illinois Press, 1980.

Mewes, Horst. "The West German Green Party." *New German Critique* 28 (winter 1983): 51–85.

Meyer, David. "Protest Cycles and Political Process: American Peace Movements in the Nuclear Age." *Political Research Quarterly* 46, no. 3 (Sept. 1993): 451–80.

Mez, Lutz, and Ulf Wolter. "Wer sind die Grünen?" In *Die Qual der Wahl,* ed. Lutz Mez and Ulf Wolter, 6–32. Berlin: Olle and Wolter, 1980.

Molotch, Harvey. "Media and Movements." In *The Dynamics of Social Movements,* ed. Mayer Zald and John McCarthy, 71–94. Cambridge: Winthrop Publishers, 1979.

Molt, Peter. "Die neutralistische Opposition." Ph.D. diss., University of Heidelberg, 1956.

Müller, Harald. "German Foreign Policy after Unification." In *The New Germany in the New Europe,* ed. Paul Stares, 126–73. Washington: Brookings Institution Press, 1992.

Müller, Harald, and Thomas Risse-Kappen. "Origins of Estrangement: The Peace Movement and the Changed Image of America in West Germany." *International Security* 12, no. 1 (summer 1987): 52–88.

Müller-Rommel, Ferdinand, and Nicholas Watts. "Zur elektoralen Verankerung der Anhaenger neuer sozialer Bewegungen: eine vorlaeufige Forschungsnotiz." In *Politische Willensbildung und Interessenvermittlung: Verhandlungen der Fachtagung der DVPW vom 11.–13. Oktober 1983 in Mannheim,* ed. Juergen Falter, Christian Fenner, and Michael Greven, 602–9. Opladen: Westdeutscher Verlag, 1984.

Mühleisen, Hans-Otto. "Grundstrukturen der Friedensdiskussion in der katholischen Kirche." *Politische Studien* 33, no. 261 (Jan./Feb. 1982): 28–46.

Mushaben, Joyce. "Feminism in Four Acts: The Changing Political Identity of Women in the Federal Republic of Germany." in *The Federal Republic of Germany at Forty,* ed. Peter Merkl, 76–109. New York: New York University Press, 1989.

———. "Grassroots and *Gewaltfreie Aktion:* A Study of Mass Mobilization

Strategies in the West German Peace Movement." *Journal of Peace Research* 23, no. 2 (1986): 141–55.

———. "The Struggle Within: Conflict, Consensus, and Decision Making among National Coordinators and Grassroots Coordinators in the West German Peace Movement." In *Organizing for Change: Social Movement Organizations in Europe and the United States,* ed. Bert Klandermans, 267–98. Greenwich, Conn.: JAI Press, 1989.

Nissen, Peter. "Prospects for a Realignment of the West German Party System." Paper presented at the conference "When Parties Fail: Paths of Alternative Political Action," University of California at Santa Barbara, 19–20 May 1982.

Noelle, Elisabeth, and Erich Neumann. *Jahrbuch der öffentlichen Meinung 1947–1955.* Allensbach am Bodensee: Verlag für Demoskopie, 1956.

Noelle-Neumann, Elisabeth. "Drei Viertel gegen die Raketenstationierung?" *Frankfurter Allgemeine Zeitung,* 16 Sept. 1983.

Oberschall, Anthony. "Protracted Conflict." In *The Dynamics of Social Movements,* ed. Mayer Zald and John McCarthy, 45–71. Cambridge: Winthrop Publishers, 1979.

———. *Social Conflict and Social Movements.* Englewood Cliffs, N.J.: Prentice-Hall, 1973.

Offe, Claus. "New Social Movements: Challenging the Boundaries of Institutional Politics." *Social Research* 52, no. 4 (1985): 817–68.

Olson, Mancur. *The Logic of Collective Action: Public Goods and the Theory of Groups.* Cambridge: Harvard University Press, 1965.

Otto, Karl. "Der Widerstand gegen die Wiederbewaffnung der Bundesrepublik." In *Unsere Bundeswehr? Zum 25jährigen Bestehen einer umstrittenen Institution,* ed. Reiner Steinweg, 52–105. Frankfurt: Suhrkamp Verlag, 1981.

———. *Vom Ostermarsch zur APO: Geschichte der ausserparlamentarischen Opposition in der Bundesrepublik 1960–1970.* Frankfurt: Campus Verlag, 1982.

Overby, L. Marvin. "West European Peace Movements: An Application of Kitschelt's Political Opportunity Structures Thesis." *West European Politics* 13, no. 1 (Jan. 1990): 1–11.

Parkin, Frank. *Middle Class Radicalism.* Cambridge: Cambridge University Press, 1968.

Pfister, Hermann, and Alfred Walter. *Friedensforschung in der Bundesrepublik Deutschland.* Waldkirch: Pädagogische Informationen, 1975.

Philipsen, Dirk. *We Were the People: Voices from East Germany's Revolutionary Autumn of 1989.* Durham, N.C.: Duke University Press, 1993.

Pirker, Theo. *Die Blinde Macht: Die Gewerkschaftsbewegung in der Bundesrepublik.* Berlin: Olle and Wolter, 1979.

Rabier, Jacques-Rene, Helene Riffault, and Ronald Inglehart. *Euro-barometer 17: Energy and the Future, April 1982.* 1st ICPSR ed. Ann Arbor, Mich.: Inter-University Consortium for Political and Social Research, 1983. Machine-readable data file.

Raschke, Joachim. "Ursachen und Perspektiven des Protests." In *Protest: Grüne,*

Bunte und Steuerrebellen, ed. Detlef Murphy et al., 156–89. Reinbek: Rowohlt, 1979.

Rattinger, Hans. "The Federal Republic of Germany." In *The Public and Atlantic Defense,* ed. Gregory Flynn and Hans Rattinger, 101–74. London: Croom Helm, 1985.

Rausch, Wolf Werner, and Christian Walther, eds. *Evangelische Kirche in Deutschland und die Wiederaufrüstungsdiskussion in der Bundesrepublik 1950–1955.* Gütersloh: Gütersloher Verlagshaus Gerd Mohn, 1978.

Reuband, Karl-Heinz. "Die Friedensbewegung nach Stationierungsbeginn: Soziale Unterstützung in der Bevölkerung als Handlungspotential." *Vierteljahresschrift für Sicherheit und Frieden* 3, no. 3 (1985): 147–56.

Risse-Kappen, Thomas. "Anti-Nuclear and Pro-Detente? The Transformation of the West German Security Debate." In *Debating National Security: the Public Dimension,* ed. Hans Rattinger and Don Munton, 269–99. Frankfurt: Peter Lang, 1991.

Ritter, Gerhard, and Merith Niehuss. *Wahlen in der Bundesrepublik Deutschland.* Munich: Verlag C. H. Beck, 1987.

Rochon, Thomas. *Mobilizing for Peace: The Antinuclear Movements in Western Europe.* Princeton: Princeton University Press, 1988.

Rolke, Lothar. *Protestbewegungen in der Bundesrepublik.* Opladen: Westdeutscher Verlag, 1987.

Rosolovsky, Diane. *West Germany's Foreign Policy: The Impact of the Social Democrats and the Greens.* New York: Greenwood Press, 1987.

Roth, Roland. "Notizen zur politischen Geschichte der Bürgerinitiativen in der Bundesrepublik." In *Parlamentarisches Ritual und politische Alternativen,* ed. Roland Roth, 74–97. Frankfurt: Campus Verlag, 1980.

Ruh, Ulrich. "Schwierigkeiten mit dem Frieden." *Herder Korrespondenz* 35, no. 2 (Feb. 1981): 53–55.

Rupp, Hans Karl. *Außerparlamentarische Opposition in der Ära Adenauer.* Cologne: Pahl-Rugenstein, 1980.

Scharffenorth, Gerta. "Konflikte in der Evangelischen Kirche in Deutschland 1950 bis 1969 im Rahmen der historischen und ökumenischen Friedensdiskussion." In *Konflikte zwischen Wehrdienst und Friedensdiensten,* ed. Ulrich Duchrow and Gerta Scharffenorth, 17–116. Stuttgart: Ernst Klett Verlag, 1970.

Schellenger, Harold Kent. *The SPD in the Bonn Republic: A Socialist Party Modernizes.* The Hague: Martius Nijhoff, 1968.

Schlaga, Rüdiger. "Polen: Beginn vom Zerfall der Friedensbewegung?" *Graswurzelrevolution* 62 (May 1982): 25–26.

Schlaga, Rüdiger, and Hans-Joachim Spanger. "Die Friedensbewegung und der Warschauer Pakt: Ein Spannungsverhältnis." In *Die neue Friedensbewegung,* ed. Reiner Steinweg, 54–86. Frankfurt: Suhrkamp Verlag, 1982.

Schlicht, Uwe. *Vom Burschenschaften bis zum Sponti: Studentische Opposition gestern und heute.* Berlin: Colloquium Verlag Otto Hess, 1980.

Schonauer, Karlheinz. *Die ungeliebten Kinder der Mutter SPD: Die Geschichte der*

Jusos von der braven Parteijugend zur innerparteilichen Opposition. Hagen: Karlheinz Schonauer, 1982.

Schou, Angela. *Die Friedensbewegung in der DDR.* Aalborg: Aalborg Universitetsforlag, 1986.

Schwarz, Hans-Peter. *Die gezähmten Deutschen: Von der Machtbesessenheit zur Machtvergessenheit.* Stuttgart: Deutsche-Verlags-Anstalt, 1985.

Scott, Alan. *Ideology and the New Social Movements.* London: Unwin Hyman, 1990.

Seiterlich, Thomas. "Basisgemeinden in der Bundesrepublik." *Frankfurter Hefte* 37, no. 9 (Sept. 1982): 35–42.

———. "Gruppierungen innerkirchlicher Opposition." *Frankfurter Hefte* 36, no. 5 (May 1981): 10, 11.

Senghaas, Dieter. *Abschreckung und Frieden.* Frankfurt: Europaeische Verlagsanstalt, 1969.

———. "Einleitung." In *Friedensforschung und Gesellschaftskritik,* ed. Dieter Senghaas, 1–22. Munich: Carl Hanser Verlag, 1970.

Smelser, Neil. *Theory of Collective Behavior.* New York: Free Press, 1963.

Snow, David, and Robert Benford. "Ideology, Frame Resonance, and Participant Mobilization." In *From Structure to Action: Comparing Social Movement Research Across Cultures,* ed. Bert Klandermans, Hanspeter Kriesi, and Sidney Tarrow, 197–217. Greenwich, Conn.: JAI Press, 1988.

Soell, Hartmut. *Fritz Erler: Eine politische Biographie.* Vol. 1. Berlin: Verlag J. H. W. Dietz, 1976.

Sozialwissenschaftliches Institut Nowak und Sörgel [SINUS]. "Sicherheitspolitik, Bündnispolitik, Friedensbewegung: Eine Untersuchung zur aktuellen politischen Stimmungslage im Spätherbst 1983." Munich, n.p., October 1983.

Sperling, James. "German Security Policy After the Cold War: The Strategy of a Civilian Power in an Uncivil World." In *European Security without the Soviet Union,* ed. Stuart Croft and Phil Williams, 77–98. London: Frank Cass, 1992.

Spotts, Frederic. *The Churches and Politics in West Germany.* Middletown, Conn.: Wesleyan University Press, 1973.

Stankowski, Martin. *Linkskatholizismus nach 1945: Die Presse oppositioneller Katholiken in der Auseinandersetzung für eine demokratische und sozialistische Gesellschaft.* Cologne: Pahl-Rugenstein Verlag, 1974.

Strässer, Christoph. "Der Krefelder Appell." In *Frieden in Deutschland,* ed. Hans Pestalozzi et al., 87–92. Munich: Wilhelm Goldmann Verlag, 1982.

Tarrow, Sidney. *Democracy and Disorder: Protest and Politics in Italy 1965–75.* Oxford: Clarendon Press, 1989.

Tauber, Kurt. *Beyond Eagle and Swastika: German Nationalism since 1945.* Middletown, Conn.: Wesleyan University Press, 1967.

Tholen, Norbert. "Die Höhe des Glaubens und die Niederungen der Politik: Bishöfe schweigen zum Polenvertrag." *Frankfurter Hefte* 31, no. 5 (May 1976): 4, 5.

Tilly, Charles. *From Mobilization to Revolution.* Reading, Mass.: Addison-Wesley Publishing Company, 1978.

————. "Repertoires of Contention in America and Britain, 1750–1830." In *The Dynamics of Social Movements,* ed. Mayer Zald and John McCarthy, 126–55. Cambridge: Winthrop Publishers, 1979.

Verheyen, Dirk. *The German Question: A Cultural, Historical, and Geopolitical Exploration.* Boulder, Colo.: Westview Press, 1991.

Vogel, Johanna. *Kirche und Wiederbewaffnung: Die Haltung der Evangelischen Kirche in Deutschland in den Auseinandersetzungen um die Wiederbewaffnung der Bundesrepublik 1949–1956.* Göttingen: Vandenhoeck and Ruprecht, 1978.

Wasmuht, Ulrike. *Friedensbewegungen der 80er Jahre.* Giessen: Focus Verlag, 1987.

Wette, Wolfram. "Sozialdemokratische Sicherheitspolitik in historischer Perspektive." In *Jungsozialisten und Jungdemokraten zur Friedens- und Sicherheitspolitik,* ed. Reiner Steinweg, 22–42. Frankfurt: Suhrkamp Verlag, 1977.

Wieczorek-Zeul, Heidemarie. "Jungsozialisten und Sicherheitspolitik." In *Jungsozialisten und Jungdemokraten zur Friedens- und Sicherheitspolitik,* ed. Reiner Steinweg, 13–22. Frankfurt: Suhrkamp Verlag, 1977.

Wiedenmann, Wolfgang. "Evangelische Studentengemeinde—Kirche an der Hochschule?" In *Christen in der Demokratie,* ed. Heinrich Albertz and Joachim Thomsen, 121–55. Wuppertal: Peter Hammer Verlag, 1978.

Wilker, Lothar. *Die Sicherheitspolitik der SPD 1956–1966: Zwischen Wiedervereinigungs- und Bündnisorientierung.* Bonn: Verlag Neue Gesellschaft, 1977.

Young, Thomas-Durell. "The 'Normalization' of the Federal Republic of Germany's Defense Structures." Strategic Studies Institute, US Army War College, Carlisle, Penn., 1 Sept. 1992.

Zald, Mayer, and John McCarthy, eds. *The Dynamics of Social Movements.* Cambridge: Winthrop Publishers, 1979.

Index

DATE DUE

GAYLORD